ASTROLOGY AND ITS UTILITY

ASTROLOGY AND ITS UTILITY

Dr. Onkar Lal Sharma "Prmad"

Publications

KALPAZ PUBLICATIONS

Delhi - 110052

Astrology and its Utility

ISBN : 81-7835-417-9

Rs. 890

Published in 2006 in India by
Kalpaz Publications
C-30, Satyawati Nagar,
Delhi - 110052
e-mail : kalpaz@hotmail.com

Laser Typesetting at : Global Printers, Delhi
Printed at : Salasar Imaging System, Delhi

Dedicated to

My Spirithal Teacher and Guru Parampujya Late Shri Bal Krishna Haksar Professor of Philosophy

(Victoria College, Gwalior (M.P.) 1953-1955)

ॐ *OM OM OM OM OM*

Contents

Preface

Astrology is a wonderful Science. Its accurate knowledge reveals the truth hidden in our future life. This book is the collection of my English articles published in English magazines from time to time since 1969 to 2003. Some articles are newly written. I experienced the truth in Astrology through Horary Astrology, Varshaphala Charts, GOCHAR and VIMSHOTTARI MAHADASA system as experienced and expressed in these articles. Horoscopic examples made the subject clear to understand. One article on ACHARYA CHATURSEN SHASTRI is specially given as he wandered here and there from Delhi to Kashi, Ajmer to Lahore, Jaipur, to Mumbai and at last to Delhi and wrote 186 works in Hindi and married 4 times. His courageous life is an example to young to burn their lamp of life in struggle leaving footprints in the way of human life's History and Literature. Mistakes may kindly be corrected by wise readers. I am grateful to Kalpaz Publications, Delhi, to publish this book for the welfare of HUMAN KIND.

30th September, 2004

Dr. Onkar Lal Sharma Prmad

1

What is Astrology

Astrology is very mystic and useful science. Astrology is an important of Vedang (वेदांग) due to which we get the information about the changing in nature by the planetary position. In finding out the conclusion in Astrology major discipline, labour and patient is necessary. It is said about Astrology.

"अप्रत्यक्षाति शास्त्राणि विवादस्तेषु केवलं
प्रत्यक्षं ज्योतिषं शास्त्रं चन्द्राकौं यस्य साक्षिणौ"

Means other texts of knowledge has dispute among them because they are indirect and not clear but Astrology is a direct and clear subject of which witnesses are SUN and the Moon.

24 hours of a day night are divided in 12 signs from the Sunrise of a day to the Sunrise of the other day within 24 hours.

From time immemorial India has been the birth place of this great knowledge branch of science. From India this science spread in China, Japan, Egypt, Arabia, Persia, Italy etc. Astrology has been directed by 18 Rishi-Muni's as Sun, Pitamaha, Vyas, Vashishtha, Atri, Parashar, Kashyap, Narad, Garg, Marichi, Muni, Angira, Polish, Lomash, Chyavan, Yavan, Bhrigu, Shaunak. They have written grand volumes of books which are known as recognised books in the form of Samhita संहिता as Lomash Samhita, Narada-Samhita, Bhrigu-Samhita, Pulashtya-Samhita, Kashyap-Samhita. King Ravana of Shri Lanka was very wise man of Astrology. He wrote Ravana-Samhita.

The famous emperor of Ujjain king vikamaditya had 9 jewels in his court each of them was the unique wise man of a particular subject. Varah-Mihir was one of these 9 jewels of his court. First of all in India he assembled all the knowledge of Astrology of all the 18 directors of this great science and wrote वृहज्जातक "Vrittatjatak". He also wrote "Varahi-Samhita" "वाराही-संहिता" "After Varah Mihir, Aryabhatta, Bhattot Pal. Kalyan Verma, कल्याण वर्मा, Bhaskara Charya were the famous Astrologers.

Kalyan Verma has written सारावली Sarawali, Bhaskaracharya has written Lilawati लीलावती, Veej Ganit,बीजगणित, Siddhanta Shiromani, सिद्धात शिरोमणि, Karan Kutuhal, करण कुतुहल and Arya Bhattiya आर्य भट्टीया Maha Siddhanta महा सिद्धांत etc. Valuable volumes. Varaha-Mihir's son Prithu Yasha wrote 56 verses called as षट पंचासिका Shat-Panchasika.

After that the research work on Astrology went on and Kashinath काशिनाथ has written शीघ्र बोध Sheeghra Vodh Lagna Chandrika, लग्न चंद्रिका, Yavanacharya यवनाचार्य had written Vrihadyavan, बृहद्यवन, Ram Daiyagya रामदैवज्ञ has written Muhurta Chintamani, मुहूर्त चिन्तामणि, Rahim has रहीम written Khetu Kantak, खेटु कौतुक, Dhundhi Raj ढुंढिराज has written Jataka Bharan, जात का भरण, Neelkantha नीलकंठ had written Tajik Neelkanth, ताजिक नीलकंठी Jeevnath Jha जीवनाथ आ has written प्रश्न भूषण Prashna Bhushan. मंत्रेश्वर Mantreshwar has written Phala Deepika, फल दीपिका, वैद्यनाथ दीक्षित Vaidyanath Dixit had written Jatak Parijat, जातक पारिजात, Mahadev Pathak महादेव पाठक had written Jatak Tatwa, जातक सत्व, Kalidas had written कालिदास कृत Uttar Kalamrit उत्तर कालामृत . In 18-19 centuries Param Hansa, Sitkantha, Kriparam Mishra, Phatah Singh, Shambhu Singh king of Suthalia Naresh सुठालियानरेश शंभुसिंह etc has written Muhurta Muktavali, Tatwa Muktawali, Samay Bodhi, Kripa Sudhu, Jyotish Kalpadrvama etc. Pandit Laxminarayan Tripathi of Narsingharha was also a great Palmist and Astrologer. He wrote a very famous Book on Hasta Samudrika Shashtra हस्त सामुदिक शास्त्र.

Pandit Surya Narayan Vyas of Ujjain was the great scholar of Astrology of Modern Age. Dr. B.V. Raman of Bangalore and Pandit Krishna Murti of Madras Pandit Hardeo Trivedi were the great scholars of to day of this great science. In this way the great divine science of Astrology has been our valuable heritage of which studying, thinking, experiencing, creating is necessary. Dr. Narain Dutta Shrimali, K.A. Dubey "PADMESH", Dr. Radha Krishna Shrimali advanced Astrology Dr. Bhoj Raj Dwevedi.

Sun transits 12 signs in 12 months. When sun transits one sign to other it is called Samkranti सूर्य संक्रांति, e g , Sun when comes in Capricorn on 14th January every year it is called Makar Samkranti मकर संक्रांति . There are 12 signs as following according to Sayan सायण System.

No.	*Sign*	*From to*	*Hindu Month*
1.	Aries मेष	14th April to 14th May	Chaitra चैत्र
2.	Taurus वृषभ	14th May to 14th June	Vaishakha वैशाख
3.	Gemini मिथुन	14th June to 15th July	Jyeshtha ज्येष्ठ
4.	Cancer कर्क	16th July to 16th August	Ashada आषाढ़
5.	Leo सिंह	16th August to 16th September	Shravana श्रावण
6.	Virgo कन्या	16th September to 17th October	Bhadrapada भाद्रपद
7.	Libra तुला	17th October to 16th November	Ashwin आश्विना
8.	Scorpio वृश्चिक	16th November to 15th December	Kartik कार्तिक
9.	Sagittarius धनु	15th December to 13th January	Margsheersha मार्गशीर्ष

10.	Capricorn मकर	14th January to 12th February	Paush पौष
11.	Aquarius कुंभ	12th February to 14th March	Magh माघ
12.	Pisces मीन	14th March to 13th April	Phalguna फाल्गुण

Rulers of these 12 signs are *Mars* of Aries, Scorpio, *Venus* of Taurus, Libra, Mercury of Gemini and Virgo, *Moon* of Cancer, *Sun* of Leo, Saturn of Capricorn and Aquarius, Jupiter of Sagittarius and Pisces. There are 27 Nakshatras. Each Nakshatra or Star or constellation has 4 padas in this way 12 signs are divided in 108 parts and each sign has 2 ¼ Nakshatras. Nakshatras have their lords and Months, Name, Habit, Lochan, Shape etc. as following:

Whose horoscope is prepared is called Jatak or Native on the day, Tithi, Star, Yog, Karan the native is born in the horoscope of that native in which sign and house the planets and sign are found according to that virtue, vice, habit, shape, size, nature, profession etc. are described. Moon, mercury, Jupiter, Venus are natural benefics and Sun, Mars, Saturn, Rahu, Ketu are natural malefics effecting each other by rulership, occupation, representation etc. and accordingly giving the results of deeds done in the previous life.

In horoscope first house is called Tanu तनु from first house colour, behaviours, shape, nature, height, and second house is called Dhan धन, family, bank balance, money third house is called sahaj सहज and friendship, younger brother and sisters, braveness, neighbourhood etc. are considered from 3rd house. Fourth house denotes immovable property as house, land, farm, field, road, mother, place, vehicle, education. Fifth house denotes primary, middle, higher secondary education progeny, intellect, intelligence, knowledge, student, genius, love affairs etc. Sixth house denotes maternal uncle, diseases, debt, animals, servants government or semi-government service, foreign contact etc. seventh house denotes wife, journey, eighth house denotes age, death, Archeology, Ninth house denotes Luck, Religion, Guru (preacher) pilgrimage, long journeys, father, tenth house denotes profession, prestige, business, fame, deeds, father, eleventh house denotes income, uncle, elder brother, sister, reunion, Twelfth house denotes Expenditure, loss, jail, dacoits, ground parents and maternal parents, foreign concerns etc.

Twelfth houses also denote parts of body of Kalpurusha e.g. Head, brain from Aries and first house, face, mouth, eyes from Taurus and second house, shoulders, throat, teeth, ears, lungs, from Gemini and third house, lower parts of lungs, upper part of heart, chest from cancer and fourth house, stomach, belly, backbone, liver, gastric part from fifth house and Leo, Intestines, kidney, spleen from sixth house and Virgo, life partner, secret part of body, urine from seventh house and Libra, uterus, sexual diseases from eighth house and Scorpio, thigh from ninth house and

NAKSHTRAS

There are 27 Nakshtras with particulars are as following:

Sl. No.	Name	Lords	Noun	Name	Habit	Sign
1.	**Ashwini**	Ashwhini Kumar	Good	Short	Hard	अ-भ-कृ-1 Aries मेष
2.	**Bharni**	Yam	Destroyer	Hard	Ordinary	कृ-इ-दौ-मृ-2 Taurus वृषभ
3.	**Kritika**	Fire	No work	Mixed	Fixed	मृ-2अ-पुन-3 Gemini मिथुन
4.	**Rohini**	Brahma	Success	Dhruva	Friend	पुन-1 पु उ-2 ले Cancer कर्क
5.	**Mrigsira**	Moon	Good	Kind	Very Hard	म-पु उ०फा-1 Leo सिंह
6.	**Aridra**	Shiva	Good	Sharp	Moving	उ. फा. 3 हस्त चि-2 Virgo कन्या
7.	Punarvasu	Aditi	Medium	Moving	Sudden	चि-2 स्वा-4 विरप-3 Libra तुला
8.	Pushya	Jupiter	Good	Short	Very Hard	विथा-1 अनु-ज्यष्ण Scorpio वृश्चिक
9.	Ashlesha	Snake	Sorrow	Sharp	Hard	मूल-पू.षा.उ.षा-1 Sagittarius धनु
10.	Magha	Pittra	Destroyer	Hard	Hard	उ.ष.-3 श्र द्य-2 Capricorn मकर
11.	Poorva phalguna	Bhag	Death giver	Hard	Fixed	द्य-2 थत-पू०मा०3 Aquarius कुम्भ
12.	Uttra phalguna	Aryma	Wisdom	Dhruva	Sudden	पू०मा.-1 उ०मा०रे० Pisces मीन
13.	Hasta	Ravi	Laxmi	Short	Friend	
14.	Chitra	Twashta	Good	Kind	Moving	
15.	Swati	Air	Bad	Moving	Ordinary	
16	Vishakha	Indragni	Bad	Mixed	Friend	
17.	Anuradha	Mitra	All Success	Kind	Sudden	
18.	Jyeshtha	Indra	Destruction	Sharp	Very Hard	
19.	Mool	Rakshasa	Wealth Destroyer	Sharp	Very Hard	
20.	Poorva Shada	Udaka	Loss	Hard	Hard	
21.	Uttra Shada	Vishwe Deva	Intellect giver	Dhruva	Fixed	
22.	Shravana	Vishnu	Giving happiness	Moving	Moving	
23.	Dhanishtha	Vasu	Good	Moving	Moving	
24.	Shatbhisha	Varuna	Welfare	Moving	Moving	
25.	Poorva Bhadrapada	Ajaik	Death giver	Hard	Hard	
26.	Uttra Bhadrapada	Ahir Badinu	Laxmi	Dhruva	Fixed	
27.	Revti	Poosha	Fulfill of desire	Kind	Friend	

Sagittarius, knees from tenth house and Capricorn, upper part of feet, legs left eye from eleventh and Aquarius, Eyes, freedom. Moksha from twelfth house and Pisces Sign.

Born in any sign is called Lagna or Ascendant and where Sun is posited in any sign that is sunrise, noon will be in fourth sign of sun rising Lagna and evening in the 6th sign of sunrising Sun.

There are 27 Yogs Vishkambh, Preeti, Ayushyman, Saubhagya, Shobhan, Atiganda, Sukarma, Dhriti, Shool, gand, Vriddhi, Dhruva, Vyaghat, Harshan, Vajra, Siddhi, Vyatipat, Variyan, Parigh, Shiva, Shiddha, Sadhya, Shubh, Shukla Bramha, Endra, Vaidhriti.

YOG – In finding auspicious period for beginning of any Job Yogs are to be considered good and bad. The half period of Parigh is Ominous, last half is auspicious. 5 ghatis of Vishkamah, 7 ghatis of shool, Ist 6 ghatis of gand and vyaghat, 9 ghatis of Harshan and vajra and all period of Vaidhriti and Vyatipat is ominous hence should be avoided.

Vishkambh, Shool, gand, atigand, vyaghat, vajra, sadhya, are to be considered. Those born in yogs suffer some how in their lives.

KARAN – Half part of a tithi is called Karan. They are 11 eleven e.g. Vava, Balav, Kaulav कौलव, Taitil, Gar, Vanij, Vishthi, Shakuni Chatushpada, Nag, Kimstughna. Ist seven are moving (Char) and final 4 (four) are fixed (Sthir).

Lords of Karans are as following :

No.	1	2	3	4	5	6	7	8	9	10	11
Karan	Van	Balav	Kamlav	Taitil	Gar	Vanij	Visht	Shakuni	Chatushpada	Nag	Kimsthghna
Lord	Indra	Bramha	Sun	Sun	Earth	Laxmi	Yama	Kaliyug	Rudra	Sarpa	Vayu

Lords of 27 Yogs are as following :

Yog	Vishkambh	Preeti	Ayushman	Saubhagya	Shobhan	Atigand	Sukarma	Dhriti	Shool
Lord	Yama	Vishnu	Moon	Bramha	Jupiter	Moon	Indra	Water	Sarpa
Yog	Gand	Vriddhi	Dhruva	Vyaghat	Harshan	Vajra	Siddhi	Vyatipat	Variyan
Lord	Fire	Sun	Land	Vayu	Bhag	Varun	Ganesh	Rudra	Kuber
Yog	Parigh	Shiva	Siddha	Sadhya	Shubh	Shukla	Bramh	Endra	Vaidhriti
Lord	Vishnu Karma	Mitra	Kartikeya	Savitri	Laxmi	Parvati	Ashwni	Pitra	Diti

Days

Days	*Name*	*Noun*	*Good For*
Sunday	Krur	Sthir (Fixed)	Music, Health, Vehicle, Purchasing
Monday	Saumya	Char (Movable)	Agriculture, Art, Journey, Music
Tuesday	Krur	Ugra (Hard)	C.I.D. work, fighting, Legal case
Wednesday	Saumya	Sam (Even)	Business, Education, Cloth
Thursday	Saumya	Laghu (Short)	Education, Justice, Service
Friday	Saumya	Mridu (Kind)	Love affairs, Music, Ornaments
Saturday	Krur	Teekshna (Sharp)	Surgery, Servant, Iron, etc.

Knowledge of Profession through Nakshatras

Sign	Nakshatra	Profession
ARIES	*Ashwini – 4*	Police, Military, Medical, Crime Branch, Railway, Iron
	Bharhi – 4	Sport, Music, Cloth Industries, Hotel, Building, Optical, Agriculture
	Kritika – 1	Land, building, Speculation, Police, Military, Bank, Medical
TAURUS	*Kritika – 3*	Government service, Jewellery, Music, Dance, Drama, Poetry, Photography, Medical.
	Rohini – 4	Public works, Hotel, House, Lands, Oil, Milk, Water, Colour, Law, Polities, Garden.
	Mrigsira – 2	Machinery, Electricity, Telephone, Mathematics, Building, Press, Agency, Brokery, fragrant things etc.
GEMINI	*Mrigsira – 2*	Stockkeeper, Bookseller, Post Telegraph, Transport.
	Aridra – 4	Publicity, Author, finger expert, drugs etc.
	Punarvas – 3	Journalism, Religion, Law, Judges, Teacher, Priest, Astrology, Mathematician, Computer operator.
CANCER	*Punarvas – 1*	Bank, Medical, Statistics, Judge, Professor, Manager, Merchant of Vehicles, Nurses.
	Pushya – 4	Petrol, Kerosene, Oil, Well, Tubewell, Dam, Bridges, Mines, Agricultural, Lands.
	Ashlesha – 4	Business agent, Salesman, Author, Paints, Accounts, Teacher, Astrologer, Mathematics, Nurses etc.
LEO	*Magha – 4*	Contractors, Service in Crime and defence department, Medical, Army, Jewellery.
	Poorva Phalguna – 4	Transport, Archaeology, Film Industries, Veternary, educationists, service in girl school College, Photography etc.
	Uttra Phalguna – 1	Government service, Medical, Navy, Stock exchange, Medical, heart specialist.

Sign	Nakshatra	Professions
VIRGO	*Uttra Phalgune –3*	Education, Information and Publicity, Tourism, Telephone Public Health, Newspaper, Embassy.
VIRGO	*Hasta – 4*	Commerce, Communication, Agent, Engineer, Press, Advocate, Artist, Painter, land and ornament, mortgages.
VIRGO	*Chitra – 2*	Law department, Medical, Education, General Merchant, Scents, Perfumes, Jewellery, Tailoring etc.
VIRGO	*Chitra – 2*	Advocates, Doctors, Philosophers, Military, Defence, Sport, Music, Information, Broadcasting Radio, T.V. etc.
VIRGO	*Swati – 4*	Tourism, Transport, Bakery, Theatre, general merchants of sales and Purchasing toilet, Judge, Poetress.
VIRGO	*Vishakha – 3*	Partnership, touring travelling agent, Speculation, Related to foreign, Teacher, Judge, perfumers, mining etc.
LIBRA	*Vishakha – 1*	Law, Judge, Bank, Drug Manufactures, Land Owner, Agriculturist, Defence, Ayurvedic Medicines.
LIBRA	*Anuradha – 4*	Medical Surgery, Homeopathy, Service Jail, Judges, Industrial mechanical engineer, heads of Corporations.
LIBRA	Jyeshtha – 4	Press Publication, Machinery, Canals, Thermal Station Insurance, Surgeon, Judges, Postmaster.
SAGITTARIUS	Mool – 4	Advocates, Judges, Commanding Authority, God fearing, Congressmen, International trade, Export and Import, Flowers, Purohitas.
SAGITTARIUS	Poorvashada – 4	Banking, Accountancy, Railway, Road, Building, Excise, Medical, Foreigners, Advocates, Judges etc.
SAGITTARIUS	Uttrashada – 1	Politician, Agriculture, Irrigation, Post and telegraph, Telephone, Religion, Education Judges, Embassy etc.

Sign	Nakshatra	Professions
CAPRICORN	Uttrashada – 3	Income Tax, Estate duty, Research work, Archaeology, Monuments, Homeopathy, Jail, Engineer, Ancient, Languages.
	Shratana – 4	Files, Kerosene, Liquids Agriculture Secretary, Minister, Mining, Geology, Pearls, Mining, Excavation, Fisheries.
	Dhanishtha – 2	Mining, Insurance, Murderers, Postmaster, Labour, Welfare, rehabilitation, Distilleries.
AQUARIUS	Danishtha –2	Agriculture, Ration, Leather, Skin, Postmaster, Police, Military, War, Riots, Revolts, Monuments, Archaeology, building, Television, Telephone, Atom energy.
	Shat Bhisha – 4	Science, Mystical subjects, occult, Astrologer, Revolution of ancient science, Jail, old places.
	Poorva Bhadra Pada – 3	Teaching, Astrology, Medical, Airship, Municipalities, Broker, Air travel, Research.
	Poorva Bhadra Pada – 1	Politics, Professor, Minister, Legal cases, Education, religion, Trusts, Hospitals, Famine, Planning, Touring, Bank, Medical, Foreign exchange.
	Uttra Bhadra Pada – 4	Prison, Sanatorium, Hospital, Jail, Export Import, Inheritance, religions and Charitable Institutes, C.I.D. education, fisheries, Photography.
	Revti – 4	Publication, Editing, Religion, Journalism, Politician, Professor, Lawyer, Typing, Radio, University, Purohits, Astrologer, Mathematician, Forest, bank etc.

SUN

Sun – Sun is the parent of the entire solar system. It is 93 million miles away from Earth. It is 750 times larger than all the Planets put together. Its diameter is 110 times of the earth and 27,19,000 miles in circumference. Sun is giver of 'Prana' and is worshipped as 'Sun God'. Gayatri Mantra is the main basic of Sun-worship. The greatest Astrologer Varaha mihir worshipped only 'Sun God'. He was one of the 9 gems of King Vikramaditya of Ujjain.

Sun is the symbol of spirit, soul of Kalapurusha, Moon of mind, mars of strength, Mercury of Speech, Jupiter of knowledge Venus of desire or lust, Saturn of misery.

Sun is lord of East and Leo sign. Sun is masculine, red in colour, Bilious. It denotes father, profession, Government, it also commands state, temples, eyes, spinal cord, nerves are affected by Sun : Sun is strong in the 7th house, cheshta Bali from capricorn to gemini. Headache, constipation, T.B. typhoid, dysentery, eye diseases, mental diseases, insult, conflict, etc are considered through Sun. Sun is the karak for Lagna, religion (9th house), karma (10th house). Sun is Digbali in 10th house. Sun is exaltation in Aries and debilitation in Libra sign. The planet which is karak of particular house, if in that house that karaka planet is alone then it does not give good result. Sun is also the karaka for heart.

Sun in 12 Signs

Sun in Aries: Sun is exalted in this sign in 10°. The native is of strong individuality, self-reliant, bold, brave, clever, bilious, kind, serious natured, independent, strong mentality.

Sun in Taurus: Self reliant, peaceful, good behaviour, mouth-disease and have jealousy with wife.

Sun in Gemini: Sweet tongued, wise, polite, wealthy, lover, Astrologer, Historian and Mathematician, kind-hearted.

Sun in Cancer: Famous, dutiful, movable, communist, historian with diseases of cough, philanthropic.

Sun in Leo: Good friends, faith in Morality, good conduct, honest, patient, courageous, angry, living in forests, labourious, brave and bold.

Sun in Virgo: Less powerful, physically weak, patient of constipation, writer, out spoken, wise, thinker.

Sun in Libra: Less self-strong, patient of constipation, desirous of going outside from mother land, adulterous, dry nature, yogic-acts.

Sun in Scorpio: Industrious, disease in stomach, popular, angry, mentally brave, miser, doctor, secret-hoarding, intelligent.

Sun in Sagittarius: Doing yogic acts, intelligent, intellectual, wealthy, kind hearted, good behaviour, peaceful, faith in god.

Sun in Capricorn: Quarrelsome, swift, misbehaviour, miser.

Sun in Aquarius: Broad minded, dutiful, angry, somewhat selfish.

Sun in Pisces: Intellectual, doing yogic-exercises, wise, Intelligent, famous, Businessman.

Sun in 12 Houses

Sun in Lagna: Independent mind, Angry, patient of bile and constipation, swift, traveller, physically weak, high nose, broad and wide face, brave, moving, wealthy, little hair on body.

Sun in 2nd house: Patient of mouth, wealthy, lucky, quarrelsome, patient of eye-ear, fear from king.

Sun in 3rd house: Bold, Brave, courageous, poet, recognised by king, famous, strong, brotherless.

Sun in 4th house: Anxious, beautiful, rigorous, destroyer of parents wealth, hate with brothers, believing in secret-knowledge, vehicle-less, no kind-heart.

Sun in 5th house: Ill, less-progeny, good conduct, Intelligent, anxious, haste in anger.

Sun in 6th house: Killer of enemies, Brave, bold, trouble some to mother, just, wealthy, healthy.

Sun in 7th house: Troublesome to wife, Independent, Rigid, selfish, insult by Government, Anxious.

Sun in 8th house: Bilious, Anxious, Angry, wealthy, weak patient and intellect.

Sun in 9th house: Good behaviour, leader, Astrologer, brave, having vehicles, servants, faith in God.

Sun in 10th house: Brave and Bold, Professionally clever, Recognition from Government, Famous, Minister, Kind-hearted, popular and wealthy.

Sun in 11th house: Happy, strong and wealthy, independent, Less-spoken, good conduct, Less-progeny, stomach-diseased.

Sun in 12th house: Sad, Left-eye troubled, headache, Idol, living out from mother land, jealousy in friendship, weak body.

Aspect of Sun on 12th Houses

1st house: If sun aspects the first house the native is eye-patient, materialistic view, generally wealthy, devotee of Saints, Vedanti, Devotee of father, Doctor or Government Officer.

2nd house: Aspect of Sun on second house shows that the native is generally happy with family and wealth, eye-patient, destroyer of hoarding money, little earning from labour, profession by animal help, tolerant in troubles.

3rd house: Aspect of Sun on third house shows that the native is from good family, no happiness from elder brother, recognition by Government, Industrious, Administrator, leader and bold.

4th house: Aspect of Sun on fourth house shows that the native was void of happiness till the age of 22-23, generally getting mother's happiness, after the age of 22 gainer of vehicles and other happiness, independent.

5th house: Full aspect of Sun on fifth house shows that the first child will destroy, anxious for Son, wise helpful to have progeny at 20-21 age.

6th house: Full aspect of Sun on sixth house shows that the native is somehow unhappy through enemies are afraid of him, left-eye disease, having debt and destroyer of maternal uncle.

7th house: Full aspect of Sun on seventh house shows that the native is debt ful throughout life, destroyer of wife in 22-23 years age, businessman, rigid nature, unhappy in beginning life, happy in last days of life.

8th house: Aspect on 8th house shows that the native is patient of pile, adulterous, speaking a lie, doing evil acts, proudy having bad habits.

9th house: Aspect on 9th house of Sun shows that the native is afraid of religion and God, Devoid of happiness from elder brother and brother-in-laws.

10th house: Full aspect of Sun on 10th house shows that the person is wealthy, Gazetted Officer in Government, destroyer of mother but if Sun is exalted and aspects the 10th house then full happiness of mother, vehicles, Money, house, landed property.

11th house: Full aspect of Sun on 11th house wealth and famous in business, destroyer of first child, intelligent, wise, having good family and kind-hearted.

12th house: Having full aspect on 12th house Sun makes the native going on travels, eye-patient, having sign of mole of nose or ear, expenses on good works, fond of vehicles and troublesome to maternal uncle.

Combination of Planets with Sun (Sun with One Planet)

Sun-Moon: Iron and Stone merchant, technician having knowledge of house-construction, Idol maker, painter, photographer, etc.

Sun-Mars: Famous, brave and bold, Industrious and out spoken of self-action.

Sun-Mercury: Sweet speaker, wiseman, Lucky, wealthy, artist, writer, thinker, modificator.

Sun-Jupiter: Preacher, Teacher, religious, faith in God, respected by King for wisdom and knowledge.

Sun-Venus: Painter, eye-diseased, luxurious, sexual, Bad-thinker.

Sun-Saturn: Physically weak, mentalist, faith in God.

Sun with Two Planets

Sun-Moon-Mars: Patient, Brave, Bold, Strong, Scientist, technician, clever in Action.

Sun-Moon-Mercury: Dignified, wise, lucky, Ethical, fond of knowledge, recognised by Government.

Sun-Moon-Jupiter: Yogi, wise, happy, broadmind, thinker, good worker, and having full faith in God, lover of mankind.

Sun-Moon-Venus: Physically weak, merchant, happy, avoid of progeny or less children, miser, less wealthy.

Sun-Moon-Saturn: Cunning, innocence, out spoken, proudy, swift, unreliable.

Sun-Mars-Mercury: Courageous but rigid, misconduct, out spoken, proudy, poor.

Sun-Mars-Jupiter: Respected by Government, truthful, wealthy, dignified, influential and honest.

Sun-Mars-Venus: Native of good family, rigid, luxurious, clever, eye-patient.

Sun-Mars-Saturn: Avoid of family and wealth, sorry, miser, insulted.

Sun-Mercury-Jupiter: Intelligent, wise, clever, poet, writer, luxurious, weak digestion, eye-patient.

Sun-Mercury-Venus: Unhappy, outspoken, travelling, jealousy, evil acts.

Sun-Mercury-Saturn: Jealousy of Art, rigid, destroyer of wealth, in childhood beautiful but at the age of 36 disturbed-body, evil-acting.

Sun-Jupiter-Venus: Helping others, broadminded, famous, doing good works, respected by the King and good kind-hearted man.

Sun-Jupiter-Saturn: Loose character, suffering from enemies, living with bad person, patient of Leprosy.

Sun-Venus-Saturn: Bad character, misconduct, disrespect by Public suffering from hated disease.

Sun with 3 Planets

Sun-Moon-Mars-Mercury: Writer, attached with family, ill, clever and dutiful.

Sun-Moon-Mars-Jupiter: Living like King, wealthy, ethical and captain or Head of an Institution.

Sun-Moon-Mars-Venus: Wealthy, dignified, ethical, dutiful. humorous, wise, tactful.

Sun-Moon-Mars-Saturn: Eye-diseased, Technician, Goldsmith, wealthy, patient and ethical.

Sun-Moon-Mercury-Venus: Happy, virtuous, famous, pandit, wise, and average wealthy.

Sun-Moon-Mercury-Saturn: Troubled body, clever in speaking, good conduct, swift, dutiful and engineering-mind.

Sun-Moon-Jupiter-Venus: Philanthropic, Head of religion, constructor of Dharmashala, Dam, etc, good man, helping nature, highly ambitious.

Sun-Moon-Jupiter-Saturn: Rigid, bad conduct, happy belonging, to good family but speaking ill of others though, dutiful and industrious.

Sun-Moon-Venus-Saturn: Physically weak body, sexual, adulterous, devoted to wife.

Sun-Mars-Mercury-Jupiter: Theft of other person's wives, thief, speaking ill of others, getting insult in life, wealthy through business.

Sun-Mars-Mercury-Saturn: Poet, Secretary, Minister, famous, happy, respected, good and wise person.

Sun-Mars-Jupiter-Venus: Popular, luxurious, ethical, dutiful, and loved by all.

Sun-Mars-Jupiter-Saturn: Respected by the Government, Dear to family, devotee of Saint, dutiful, Mill-owner, Businessman, teacher, administrator, and knowledge of constitution.

Sun-Mars-Venus-Saturn: Jealous to brothers, badname, evil acts, dirty low-action.

Sun-Mercury-Jupiter-Venus: Wealthy, having brothers, happy dutiful-worker, chairman, popular, ethical.

Sun-Mercury-Jupiter-Saturn: Respected but weak, quarrelsome, poet, reviser, editor, literary.

Sun-Mercury-Venus-Saturn: Outspoken, virtuous, little happy, living in forests, traveller, having all means necessary to life.

Sun-Jupiter-Venus-Saturn: Miser, poet, leader, head, selfish and clever, famous.

Sun with Four Planets

Sun-Moon-Mars-Mercury-Jupiter: Clever in fighting, cunning, authoritative, having no peace, dogmatic, proudy.

Sun-Moon-Mars-Mercury-Venus: Pure selfish, faith in other religion, brother-less, weak.

Sun-Moon-Mars-Mercury-Saturn: Living no more years (short life), unhappy, avoid of wife-wealth-son, suffering from being away from family.

Sun-Moon-Mercury-Jupiter-Venus: Avoid of parents and brothers, thief of other wealth, cruel, eye diseased, brave but tricky.

Sun-Moon-Mars-Venus-Saturn: Able fighter, conductor, avoid of wealth-fame-influence, trouble giver to others.

Sun-Moon-Mercury-Venus-Saturn: Brave, wealthy, dirty, misbehaviour, attached with others wives.

Sun-Moon-Mercury-Jupiter-Venus: Minister, wealthy, strong, brave and distinguished.

Sun-Moon-Mercury-Jupiter-Saturn: Timid, beger, cruel, angry, sinner, dependent for food on others.

Sun-Moon-Mercury-Venus-Saturn: Poor, avoid of son, ill, long-life, suicider.

Sun-Moon-Jupiter-Venus-Saturn: Happy with wife, strong, fearless, clever, magician, unstable mentality.

Sun-Mars-Mercury-Jupiter-Venus: Army commander, leader, attached with others wives, humourous, happy bold and brave.

Sun-Mars-Mercury-Jupiter-Saturn: Patient, dirty, aggressive, a little wealthy.

Sun-Mercury-Jupiter-Venus-Saturn: Religious, wise, lover of wisdom, lucky, happy and wealthy.

Sun with Five Planets

Sun-Moon-Mars-Mercury-Jupiter-Venus: Pilgrimager, virtuous, having wealth-wife-son, living in forests, famous.

Sun-Moon-Mercury-Jupiter-Venus-Saturn: Headache, living in far off countries, somewhat mad-natured, living near temples, character - loose.

Sun-Mars-Mercury-Jupiter-Venus-Saturn: Wise, ever going on travels, jealous of brother, ill and servant of others.

Sun-Moon-Mars-Mercury-Jupiter-Saturn: Leprosy-diseased, insulted by brother, son-less, sufferer, servant of others.

Sun-Moon-Mars-Jupiter-Venus-Saturn: Leader, Secretary, Minister, Low-mentality, influential, patient of T.B., little wealthy.

Sun-Moon-Mars-Jupiter-Venus-Saturn: Kind hearted, peaceful, wealthy, administrator.

Moon

Sun is said to be generator of power where as moon is considered as the conductor of power lent by Sun. Moon is 2,38,000 miles away from Earth. It moves round the earth which revolves round the Sun. Moon is small in size. Diameter of earth is 7800 miles whereas that of the moon is only 2200 miles. Sun gives the spirit and life to all the planets and moon rules over the lives of beings on earth. Sun represents individuality, Moon shows personality. Moon also represents mother while Sun represents father. Sun is masculine and moon is feminine. Sun is fiery, while Moon is watery so moon is a fruitful planet.

Moon transits through all the 12 signs of the Zodiac in 27 days, 7 hours and 43 minutes. Moon is a nocturnal, cold, changeable, moist, receptive and feminine planet. Cancer sign is ruled by Moon. Moon gets exalted in Taurus. In Taurus it is very strong. It gets weak and debilitated in Scorpio sign.

Moon is a cold planet. So often causes cold and fever. Changeability is the main characteristics of Moon. The people born with moon as their ruling planet will ever be unsettled. Moon represents mother, owns the 4th house indicating love for home and motherland of the native. Mind is ruled by Moon. Mercury governs intelligence hence if *Moon-Mercury* aspects each other they give the native fertile imagination, deep feelings, etc. *Moon-Venus* aspecting each other give taste for music, painting, scented oils, keen imagination, love for all pleasurable things. Moon-Mars in favourable disposition offer extreme liberality and frank nature. *Saturn-Moon* beneficial relations makes one patient, persistent, steady cautious, ever inclined to hoard money. *Jupiter-Moon* aspecting favourable give hopeful disposition good, imagination, optimism. *Mercury and Sun* framing good aspect with moon gives proper digestion and assimilation.

Moon is the lord of West-North Direction, feminine, watery, white in colour. It rules cold, cough, gas, blood in body, parents, mentality, vitality, grace of the King or Government, wealth and property and 4th house are considered from moon. It is strong in 4th house and Cheshta Bali from Capricorn to Gemini sign. Physical deficiency, disease of cold, cough, gonorrhoea, ladies illness, mental diseases, travels, stomach, mind are considered by moon. From the 6th day of Black Night (कृष्ण पक्ष) to 10th days of light night (शुक्ल पक्ष). Moon is weak and malefics and from 11th of Shukla Paksha to 5th of Krishna Paksha it is benefic and strong. Strong and beneficial Moon gives full success when in 4th house, otherwise not. Moon gets exalted in Taurus on 3 degrees and debilitated in Scorpio on 3 degrees.

Moon in 12 Signs

Aries: Moon in Aries gives strong body, stable wealth, brave, sexual, fear from water.

Taurus: Handsome, happy mood, sexual, donator, daughters more, peaceful, cough-diseased.

Gemini: Clever in sexual intercourse, worldly wise, eye-doctor.

Cancer: Having progeny, Prosperity, wealthy, best intellectual, sexual, faithful, astrologer, somehow mad.

Leo: Strong body, patient of teeth and stomach, devotee to mother, less progeny, donator, serious in working.

Virgo: Handsome, sweet-speaking, virtuous, patient, wise, happy, fond of learning, teaching and journalism.

Libra: Strong and large body, faith in God, Corn-Doner, wealthy, landlord, philanthropic.

Scorpio: Miser, no faith in God, brotherless, fond of others wives, clever in hoarding money.

Sagittarius: Beautiful, speaker, technician, destroyer of enemies.

Capricorn: Famous, religious, poet, angry, miser, musician.

Aquarius: Little body, tall, drinker, idol, technician and sufferer.

Pisces: Technician, handsome body, religious, wise, sexual, happy, kind-hearted.

Moon in 12 Houses

1st house: When is in Lagna the native is physically strong, luxurious, happiness, Industrious, fond of Music, Fat body.

2nd house: Sweet speech, handsome, materialistic, living in far off lands, tolerant, lucky, peaceful.

3rd house: Smiling, faith in God, hardworker, sweet tongued, Lover, Coughy.

4th house: Doner, distinguished, happy, kind-hearted, Healthy, Avoid of Attachment and envy, Agriculturist, Rising Luck after marriage Intelligent and earning living by water.

5th house: Swift, daughters more, virtuous, earning from speculation, and forgiver.

6th house: Cough-patient, Short lived, Attached, Extravagant, disease of eyes, lover of servants.

7th house: Civilized, Patient, Leader, Thinker, Travelling generally, Seavoyage, Proudy, Advocate, famous, cold and smart.

8th house: Disturbed body, sexual, earning from Business, out spoken, independent, envy, unhappy from Boundage.

9th house: with Progeny-Prosperity, Religion, Active, fond of travel, just, swift, wise, fond of wisdom, knowledge, courageous and less-brothers.

10th house: Active, dutiful, kind-hearted, Less intelligence, Businessman, happy, popular and famous, wise, rising name and fame of the family, satisfied, well wisher of humanity, dignified, courteous, smiling, Long life.

11th house: Swift intellect, man of quality, prosperous with progeny and property, happy, popular, famous, Long life, knowing Mantras, fond of living in far off lands, expert in government job.

12th house: Patient of eyes, swift, patient of cough, Angry, solitude, anxious, sweet speech, extravagant.

Aspect of Moon on 12th House

1st house: Full aspect of moon on Lagna makes traveller, Industreious, Lucky, miser, fond of Luxury and Lover of wife.

2nd house: More children, generally happy, Physically troubles from 8-10 years of age, loss of wealth, fear of drowning in water, suffering from wounds, hurt.

3rd house: If moon aspects fully the 3rd house the native is religious, Traveller, less brother, more sister, Lucky from the age of 24, lover of good persons society, broad minded.

4th house: Happy from the age of 24, Respect by Government, happy from vehicle and house, devotee of mother.

5th house: Good behaviours and fine conduct, wise, First child is male, Artistic mind.

6th house: Peaceful, Patient, fear and trouble from foes secret illness, extravagant, fear from water at the age of 24 years.

7th house: Happy and handsome, beautiful wife, Truthful, earning from business, miser.

8th house: Destroyer of paternal wealth, opposition to family, eye patient, Avoid of goodness.

9th house: Full aspect of moon on 9th house makes the native religious, Lucky, devoid of brothers, and wise, intelligence.

10th house: Laying and selling of animals, change of religion, hate and enmity with father, disturbed nature.

11th house: Gaining profit, expert industrious, more daughter, Lover of friends.

12th house: Expenditure by enemies, Anxious, Respect and service in government job, happy in olden days.

Combination of Moon with One Planet

Moon-Mars – Victorious, good in speech, Brave, Bold, Artist.

Moon-Mercury – Religious, wise, psychic, Pure intellect, Reviser.

Moon-Jupiter – Virtuous, love, religious, good behaviour and conduct, Philanthropic, Servant of Pure humanity through wisdom, knowledge.

Moon-Venus – Businessman, happy, wealthy, materialistic, lover of Music, Art, Painting, Poetry, drama, literature, etc.

Moon-Saturn – Vicious, Void of Virtues, food, inclined towards, hoarding money, fool

Two Planets with Moon

Moon-Mars-Mercury – Rigid, Sinner, Cunning, Cruel, evil acts tendency to harm others.

Moon-Mercury Jupiter – Happy, healthy, wealthy, dignified, Active in sweet speaking, dutiful.

Moon-Mercury-Venus – Miser, Jealous, Vicious, Proudy, cunning and clever in deceiving others by sweet speech.

Moon-Mercury-Saturn – Restless, Intelligent, Successful in keeping words, dutiful, respected by those superious in government.

Moon-Jupiter-Venus – Virtuous, happy, wealthy, Luxurious, Leader, dutiful, Quick witted.

Moon-Jupiter-Saturn – Leader, fond of wisdom, Industrious, teacher, Advocate, ethical works.

Moon-Venus-Saturn – Writer, teacher, Astrologer, good works, editor, labouorious, industrious, good behaviour.

Three Planets with Moon

Moon-Mars-Mercury-Jupiter – Intelligent, Virtuous, happy, Technician, Wise, Helping people by speech and good actions.

Moon-Mars-Mercury-Venus – Quarrelsome, Idle, lazy, happy but non-cooperative with others.

Moon-Mars-Mercury-Saturn – Brave and bold, many sons, good family, Virtuous but physically weak and trouble-some.

Moon-Mars-Jupiter-Venus – Patient, brave, wealthy and respected, religious and social worker, happy from wife.

Moon-Mars-Jupiter-Saturn – Brave, bold, Patient, Wealthy, labourious, knowing wisdom and use of weapons.

Moon-Mars-Venus-Saturn – Avoid of teachers, sad, troublesome, devotee to parents, wise, wealthy, happy and dutiful.

Moon-Mercury-Jupiter-Saturn – Brave, famous, Lover of brother, Respected, famous poet, writer, Literary.

Moon-Mercury-Venus-Saturn – Character less, envy of people, void of society.

Moon-Jupiter-Venus-Saturn – Travellers disease of skin, outspoken, troubled, poor.

Moon with Four Planets

Moon-Mars-Mercury-Jupiter-Venus – Happy, wise, writer, goodman, lucky and powerful, dutiful, reviser.

Moon-Mars-Mercury-Venus-Saturn – Troubled, ill, Philanthropic, Stable-mind, famous, helping to the needy person.

Moon-Mercury-Jupiter, Venus, Saturn – Respected and worshipable, popular, mechanic, living like a king, eye-diseased.

Moon with Five Planets

Moon-Mars Mercury-Jupiter-Venus-Saturn – Religious, wealthy, Luxurious-good character.

MARS

Mars is one of the outer planets. It is nearer to the earth than any other outer planets. The distance between Sun and Earth is 93 million miles where as the distance between Sun and Mars is 141 million miles.

Mars completes its Journey around the sun in 687 days. Mars is smaller than earth and its diameter is around 4200 miles. It is just double of moon. Mars is Red in colour. Mars is known as GOD of war and hunting. He is also GOD of dispute, destruction, force, energy He is the commander in chief of the planets-army.

Mars is fiery, dry planet, masculine by nature. He rules over 2 signs Aries and Scorpio Positive in one negative in second, exalted in Capricorn, debilitated in Cancer detrimental in Taurus and Libra Mars is significant of energy both constructive and destructive depend upon the position in Horoscope. He also rules over the animal's instincts in man. Though mars has generally malefic view but when aspected favourably by benefics it gives in man self-confidence, endurance, impulse for all ventures and heroic deeds, strength, courage, sharp wit, faculty to argue, to go ahead spirit etc. Quick mental Activity, muscular strength, great organising ability, power for practical execution, independent spirit, force of character, strong determination, ambition to come out successful in the material field inspite of any opposition and above all leadership in all pursuit, bestows on men.

In weak and afflicting position Mars will give the native Rash, lose temper quickly and will be fore-hardy. One will be quarrelsome. He may be fond of drink. He is always ready for violence. Worst type of sexualities is also governed by mars. Martious are extremists when they are true to anybody they will sacrifice their lives to save their friends. They take large projects.

Mars is the chief governor of brothers and Landed property. Good aspect between Sun and Mars gives abundant energy and good health, self reliance and luck. Forming good aspect with moon indicates the native to be generous, ambitious, hold and enthusiastic.

Having good aspect from mercury one will envince love for work. Good aspect from Jupiter makes the native determined. Logicians and lawyer have good aspect between Mars and Jupiter. Good aspect from Venus will make the native Courteous, upright, accommodative and diplomatic. Favourable aspect between Mars and Saturn is very beneficial then the native is bold, courageous and gives the native force and character, patience, endurance, health and activity.

Mars in 12 Signs

Aries – Truth-speaker, brave and bold, Leader, courageous, doner, respected by public and by government, popular.

Taurus – Envy of son, Traveller, Unhappy, Sinner, Quarrelsome, void of Virtue.

Gemini – Technician, Living in other place then mother-land Dutiful, happy, well wisher of the public.

Cancer – Desirous of happiness, Poor, Servant, Agriculturist, ill, evilness.

Leo – Brave and Bold, Virtuous, Philanthropic, expert in deeds, lover.

Virgo – Respected by Public, Good behaviour, fear from Sin, happy, technician.

Libra – Traveller, Speaker, Sexual, thief of other's wealth.

Scorpio – Businessman, Leader of thieves, Sinner, rigid, Vicious, evil-minded.

Sagittarius – Hard, Rigid, Cruel, labouorious, dependent on others.

Capricorn – Famous, Bold, Leader, Luxuries, happy, Ambitious.

Aquarius – Vicious, inclined to do evil deeds, destroyer from speculation bad habits, Miser.

Pisces – Ill, Traveller, envy of brothers, no faith in God, Cunning, out spoken.

Mars in 12 Houses

Lagna – Cruel, Courageous, Swift, Secret diseases, trouble from Iron and Wounds, hurt etc. loss in Profession does not think seriously.

2nd House – Hard-speaking, Wealth less, not intelligent, growing animals, troubles in the family, diseases in ear-eye, religious.

3rd House – Famous, brave and hold, patient, Courageous, Having all Virtues, Brother less, powerful, good digestive system trouble some to brother, speaking hard.

4th House – Happy from vehicle, progeny, unhappy from mother's side, Traveller, fear from fire, Short lived or having accidental death. Agriculturist, opposition to brother, having profit from land, house, etc.

5th House – Aggressive intellect, Insincere, ill from stomach, weak body, disease in secret parts of body, swift, intelligent, troubled from Progeny.

6th House – Strong digestion, powerful, patient, member of good family excessive strong, killer of energy, debtful, police officer, angry, suffering from eczema, wounds, blood, extravagant.

7th House – Unhappy from wife, gas trouble, fear from Government, sudden anger, Hard speech, cunning, fool, poor, revengeful, envy, destroyer of wealth.

8th House – Affliction from obstruction, Drinker, Hard Speaking, eye diseased, madly behaviour, thief of weapon, Afraid of fire, Shy, defect in blood, Anxious for money.

9th House – Envy, Proudy, Angry, Leader, Officer, Jealousy, famous, less-profit, unsatisfied, opposite to brother.

10th House – Happy, Wealthy, famous, Arousing the name of family, happy from vehicles, Independent, suffering from progeny.

11th House – Speaking hard, proud, Struggle some, angry, Brave, traveler, with profit, just, patient.

12th House – Eye-diseased, destroyer of wife, Debty leftist, Quarrelsome, fool, extravagant, low mentality.

Aspects of Mars in 12th House – If Mars Aspects the House:

1st House – Aggressive Nature, Death of first wife in 21 or 28 years of age Recognised by the state, getting money from land.

2nd House – Disease of Piles, Less profit, separated from family, labourious and angry-anxious minded.

3rd House – No happiness from elder brother, bold and brave, Lucky, having a widow sister.

4th House – Avoid of parents happiness, Physically troubled, sorrow till 28 after that doing no labour.

5th House – Knowing many language wise man, troubles to progeny, adulterous, diseases of Updansh.

6th House – Killer of enemy, troublesome to maternal uncle, famous and bloody illness.

7th House – Fond of other's wife, sexual, Death of first wife at the age of 21 or 28 years of age, Drinker.

8th House – When Mars aspects 8th house the native is destroyer of wealth and family, afflicted by debts, labourious, unhappy, unlucky.

9th House – 9th house aspected by mars makes the native intelligent wealthy, courageous, not interested in religion.

10th House – Government servant, troublesome to parents, happy, lucky.

11th House – Wealthy, trouble to progeny, suffering from family trouble.

12th House – Diseases of piles and fistula, destroyer of maternal uncle, Vicious, Victorious over enemies, leftist nature.

Combination of Planets with Mars

Mars-Mercury – Wealthy, Speaker, Doctor, Technician knowing old texts.

Mars-Jupiter – Mathematicians, Technician, Wise and fond of Music.

Mars-Venus – Expert in Business, Mentalist, doing exercises of Yogas, dutiful, pilot of airplane, unhappy married life.

Mars-Saturn – Impostor (Kapti) cunning, Magician, Unreliable, Crafty (Dhongi)

Mars-Mercury-Jupiter – Goodman, Poet, Well-Versed in Music, Happy with wife, philanthroponic, progressive, ambitions, great worker in life.

Mars-Mercury-Venus – Traveller, Mouth-diseased, Void of duty.

Mars-Jupiter-Venus – Friend of Government, Passionate, good son, luxurious, businessman.

Mars-Jupiter-Saturn – Luxurious, Wealthy, Virtuous, happy, doing great job in last days of life.

Mars-Mercury-Jupiter-Venus – Respected by the public, wise, brave, clever, wealth less, labourious.

Mars-Mercury-Venus-Saturn – Strong body, Athlet, victory in fight, brave.

Mars-Jupiter-Venus-Saturn – Wealthy, dignified, Miser in case of woman, Courageous, Swift.

Mars-Mercury-Jupiter-Venus-Saturn – Ever smiling, Satisfied, distinguished, famous.

Mercury

Mercury is dualist planet bigger then moon but smaller than earth. It is 36 million miles away from Sun. It takes round the sun in 88 days. Its diameter is nearly 3200 miles. Mercury represents speech, wisdom and duality. He is also known as GOD of Commerce. Though Mercury is an intellectual Planet but he is Convertible and mutable planet due to his dual behaviour. Mercury is feminine, neutral and dualistic planet. He becomes malefic if he is connected in Horoscope with evil planets.

Mercury is the ruler of Gemini and Virgo exalted in Virgo debilitated in Pisces. Saturn, Venus are his friends. Sun, Moon, Mars, Jupiter behave as enemy. He rules over the nervous system. He gives the native retentive power and reproductive ability. With good aspects it represents political brain and intellect, a logician with learning and discretion. He makes the native searcher into mysteries and learning, sharp and witty, learning almost anything without a teacher and ambitious of being exquisite in every science. He also gives curiosity to master occult science also. Perseverance and steadiness is necessary because Mercurian is Restlessness and Variable.

Afflicted mercury will make one clever, cunning and mischievous. He may be a gambler too, the worst liar, conceited, showy person. With vain glorious statement. He will be a talkative person. He will also commit mistakes due to forgetfulness. He is a man of mood.

Receiving favourable aspects mercury makes one versatile, good in mathematical calculations, engineering, accounts, correspondence etc. He finds pleasure in Variety. Though he has keen intuition but he himself allows wandering in the way of his grand success. Mercury being a talkative planet hence persons ruled by mercury will prove to be good salesmen, insurance agent, publicity officer, Propagandists, orators, Lecturers, Professors, Advocates, can learn many languages. Mercury indicates North direction so in mercury's period the native will go to North for good fortune or bad as the case may be depends on good or bad aspects. Mercurian appear younger then their actual age.

Sun-mercury with in 3 degrees produces Chief engineers, Accountant general, Publicity officers etc. Moon-mercury have fertile imagination hating original ideas. Mars forming good aspects with mercury shows that the native will be healthy, active and alert. He will never be lazy. Good aspect with mercury and Jupiter gives the native clear thinking, correct forethought and good judgments his out look will be Philosophical and broad-minded. He may be good journalist, Copyist, writer, cashier, auditor, inspector etc. He also may be a good astrologer. Venus and Mercury having good aspects indicate that the native will be very cheerful. Saturn farming good aspects with Mercury offers the native steadiness, Carefulness, good judgement. Precision methodical approach to any subject good memory etc.

Mercury in 12 Signs

ARIES—Weak Physical appearance, clever, lover, dramatist, truthful, sexual, writer, having debt.

TAURUS—Knowing old cultural Texts, lover of exercise, wealthy, serious sweet-speaker, passionate sexologist.

GEMINI—Sweet-Speech, learned, famous, orator, writer, Less-Progeny, wise, virtuous.

CANCER—Talkative, Singer, devotee to woman, Sexy, Living in far off lands, famous, executive, labourious.

LEO—Liar, evil-doing, cheater, sexy,

VIRGO—Lecturer, Literary, Writer, editor, Happy, Journalist.

LIBRA—Technician, clever, orator, poet, literary, Businessman, Kind hearted, faith in GOD, family-loving.

SCORPIO—Vicious, fool, debty, beggar, Liar, mischievous.

SAGITTARIUS—Kind, famous, wise, writer, respected by King, editor, orator.

CAPRICORN—Lower family, not virtuous, liar, debty, fool, timid. Dogmatic.

AQUARIUS—No family, Sorry, unwealthy.

PISCES—Virtuous, Lucky, happy in travel, Money-hoarder, dutiful, Sweet-Speech, tolerant, Independent.

Mercury in 12 Houses

Lagna—If Mercury is in Lagna then the native is long-lived, has faith in God, Mathematician, Humorous, kind, Doctor, wise, dear to wife, Sweet-speaker and thrifty.

2nd House—Beautiful, orator, happy, virtuous, Sweets-eater, Broker Advocate, Thrifty, Courageous, Hoarder.

3rd House—Expert in work, Labourious, Timid, writer, Palmist, Editor, Poet, Having Progeny, Passionate, Less-brothers, Swift, Businessman, Traveller, Religious minded, Friend's lover, Virtuous.

4th house—Pandit, Lucky, happy from vehicles, Doner, fat body, Lazy,fond of Singing, kind, Brother's lover, wise, writer, ethical.

5th house—Happy, quick witted, famous and Respected, Smiling, Virtuous, Musician, Poet, learned man, industrious.

6th house—Good knowledge, struggle Some, lazy (आलसी), ill, proudy, labourious, weak, sexy, lover to wife, Plaintiff (वादी).

7th house—Beautiful wise, coming from good family, Expert in profession, wealthy writer, editor, kind, happy, religious, weak, long-lived.

8th house—Long-lived, famous, Proudy, Respected by Government, agriculturist, mentally unhappy, Poet, orator, judge, mentally wise, wealthy and religious.

9th house—Virtuous, Poet, Singer, Editor, Writer, wise, Astrologer, Afraid of religion, busy in business, Lucky.

10th house—Truthful, wise, Popular, mental thinker, Expert in business matters, poet, writer, just, lucky, respected by the government, landlord and devotee to parents.

11th house—Long-lived, yogi, Virtuous, wealthy, famous, wise, found of music, Leader, honest, beautiful, thinker, enemy-killer, having sons.

12th house—Wise but lazy, speaking a little, having knowledge of old religious texts, writer, vedanti, beautiful, Vehicle and religious.

Aspect of Mercury on 12 Houses

1st house—If Mercury aspects fully the first house then the native is Mathematician, beautiful, businessman, Good behaviour, famous, loving everybody.

2nd house—Wealthy from Business, opposite to family, Dogmatic, Proudy.

3rd house—Lucky, Traveller, Virtuous, religious, Happy from brothers.

4th house—Happy from profit from Government, Happy and wealthy from land and vehicles, good intellect and wise.

5th house—Wise and clever, Technician, wealthy, first child born is son.

6th House—Gastric trouble, expenses on evil acts Suffering from enemies, wealthy in last-olden days.

7th house—Having a handsome and good wife, Businessman Mathematician, clever and expert in his work.

8th house—Ever wandering, opposite to family, troubled, traveller.

9th house—Always smiling face, earning wealth, envy of brother meeting with Royal persons, found of music and passionate.

10th house—Respected by kings famous, happy, coming from high family, light of the family.

11th house—Wealthy, having progeny, wise and Artist.

12th house—Liar, blame to the family, wine-drinker low mentality and having bad habits.

Combination of Mercury with other Planets

Mercury-Jupiter -Poet, famous orator, Reviser, Respected by people.

Mercury-Venus-Clerk, passionate, happy, respected by Government Administrator, sexy.

Mercury-Saturn Poet, orator, Artist, thinker respected by association.

Mercury-Jupiter, Venus, Saturn-Learned man, devotee to father, Religious, happy, high character, Expert in his work.

Jupiter

Jupiter is 500 million miles from the Sun. It has diameter of 88000 miles. It takes about 12 years to go once round the Sun-Jupiter is planet of dignity and shines brilliantly. Jupiter has 11 Moon, earth one and Mars has two Moon. Jupiter is teacher who removes ignorance and darkness. It is the Symbol of wisdom and God of Righteousness and justice. Jupiter is Dev-Guru and Venus is Asur-Guru.

Jupiter uplifts the soul and does not attach much to domestic life. Jupiter rules finance and family. Jupiter is a fiery, noble benevolent, fruitful, masculine, optimistic, expansive, positive and dignified planet. He rules the Signs Sagittarius and Pisces Jupiter is exalted in Cancer, Debilitated in Capricorn.

Sagittarius being the 9th sign of Zodiac indicates long journeys coming and going from one place to another. Pisces is also ruled by Jupiter which is watery Sign-Pisces born native will be Quiet unassuming, social, ease-loving, disposed of long journeys and life in foreign place. Jupiter and the 9th house indicates meritorious deeds done in previous birth. In religion one will have sincere faith in God.

Hence those who are ruled by Jupiter will be law-abiding, true, honest, sincere and dutiful, will be logical and broadminded. Jupiter is the most beneficial and divine planet which offers generosity, joy, honesty, purity, truthful men, morality. During Jupiter's period respect and reputation can be expected. Peace, Prosperity, health and wealth are offered by Jupiter.

Afflicted Jupiter makes one extremist, will be very liberal, extravagant, over optimisty false hopes, carelessness, debts, disputes, failure in speculation, gambling, worries through children and many other evil signs. Jupiter is said to be a judge.

Jupiter rules over Liver, Tumours, Circulation of blood in the arteries and fat in the body. Sun forming good aspect with Jupiter gives the native a broad outlook recovery from serious diseases are offered. Earning will be made only by fair means.

Mercury forming good aspect with Jupiter gives the native promotion and higher official will be transferred, vacancy will be filled by him. Saturn forming good aspect with Jupiter his senior mostly will pass away and he will be promoted. If Jupiter is strong he will be promoted during Jupiter's period there may be expansion, may be lifted by creating a post. The person will be religions.

Law, finance, education, Bank, executive posts may be his occupation. President, Major Counsellor M.P., M.L.A., Chief Justice, Vice-Chancellors etc honourable posts may be got through Jupiter's good position.

General success in his life will be mainly due to the good aspect between Moon and Jupiter's. Mars forming good aspect with Jupiter makes the native sincere, noble and honest, may be a good sportsman, a police officer, a military man etc.

Venus forming good aspect with Jupiter promises ground success and good fortune. He will be healthy, wealthy, happy, will enjoy happy married life. Venus gives all round success in worldly matters.

JUPITER in 12 Signs

ARIES—Jupiter in Aries make the native Plaintiff, Advocate, Luxurious, dignified, famous, victorious.

TAURUS—Having faith in God, Strong Body, Virtuous, Wealthy Doctor, Wise, intelligent and diplomat.

GEMINI—Scientist, Suddenly getting wealth, Popular, worshipped by public, writer, good behaviour.

CANCER—Wise, Good deeds, Truth-speaking, distinguished, famous, social reformer, yogi, leader, happy, wealthy.

LEO—Good Speaker and orator in Society, conference, seminar etc. Victory over enemies. Religious, Lover, dutiful.

VIRGO—Happy, Passionate, Painter, Wise, Poet, Writer.

LIBRA—Wise, good businessman, poet, writer clever, swift editor, many sons happy.

SCORPIO—Knowing old cultural text words, dutiful, minister religious soul.

SAGITTARIUS—Head of religion, proudy, cunning, sexy.

CAPRICORN—Wealthless, Traveller, useless, labourious, swift, cunning but if Jupiter is retrograded then good.

AQUARIUS—Timid Traveller, is sincere, ill.

PISCES—Writer, Knowledge of Cultural Old texts, not Proudy, Noble, Prideless, respected by king and Government Peaceful, King, good behaviour, Literary.

JUPITER in 12 Houses

Lagna—If Jupiter is in Ist house the native is Astrologer, Long-lived, dutiful, wise, social worker, dignified, outspoken, independent, happy healthy, handsome, polite, having sons, religions, respected.

2nd House—Beautiful body, Sweet-speech, wealthy, having progeny, respected by Government, Popular, Good deeds, Virtuous, Lucky Destroyer of enemies, Long-lived and businessman.

3rd house—Victory over senses, weak digestion, knowledge of old religious texts, writer, Traveller, Yogi, having faith in God, Luxurious, sexy, Lover of wife, dutiful, Industrious, Lover of foreign countries, Traveller, with vehicles.

4th house—Happy with all worldly materials as house, vehicle, mother, peace etc, handsome body, dutiful, Industrious, Astrologer, Family Planner, Respected by Government and Public, devotee of Parents, Famous and Good behaviour and Conduct.

5th house—Faith and belief in God, Astrologer, Popular, the best in family, wealthy from speculation, having progeny, ethical conduct.

6th house—Sweet Speaker, Astrologer, Quick witted, wise, famous, good work, weak, kind, popular, healthy, brave.

7th house—Lucky, wise, orator, head, Polite, Astrologer, Patient Traveller, Beautiful, Lover of wife and fond of others wives.

8th house—Long-lived, virtuous, happy, peaceful, Sweet speaker, wise, writer, light of the family (कुलदीपक), studying astrology, miser, secret disease, destroy of money through friends

9th house—Ascetic, famous, devotee to God, Yogi, Vedanti, Lucky, wise, worshipped by kings, courageous, brave, intelligent, having sons, religious.

10th house—Doing good deeds, morals-worker, religious, luxurious, saint, clever, just, happy, smiling, Astrologer, Truth-speaking, killer of enemies, recognised by Government, Independent thinker devotee to parets, wealthy lucky.

11th house—Healthy, happy and handsome, industrious, satisfactioned, less progeny, worshipped by kings, wise, many wives, expanses on good work, courageous and brave.

12th house—Lazy, speaking-less, happy, economic, yogi, philanthropic kind, knowledge of old religious texts, editor, virtuous, miser, traveller, cruel and cunning, wicked mentality.

Aspect of Jupiter on 12 Houses

Lagna—If Jupiter aspects Lagna the native is religious. Reputated, glorious, owing to good family, wise, husband of devoted fully to husband lady.

2nd house—Destroyer of Paternal, wealth, earning money, with family, the best among his friends, recognised by the state Government.

3rd house—Lucky, bold, happy with brother, Traveller, Virtuous.

4th house—The best reader, fond of knowledge, landlord, with vehicles happy, Happiness of parents and house, peacefully living.

5th house—Wealthy, luxurious, wise, lecturer, having five sons, Artist,

6th house—Living in troubles, destroyer of wealth and money, Angry, cunning .

7th house—Handsome, wealthy, glorious lucky.

8th house—Fear from Government death like trouble in the age of 8th year, in 26 years of age trouble from jail.

9th house—Lucky, member of good family, learned, religious, independent, having progeny, donor, having fast and Vrit, upwas. (fast)

10th house—Happy, wealthy with family and sons, land lord, Luxurious respected and recognised by the Government.

11th house—Intelligent, father of 5 sons, wise, Artist, lover, long life till the age of 70 years.

12th house—Troubled, extravagant, not intelligent, not broad minded.

VENUS

Venus is the most brilliant Planet in the Solar-world. It is much closer to the Sun than the earth. The distance between Sun and Venus is 67 million miles and between Earth and Venus during interior conjunction will be only 25 million miles. Venus has a diameter of 7600 miles while that of earth is 7200 miles. Its period is 225 days.

Venus is Considered to be the Goddess of love, marriage, beauty and Comforts. Venus is a feminine Planet. It rules 2 Signs of Zodiac Taurus and Libra. Taurus is an earthy and fixed sign whereas the latter i.e., libra is an airy and movable one. Being a Feminine Planet Venus governs the gentle and refined attributes. So the people ruled by Venus are kind and social. A Taurusan is pleasant and handsome while a Libran will try to have peace at any cost. They are calm and patient. Venus tries to have sympathy and kindness in family with all the members of the family.

Venus gets exalted in Pisces. Mooltrikona Sign is Libra, it gets debilitated in Virgo. Aries and Scorpio are detrimental to it strong Venus attracts the other sex very early in life. Venus bestows on one all comforts, enabling one to lead a pleasant life in this world. Pleasant eye and sweet voice, smile will attract anybody because he is the Super Quality of Venus. Generally Venusious are the winner in any competition. Affection in the eyes is the main disease which venus gives when afflicted.

Venus gives all the happiness of world. So when the native is over indulgence in amusements, eating, drinking, the Common diseases are Gonorrhea, Syphillis, diseases of ovaries, Skin diseases, Bright's disease swelling, Goitre, Anaemia, afflicting.

Sun and Venus Indicates Cancer

Afflicted Mercury aspecting Venus will give the native nervous disorders which may lead to Hysteria. When Venus is afflicted by Saturn or Ketu one suffers from Eczema.

Musicians, Cinema actors, actresses, film producers, Dramatists, dealers of musical instruments, when second house is strong Venus indicates that the native will be a vocal musicians, a singer or a poet.

Venus as Chief Governor for Marriage

Venus is Karaka for life partner wife/husband. It is also Karaka for business Karaka for vehicles. Daytime born Children's Karaka for mother is Venus.

Sun forming good aspects with Venus indicates that the native will be delighting in sociability, pleasure, easy life, comfort, luxury, clubs, societies. One will be fond of company of the opposite Sex. A venusian will be hospitable, It makes the native generous courteous and cheerful nature. It makes the person fond of art, music and poetry. Marital bliss is the result of positive Venus. Gain of money through business, profession, speculation, holding public office. Sun-Venus combination in 5-7-9 houses indicate that the wife has defect in the generative system.

If sun has adverse aspect with Venus delay in marriage, no pleasant in domestic life.

Moon forming good aspect with Venus will make the native polished and refined will wear neat dron, use fragrant scent, fond of music will be respected among young opposite sex. They will be fond of music, light literature, cinema, drama etc. They will be affectionate and attractive, gentle and good, social and sympathetic. They may be rich through their mother or wife. They will possess luxurious articles, furniture and vehicles. If moon is a significator of marriage wife's star may be Rohini. They will enjoy happy married life.

Mars forming good aspect with Venus indicates that the native will be courteous, well behaved. It gives courage and confidence. One will be fond of adventure, ambitious. He may be expert in music. He may be extravagant. Mars gives energy, authority, responsibility, tact, push and activity. If Mercury forms good aspect one will not mind spending money on advertisement, display, show and propaganda. They are connected with club, societies, etc.

Adverse aspect of Mars to Venus will make life immoral, rivalary, jealousy create enemies. Passion cannot be controlled. There may be separation and dispute. Divorce may be in the end. Accidents from vehicles too may take place.

Good aspect of Mercury with Venus will make the native Cheerful, pleasant and humorous. They may be good artists, having taste in fine arts, music. They may be imaginative and proficient in literature. Sanitary engineering Poetry, comedy, drama writing may also be their taste. They can gain money as agent, broker, salesman, to ladies, assistants to actresses etc.

In adverse aspect of Mercury to Venus mental worry and ill reputation may be results. Secret acts will reveal, letter may be delivered to a wrong person.

Jupiter forming good aspect with Venus the native will be polite dutiful, honest, chaste and faithful. They will have faith in God, occult science etc. They will follow tradition, may not break the law, nor destroy the peace. They will be just and fair, very hospitable. Charity, Purity, piety, equity, are bestowed on the person having this beneficial aspect. Good health and smooth life is bestowed. One may gain success in law court, income tax, sales tax etc. bank, women's college, honour and reputation will increase one may become a trustee of a temple, director, manager of a company, cashier in Transport department. By marriage position many increase. This aspect is the most auspicious for the person to have.

Saturn forming good aspect with Venus. Saturn is a serious thinker so one will consider deeply, before launching an enterprise. Fertile imagination and far sightedness, steadiness, and perseverance, honesty and sincerity. Will make one to plan good scheme. Though he will be economical but not miserly. Good aspect of Saturn to Venus shows marriage in proper age and mutual love between the couple. Adverse aspect will make delay in marriage, disappointment, The moral backbone will be lost. Financial loss, domestic worry, separation, ill health eczema and many other secret diseases may suffer the native. There will be scandal. The native may have litigation and divorce the partner.

Venus receiving good aspect from Rahu and Ketu. The Star and sign in which Rahu and Ketu are posited. The lords of the star and the sign of Rahu and Ketu if aspected by Venus the results will be enjoyed specially in the period of the lord of the star and sign during Venus dasa or Bhukti.

VENUS in 12 Signs

ARIES—Unreliable, fond of other wives, vicious, struggle some prosititute going.

TAURUS—Beautiful, luxurious, donor, virtuous, good conduct, helping others, knowing many old cultural texts.

GEMINI—Clever in drawing and painting, literary poet, lover goodman, well wisher of the world.

CANCER—Religious, well versed in knowledge, beautiful, desirous of wealth and happiness, knowing ethical manners.

LEO—Less happiness, well-wisher and well doing to others, anxious, technician.

VIRGO—Wise man in assembly, more sexy, happy, weak, ill, destroyer of wealth through speculation, sensual.

LIBRA—Traveller, reputated, clever in work, Artist.

SCORPIO—Vicious atheist, angry, debty, poor, secret disease, envy of wife.

SAGITTARIUS—Donator of self-earned money, wiseman, beautiful, popular, respected by Government, happy.

CAPRICORN—Miser, weak, heart-trouble Proudy, sad.

AQUARIUS—Careful, troubled from diseases, unreligious, fond of other's wives, lower mentality.

PISCES—Technician, Peaceful, wealthy, dutiful, Agriculture landlord or jewellers.

VENUS in 12 Houses

Lagna—If Venus is in Lagna the native is long-lived, happy, luxurious, sweet-speech, traveller, wiseman, passionate, sexy and happy from government.

2nd House—Wealthy, sweets-eater, glorious, popular, happy jeweler, with family living, poet, long-lived, brave and lucky.

3rd House—Happy, wealthy, miser, lazy, painter, courageous, wiseman, lucky, traveller.

4th House—Beautiful, powerful, philanthropic, faith in god, happy, clever in conduct and behaviour, passionate, lucky, having son, long-lived.

5th House—Happy, healthy, wealthy, virtuous, just, faith in God, donor, kind, wise, genius, orator, poet, having son, gaining profit, businessman, destroyer of enemy.

6th House—No happiness from wife, having many friends, vicious, urinal diseased, poor, sad, secret diseases, dear to wife, destroyer of enemy, economic.

7th House—Happy from wife, kind, popular, wealthy, anxious, rising luck after marriage, devotee to saint, sexy, adultery, swift, passionate, musician, lucky.

8th House—Living foreign countries, cruel, ill, angry, astrologer, man of mind, sad, secret diseased, traveller, lover of others woman.

9th House—Faith in God, virtuous, happy from house, lover, kind, pilgrimage of pure cities, respected by government religious.

10th House—Passionate, Luxurious, just, Astrologer, Victorious, Miser, religious, Musician, Lucky, kind and virtuous.

11th house—Passionate, Happy from vehicles, steady health, popular, philanthropic, jeweller, wealthy, wise, sexy and having sons.

12th House—Just, lazy, sinner, fat, fond of other wife, much-eater, wealthy, miser, destroyer of enemy semen-diseased.

Aspects of Venus on 12 Signs

Ist House—If Venus aspects fully the Lagna the native is beautiful, lover of others women, fond of sexy job, lucky and clever.

2nd House—Happy with family and from wealth. Earning money, laborious and passionate.

3rd House—Administrator, having many brothers, and sisters, less semen, rising luck at the age of 25.

4th House—Happy, handsome, social server, lucky, obedient, government servant.

5th House—Wise, wealthy, father of a daughter and three or 5 sons, lover, intelligent.

6th House—Brave and bold, destroyer of enemies, vicious, troubled with semen, whitelesprosy, and talkative.

7th House—Sexy, adultery, dogmatic, beautiful wife, independent life passing from the age of 25.

8th House—Poor, troubled, family-less, devotee to saints, suffering from cough and gastric troubles.

9th House—Bringing name, fame and light to the family (कुलदीपक), Head of a village, triumph over enemies, religious, reputated, wonderful.

10th House—Lucky, happy, wealthy, Government Servant, Land-lord.

11th House—Gaining profit by many means, Leader, Head, fond of others wives, poet.

12th House—Semen, diseased, expenditure on marriages, suffering from enemies, Anxious and Jealous of wife.

SATURN

Saturn is known as Shanisnchara which means going slowly. It is surrounded by a system of 3 concentric rings. It appears like a blue ball with 3 rings. Saturn is 886 million miles away from Sun. It is smaller than Jupiter and its diameter is around 75000 miles. It has 9 Moon. Saturn takes 30 years to go round the Sun. It takes about 2 years 6 months in passing through each Sign.

Saturn is Son of Sun and brother of YAMRAJ the God of Death. He is the Chief Governor of Longevity. Saturn is cold and Icy Planet. He is also said the father of 2 evils known as Gulika and Mandi. Saturn is known the enemies of Sun and Moon both Lumanaries. So their Sign Cancer and Leo are opposite Capricorn and Aquarius as Capricorn and Aquarius both Signs are ruled by Saturn.

Saturn is a barren, binding, cold, constant, dry, hard defensive, nervous and secretive Planet. Saturn's might house is Capricorn, day's house and mooltrikona sign is Aquarius. Saturn's exalted Sign is Libra, debilitated Sign is Aries.

Saturn is friendly with Gemini, Virgo, Taurus, Libra ruled by Mercury and Venus as both are considered friend's of Saturn. Saturn is beneficial when in its own Signs Capricorn, Aquarius, or when in Signs of Jupiter Sagittarius and Pisces, exalted in Sign of Venus Libra. Saturn may be how much strong but in Venus period (Such Period) will make one beg always in the street whether the person may be a king or Kuber (Lord of Money) *we have seen Practically in case of Indira Gandhi and Digvijay Singh when both were to leave their Chair of P.M. and C.M. In Saturn mahadasa such Period of Venus in 1977-1980 to Indira Gandhi and in December 2004 to Digvijay Singh.*

Saturn is the most strong and most kind among all Planets so if represents Lord Shiva Lord of Death and giver of Luck calling Rudra and Shiva. Saturn may cause delay, deny, disappoint as they are the evil results of Saturn. When Saturn is benefic patently working, Produce economy saving, Industry, thrift, power to keep secrets Stability and self control, sense of duty are good results of Saturn.

When Saturn is malefic the native will be Lazy will not do work well. hindrances, difficulties, will stop the way of native. Saturnian are very Lazy often miss the bus, they are anxious, distrust, late to start a joli.

People born on Saturday in Capricorn, Aquarius Signs as Lagan and in the nakshatra of Saturn Pushya Anuradha, Uttra Bhadra Pada will work according to the position of Saturn during its period good or evil. This is very Important. Jupiter Produces, Saturn destroys.

Saturn when benefic makes a person true, reliable, honest, sincere, faithful etc. The veil of Saturn can be warded off by the powerful Mars and Saturn. Saturn is depress or hence when Moon, Mercury are afflicted by Saturn they feel inferiority Complex. In such condition use red colour.

Saturn indicates all hidden things in secret, mines, tunnels, burial grounds etc. Geology is studied under rulerships of Saturn. Jupiter in for expansion, improvement but Saturn never cares for others opinion and is economical and calculating.

Saturn governs Pure blue colour. When one run's Saturn's period blue colour will attract.

Saturn and Sun Show those who organise and manage big Componies assisted by Government service in local board, Panchayat Board, District Board etc. Moon-Saturn show agriculturists, preacher of old customs Mars and Saturn engravers, Surveyors, engineers, Contractors, Builders, X-ray technicians. Combination of Saturn with other Planets show the Profession according to the Qualities of Planets.

SATURN in 12 Signs

ARIES—Adulterous, Poor, No self-confidence, Dogmatic, no faithful,
TAURUS—Liar, wealth less, fool, speechless
GEMINI—Insincere, Vicious, Proudy, poor, sexy.

CANCER—Troubled in Childhood, no mother's happiness, Intelligent, wise, progressive.

LEO—Writer, teacher, dutiful, heart. Trouble.

VIRGO—Powerful, less-speaking, wealthy, editor, writer, philanthropic, steady worker.

LIBRA—Nice-Speech, Leader, famous, Independent, Progressive.

SCORPIO—Wife—Less, Angry, Hard, Violent, miser.

SAGITTARIUS—Good behaviour and conduct, famous from the name and fame of Son, Virtuous, happy in olden days.

CAPRICORN—Liar, Faith in God, Labourious, Technician, Traveller, materialistic.

AQUARIUS—A theist, Labourious, Thinker.

PISCES—Pessimist, Technician, Nervous, not thinking systematically.

SATURN in 12 Houses

Lagna—If Saturn is in Lagna of Capricorn, Aquarius, Libra than the native will be happy, wealthy. In other Signs if lagna falls then the native is poor.

2nd House—If Aquarius and Libra is in 2nd house and Saturn is there then the native is wealthy, If other Signs are in 2nd house then mouth-illness, envy of Saints, Hard-Speech, apart from family and brothers.

3rd House—Yogi, healthy, wise, Athelet, Suddenly doing job, clever in Assembly, meeting, society etc., knowing easily, Destroyer of enemies, lucky and swift.

4th House—Not powerful, defame, weak body, early angry, tricky, cunning, lucky, bilious and gastric trouble, sad.

5th House—Gastric illness, Traveller, wiseman, neutral, with progeny lazy and swift.

6th House—Killer of enemies, Poet, Yogi, Bhogi, Throat and breath illness, opposite to caste, wounded, Powerful, Vicious.

7th House—Angry, void of wealth and happiness, Traveller, Low-mentality, Lazy, devotee of wife, passionate and sexy.

8th House—Insincere, talkative, Leoprosy-illness, Timid, Cunning Secret diseases, wise, Fat body and kind hearted nature.

9th House—Gastric trouble, Talkative, Traveller, weak body, timid, Religious, brave brotherless, destroyer of foes.

10th House—Leader, just and fair, wise, Astrologer, Rajyogi, officer, clever Ambititious, Labourious, Lucky, Stomach trouble, Respected by Government, wealthy.

11th House—Long life, Angry Swift, Technician, Happy, wise, Yogi, ethical, labourious, son-Less Healthy, Powerful with Intelligent.

12th House—Saturn in 12th house makes the native ill through Epilepsy. hysteria, extravagant, wicked, hard-speech, unreliable, troublesome to mother and Lazy.

Aspect of SATURN on 12 Houses

Ist House—If Saturn aspects fully the Lagna then the native is black, far from own wife loves the woman of low caste, prostitvte.

2nd House—Destroyer of money till the age of 36, opposite to family, Physical trouble in the age of 19 years having diseases of many kinds.

3rd House—Brave and bold, unreligious, no happy from brothers, low society and doing evil acts.

4th House—Physically ill in one years age, respected by Government Increase in Government Power in 35-36 years of age, Reputated.

5th House—No Progeny, low mentality, low-society, low work.

6th House—Destroyer of enemies, troublesome to mother, eye-diseased far from religion, busy in evil-doing.

7th House—Struggle-some, equal to death trouble at the age of 36, destroyer of money, low mentality.

8th House—Opposite to family, loss from Government, destroyer of Paternal money at the age of 36, ill.

9th House—Traveller, opposite to brothers, earning money in journeys, low-worker, Brave, Religion-less, speaking ill of others.

10th House—No happiness of father, trouble to mother, land lord, happy, respected by Government.

11th House—Having son in old age, knowing many languages, Profit through ordinary business.

12th House—Expenses in bad work, troublesome to mother, destroyer of enemies, having general profit.

RAHU-KETU

Rahu and Ketu are called Chhayagraha or Shadow Planets. They are not independent Planets. They are also called Dragon's Head and Dragon's tail. They are also called Nodes RAHU as ascending node and Ketu as descending node. They have retrograde movement. Some Astrologer say that Rahu is benefic while Ketu is malefic.

Rahu Ketu indicate a person born in lower caste, plot secret with girls. He is fully evil, has friendship with other low caste-fellow, who is fond of travelling, lives in forest, speaks a lie, harsh in speech.

Rahu and Ketu affect the Spleen. Gas trouble and Sharp acute pain is given by them. For both the nodes agate (सुलेमानीरत्न) is the precious stone.

Rahu indicates Paternal grandfather (दादा) whereas Ketu shows the maternal grandfather (नाना) both are Karaka for imprisonment (Jail) living in rented house, enjoying life at other's expense, to use other's vehicles, to have an office car, to take one in adoption, danger to offspring, Pilgrimage, ill health, defect in vision etc are judged from the position of Rahu Ketu in Horoscope.

Rahu and Ketu represent the lord of the Sign. Only when they are not conjoined or aspected by any other planets. Hence to get the result of Position of Rahu Ketu 4 things are important:

1. The Lord of the Sign in which Rahu and Ketu.
2. With which Planet they are conjoined.
3. By which Planet they are aspected. They will give the result of that planet.
4. The Lord of the Star in which they are posited.

Among these 4 Principles the most important is the Planet with which they *are conjoined,* If Rahu and Ketu are not Conjoined with any one Planet then they will give the result of the Planet *which aspect them.* They may be 2, 3, or more in number. Thirdly the Lord of the Sign in which they are will give the result. Fourthly the Lord of Star. In this way in Mahadasa, antardasa of those Planet result will occur with which Rahu Ketu are related as mentioned above.

For example if Rahu and Ketu are in 5 or 9 houses and are Conjoined or aspected by the Lords of 2-7 (Marakas) houses then in the period of Dasa, Mahadasa, antardasa of 2-7 house-lords death may take place. But if Rahu, Ketu are posited in 2-7 houses and are Conjoined-aspected by Lords of 5-9 houses they do not cause death, but will be helping in increasing health and wealth for a long time.

If Rahu or Ketu are in Gemini or Virgo or Pisces or Sagittarius Conjoined with Lords of 1-4-5-7-9-10 houses then the person will gain wealth in their periods-sub-periods. In the same way if Rahu and Ketu are in 3-6-9-12 Signs and if their Lords, i.e., Mercury and Jupiter are in 1-4-5-7-9-10 houses then also in their periods-sub-periods promotion, prosperity-power is given to the Navie.

But if Rahu and Ketu are in 3-6-9-12 dual Signs and are Conjoined with or aspected by any of the Lords of 6-8-12 houses then no benefit will be gained in their periods but any elder member of the family belonging to his or maternal side may die.

If Rahu and Ketu are in movable Signs 1-4-7-10 or fixed Signs 2-5-8-11 with Lords of 1-4-7-10 or 5-9 they give the native wealth and Power.

Rahu and Ketu in 6-8-12 Evil houses cannot produce beneficial results even conjoined with Lords of 1-4-7-10 or 5-9 houses. In 6-8-12 houses Rahu and Ketu may cause death. Being in 6-8-12 houses and conjoined with or aspected by Lords 2-7 (Markesh) may affect the longevity of the native.

Rahu and Ketu in 1-3-4-7-9-10 houses with Rajyoga Karaka Planets or aspected by them one will be happy, healthy, wealthy, will enjoy power, Prosperity and children, vehicles etc.

Rahu is exalted in Taurus, debilitated in Scorpio. Aquarius is the own sign of Rahu and Scropio of Ketu. Mooltrikona of Rahu is Gemini and of Ketu is Virgo. Cancer and Leo are their inimical Signs. Friendly Signs are Libra and Capricorn, Neutral Signs are Aries, Sagittarius, Pisces. Pandit Ram Dayalu says that Gemeni is exaltation Sign of Rahu, Virgo is own Sign of Rahu. Sagittarius is the exaltation sign of Ketu, Pisces is the won sign of Ketu. Some Astrologer say that Scorpio is exalted Sign of Rahu and Aquarius is the exalted Sign of Ketu.

Rahu is beneficial in 4-7-9-10-11 houses, Ketu favourable in 3rd house.

RAHU in 12 Signs

ARIES—Braveless, Lazy, innocent, knowledgeless.

TAURUS—Happy, Swift, not beautiful but beautyless.

GEMINI—Doing yoga-exercises, Singer, Powerful, Longlived.

CANCER—Kind, ill, poor, Impostor, defeated.

LEO—Clever, Ethical, good man, Thinker.

VIRGO—Popular, Sweet-Speech, Poet, Writer, Singer.

LIBRA—Short-life, Dental-illness, having property of dead person, dutiful.

SCORPIO—Cunning, Poor, ill, destroyer of wealth.

SAGITTARIUS—Happy from early age, Adopted, Conflict with friend.

CAPRICORN—Economic, family-less, Dental-Diseased.

AQUARIUS—Wiseman, writer, little-speaking.

PISCES—Faith in God, Born in good family, Peaceful, Artist, Expert.

KETU in 12 Signs

ARIES—Swift, Knowing many Languages, If Aries is Lagna then Poet.

TARUS—Sad, not doing anything, Lazy, Talkative.

GEMINI—Having Gastric troubles, Less satisfied, Proudy, Short life, Angry.

CANCER—Gastic troubles, sad, suffering from ghost.

LEO—Knowing many languages, Timid, Intolerant, fear of snake-bite, Artist.

VIRGO—Ever ill, Fool, Dyspepsia, useless plaintiff.

LIBRA—Patient of Leoprosy, Sexy, Angry, Sad.

SCORPIO—Angry, Leoprosy disease, Cunning, talkative, poor, Bad habits.

SAGITTARIUS—Liar, Swift, Cunning,

CAPRICORN—Traveller, Laborious, Bold.

AQUARIUS—Patient of ear, sad, Travelling, Extravagant, a little wealthy.

PISCES—Patient of ear, Traveller, Swift, Dutiful.

RAHU in 12 Houses

Lagna—Father of still-born child, Male or Scar in the head, wicked unsympathetic, diseased. Selfish, envy of Government, Low-worker, weak but mentally strong, sexy, Less-Progeny.

2nd House—Going far from motherland, Less Progeny, family-less, Hard in speech, less wealthy, hoarding of money, Jealousy, Dark body, may have more than one wife, Quarrelsome.

3rd House—Agriculturist, bold, rich, Exercising of Yoga, destroyer of hindrances, Traveller, Powrful, wise, Businessman, ever store of food at home.

4th House—Troublesome to mother, Suspicious, minded, may be married 2 times one may be Concubine, not reliable, sad, dissatisfied, cruel insincere, Stomach-trouble, liar.

5th House—Void of wealth and intellect, destroyer of wealth and family, unlucky, fond of knowledge, Danger to Children, funky, Sympathetic, Miser

6th House—Very Bold, Brave, Victorious, Long Life, will enjoy life. Profit by other religion's persons, good health, trouble in waist, enemy-destroyer.

7th House—Wife-destroyer, loss in business, Traveller, gastric trouble, clever, miser, evil deeds Adulterous, If there is another malefic then may have two wives, Proudy, arrogant, diseased.

8th House—Ever ill, Ever worried, Confused, depressed, delay in achieving aim. Secret diseased, Angry, fool, Stomach trouble, Sexy.

9th House—Traveller, gastric trouble, useless labour, Pilgrimage-going, Unlucky, religious, wicked. Unhelpful to children, will have servant. No obligation to any one, hate parents, rich, popular.

10th House—Living with widow in dirty Place, wicked person, Lazy, Talkative, irregular worker, economic, troublesome to Progeny. If Moon combines Rahu in 10th house then RAJ-YOGA-KARAKA.

11th House—Wealthy, many children, Owner of land, Building, reputated in war, Victory over enemies, Laborious, Businessman, Sudden Profit.

12th House—Fool, Servant, Expensive, Anxious, Sexy, Few Children, defective vision, Sinner, helpful to other, useless wandering.

KETU in 12 Houses

Lagna—Father of Still-born child, diseased, miser, if connected with benefic then rich and having long-living children, Swift, Timid, Adulterous but if it is Scorpio Lagna then happy, Wealthy, Laborious.

2nd House—Unhealthy, worried for family, may marry two times, fear from Government, mouth-diseased hating others.

3rd House—Swift, Gastric-ill, devotee of ghost, useless talking, Agriculturist, rich, successful contractor, messenger.

4th House—Wealthy, may marry two times, illness to mother, Swift, talkative, Lazy, incourageous useless.

5th House—Evil habits, gastrouble, delay in the pleasure of married life, in auspicious to children, living with low minded people, cunning.

6th House—Courageous, Clever, famous, learned, Studious, but if Moon is conjoined with Ketu in 6th house then no gain, No savings economic, happy some what struggle some, secret diseased.

7th House—Loss of happiness, wife, wealth, fool, defeated by foes, always sleeping, No principle in Life, always touring, cruel.

8th House—Cunning, jealousy of wife, miser, venerable diseased. If with benefic or aspected by benefic may give wealth and long life.

9th House—Finds pleasure with law clan ladies, and servants, no donation, irritated, nice talk, also talk ill of others, evil minded though bold, self-boasting, fond of happiness, useless labour, infamous.

10th House—Envy of father, Bad Luck, foolish, Proudy, Living-dirty Place, living with widow, clever, diplomatic, brave, social success will always be touring

11th House—Gastric trouble, loss, foolish if with or aspected benefic then rich, Courageous, social success, economic, good deeds.

12th House—Few children, defective vision, Sinner, weak mind, unprincipled, no reputation, cunning, superstitious, cheater.

Aspect of RAHU-KETU on 12 Houses

Ist House—If Rahu aspects fully the Lagna then the native is Physically ice, gastric troubles, Cruel and dogmatic, sad mentality unreligious, less-Industrious

2nd House—No happiness from family, destroyer of wealth, suffering from wounds by Stone and Swift.

3rd House—Brave and Bold, No Son, Diplomatic, Victorious.

4th House—Patient of Stomach, ordinary happy, neutral.

5th House—Lucky, Wealthy, Good Behaviour and Happy from Progeny.

6th House—Destroyer of enemies, Brave, suffering from wound in Anus. Expensive, sign of little wound o eye, brave and Bold.

7th House—Wealthy, Sensual, Sexy, having low-society.

8th House—dependent, Destroyer of wealth, suffering from illness in throat, illreligious, busy in low-deeds living separate from family.

9th House—No happiness from elder brother, Luxurious, bold and having progeny,

10th House—No happiness of mother, troublesome to father, Respected by Government, Industries.

11th House—Suffering from Progeny-trouble busy in low-deeds, getting a little profit.

12th House—Secret illness, destroyer of enemies, doing expenses on evils, poor.

Note—Aspect of Ketu on 12 houses is as Aspect of Rahu mentioned above.

Results of Rahu in Stars of other Planets

Rahu-Ketu are Shadowy Planets as they are not independent hence they give the result of that Planet in which Star's Rahu is posited. This is very important to Know.

RAHU IN SUN'S STARS—Sun is the Lord of 3 Stars—Kritika, Uttra Phalguna, Uttra Shada. These 3 stars have 2 signs e.g.

Kritika-1st Pada Sign Aries

Kritika-3 Padas Sign Taurus

Uttra Phalguna—1st Pada Sign Leo

Uttra Phalguna—3 Padas Sign Virgo

Uttra Shada—1st Pada-Sign-Sagittarius

Uttra Shada—3 Padas-Sign-Capricorn.

Hence when Rahu is in Horoscope in these stars the following diseases activities are common which attack suddenly on the native High fever, Heart disease, giddiness, enmity, Quarrels, unhappy environment, fear, suspension about partner, unreliability, change in residence and occupation, unrest, If Sun is Raj Yoga Karak then Promotion, Progress is Business, Profession, name, fame loss of enmity and charity, donation are indicated.

Rahu in Moon's Stars—Rohini, Hasta, Sravana these 3 Sign have 4, 4, Padas in Taurus, Virgo, and Capricorn. When Rahu is in these Stars Success in farming, good crops, purchase of Cow, increase in income, pleasant life, peaceful sea voyage, Purchase of lands, but if moon is afflicted then danger of drawing, change of residence, transfer in service, loss or danger to wife, pain and swelling, injury, mental writers, Anxiousmen etc. are indicated.

Rahu in Mars Stars— Mars Stars are Mrigsira, Chitra, Dhanishtha, If Rahu is in these Stars it gives the result of Mars e.g. loss by fire, robbery, litigation, loss of money, difficulties, animal activities, disputes, irritation, rash action, violence, calamities, dishonesty, danger from Government, Police, military, chances of Imprisonment. Loss in agriculture, disputes of houses, lands, fields, etc, as these are the subjects of Mars. If mars is benefic service in Jail, Police, military P.W.D. agriculture etc. are indicated.

Rahu in Mercury's Stars—Ashlesha, Jyeshtha, Revati are ruled by planet Mercury, when Rahu is in these stars. It will give the result of Mercury. e.g. large number of friends, benefactors, short tourings, saving will be by royal favour, gain from stranger. Life will be happy, birth of many children of gain in business, purchase of vehicles etc. but if Mercury is afflicted the native will be found cheater, dishonesty, cunningmen, increase in enemity, fall of social reputation etc.

Rahu in Jupiter's Stars—Punarvasu, Vishaka, Poorva Bhadrapada are the stars ruled by Jupiter. If Jupiter is beneficial end of enmity, Victory in election, litigation help from Government, Pleasure, acquire of Land wealth, birth of Children increase in wealth and power, good relations and help from high politician, Visits to holy places, social, religious ceremonies in the family etc. If afflicted Jupiter aspects Rahu the position will be just opposite to the above.

Rahu in Venus's Stars—Bharni, Poorva Phalguna, Poorva Shada are the stars of Venus. The purchase of vehicle, furniture, decorated things, good relations, wealth, happiness, friendship will increase. Advantages from superiors, Promotion, Popularity, Prosperity, Property, marriage, birth of children etc will take place. If Venus rules over 6-8-12 houses deception diseases, troubles from enemies, breaking of friendship with other sex, scandal through ladies, loss of money, honour etc. will take place.

Rahu in Saturn Stars—Pushya, Annuradha, Uttra Bhadrapada are the stars ruled by Saturn. Saturn is a naturally malefic hence when Rahu is in these Stars ill Reputation, injury to person, bad Association, struggle with partner and even divorce, disputes, Chronic diseases, rheumatism, biliousness gastric troubles, Depression, Friends, well wishers will go against may have to leave the birth place residence, living in Salitude etc.

Rahu in Own Stars—Aridra, Swati, Shatbhisha are ruled by Rahu. Rahu in these Stars will disturb the mind, Produce anxieties, Quarrels, misunderstanding death of elder or partner, danger of poisoning, transfer atundesirable place; Scandal, ill reputation, ill-health, pain in joints, injury, biting by snakes, loss of wealth. If Rahu is in sub of a benefic the native may be head of the family, enjoy life, may go foreign place, many have promotion etc.

Rahu in Ketu's Stars—Ashwini, Magha, Mool are the Stars ruled by Ketu when Rahu is in Ketu's Stars danger from insects, fracture, piles, fistula, infectious diseases, illness in family, troubles through partner, enmity with superiors, loss of money, honour children etc. But if Ketu is well posited Purchase of jewels, marriage, promotion, land, vehicle etc. birth of child, starting of business, etc., are indicated.

Results of Ketu in Stars of other Planets

Ketu in Sun's Stars—Kritika, Uttra Phalguna, Uttra Shada are ruled by sun When Ketu is in these stars bodily pain, nervousness, danger, blood poisoning, unsuccess, obstacles, hindrances in profession, enmity, trouble in service, parent's relative's sickness, long journey, separation from family secret plans against the native dissatisfaction, opposition, loss etc.

Ketu in Moon's Stars—When Ketu is in Rohini, Hasta, Sravana then mental depression, disputes, worries, troubles through fair sex, wife, daughter, mother. Cold, pleurisy, Bronchitis, Pneumonia, T.B. Loss of relatives, money. If Moon is in 1-4-7-10 or 5-9 houses then social and economic gain is indicated.

Ketu in Mars Stars—Mrigsira, Chitra, Dhanishtha, Stars ruled by Mars and when Ketu is in these stars trouble due to Rash action, injury, dispute with brothers, partition, enemies, difficulties through lands, house, field, fever, headache, typhoid, theft, imprisonment piles, B.P. bleeding, abortion, but if Mars owns beneficial then purchase of land, house, marriage, good health, good relation with brother are indicated.

Ketu in Mercury's Stars—In Ashlesha, Jyeshtha, Revati ruled by Mercury. Ketu in these stars gives no more troubles but favourable with relatives, friends, no anxiety, no jealousy, no deception but gain of knowledge, marriage, child's birth, starting new job etc.

Ketu in Jupiter's Star—Punarvasu, Vishaka, Poorva Bhadrapada are Jupiter's Stars. When Ketu is in these stars then discharge from illness, end of debt, earning of money. Sastisfactory bank balance, birth and marriage of children, success in effort pilgrimages and many other kinds of success are gained.

Ketu in Venus Stars—Bharni, Poorva Phalguna, Poorva Shada are ruled by Venus. When Ketu is in these stars the person will enjoy life fully will have good house with all the facilities in it increase in income, will have vehicle, a beautiful and healthy wife, will have money and jewels, will be devotee to Goddess Laxmi the deity of wealth.

Ketu in Saturn's Star—Pushya, Anuradha, Uttra Bhadrapada are Saturn's Stars, When Ketu is in these stars loss of near related persons, trouble from foes, loss of money, danger of Jail, sale of landed property, loss through calamities, loss of crops, attack of diseases, litigation with landlord , mental disturbance, Secret relation with servant maid. Opposition with relatives etc.

Ketu in Rahu's Stars—Aridra, Swati, Shatbhisha ruled by Rahu when Ketu is in these Stars litigation, sale of Property, other things, chances for jail, disagreement with friends. Loss of Prestige, Power and Property, Punishment by Government, Loss by theft, failure in Business, adultery with low class ladies, ill reputation and reversion in service, disappointment.

Ketu in Ketus Stars—When Ketu is in own Stars Ashwini, Magha, Mool. Then the native gets worries, confusion, loss, delay, separation, extravagants, blood poisoning, depression etc. If Ketu is in good house, its Lord well posited then the above mentioned evil effects will be less.

What the Twelve Houses Tell?

There are 12 houses in a horoscope. Every thing is known through these 12 houses.

First House

The first house is called Ascendant or Lagna. General appearance, character, temperament, colour all these things of a native are known through first house or Lagna. Aspect of benefics on Lagna shows good health aspect of malefics indicates ill health. The result of good and bad aspect of benefics or malefics is known during the Mahadasha, Antardasha and Pratyantar dasa period of the concerning planets Native's habits, disposition, tendencies, personality etc. are also known through Lagna. Honour, dignity, well being, prosperity, courage, fortune in motherland or outside from birth place etc. are known through Lagna. The condition of face is indicated by first house. In mundane Astrology people in the country e.g. in the Horoscope of Independent India. First house is Taurus sign where Rahu is posited and have no aspect hence in India after 15th

August 1947 the influence of foreign culture, foreign Language, foreign civilization etc., may be seen clearly. The individuality of Indian people have been governed by the foreign influence special English language and English culture. In horary Astrology the first house indicates Querist (The person who asks question) Longenity, age, health, happiness, virtues, vices, sufferings are known from Lagna.

The position of planets in Lagna also influences the life of the native e.g. Saturn in Lagna with malefics will make the native Lazy, Mars with Venus or Mercury the person will be ever active e.g. in the horoscope of honourable Chief Justice of India. Shri R.C. Lahoti has Mars, Venus, Rahu in Lagna. If lord of 6th house is present in Lagna with Lord of Lagna the person will be insulted by enemy. Blame on his career may harm the life.

Gains to younger brothers, friends are also indicated by Lagna. Name, fame, higher education, Long Journey relation with foreigners, first child are judged from Lagna. Demise of partner, wife or husband, father's position etc. are known through Lagna.

Second House

The second house of the horoscope indicates economic condition, family position, profit or gain, loss or damage etc. In money matters Jewellary, metals (gold, silver, diamond) bonds, Bank Balance etc.

In family matters second house includes own family relatives, father, mother, grandfather, grandmother, brothers, sisters, children, wife etc.

Moon and Jupiter or their aspect on second house denote good and cultured family. Moon in 2nd house with beneficial aspect of Saturn denotes small family. Rahu in 2nd house shows birth control. Second house is also known as house of speech. Ketu in Cancer, Scorpio or Pisces Signs makes the native dumb. Mars aspected by Mercury and Jupiter shows the native is expert in good conversation. Moon aspected by Mars the person is out spoken aspect of Mercury on moon clear speaking ability aspect of Jupiter on moon-wise speaker, aspect of Venus on moon show talks on sex, cinema, pleasurable pursuits. Saturn's aspect speaks less, Sun's aspect on moon dignified speaker. Mercury in 3-7-11 sign good conversationalist. The second house also shows second marriage. The second house also represents observing power, right eye, memory, imagination. The nail, tongue, nose, teeth, cheeks and chin are also related to 2nd house. Benefics in second house denote good understanding with family. Besides malefics in 2nd house misunderstanding with family members in the period of those malefics. Saturn in second house makes economical and slow in speech. Mars in 2nd extravagant and outspoken in speech. Jupiter in 2nd earning by right means. Second house is a marakasthana being 12th from 3rd as 7th house is 12th from 8th. Aptitude for music is also known by this house.

In mundane astrology this house relates to national affairs, national wealth, banking activities, matters concerting with revenue.

In horary astrology second house denotes money of the querist, his loss or gain. Second house is the 12th house from 3rd house and 11th house from 4th house, denoting younger brother, sisters and mother respectively. Hence their profit and losses are also known through 2nd house.

Third House

The third house in a horoscope denotes courage, firmness, right-ear, boldness, younger brother or sisters, mental strength etc. It indicates inclination to study. If lord of 10 or 6 has related with 3rd house in any way the native may be a soldier or an army officer. Assistance from friends, neighbours, short travels. All kinds of correspondence, letters, paper, writings, accounts etc. means of communication. If third house has any connection with 2, 6 or 10 houses one can become an agent of commission business. If the lord of 4th house is connected with the 3rd house the native may be an estate broker (property or house broker).

The third house is significant of books and magazines and lord of third house is strong then the native may be editor, newspaper agent, Reporter, Journalist, Information officer etc.

If in a lady's chart lord of 3rd is in 2nd then the lady put on jewels on ear, hand, and neck.

If Rahu or Ketu joined with Mars or with lord of 6th house in 3rd house ear disease may be to the native. Lord of 10th house in 3rd house employs in service.

In mundane Astrology the third house denotes the position and behaviour of neighbouring countries. Transportation in the state such as rail, postal, road, telegraph, telephone, etc. Public education also deals by 3rd house, Saturn in 3rd house makes one cautious but not bold but Mars in makes the native brave and actively bold Rahu in 3rd house denotes death of the father of the native during dasha, antardasha of Rahu.

Fourth House

Mother, happiness, vehicle, land, home, learning are known through fourth house. Landed or immovable property taken on rent or given on rent are concerned with this house. Fields, farm, garden, building old monuments are the subject of 4th house. Hereditary properties, treasurers hidden under ground (secret money) are also the subject of this house.

In horary astrology this house signifies termination end of every undertaking, where is stolen property is kept is known through the lord of 4th house and its position. Mars is the Karak for land, house, garden, etc. hence when Mars period or the lord of 4th house's period is running one may buy land, house, garden and other things related to land. In unfavourable condition the land may be sold. If Lord of 4th house and Venus are beneficial one may possess a vehicle. By aspect of malefics on 4th house or on lord of 4th house heavy expenses may occur on vehicle or house construction etc. The Karak for mother is moon and if moon and lord of 4th house are with benefics or have beneficial aspect the native will have long-living and helpful mother. In 4th house is affected by malefics the health of mother may be in trouble or loss of mother and vehicle and happiness may be result.

Fifth House

The fifth house is the house of progeny. Benefics and moon in the fifth house increase the strength of the house and number of children may be increased. Cancer, Scorpio, Pisces are supporting signs in fifth house while Aries, Leo, Virgo are barren signs. If Moon or Lagna are not in fruitful sign or lord of Lagna is not with benefics or no fruitful planet in 5 or 11th house then there is no chances of children.

Property derived through wife or partner, all pleasures physical or mental, games, sports, artistic talent etc., are known through this house. The fifth house is one of trine house (1-5-9 are trine houses) so it denotes previous life's fruits of good deeds.

All the subjects corresponding to opposite sex are given to this house, e.g., love affairs, courtship, legitimate, illegitimate attraction, sexual relations prior or after marriage, kidnapping, raping, etc., are known through this house. Good morals, virtuous life, prayer, vedic and cultural knowledge, ambassadors are matters related to national affairs in Mundane Astrology are known through this house. Profound wisdom, literary production, religious acts, scholarship, etc are the subject of fifth house. Short journeys and so many other portfolios are connected with this house.

Sixth House

Enemy, Disease and debt, arms, wounds, sin, wicked acts, fear, humiliation and danger are known from sixth house. Sickness, its duration, recovery are the subject of this house 6th to 6th house is 11th house which governs the discharge from hospital. The following planets in sixth house show the following.

Mercury	-	Native has many fads and fancies regarding diet.
Saturn	-	Under nourishment generally
Mars	-	Over indulgance in eathing
Jupiter	-	Good for health, it also denotes ill health through love feasting
Moon	-	Native will be whimsical and fanciful in the matter of eating and over fond of liquids and spirits specially when there is a watery sign such as Cancer, Scorpio or Pisces in 6th house and is connected with Mars.
Venus	-	Venus in sixth shows that the native has a taste for nice food and drinks and may cause trouble to health through excess.

As diseases are mostly due to food we eat and thoughts we have in mind. In the period of lord of sixth or the planet occupying sixth house sickness may be felt.

Sixth house also denotes employees, servants and subordinates. Whether the native is in service or he has employed others in his service. Benefics in 6th may cause gain by servants, malefics loss through servants. So in the case in borrowing loans either by benefics or by malefics as the case may be.

Sixth house is also called *'Upchaya'* hence favourable result in competition or otherwise may be known through this house. Miserliness, anguish, prison calamity have to be studied from sixth house.

In Mundane Astrology working class labour, Industries, sanitation and public health are described through sixth house.

Being second to 5th house and 12th house from 7th, the Bank balance of first issue and loss to partner, life in a foreign place, disharmony with or separation from the partner. Father's occupation, name and fame are also known through the 6th house and its lord. This is the house of diseases, enemies, debts hence roll of Doctor, Court cases, Banking etc., are also concerned with sixth house.

Seventh House

The seventh house is the house of union wife, desire, love, passion, way, dowry, coming and going etc are known through the seventh house. Happy and harmonious wedded life is necessary for leading a good family life. Partner in trade business, contract or agreement, conflicts and quarrels, litigation, rival in contest in election or in any other cases are discussed through seventh house. Relation with public such as doctor, engineer, contractor, borrowers etc. should be studied carefully.

Fines, divorces, Legal bondage are ruled by 7th house. Seventh house shows break in journey. 3rd house denotes short Journey, 9th long

Journey. Influence in foreign countries, honour, reputation received their depends on 7th house, its lord and aspect of benefics or malefics.

The seventh house is a marakasthan being 12th to 8th house.

In horary astrology queries relating to the recovery of lost property describes the thief, pick pocketeer etc. The lagna is the owner of stolen property, 4th place of stolen article, 7th house thief, 8th house thief's wealth. When planet in 7th or lord of 7th is weak or among malefics the thief will be caught.

In mundane Astrology international relations war, foreign affairs, international trade, general condition of woman, laws relating to marriage, divorce, public relation, national policies, public meeting etc. are dealt with seventh house. Being 4th to 4th house it deals with mother's immovable property. Honour and credit of the government being in 10th to the 10th house also dealt.

Eighth House

The eighth house is the house of longevity or span of life. Mental pain, defeat, sorrow, scandal, death, impurity, obstacles. For ladies this house is the mangalyasthana or house of luck in case of life of husband. How death is occurred natural or unnatural by drowning, fire, accident, suicide, chronic diseases etc.

Whether the native will have long, medium or short life?

Causes of Death

1. Lord of Lagna in 8th house, planet in 8th in the nakshatra of lord of Lagna or Lagna lord or 8th lord joined, the native himself will be the cause of his own death.
2. Lord of 3rd house in 8th house in the nakshatra of the lord of 12th then younger brother/sister may be the cause of death.
3. If 3rd house is connected with 8th house death may happen during travel.
4. If 12th house is connected, death may take place in a nursing home, sanatorium or in unknown place.
5. If 11th house is connected the native may die in a friend's or elder brother's residence.
6. If the 9th is connected with the 8th house the native may die in a far off place or while going on a long journey.
7. Rahu connected with 8th house may give strange and sudden death or death by incurable disease.

8. Ketu connected with 8th house may cause mysterious death by gas, by unconsciousness etc.
9. If 8th house is in Cancer, Scorpio, Pisces death may be by water through drowning or drinking water, milk etc.
10. Saturn in 8th may cause death due to colds, bone trouble, chronic disease, rheumatism.
11. Jupiter in 8th or with 8th lord or connected in any way with 8th house may give natural death. But if afflicted by evil aspect then death may occur due to poisoning, cancer, liver trouble or inflammation of the lungs.
12. Mars as a fiery planet may cause death by fire, accidents, smallpox, bladder trouble. If mars is in fiery sign at birth then death may take place by fire, violence, if in watery signs 4-8-12 death may be by drowning if in airy sign 3-7-11 haemorrhage may be the cause of death.

Income derived through husband wife is shown by the 8th house. 8th house is called Dushtsthan. As 2nd house shows the money earned by native him self and the 8th house tells about the unearned wealth of the native Eighth house is also connected with medical department as surgeons, medical and health officer, slaughter houses etc. Mercury in 8th denotes an enquiring mind. Jupiter and Saturn in 8th show deep interest in occult sciences.

In mundane astrology 8th house deals with national death rate, public morality, suicide, accidents, food, fire, famine, earthquake national calamity or grief, financial relation with foreign countries, export, import, public loans debts budget etc.

In horary Astrology 9th house shows information of difficulties in Journey, sufferings caused by enemies, death, corruption etc.

Ninth House

Ninth house in a horoscope denotes position of father, teacher, previous luck, worship, virtue, god, grandson, prayer, noble family, faith and wisdom. Ninth house in known the most auspicious house in the horoscope as it is related to the luck, fortune of the native. Jupiter and Saturn aspected by sun or mercury gives one intuition and fore thought religious places as Temple, Church, Mosques, Gurudwara, pilgrimages to the holy places, sacrifices and charity, higher education, higher thought research, inventtion, discovery etc. all these subjects are concerned with 9th house.

Association with good people, devotion to God and elders blessing from the family deity are to be considered from this house.

In mundane Astrology Ninth house relates to travel to long distances such as seavoyage, air and land travel by train and Bus. Judges relating to matters of religion temples, import, export, of the nation, national trade etc. If lord of 9th is strong, the native will be lucky. If lord of 9th is in 6-8-12 houses then there will come many hindrances in the way of luck of the native. If lord of 11th is in 9th the native gets service. Lord of 10th and 11th in 9th house makes the native lucky and wealthy. If ninth house is aspected by Jupiter or Venus or lord of 9th is with Jupiter or venus or lord of Lagna, Lord of 2nd are in 5th house or 9th house, lord of 9th in Lagna then the native is lucky.

If lord of Seventh or Venus is in 3-6-7-10-11 houses the luck of the native will be fruitful after marriage.

If lord of 9th is Sun, Moon, Mars, Mercury, Jupiter, Venus, Saturn or Rahu then rise of luck will be in 22, 24, 28, 32, 16, 25, 36 or 42 years respectively.

If there is exalted Jupiter or Venus in 9th than the native may be minister, member of the council, parliamentary – secretary, Chief Justice, etc.

If Jupiter is in 9th house aspected by Sun and Mars then the native is M.L.A., M.P., if moon aspects Jupiter in 9th then the native is beautiful and passionate. If Mars aspects Jupiter in 9th then the native has gold, diamond and jewels etc. If Mercury aspects then wealthy, if Venus aspects then the native is the owner of movable and immovable property.

Tenth House

Tenth house is the most important house of the horoscope as one's name, fame, honour, recognition, profession, are related to the 10th house. 10th house is the house of lordship, honour, dignity and public esteem. It is the apex of the Horoscope as all the worldly attainments achieved through name and fame, power and prestige, credit and conduct, success and status, respect and reputation, ambition and authority, popularity and public life, etc. are concerned with the tenth house. Appointment in Government service, promotion, superiority etc known through this house, its lord, planet in 10th and nakshatras which falls in 10th house and nakshatras of Lord of 10th, aspecton 10th house etc. are the subject of 10th house.

To judge the profession, business, service, etc one has to study houses 2-6-10 together to reach at the point of conclusion in case of profession or business. The second house denotes result of one's labour in economic advantages. 6th house shows service, routing monotonous work. 10th house shows permanence or change in profession. Saturn in 10th show slow, steady and patient industry. Good and bad aspect on Saturn show a good rise and sudden fall. Jupiter in 10th house shows high honour and favour of those who are in high position. One's moral standard will also be high. He will earn honestly. The native may be a good judge, trustee, minister, ambassador, philosopher, banker, merchant etc. But Jupiter must be well aspected by benefics and be strong then only these results may occur. Distinction, trust and high responsibility are the result.

Mars in 10th with good aspect, strongly posited gives courage, and executive ability. Commanding ability in native comes through mars. Hence those who have mars in 10th house earn name and fame by military, police service or where fire, iron, sharp tools are used.

Mercury in 10th gives success in commission business or agencies. All mental and occult occupation will be fruitful. Mercury empires the native in plural jobs at a time. Mercury works well as a messenger and not a master. One may be employee in engineering, postal, communication, export, import, international trade, contractor or supplier etc.

Venus in 10th well-placed, aspected by benefics indicates good will and patronage among ladies as success in social, artistic and musical pursuits. The native becomes more popular by good humoured nature then by merit.

Sun in10th gives success, honour, distinction, power, prosperity, high patronage and public support, success in Government Service. Favour of superiors, the native makes the trustworthy and responsible position. If Sun is strongly posited in 10th house one will be honest and possess a good moral standard.

Moon in 10th house rules public commodities, travelling, affairs connected with common people.

10th house is known as the house of *"Karma"*. Hence actions as last right in one's parents, religious function and yogya, etc. It is also generally seen that when one gets advancement in his work one loses either of the parent. Such as in the case of Late Mr. Rajeev Gandhi, his mother Mrs. Indira Gandhi was assassinated and he became P.M. of India. So in the case of Jyotiraditya Sindhiya, his father Late Mr. Madhav Rao Sindhiya was killed by air crash and just after this he became the member of Parliament.

The 10th house rules orders or commands. Pilgrimages to holy places are also known from 10th house.

In horary Astrology this house concerns the Judges, judgement and the things taken away by thieves as 10th house is the 4th house from 7th house.

In mundane Astrology 10th house deals with the Government as head of the State whether monarch or President National Leaders eminent and distinguished personalities as Prime Minister, President, Chief Justice, etc. Nation's honour, political parties, their leaders etc are known through

10th house. 10th house is the maraka house to both father and mother being 2nd to 9th house (house of father), being 7th to 4th house (house of mother).

The Navamsa lord of 10th house from Sun, Moon and Lagna the way of living or professional earning may be known as following:

If the Navamsa lord of 10th house from Sun, Moon or Lagna is Sun then the native may be a Doctor, a Physician, or may be businessman of Gold, woolen cloth, ghee, gud, sugar, grain, grass and wood.

If the Navamsa lord of 10th house is moon then cement, mud pots, agriculture, garden, oil, wine, cloth's many be the business of the native.

If there is Mars then gun, top, sword, knife, fiery work of Goldsmith, ironsmith, woodsmith, known as Sunar, Lohar, Badhai, etc. or by serving in electricity department or by machinery work the native may earn his livelihood.

If there is Mercury in above position then Clerk, Writer, Poet, Painter, bookbinder, Teacher, Astrologer, Bookseller, Editor, Translator, Journalist, Advocate, Press worker or soap, agarbatti, flower garlands, toys of paper etc., may be profession.

If there is Jupiter then teacher, religious preceptor, professor, judge, barrister, etc., may be the profession.

If there is Venus then silver, iron, gold, cow, buffalo, milk, curd, scents, diamond, ruby, pears, etc., and cinema, film, drama, wineseller, etc may be the profession.

If there is Saturn in above position then the 4th clanss Government servant as peon, postman, watchman, messenger and service done in the form of theft, violence, home servant, etc.

The sign and planet and lord of Sign in 10th house also indicate the profession of the native.

If lord of 10th house is weak then the person is vicious. If there is Pisces in tenth house and Mars and Mercury are there the person in Tapasi or hardworker. If from lord of 10th in 10th house is Rahu then the person doet not get success even when the lord of 10th be in exaltation in 6-8-12.

Eleventh House

Eleventh house deals with Income, elder brother, profit, desire, wealth. It is also called the house of friends. In horoscope 1 to 8 houses show the story of a native from birth to death. The Ist sign Aries to 8th sign Scorpio all the world's materialistic gain or loss describe by the 8 houses. Mars is the lord of Aries and Scorpio. Mars is called the Son of Earth or Land.

The houses 9, 10, 11, 12 are known as Dharma, Artha, kam and Moksha. The lord of Kalpurasha Rasiln 9 is Dhanu (Sagittarius) in 10 capricorn in 11 Aquarius and 12 pises. The lord of Sagittarius and Pisces is Jupiter while 10 Capricorn and 11 Aquarius are owned by Saturn. Both are philosophical planets Jupiter and Saturn. Hence from 11th house one's hopes, desires and their fulfilment is known. Net profit is shown by this house. Hope of union in friendship, in partners or lovers is known through 11th house. While setting marriages 2nd and 11th houses should also be judged alongwith the 7th house. Benefic in 11th shows the right means income and malefics in 11th house shows income through unfair means.

Sun in 11th house benefit from the person of high rank and position. It is good position for social success depending on the position of sign in 11th in which Sun is posited.

Moon in 11th house aspected by benefics shows large circle of friends specially among the females. As moon is changeful in nature, so in movable sign or common sign it may not give so much support as in fixed sign.

Mars in 11th house shows friendship with martial and athletic class, police, military, army, etc. If Saturn or Mercury aspect Mars in 11th house treachery in friendship may be shown. Unfavourable aspect of Sun, Jupiter or Mercury may offer wrong advice finding one in trouble. Venus or Moon afflicting indicates over indulgence with female friends. So friendship must be maintained carefully when Mars is in 11th house.

Mercury in 11th house – Friendship may be with literary and scientific minded people. Friends may be harmful if mercury placed in 11th house is with malefics or in debilitation or writing, accounts work enemy camp. Income may be by banking and other subjects concerned with mercury.

Jupiter in 11th house. Source of income will be fair. If Jupiter is in good position and favourable than social success, popularity, credit will be gained through friendship and elder brothers. But if Jupiter is afflicted fulfilment of desires by friends may not be completed.

Venus in 11th house with good aspect shows friendship with opposite sex and those in social circles full of humanity and sympathetic. Marriage is also fruitful as venus is a social planet hence success in social affairs is sure. Afflicted venus will give opposite result as shown above.

Saturn in 11th house with good position attracts old and serious friends. It shows friendship with working under native. Though Saturn in 11th shows few friends but Jupiter more. If Saturn is afflicted the native should be careful by his/her old aged friends as they may go against him/her in bad times. Saturn shows delay in achieving ambition of a native even placed in good position.

In mundane Astrology 11th house deals with the parliament or legislative assemblies. It rules the lower and upper houses of parliament, municipal and district boards, corporation, panchayats in janpada and district etc. It also shows relation with political parties, international friendship, governing bodies and companies involved in economic cases of the Government. In horary astrology 11th house deals with hopes and desires and their fulfilment of the native.

Rahu and Ketu are known as chhayagrah hence they give results of the planet who is lord of the sign and constellation in which Rahu, Ketu are present.

Twelfth House

12th house is the house of expenses, which shows loss, disappointment, bondage, bed, sin, poverty, back biter, misery, left eye, leg and jail. Our sages have called 1st to 8th houses *"LOK SUKH"* and 9th to 12th house *"PARLOK SUKH"* Hence the last four houses 9,10,11,12 are called the houses of Dharma, Artha, Kam and Moksha. The 12th house is the final house which shows divine worship and the future state of existence after death.

If the 2nd house is connected with 12th house the native spends money on purchasing jewels, when connected with 3rd house it shows expenditure on short journey and writings and publication. When 4th house is well connected with 12th house the native may purchase land or vehicles, expenditure on mother going on pilgrimage when connected with 5th house expenditure, on children's education, marriages etc.

When connected with 6th house repayment of loans borrowed by the native is made. 6th house is the service or help to ordinary person while 12th house represents service to mankind. It is the house of sacrifice for wrong action committed in previous life as it indicates the house of moksha (freedom). 6th house is the house of enemy too but the 12th house shows the secret enemies. It is the house of secret conspiracy, envy, fraud and treachery, exile etc.

Sun in 12th house Well aspected and in strong position sun gives success in psychic matters. Sympathy from father and help in economic matters, triumph on enemy etc are also shown through strong sun in 12th house. Weak sun shows enmity with influential people, separation from family members.

Moon in 12th house – Success in works performed in hospitals, prisons and such other institutions related with general help. Moon in 12th house shows expense through charity, gift, donation, virtuous action.

Mars in 12th house. If dignified, well aspected mars is in 12th house it makes the native an administrator of an estate or in a public institution. Though mars in bad position gives loss of reputation or treachery from enemies even danger of violence or from big animals. Well mars if connected with sun and 10th house may make the native a surgeon in hospital as mars represents surgery and sun represents medicine. Mars in 12 afflicted by Saturn may give jail or illness caused by a long-run disease and long treatment in a hospital.

Mercury in 12th house – Mercury well placed in 12th house may incline the native towards mysteries and scientific research work. Mercury represents wisdom and publication. Enmity by writing in newspapers, book may also take place.

Jupiter in 12th house Well placed or aspected Jupiter in 12th house gi' .s gain and success through service work in hospitals, public institutions far from birth place of the native. Even gain and triumph over enemies may be seen when Jupiter is strongly placed in 12th house. Give and take in case of charity, donation may be known through Jupiter in 12th house.

Venus in 12th house. Shows comforts in bed with opposite sex as venus is the representative of love and pleasure with ladies if afflicted venus then shows enmity with women. Saturn afflicting venus causes separation. Mars over indulging in passion.

Saturn in 12th house well aspected and strong in position gives success in laborious occupation. Saturn in 12th wants the native to work alone and peacefully. Badly afflicted by mars there may be danger of violence, robbery or even suicide. Mercury's affliction to Saturn may cause mental disturbance and loss by theft.

In mundane Astrology 12th house deals with charitable institutions, jails, hospital, crime in general, secret enemies of the nation, secret and occult societies are governed by 12th house.

In horary astrology 12th house deals with question of grief, persecution, secret mental toil, envy, misery etc., also suicide, assassination an l all matters convecting with decent, sorrow, weeping, blackmailing are death with 12th house.

Significance of Twelve Signs

Benefics as Jupiter and Venus in Lagna mitigate the evil and generally give moderate results. Malefics like Saturn, Mars, Rahu, Ketu, Sun in Lagna spoil the good Qualities and give bad qualities if they are aspected by malefics. General physical features may be different due to occupying the sign by planets in each Sign.

ARIES

Aries is the first or head sign of the Zodiac. It is fiery and hot, movable, masculine, positive and short in size. It represents head and face, ruled by Mars. Sun in Aries is exalted, Saturn is debilitated.

People born in this Sign are active and ambitious, bold and impulsive. If Aries Lagna is under malefic influence too native will be rash and aggressive. Only aspect of benefic can make them Confidence and Courageous. Their aim is high and are ever enterprising. They will desire always to be at the Head of all affairs. They do not want suggestions from others but act according their own judgement. As they want to be leaders in action and thought hence they neglect any kind of subordination. If Lagna Aries is in good aspect of benefics then the native is best fitted to guide, Control and govern others. Aries is positive Sign So it gives determination and force of character. They have unbound confident so they act quickly. They are fit for executive works. Aries is movable Sign so the native may change their liking at the very moment. As fiery Sign the native wants sudden obedience of his order. For fulfilment of their desires they can have Quareces if afflicted. They underestimate others. They are over-optimistic. They are ardently demonstrative and passionate. Their attention is on the ends and not on the means. As Mars rules this Sign who represents blood so minor injuries or serious accidents particularly to the head. They should be careful in driving car and working with sharp instruments. They are fond of games and Sports. An Aries represents face and head in human body so headaches, burn, brain affection, Coma, high fever, paralysis, apoplexy, ringworm, small pox, malaria etc diseases may attack. So the native must take rest and eat good food with more vegetables. They should control their feelings and emotion and avoid worries.

Aries Native think only of today and not of tomorrow, and so they fail in their budgets.

Aries have charming, attractive nature so the opposite sex is attracted by them.

Aries ladies are witty and Independent. Afflicted Aries will make Aries Ladies Proudy. Jealousy and Pride her weakness will speak high. For Aries ladies born should have husband born in Leo and Sagittarius fiery Sign.

Aries born persons are ruled by Mars hence their occupation should be connected with fire and land as Police, Military, Army Officers, Soldiers, Surgeous, thinker, Watchman, cooker, Physician, Iron, Steel worker, Fireman, guard, mechanics, wrestlers, workers in Lime & brick dealers of sports and red articles. Government servants in P.W.D. agriculture, land revenue, Police etc connected with Land. As Mars is known as son of the Earth (Land). So Agriculturist also come in this category.

The famous persons born in Aries are Prithvi Raj Chauhan, Alexander the great, Subhash Chandra Bose, Sardar Ballabh Bhai Patel, Rashtra Kavi Shri Krishna 'Saral';

TAURUS

Taurus Lagna is an earthy, fixed, feminine, Short fruitful sign governed by Venus. Moon is exalted in this Sign. Venus, the Lord of this sign is passionate and peaceful. plumpy and middle Size forehead broad. They can endure and are very patient. Taursan if Provoked to anger he becomes very wild and dangerous, though they are slow and steady preserving, patient and persistent, enduring and executive. They are conservative in their thoughts. They never waste their energy hence they like to be busy with their work silently.

They have strong will power. When Taurus is afflicted the native is lazy, dull and selfish. They are clever in worldly matters, keeping an eye on money. They prefer sweets. They take any action in their hands after sufficient consideration. They are honest and have good will with each and every native of society. Venus is a cheerful, Pleasant, full of humanity So the Taurus born native also will always smile and he may be highly diplomatic and it is not easy to understand him. He will find everything at time e.g. jewels, gems and ornaments, land, vehicle, garden. Beautiful things will attract him. He will feel happy in natural places as rivers, mountains, green lands etc. If Saturn aspects the Lagna then he may lead a solitude and rural life busy in Horticulture. They have deep knowledge and have intution they are origin in their thoughts. Generally they do with trust and honesty each work.

They are loyal in love affairs. They are fond of music, Poetry, drama, cinema, etc. They are less sensitive to pain.

When Taurus is afflicted the native suffers from tonsils, diptheria, Pyorrhoea, diseases of throat, Palate and necks cold and apoplexy is Common disease to them.

In case of finance they are lucky as they hoard money. They spend money only in need. They have reserved funds for their bad days.

Saturn though a malefic but being the ninth and tenth lord is most favourable. The meritorious deed of previous life realised by ninth house and present deed done from tenth house are known through the position of Saturn being the Lord of 9th and 10th houses. They are practical and build their fortune on a firm foundation.

As Taurus is the Second Sign of Zodiac indicating finance hence Taurus born may be bankers, stock-brokers, treasurers, Cashiers, Speculators gamblers, race goers etc.

Music, drama, poetry, painting etc., are the subject of Venues hence they may be excellent musicians, Actors, film producers, owner of Cinemas. Their other profession may be agriculture, bookbinder, dressmaker, painters, decoraters, Beauty parlour. They may be flower sellers, scent seller, milk seller, vegetable, Petrol, Sugarcane and Sugar etc. may come in the category of Venus Lord of Taurus. One may be employed in girls school, colleges and Ladies club as Taurus is a feminine Sign.

Those born in Virgo, Capricorn (earthy Signs) and Cancer, Scorpio, Pisces (watery Sign) will prove better partners to lead a happy life. They are affectionate, warm and everloving to each other. Taurus wives behave like a mother and also a wife. Great persons born in Taurus are Bhagwan Krishna, Shukuracharya, Kabirdas, Rajneesh, Lata Mangeskar, Shyama Prasad Mukherjee, Queen Victoria, Jagdish Chandra Basu, Warnard Shaw, Tej Bahadur Sapre, Independent India's Birth Lagna is also Taurus.

GEMINI

GEMINI is the airy Sign. It is masculine and positive. It is also known as barren Sign. Dual in nature Gemini is ruled by Mercury an intellectual Planet. Saturn and Venus are friends to this Sign. Jupiter is in its detriment in this Sign. Geminian has a tall, up right and straight body. What planet is in Gemini determines the colour of the native. Gemini as an airy sign hence the Native lives in mind positive and strong. As dual in nature they are fond of change. Mercury the Planet of wisdom is the Lord of this Sign hence reading writing is necessity to them. They can adapt in any circumstance but cannot command or manage successfully. They cannot take decision easily hence opportunities come and go and they cannot be benefitted by them often.

Being a dual sign they can follow more than one occupation at a time. Leaving one work unfinished, they allow themselves to do another work. They are generous but timid and nervous too. They have no any kind of anxiety in their mind. They love diversity. Like air they move from one place or thought to other place and thought. They are super intellectuals and horse reproductive ability. They are Quick witted and clever. They cannot Concentrate on any one subject. Good personality having fondness for good company. They lack concentration and Quick decision. They are hasty in their nature and wants to know the result then and there.

They are as active as their mind. Sometimes they Spoil their health by unnecessary and unavoidable worries. They should not take of once more variety of works.

Gemini rules over the lungs hence cold, Influenza, Pleurisy, Bronchitis, T.B. etc are the diseases they often have to face. From Gemini

6th house is in Scopio hence diseases indicated by Scorpio such as Piles, Fisthula, bladder etc.

Changes in life sometimes may have misfortunes to Gemini Sign born people due to the love affairs with the other sex. Secret cases of love affairs may bring loss and difficulties. Hence natives born in Gemini should be very careful from the influence of opposite sex in their lives.

As regards occupation Bookseller, accountant, clerk, Salesman editors, reporters, teachers, photographers, tutors, cashiers, treasures, speakers etc are the profession suitable to Gemini born people. Geminian are active and industrious, Sense of humour makes them good orators, Successful brokers and diplomats. As they have institional power so they can know likings of their customers. If Mercury is retrograde they may prove good Critics with beneficial aspect of Jupiter if aspected by Mars they may have their own press. Mercury represent art, publicity, mathematics changing in profession and travelling is necessary for Gemini born persons. They may be good Advocates, travelling Agents, etc. Generally Geminians are jack of all trades. Being a dual Sign they are today in press, tomorrow they may be in Court or travelling elsewhere. Side business is necessity for them to increase their income.

Gemini brides are generally intelligent. Born in airy sign Libra and Aquarius Partners will have good understandings Aries and Leo these 2 fiery Signs will match with Gemini satisfactically. For Geminians it is necessary that they should not do many things at a time. They should try to do one thing of a time. Great persons born in Gemini Sign are the great industrialist jugalkiishar Birla, Ramkrishna Dalmiya, Nathu Ram Godse, George Washington, Kaka Hathrasi (the Hindi poet of Humour) Morarji Desai, Dr. Zakir Husain, Dalai Lama, Arjun Singh.

CANCER

Cancer is a watery, Cardinal, movable, feminine and fruitful Sign. Cancer is Prishthodaya rasi. Other Pristhodaya rasis are Aries, Taurus, Sagittarius, Capricorn. They rise with their back.

Cancer's ruler is Moon. Jupiter in Cancer is exalted, Mars is debilitated. Jupiter is Param Uchcha in 5 degrees of Cancer and Mars is Param Neecha in 28 degrees of this sign. Sun is friend's Sign, Mercury, Venus and Saturn are inimical. Generally, Cancerian have a large upper body, wide face, big abdoman. As Lord of Cancer is Moon a changing Planet, so the life of native born in Cancer is also changeful. They see many ups and downs in their life. They are pure imaginative, emotional, over sensitive and sympathetic. They easily absorb other's ideas. Some what sentimental and talkative too. Due to high sensitivity they are highly nervous too. As Moon is waxing or waning so is with the native born in Cancer that at sometime they are timid but at the other time courageous like full or new man. They are Physically weak, but mentally brave and their attitude is morally strong.

Cancer Born are fond of family and comforts. They have strong memory, kind behaviour with them encourages them. Their beginning of life may be hardship but finally their latter life is remarkably progressive and advanced. They have psychic faculty with intuition.

As watery Sign Cancer born people are influenced easily will adjust easily anywhere, any time. Like water their life is too wandering and restless. They are kind in charity and famous in hospitality.

They are loyal and their responsibility is praised. They are fortunate. They are magnetic and impressionable. Mars in Cancer Lagna makes the native short-tempered, Saturn in Cancer Lagna makes them patient and feeling loneliness. Chest and Stomach are ruled by Cancer hence Cancerian suffer from asthma, gastric trouble, weak digestion, flu, cough, bronchitis pleurisy, T.B. dropsy, nervousness. Jaundice, gale stone etc. They should keep away them with alcohol.

Their occupation is mostly concerned with water so restaurants, coffee houses, Hotels, fruit stalls are managed well by cancerian. If in Government Service, they may be fit in Irrigation, water supply, and agriculture department purely connected with water, tank, river, sea sides etc. great sailors, sea-captains, navy-servants, shipping department, industry dealing with water, milk or oil etc.

Exalted Jupiter in this Sign makes the native Teacher, Preacher, orator, State minister etc. debilitated Mars in Cancer makes farmer, agriculturist, gardener, or Government servants in Agriculture Department.

Cancer borns are very honest unless aspected by malefic. They cannot tolerate dishonesty. They are fond of family comforts. They should avoid inferiority complex, should not be over-anxious about the future.

Cancer is the best sign of all the signs as Bhagwan. Ram was born in this Lagna and had 6 exalted Planets in his horoscope. Other great persons born in Cancer are Gautam Buddha, Arvind Ghosh, Ramanujacharya, Ranjit Singh, Jawaharlal Nehru, Indira Gandhi, Lokmanya Tilak, Jai Prakash Narayan, Kam Raj.

LEO

Leo is fiery, hot, dry, masculine, positive, bestical barren and fiexed Sign. Lord of Leo is the Sun. Moon Mars, Jupiter when in Leo are considered as in friend's Sign. Saturn, Venus, Mercury are considered to be in enemy Sign.

Leo born Native will be tall, muscular with broad forehead. His appearance is majestic, imposing, commanding and dignified. Leo means

Lion so the native born in Leo Sign is Royal. Persons born in Leo are noble Large-hearted and generous. They are helpful to mankind.

Sun represents the Government aspect of Jupiter on Sun or Jupiter with Sun gives protection from Government. Saturn's aspect on Sun will produce hate by the Government. Sun is the king of all the Planets. They get full cooperation of their subordinates. Generally, Leonias become the Head of the Institution, of association, of any Public or Government body. They talk less but do more. Their judgement is wise. They desire to be honoured, forgive and forget weaknesses of others. Mercurians are the favourities of the Leonians. They have organising and commanding power. They have zeal for sports and speculation. He may be proved in best position when hindrances and obstacles are in the way. They are frank and just; noble lofty in character. They dislike subordination. They should avoid being hasty, should also consider others advices. Keep away from flattery of others.

Leo indicates the heart, the spinal cord, Spinal marrow so inflammation, sunstroke, giddiness, Epilepsy, rhematic fever are the diseases when the Lagna is afflicted by Mars and Saturn. Jupiter in Leo Protects from any surgical aid. One should not drink alcohols etc. He should take balanced diet. Leonian is able to face any hardtime. When young Leonians may improve their Career. Gambling and Speculation may tempt him. Besides high position in Government Service or in Commerce they should earn through speculation, music, jewellery, manager of great enterprises. Favourable Mars makes them Soldiers, Surgeous, Chemists, dentists, irons and copper's business, Mars and Leo favour Police, military, defence Department. Favourable Mercury may make them Share brokers, ambassadors, auditors, engineers, etc. Jupiter forming favourable aspect may make born lawyers, judges, Priests, bankers and Physician. Venus in Leo departments of transport, travels, food, agriculture etc. Favourable Saturn favours mines, coal, wood, lead, medical posts.

Leonians spend money to maintain Prestige and honour. In poverty too they never think of economy. They spend more on dress, screen, cloth, curtains, furniture.They keep their home decorated .

Leo-Borns are romantic but he does not demonstrate love. He is proud of his family. Opposite sex is attracted towards him. Leo is a fiery Sign hence Aries, Sagittarius, Gemini, Libra, or Aquarius will Suit well for marriage purposes. Geminian may be sincere and affectionate partner. Leo Lady too is ambitious and ideal successful social worker.

Children born Leo other children guide they are captain, fine organisers inspiring others.

Famous person born in Leo Sign Lagna are Chhatraptati Shivaji, Herald Wilson, Johnson, General Manik shaw, Guru Nanak, Nixon, Choudhry Charan Singh, Rajiv Gandhi, Dr. Shankar Dayal Sharma.

VIRGO

Virgo is an earthy, common Sign ruled by Mercury. It is negative, feminine, cold, dry in nature. Mercury as ruler is exalted here in this Lagna. Venus though a good friend of Mercury is debilitated in this Sign. Saturn in Virgo is known as in friend's Sign and when Sun, Moon, Mars, Jupiter are in this Sign they are known in enemy's Sign.

Exaltation of Mercury in this Sign show that Mercury prefer wisdom and debilitation of Venus in this Sign Shows that Venus prefer wealth. Wisdom make one immortal while wealth makes one immoral. Virgo is Shy and self conscious while Gemini is timid.

Virgo born is tall, voice, Quick walk, they are ever active hence they seem of less age than what they are. They are honest and frank. As Mercury is in constant so Mercurian desires change. Among all the 12 sign only Virgo-born people are Conscientious, and very capable of handling unfavourable condition. They are thorough and methodical, always Practical and discriminative. They are good and Quick at finding fault with others. You will analyse, dissect and go deep into the matter. Being an earthy sign to save money is desired by you. You have some reserved money for emergencies. Virgo-born are governed by intellect.

You are fond of studying science particularly, medicine, food diet, hygiene etc. You are clever, learned and versatile. You may be employed as a teacher, writer or as an excise officer. Virgo gives analytical nature. Hence Research scholor, wise men are born in Virgo. Though he himself a good judge even then he takes advice from others. He starts the other work while his previous work is incomplete. So he passes his time in confusions. Malefics in Virgo will make the native suffer from dysentery, typhoid, He should take plenty of rest. Your nervous system and stomach are sensitive. Hence you take in food Vitamin 'B' in Vegetables. Be on guard against gall stones, Avoid Alcohol.

You may have many ups and down in your life. Your lord of 6 is Saturn, Lord of 8 is Mars hence you should be careful about your health. You have to collect wealth and earn money through hardwork. Sun's aspect on the Lords of 2-6-10 indicates that you may be successful medical officer in Health Department you may serve as engineer, Auditor, Professor, Mar's aspect denotes own nursing home, Press, Drinking, editing etc. If Mars is afflicted the Virgo-born person may earn money by black market or robbery of theft. Malefic aspect with Mars on Mercury may put in trouble by your personal Individual. Hence be careful.

Mercury forming good aspect may make the native book-keeper, broker, teacher, lawyer, author of many books, Good journalist, As a lawyer you will be successful in cross examination. Jupiter forming good aspect with 2-6-10 Lords in Virgo indicates your intellectual pursuit. You may work in Religious Board, trust, insurance and law courts. You may be a successful ambassador too as Dr. Radha Krishnan (Ex President of India) was an ambassador in Soviet Russia was born in Virgo Lagna. Good aspect from Venus shows that the native will be a good musician, actor, Painter or artistry poet, writer etc. good aspect from Saturn expert in mathematics, statistics, accounts, etc. You may hold responsible and positions of trust. Your mother and wife born will be God fearing as Lord of 4th (mother) and 7th (wife) is Jupiter. Hence your domestic Life will be Peaceful.

Famous persons born in Virgo Lagna are Dr. Radha Krishnan, Keneddy, C.D. Deshmukh, Jimmi Karter, Justice P. Govind Menon, Present Chief Justice of India R.C. Lahoti.

LIBRA

Libra is an airy Sign, Moola Trikona Sign of Venus. Taurus is fixed and Libra is Movable Sign of Venus. It is Positive Sign and not negative as Taurus. It is the Sign of Justice or Balance. Saturn is exalted in Libra, Sun is debilitated. For Moon, Mars, Jupiter this is the enemy's camp. The Libras are tall, graceful appearance with a Sweet Smile. They are the best judge, excel others in debate as constructive critics.

The native is Courteous, modest and gentle. He is Sympathetic. He is fond of dress, perfumeries, art and music. Their profession too is Changeable being a movable Sign as Photography, gardening, drawing, painting, embroidery etc Librans work hard for the benefit of others.

Being an airy Sign Librans have fertile imagination, correct intuition, brilliant intellect, pleasant nature etc. Saturn being exalted can make a native to reach higher spiritual life. They have unasuming nature and humanitarian instincts. They lean more to the spiritual side of life. They are very affectionate and gentle, easy going, never hurt other's, feelings. They are expert diplomatic.

Librans have strong conjugal affection and enjoy life in the company of opposite sex. They adjust the situation with tact. They learn romantic music. They should try to take Quick decision. They spend much on customs. Kidneys Spines are indicated by Libra. In the case of uterus ladies may be affected. They are the best suited for business with a partner. Librans prove the best advisors as they are in reassuring, logic, foresight and judgement. The person who has 2-6-10 houses with Libra in his horoscope may be a story writer, play back, musician, poet, e.g. in Virgo, Taurus, and Capricorn born persons.

In business they may be more successful due to charming, pleasing manners smile and sweet words. Librans are seldom economical as they spend more on luxuries. For good cause they donate and are liberal and generous.

The Librans are ever lasting good friends to all those come in contact with them. They are honest, true, kind and generous. They easily make friends. As Lord of 11th is SUN so Libran will lead a public Life with Social and financial success. They forgive their friends for their mischieves.

They are the most lovable person for pleasant and happy sex life. They are sincere lovers. Their sweet smiling mouth attracts the opposite sex. They marry early and preserve old traditions. They are happy every where. Their partners may be of fiery nature as Aries-a fiery sign is in 7th house so by diplomacy and tact they should maintain peace at home.

Born in Gemini, Aquarius match the Libran very well. Pisces, Capricorn, Cancer will not agree. With others they can manage.

Generally people born in Libra do not have useful, reliable, true younger brothers as Lord of 3rd house is inimical, the Lord is Jupiter who is inimical to Venus hence younger brothers and neighbours will be inimical.

Venus is Lord of Taurus, Libra two houses being 6-8 to each other. Venus as Lord of 8th house for Libra born native will throw obstacles because as Lord of Lagna Venus being in 8th house saves life, though the life will not be smooth.

Famous persons born in Libra Lagna are Mahatma Gandhi, Atal Bihari Vajpai, V.V. Giri, Tulsidas, Christ, Chaitanya Maha Prabhu, Laxmi Bai, Hyderali, George VI, Esen Hower, Churchill, Hitler, Musolini, Stalin, Akbar, Haribans Rai Bacchan, Jain Muni Vidyananda, Motilal Bora, Acharya Binowa Bhave.

SCORPIO

Scorpio is the fruitful, fixed, feminine yet violent and watery Sign ruled by Mars. In this Sign Moon is in debilitation Sun and Jupiter in Scorpio means in Friends sign but Saturn, Venus and Mercury means in inimical Sign. Scorpians are of 2 types. One who control over their Senses and the other who are Jealous and Sensual.

Scorpian have good personality. They keep them selves busy at their target. They are at the best when they are under obstacles and hindrances. In true words they are the fighter fighting at the last moment leaving on GOD the result.

Being Watery Sign they have fertile imagination and sharp intelligence. Their talent and dynamic energy have to be aroused by others. They are quite unknown about their quality and energy as Hanuman Ji was aroused by Jamvant in Ramayana. They have intense feeling and emotion which gives them intuition. They may be good critic. They also may be successful in buying and selling.

Mars gives the Scorpian, courage, independence, excitement, forcefulness. They controls others easily. They are self made. They loose their temper Quickly being a fiery Lord Mars. Scorpio is a highly sexed Sign. They do not interfere in others matters. They can be cunning also though they are true, loyal, faithful and reliable. When anybody tries to harm them then they take revenge.

They should try to avoid secret enmity of the Ladies. In negative side of Scorpion dominates then they become dangerous. They should work above selfishness and ego. Scorpio Governs the generative organs the bladder. Mars and Jupiter in Scorpio they affect the bladder, womb, ovaries and lead to trouble enlargement of the Prostrote gland. Venereal distemper is the main disease caused by Scorpio. Stone in bladder is caused by Saturn. While Moon is Raj Yoga Karak it is Badhak too. Jupiter and Venus as Lords of 2-7 are Marak.

Scorpian are lucky in everything. They know how to make money. Do not be extravagant. Wait and invest your money seeing the favourably opportunities.

They make friends in a very short period but if there is any friction they may prove worse enemy. They make friends with whom who are in high power and authority Upper type of Scorpian are popular but lower type of Scorpian will be notorious. Mercury as Lord of 8th and 11th though is beneficial but if there is any kind of fiction they may harm you. So keep them in tie of friendship. They want demonstration of affection with their partners. Their partners will be just, honest, sincere as the lords of 2-7-11 are Jupiter, Venus and Mercury benefics.

They will be happy with Cancer or Pisces, Scorpio born people. Scorpio wives if malefics afflicted then they may be worst with their husbands. But if it receives good aspects one cannot get a better wife then Scorpio borns. Generally I have seen that Scorpian are proudy. They are cunning, clever in money making and selfish too. Hence while judging the Horoscope of Scorpio born people see the benefic aspect on Mars and Scorpio Lagna.

Lord Ganesh and Hanuman Ji were born in this Lagna. Henery Ford, Nasir, Kosygyn, Dacoit Man Singh, Baba Ram Dev, Rajgopalachari, Shekh Muzib, Satya Sai Baba, were born in Scorpio Lagna.

SAGITTARIUS

It is a fiery Sign, Common, positive, masculine, hot, dry, dual double-bodied (First half human, second half animal) ruled by the divine Planet Jupiter. Sun, Moon, Mars in friend's house and Saturn, Venus, Mercury in enemy's Camp. He is tall, high, large forehead, fair complexion and beautiful. He is bold, courageous. He is also ambitious, greedy and aspiring.

Persons Born in Sagittarius Lagna are not timid. They have self confidence in their odds. Like scorpian they are at best when they have obstacles. Being a fiery Sign they are energetic, Vigorous and bold. They act after full consideration and not in hurry. They love truth. They speak out what they feel right, they do not care for other persons settlement. They are highly educated, fond of long travel. They are philosophical, religious minded and God fearing.

Jupiter the divine Planet as lord of this Sign gives them broad mind, confidence, truth, spiritual uplifts etc. Justice, Sympathy and courage are the main features. They grasp quickly as 9th and 10th Lord of this Lagna are ruled by Sun and Mercury forming nipuna Yoga. Their intuition is Correct you cannot tolerate injustice done with the poor. Their friendship stands for a longtime. Moon as Lord of 8th house change their opinion and unnecessary distrust is produced.

They lack in tact. Try to be moderate instead of insulting or hurting others by giving your opinion. Do not hate parents & brothers. From Sciatica, rheumatic pain, fracture in the hip, gout lung trouble may suffer. Mars and Saturn in Sagittarius cause fracture of the bones and ulcer in the thigh which may need surgical aid. Jupiter in Sagittarius may cause suffer from gout, Pulmonary apoplexy. Jupiter in Poorvashada Star may cause diabetes. Saturn alone slow constructions of the hips, T.B. Chronic Pulmonary disease, asthma etc. Moon indicates bronchitis, Pneumonia, diabetes, Sun causes ear diseases resulting in poor vision and defective hearing. Venus indicates tumour diabetes etc. Mercury show high cough, asthma etc.

To Chara Rasi, fixed Rasi, Common Sign 11th, 9th and 7th houses are Badhaka Sathunas. Sagittarius does not want that others order him.

Being ruled by Jupiter the Sagittarius born people may be teacher, Public Speaker, bank employee or may be attached to religious institutions. If Jupiter is not afflicted Politics may prove Lucky. Tenth house is the house of Profession whose Lord is Mercury. Hence you may edit, Publish, audit, and have income through advertisement. May work in Foreign embassy. Planets connected with 2-6-10 houses can offer service in mines, transport, engineering also.

You do not like close relatives but may be generous towards the other sex and be friendly with them. You may be kind to others but not to your kith and kin. Like Gemini people you make friendship easily. Your Sweet Smile and Quick wit will make many friends.

People born on Friday or in Taurus or in Libra or in nakshatras Bharni, Poorva Phalguna, Poorva Shada will be long standing friends. Those born in Hasta nakshatra may bring you ill-reputation. Importance of Lords of 2-7-11 is particularly helpful in family life. Saturn, Mercury, Venus are two Lords of 2-7-11 to Sagittarius born people. If they are not aspected by Mars may give you the most reliable, faithful, dutiful, pleasant, and intelligent wife. Be tactful in dealing with your children.

Wear emerald in golden ring in lowest finger it will give you name, fame, reputation, investment profit, promotion and prosperity.

Many great persons are born in Sagittarius Lagna. Tipu Sultan, Dr. Rajendra Prasad, Neelam Sanjeev Reddy, V.K. Menon, Pandit Din Dayal Upadhyay, Kumar Bal Gandharva, Edward VII, Queen Elizabeth, Shakespeare, Lal Bhadur-Shastri, Mohan Lal Sukhadia and J.N. Vyas of Rajasthan. Film Actor Surendra Nath.

CAPRICORN

Capricorn is a movable, cardinal, tropical, negative, feminine, earthy, dry, cold, preserving, despondent sign ruled by SATURN. Mars gets exalted in this Sign, Jupiter gets debilitated, Sun, Moon are said to be in enemy's Camp. In Capricorn Mercury, Venus are said in friend's residence.

Capricorn takes birth as weak and grow slowly. If Saturn is ill-posited the native may suffer from T.B.

Being an earthy Sign the native is economical thoughtful and practical minded. The native is calculative and business like. He works after taking carefully a decision. He has special organising capacity and with hard labour, patience, tolerance and steady nature they may be the Head of Large projects.

His nature is reserved. To cheat him is difficult. Because he is optimistic and is modest and polite. He does not make friends quickly and easily for Judging a person it takes a long time to make permanent tie of friendship.

Saturn owns this house indicates that either the person will be honest, sincere, reliable or the most dishonest, selfish, greedy, miserly never hesitating to commit any crime. Repeated attempts will make the Capricorn at last successful Lord of 5 and 10 Venus shows that the native will be fond of music, drama, cinema etc. Moon as Lord of 7 shows that the native will always have a company of a friend or partner. Saturn in 10th in exaltation as Lagna Lord will make great politician, tactful, diplomatic, clever cunning and selfish. Mercury as Lord of 9 gives power to remember before election but to forget after election. Good aspect between Saturn and Mercury will make them to do great work for the sake of the country.

Either Lagna or Lord Saturn in bad aspect will make the native selfish and egoistic, pessimistic, depressed in broken hearted. Avoid nervousness and discontent and try to develop dignity and diplomacy.

Hysteria, rheumatism, and cold are the diseases found generally in Capricornian may be Pulmonary affection and trouble to heart due to Cancer and Leo as Signs in 7th and 8th houses. For Capricorn 11th house is Badhaks than and Capricorn is movable Sign. Hence Lord of 11th house Mars is not good for longevity. Saturn is also Marak being Lord of 2nd Aquarius Sign, 7th house is owned by Moon, the second marak hence Mars, Saturn, Moon are evil and they will cause death. Mercury as Lord of 6 affects health, Vitamin 'B' deficiency, gas trouble, general nervous debility may be expected during period of Mercury.

SATURN, MARS, MOON will cause danger and anxiety to one's longevity in their conjoined periods in the major period of evil Planet where Mercury will give more or less the same disease repeated by.

Capricornians have the desire to gain name, fame, reputation and money. They are industrious. They are most economical, correct, trust worthy. well informed and wide awake worker.

Houses 2-7-11 indicate marriage. Their Lords are Saturn, Moon, Mars, who is the strongest among these 3 the feature, characteristics will be known by the strongest of these 3 Planets.

Great persons born in Capricorn Lagna are Mahavir Swamy, Swamy Vivekanand, Maharana Pratap, Film Actor Ashok Kumar, Sanjay Gandhi.

AQUARIUS

Aquarius is an airy sign with high humidity, fixed moist, positive, human and voice sign. In the human system it is the distributor of water and gas. People born in this Lagna are tall. They are strong, handsome. Being an airy Sign, people born in Aquarius are intelligent. They cannot be made fool by flattery. In character reading and finding motives of others they are expert. Mercury is good as lord of 5th house.

Auarius-born people have broad out look, human understanding, are outspoken, unselfish and impersonal. Though social but make friends who are silent workers. They make efforts to bring harmony in the society. They want to improve and raise the mental standard of all. Though they are shrewd but quick witted, wide-awake and clear headed. They have new ideas and so try to originate new ideas in men. They have their own individuality, mannerism, peculiarity. They have intuition. They are constant in friendship, best fitted for research work. No Pressure from outside is allowed by them.

Leo-born are materialist and is opposite Aquarius sign is spiritualist. One for this Lok-Sukh and the other for Par-Lok-Sukh. Aquarius-born develop intuition and inspiration. They meditate and concentrate. They believe in practice, not in preaching. They are pure socialist in their views.

Jupiter the Lord of 2-11 blesses then with good family and Satisfactory economic condition, Mars Lord of 3-10 inclines towards Study, research, to be bold and courageous, to gain name fame, reputation. Venus Lord of 4-9 shows higher education and attachment to parents. Mercury Lord of 5-8, Moon Lord of 6th house show that they feed for thought, if afflicted they have melancholy. They are strong pessimists.

If this Lagna or Saturn is afflicted the native will be lazy so he should avoid solitude, should not worry, should not be pessimist, should be alert, active, should try to love all. Being an airy Sign tooth troubles and tonsils may cause trouble, can not tolerate cold weather so they have to warm up the limbs and foot, should take rest more. One should guard against Variculre veins. Their heart may cause trouble, there may be blood pressure, The legs may swell, Moon may cause dropsy. Planet in Shatbhisha may cause poor Constipation Planets in Poorva Bhadra Pada produce dropsy, irregularity of Circulative System.

9th house is Badhak to fixed Sign. Libra is the 9th house of Aquarius-born people. Venus kendradhipati is evil may affect longevity.

They will make money after using talent through machineries, invention and discoveries. They are neither economical nor liberal or extravagant. Jupiter Lord of 2 indicates that the native may be a scientist, administrator, lecturer, psychologist or Astrologer Moon Lord of 6 indicates that he may be doctor, Kerosene dealer Mars Lord of 10 shows that he may be in engineering, building construction, cement dealer, C.I.D. officer or service in Police, Military P.W.D. agriculture department. Mercury forming good aspect with 2-6-10 houses or their Lords may take interest in Bookselling, Press, accompany, Postmen, Astrologer etc. Venus having good aspect with 2-6-10 may make them poet, painter, musician, merchant. They are good partners in business and cheerful husbands for happy family life, good friends in society. Their partner will be Governed by Jupiter and Sun. They will be honest trustworthy. Harmony and Happiness is the main idea of Aquarius.

Great persons are born in Aquarius Sign. Ram Krishna Param Hansa. Yeshwant Rao Chauhan. Film Actor Shivaji Ganeshanm, The great Russian thinker Communist Karlmarx, The great Astrologer of India Dr. B.V. Raman, Sita Ram Jaipuria (M.P. in India) Mohammed Ali Jinnah, founder of Pakistan, the great king of Lanka Ravana etc.

PISCES

Pisces—Pisces is the watery, common Sign, feminine and cold. Ruled by Jupiter Venus is Exalted and Mercury is debilitated in this Sign. Jupiter inclines towards spiritual Life while Venus towards satisfying animal instincts enjoying all the fruits of life in the world. Pisces is friendly to SUN, MOON, MARS, MOON being the Lord of 5th house give full advantage in this Sign as From Cancer Sign of Moon Pisces is the 9th Sign giving in Luck full advantage of Divide Planet Jupiter.

Pisces is fruitful, pshychic, emotional, bicorporal-double legged Sign as this Sign is Symbolised with two fishes going in opposite side to each other. They are short in size. Jupiter the Chief Governor of Philosophy Progeny and Divine power is ruler of this Sign. Hence Pisces born people will be Philosophical, restless, emotional, leading a romantic life. He will be honest, outspoken, helpful and human. At a moment's call will help the needy person. He will calm down the enemies with generous behaviour and forgive them. Due to this over liberality and unbounded generosity cannot program much. These Qualities are obstacles in his way of Advancement. As he is pure Non-violence person who cannot think of harm of anybody evenin dream. It is also duel Sign puzzle to others. He is sweet tempered and socially inclined. He will be polite, modest with fresh ideas he can be led away.

Exalted Venus makes him a poet, a musician, a painter or a novelist or film actor. He is full of sympathy with the suffering people. He will have the desire to study the occult science, the divine life Naturally he is timid and lacks in self-confidence. He may go to overseas and may Visit foreign lands. Mars as Lord of 2nd house makes him extravagant. As he earns so he spends even more than earning being frank and fearless. Venus, Lord of 3rd house gives him good neighbours giving them great service and help. Mercury as debilitated makes him studious and changing ever his residence. Moon makes him dreamy and imaginative. Sun being Lord of 6th house makes him nervous taking necessary precautionary measures when there is an epidemic. In old age his friends may cheat him so he must be careful. He should not worry and be generous but not over liberal, should not hope more on other's promises, should not be dreaming always.

He should take care of the following things:-gastric troubles, affections in ankles of feet; Verilcose veins or guinea work, intestinal troubles lack of blood supply and typhoid, should not drink wine, piles, hernia, nervous debility, deafnees, T.B, Feet swollen, Tumours in abdoman. Govt., Rhennatism, fort drop, dropsy, beri-beri, enlargement of Liver.

Pisces are very kind of heart, full of sympathy, humanity to suffering person. So they help the needy person in case of health, wealth, knowledge. They are good teachers, good nurses, bankers, musician, Palmist and Astrologer too. Jupiter as Lord of 10th and Lagna may give success to the native as minister, physician, captain of ship, Port trust, custom-house, service in schools, colleges, temples, churches on hospitals, Sanotorium etc. Sun Lord of 6 may give permanent, Govt. Service. They are very affectionate at home and in society. Every Pretty face attracts them. They have many friends and worry when their friends are in difficulties. They are never treacherous.

Throughout life they will be attracted to the romantic life. If Mars is strong, the partner will be bold brave and independent, there can be no harmony at all. If Venus and Saturn form evil aspect the married life will be short. It may end in a divorce. Pisces born can lead a happy life with Virgo borns and Cancer borns.

Pisces born person should be careful from those born on Saturday or in Capricorn, Aquarius, Signs as they will be proved selfish later on in old days will cheat. Friendship should carefully be made so that no cheatry may take place.

Great person born in Pisces-Lagna are Swamy Ram Teertha, Ravindra Nath Tagore, George Vth, Princess Margerate.

Navamsha

In each Sign there are 9 Navamshas each of 3°-20′ three degrees twenty kalas. In each Sign thus there are 9 parts of each 3°-20′ thus total 9 Navamshas are 30°—00.

In each Sign there are 9 Parts e.g. in

Aries-Ashwini-4; Bharni-4, Kritika-1	Total 9
Taurus-Kritika-3; Rohini-4, Mrigsira-2	Total 9
Gemini-Mrigsira-2; Aridra-4-Punarvasu-3	Total 9
Cancer-Punarvasu-1; Pushya-4, Ashlekha-4	Total 9

Leo-Magha-4; Poorva Phalguna-4-Uttra Phalguna-1 Total 9
Virgo-Uttra Phalguna-3; Hasta-4, Chitra-2 Total 9
Libra-Chitra-2; Swati-4, Vishakha-3 Total 9
Scorpio-Vishakha-1; Anuradha-4 Jyeshtha-4 Total 9
Sagittarius-Mool-4; Poorva Shada-4 Uttra Shada-1 Total 9
Capricorn-Uttra Shada-3; Shravaha-4-Dhanishtha-2 Total 9
Aquarius-Dhanishtha-2; Shatbisha-4, Poorva Bhadra Pada-3 Total 9
Pisces-Poorva Bhadra Pada-1; Uttra Bhadra Pada-4 Revti-4 Total 9

Thus there are 108 navamsha in 12 Signs. Each Sign has 9 navamshas there characteristics different to one another e.g. in Aries Lord of Aswini is *Ketu, Bharni-Venus, Kritika-Sun*

ARIES	BSHWINI 4 Ketu	+	BHARNI 4 Venus	+	KRITIKA 1 Sun
TAURUS	Kritika 3 SUN	+	Rohini 4 MOON	+	Mrigsira 2 MARS
GEMINI	Mrigsira 2 MARS	+	Aridra 4 RAHU	+	Punarvasa 3 JUPITER
CANCER	Punasvasa 1 JUPITER	+	Pushya 4 SATURN	+	Ashlekha 4 MERCURY
LEO	Magha 4 KETU	+	Poorva Phalghuna 4 VENUS	+	Uttra Phalguna 1 SUN
VIRGO	Uttra phalguna 3 SUN	+	Hasta 4 MOON	+	Chitra 2 MARS
LIBRA	Chitra 2 MARS	+	Swati 4 RAHU	+	Vishakha 3 JUPITER
SCORPIO	Vishakha 1 JUPITER	+	Anuradha 4 SATURN	+	Jyeshtna 4 MERCURY
SAGITTARIUS	Mool 4 KETU	+	Poorvashada 4 VENUS	+	Uttra Shada 1 SUN
CAPRICORN	Uttra Shada 3 SUN	+	Shravana 4 MOON	+	Dhahishtha 2 MARS
AQUARIUS	Dhanishtha 2 MARS.	+	Shatbhisha 4 RAHU	+	Poorva Bhadrapad 3 JUPITER
PISCES	Poorva Bhadrapada 1 JUPITER	+	Uttra Bhadrapada 4 SATURN	+	Revti 4 MERCURY

NAVAMSHA CHART

ARIES	*TAURUS*	*GEMINI*	*CANCER*	*LEO*	*VIRGO*	*LIBRA*	*SCORPIO*	*SAGITTARIUS*	*CAPRICORN*	*AQUARIUS*	*PISCES*	*D/M*
1	10	7	4	1	10	7	4	1	10	7	4	3/20
2	11	8	5	2	11	8	5	2	11	8	5	6/40
3	12	9	6	3	12	9	6	3	12	9	6	10/00
4	1	10	7	4	1	10	7	4	1	10	7	13/20
5	2	11	8	5	2	11	8	5	2	11	8	16/40
6	3	12	9	6	3	12	9	6	3	12	9	20/00
7	4	1	10	7	4	1	10	7	4	1	10	23/20
8	5	2	11	8	5	2	11	8	5	2	11	26/00
9	6	3	12	9	6	3	12	9	6	3	12	30/00

Thus Sign of natives are 12 in number. There Lords are 12 e.g. of
Aries, Scorpio—Mars
Taurus, Libra—Venus
Gemini, Virgo—Mercury
Cancer—Moon
Leo—Sun
Sagittarius, Pisces—Jupiter
Capricorn, Aquarius—Saturn

Mars, Venus, Mercury, Saturn are Lords of 2 Signs while Sun and Moon are Lords of one Sign each.

Importance of NAVAMSHA

There are 12 Signs in Horoscope. Any native may be born in any navamsha of a Sign. There are 9 Navamsha in each Sign. Every Navamsha is of 3-20 i.e. Three degrees twenty Kalas. In this way each Sign which has 30^0.00. Thirty degrees in full has 9 Navamshas each of 3^0-20

3^0.20-1st Navamsha 6^0.40 2nd Navamsha 10^0.0 Third Navamsha
13^0.20-4th Navamsha 16^0.40 5th Navamsha 20^0.0 Sixth Navamsha
23^0.20-7th Navamsha 26^0.40 8th Navamsha 30^0.0 9th Navamsha

Each Navamsha contains 13-15 minutes of time. With the help of Navamsha we can correct the Lagna of Horoscope by the Characteristics of Navamshas. For Example if the birth time has not been noted correctly but has been noted at random e.g. The child was born on 30-7-2004 at about 9-00 A.M. to 10.00 A.M. (within one hour) But by the help of Signs, form of body, Height, Colour, Size we can fix the correct time by asking some Question to the father/mother of the child. The characteristics of Navamshas are as following:

ARIES Sign

1st Navamsha—The native born in 1st Navamsha of Aries Lagna has sheep like mouth, Little nose, Little arm, Hard word, not beautiful, short healthy and strong body.

2nd Navamsha—The native born in 2nd Navamsha of Aries is black, fate shoulder and arm, Little short forehead, beautiful eyes, bright Sight, long mouth and nose, sweet speech, weak feet.

3rd Navamsha—No hair, white colour, loose arms, beautiful eye

5th Navamsha—Leftist, eyes like elephant, fat nose, forehead, and brows, Fat body, hard hair.

6th Navamsha—Native born in 6th Navamsha of Aries is black in colour, kind hearted, eyes like deer, long, weak back, hard feet, loose stomach and arms, timid, talkative and common gender.

7th Navamsha—Native born in 7th Navamsha of Aries is Black, Swift, white eyes, wicked and fat body.

8th Navamsha—Born in 8th Navamsha of Aries is monkey-faced speaker, Hard and yellow body, secret-patient, violent, liar, dear to friends, and hard nature, hard behaviour.

9th Navamsha—Native born in Last Navamsha of Aries is long, weak body, touring short forehead, short eyes, horse like mouth, famous but wicked by nature.

TAURUS Sign

1st Navamsha—Native born in 1st Navamsha of Taurus is of medium size, Black in colour, in Previous position unable to do some thing in oldage doing low worker of low mentality and acute sight.

2nd Navamsha—Deep sight, lazy, low head and mouth, little intelligent, working abnormally, speaks more lie.

3rd Navamsha—Loose body, handsome nose, big eye, long size doing religious work yagya etc., strong feet and hand.

4th Navamsha—Small in Size, touring, angry, sheep like eyes, yellow colur, poor, drawing other person's money.

5th Navamsha—Wicked, highnose, like big ox body, curl hair, passionate, fate arms, shoulder and waist, whitish colour.

6th Navamsha—Nice eyes, steadfast, beautiful hair, shinning, orator, adult, humorous, weak body, expert in all works.

7th Navamsha—Lover of Still birth lady, some what long nose, eyes, strong body, envy of family members, long feet, short hair.

8th Navamsha—Eyes like a tiger, beautiful teeth, Victorious, broken nose, doing a little work, curled and black hair, sharp nails, talkative.

9th Navamsha—Popular lower strength, timid, Angry, even and nice body, cunning, hoarder of money, famous, weaknees in lower part of the body, weak and lastly weeping.

GEMINI Sign

1st Navamsha—Native born in 1st Navamsha of Gemini has hair on arm and shoulder, nice black eyes, high nose, light black colour, weak feet, and hands.

2nd Novamsha—Head like a pot, negative acts, violent, shrink nose in middle, talkative, active but expert in conflict.

3rd Navamsha—Whitish colour, red eyes, nice nose, even body, genius, long mouth, black brows on eyes, expert in speech.

4th Navamsha—Nice brows and head, sexy, black, vast chest, clean teeth, sweet-speech, beautiful hair.

5th Navamsha—Vast mouth, High hip, strong chest, fat forehead, wicked, proudy, clean and even sight.

6th Navamsha—Honey-coloured eyes, useless talks, vast forehead, medium size, beautiful body, cunning, swift, beautiful lips and teeth strong , powerful.

7th Navamsha—Red and high eyes vast-chest, well versed in education and drawing, humorous.

8th Navamsha—Black color, the best wise person, beautiful, sweet-speech, long body, vast and black eyes, having the knowledge of Art.

9th Navamsha—Black Round eyes, beautiful body, successful worker, genius, lover, expert in Science and Poetry.

CANCER Sign

1st Navamsha—Born in 1st Navamsha of Cancer the native is clean, whitesh colour, beautiful hair, vast stomach, beautiful mouth, high eyes, weak body, and arms.

2nd Navamsha—Red-whitish colour, Strugglesome, fighter, knowing Art, mouth and nose like cat, donator, weak thigh.

3rd Navamsha—White Colour, nice eyes, orator, body slim like lady, wise and intelligent, doing low job, lazy.

4th Navamsha—Black colour, slim brows, Fat and long size, nice nose and eyes, patient, donor, envy of own caste.

5th Navamsha—Speaking loudwords, lowmouth, Combined brows, long arms, server, evil doing, less intelligent, strugglesome.

6th Navamsha—Long, extent body, beautiful eye, hold, white colour, nice nose, speaker, fat teeth.

7th Navamsha—Scattered hair, vast body, thigh with nerves, living in other person's house, shape like crow.

8th Navamsha—Ghanta like head, evil worker, beautiful mouth and arms, moving like tortoise, low nose, black colour.

9th Navmasha—Whitish colour, fish like eyes, loose stomach, vast chest, long lip and head, fat thigh, weak knees.

LEO Sign

1st Navamsha—Native born in 1st Navamsha of Leo has crushed stomach Red Nose, Vast head, high and strong chest.

LEO Sign

1st Navamsha—Native born in 1st Navamsha of Leo has crushed stomach Red Nose, Vast head, high and strong chest.

2nd Navamsha—Vast and high forehead, Square body, Vast eyes, long arm, high chest, fat nose.

3rd Navamsha—Vast Arms with hair, eyes like chakor bird, Swift, Donor, saint, high nose, loose body, round throat.

4th Navamsha—White colour like cream, long, black eye, loose hair, word like crow, Fat hand's feet, frog like stomach.

5th Navamsha—Head like Ghanta घटां little hair, nice noise, and eyes, Hair on body, long stomach, leftist, scattered teeth, vast chest.

6th Navamsha—Little loose hair on body, vast and clean eyes, long size, black, loved by ladies, orator wise.

7th Navamsha—Long mouth, Fat body with veins, envy of wife, black colour, leftist, hair on body, hard speech, insincere in behaviour.

8th Navamsha—Sweet speech, fixed body, Deep sight, evilacts poor, expert in doing number two works copying etc.

9th Navamsha—Mouth like Donkey, black eyes, long arms, nice thigh, suffering from Asthma (disease of breaths)

VIRGO Sign

1st Navamsha—Native born in 1st Navamsha of Virgo has eyes like deer, orator, donor, wealthy, sensuous, black, vast heart.

2nd Navamsha—Beautiful mouth and eyes, shining, sweet speech, long stomach, vast thigh.

3rd Navamsha—Nose broken, nice feet, vast arm, speech not clear, whitish in colour, kind hearted.

4th Navamsha—Wise, too much attached with wife, loose body, dear in sight, red-white colour, leftist, intelligent weak thigh, nice head and hair.

5th Navamsha—Fat Lips and arms, high body, fat hair and shoulder, vast chest, dependent, strong thigh.

6th Navamsha—Beautiful, sweet in speech, shining body, wise, Author, happy and tourist.

7th Navamsha—Small mouth, thigh shoulders, Strong arms very white colour, long stomach, feet, hands, afraid of water.

8th Navamsha—Loose and white body, long size, high eye, leftist, proudy, long and fat arms, yellow hair.

9th Navamsha—Distinguished, loose body, beautiful, vast eyes, Brave and bold, clever, low shoulder, expert in writing essays.

2nd Navamsha—Retro and Round eyes, high teeth, lean waist, nice throat, vast heart, filthy body, joint brows.

3rd Navamsha—White in colour, mouth as horse, nice teeth, high eyes, weak, famous, long hair and nose, nice feet.

4th Navamsha—Weak arms, Timid, high teeth, weak body, swift eyes, small nose, black, saddy nature, Vicious.

5th Navamsha—Deep sight, steady intellect, dear to friends Polite, Hard hair, even eyes, nice nose.

6th Navamsha—Strong body, white colour, vast eyes, nice nose, clean nail; knowing ethics and old texts.

7th Navamsha—Red-white colour, wise, long body and hands, vast head, Miser, leftist and mentally strong in reading.

8th Navamsha—High check and shoulder, sensuous, hard body, large and black brows, peacefully speaking, beautiful chest and broken head.

9th Navamsha—Nice eyes, Happy mood, white, nice body, Artist, simple and humorous, low mentality.

SCORPIO Sign

1st Navamsha—Native born in 1st Navamsha of Scorpio has small and high lips and nose, beautiful forehead, strong body white colour, frog like stomach and the native is broker.

2nd Navamsha—White colour strong and vast heart, arms, red eyes, trimpuh on enemies, army, courageous, more hair on body.

3rd Navamsha—Pandit, wise, strong shoulder and arms, nice hair, true speaker, unmarried lady's son, white colour, nice lips.

4th Navamsha—Laning mind in others lady and conflict envy of others, directing the people in work, patient, big body, black colour, black hair and eyes perfect in dance, fat hair on body, strong shoulder.

5th Navamsha—Deep personality, red eyes, narrow nose patient, proudy, hard worker, strong body, famous.

6th Navamsha—Unhesitating, Intelligent, high nose, powerful, strong body, knowing ethics, hardworker, leftist, expert, in work little hair, combined brows.

7th Navamsha—Open mouth, strong body, small and big teeth, veins and Nerves in body, narrow stomach, left sight, shining beautiful.

8th Navamsha—Broken nose, black colour, vicious, dirty shape, high hair, less intelligent.

9th Navamsha—White colour, simple nature like deer animal, peaceful, yellow sight, strong and healthy body.

SAGITTARIUS Sign

1st Navamsaha—Native Born 1st Navamsha of Sagittarius has long nose, eyes like sheep, out spoken beautiful teeth and hair, white colour, leftist and strong hydrocele.

2nd Navamsha—High head, steady intellect, vast eyes, strong waist, thigh, broken nose, long size, fat beard.

3rd Navamsha—Intelligent wise, educated, knowing old texts, expert deeply wise, knowing ethics, beloved of wife, mentally strong, humorous, knowing technology.

4th Navamsha—Active worker, honey coloured round eyes white body, stomach, like tortoise, wise, touring, nice hair, vast body, handsome body.

5th Navamsha—Vast ears, eyes, mouth. Body like lion, long brows, strong shoulder and arms, body without hair, and keen intellect.

6th Navamsha—Nice black but vast eyes, big forehead, poet, strong and large mouth, not getting help, have faith in wise persons talk.

7th Navamsha—Black colours, simple habit, keeping his words, high head, hoarding, vast body, eyes, kind hearted good man.

8th Navamsha—Lean, pressed nose, long head, having enmity with people, disturbed sight, speaks too much, beloved by teachers.

9th Navamsha—White colour, mouth like horse black vast eyes, speaking a little, truthful, having sadness, legs not straight.

CAPRICORN Sign

1st Navamsha—Native born in 1st navamsha of Capricorn has thin teeth, black in colour, less speaking, hard hair, famous, devoted to music and humour, moving wealth and weak body.

2nd Navamsha—Lazy, wicked, nose not straight, lyrical, vast body, beloved of many ladies, speaking too much and clever.

3rd Navamsha—Expert in Music, Famous, white-colour, clean eyes, nice nose, many friends, beloved of brothers, successful in desired.

4th Navamsha—Read and black eyes, vast forehead, weak body and hands scattered hair, thin teeth, speaking a little.

5th Navamsha—High check and arms, finishing beginning work, high nose and stomach, sensual, attached with adult lady, black colour, round thigh.

6th Navamsha—Shining, beautiful shape, sexy, little and even teeth, sweet-speech, Large beard and forehead.

7th Navamsha—Black colour, lazy, good speaker, curled hair, vast body, hard tendency, loose hands and feet, wise, virtuous.

8th Navamsha—Deep sight, nice nose, red mouth, broken nails, and hair, unnatural body, forehead like a pot.

9th Navamsha—Vast heart and eyes, genius beautiful mouth, busy in singing with instruments, lovely in sight, strong, powerful, good man and knowing ethics.

AQUARIUS Sign

1st Navamsha—Native born in 1st Navamsha of Aquarius has black colour loose and weak body, fat beard, knowing old texts and poetry, sexy, lover and beautiful

2nd Navamsha—Hard skin, nail, eye and hair, helper of poor and troubled good man, long size, strange head, and less intelligent.

3rd Navamsha—Strong body, beloved of ladies, nice shining, knowing old texts and doing work according to the religion.

4th Navamsha—Attached with wife, whitish colour, vast mouth, destroyer of enemies, deep thoughts, patient, powerful, sensual and lover.

5th Navamsha—Knowing essence of life, Artist, sharp hair on feet, hard behaviour, narrow checks, ears and black.

6th Navamsha—Mouth like tiger, Adult, curled hair, strong will power, killer of tiger, serpant and deer, beloved by the king.

7th Navamsha—Mouth and eyes like sheep, sharp behaviour, living happy in village, dependent on wife, bilious, patient and powerful.

8th Navamsha—Born in 8th Navamsha of Aquarius has permanent strength, intellect, and love, either king or soldier of king, beautiful, fat teeth, big eyes.

9th Navamsha—Black in colour, black teeth, loving apart from wealth, woman and son, sweet speech, famous and expert.

PISCES Sign

1st Navamsha—Those born in 1st Navamsha of Pisces Sign are red-white shining body, kind heart, beloved of wife, swift mind, short throat and thin waist.

2nd Navamsha—Vast and Fat nose, active worker, fond of eating meat, beautiful body, touring in forest, mountain, fat head.

3rd Navamsha—White in colour, wicked, beautiful eyes, nice body, religious, wise man, kind and polite and very beautiful body.

4th Navamsha—Virtuous, helper of poor, downtrodden, Serving old persons, active worker, powerful, knowing ethics, high nose.

5th Navamsha—Long in Size, black, brave and bold, restless, small nose, violent, nice teeth, intolerant, speaking uselessly.

6th Navamsha—Visiting personality, brave and bold, wiseman, of good family, small nose, proudy, leftist mouth, famous and clever.

7th Navamsha—Proudy, lover other religion, Aristocrate, minister, powerful, cruel and Swift, full of sorrow and sadness.

8th Navamsha—Long and big head, weak body, Lazy, hard eyes, hair, busy in hoarding money, clever in fighting, having little son.

9th Navamsha—Small size, simple behaviour, patient, vast chest, eyes and nose, shining vast body, intellectual, wise and famous.

2

Electional Astrology

Our great learned Rishis have prescribed selected Mantaras for performing our different roles in daily life avoiding difficulties, barriers, in conveniences to get success and happiness in our daily life. This branch of Astrology dealing with selection of Mantaras is Called Electional Astrology which is based on tithis, days, Nakshatras, Yogas, Karans, constituting PANCHANGA or five part of Panchang in selecting auspicious time for buying, selling, stocking of every thing e.g. putting on clothes, beginning of studies, Living in or changing a house, digging a well hand pump or tubewell, to travel or opening a new shop, Putting Seed in fields, Cutting of Crops, to take medicine, Marriage etc.

1. Day – The most important thing is the Day by which our daily life is begun. Certain Signification of the days are discussed herewith.

2. Sunday – Lord of the Day is Shiva Sublord is fire, Planet Sun who is the lord of the east. On Sunday Havan, Yangnya, taking medicines, buying Cows, using Weapons, buying and selling of Gold, Copper, Wave, Cloth, Cooking gas, Woods, Putting on Shoes etc are supposed to be good and auspicious.

Monday – Lord of the Day is PARWATI, Sublord is Water. Planet moon who is the lord of Vayavya (middle of north, west) Side Purchasing Conch, Lotus, Pearls, Sugarcane, eating Sweets, Sexual deed, Plantation, digging well, to start musical study, wearing gold, silver jewels, yagnya, milk, having Cows, buffaloes, etc. are supposed to be good. *No operation is suggested to be on Monday.*

Tuesday – Lord of the Day is Shadanan or Kartikeya. (Elder brother of Ganesh Ji) Planet Mars who is the lord of South.Tuesday is auspicious *for bad* and *unsocial* deeds as theft, diplomacy, toxic, firing, use of weapons, destruction, Killing, Struggle, Police, Military, Camping, Mines, deeds, litigation, gambling, *Loan should not be taken on Tuesday but paying of loan must be on Tuesday if you want to get rid of loan soon.*

Wednesday – Lord of the day is Vishnu Sublord is Earth, Mercury is the planet who is lord of North. On Wednesday admission in Schools for the first time, beginning of religious deeds which earn PUNYA by means of donation, beginning of service, technology, drawing, art, metal, to begin friendship, exercise debating, Putting on new clothes, writing work etc. are treated to be auspicious on Wednesday.

Thursday – Bramha is the lord, sublord is Hari of this day. Jupiter is the planet who is the lord of ISHAN (middle of North east). All the high Class religious, Spiritual deeds, worshipping of deities, Guru, Yagnya, Study, house jobs, travelling, medicines, jewelley, Vehicles, meditation, Judiciary etc. are supposed to be auspicious. All good deeds, education, marriage, worshopping etc are generally prescribed on Thursday.

Friday – Lord of the day is Indra, Sublord is Indrani, Venus is the Lord of South-east direction. On Friday matters related to fair sex, marriage, love affairs music, song, bed, jewellary, perfumery, clothing, inspiration, beginning of shop, land, animals, agriculture, money matters, diplomatic matters, foreign travels, digging of well, Hand pump, tube well etc. are supposed to be auspicious on Friday.

Saturday-Kaala is the lord and Bramha is sublord. Saturn is the lord of western direction. Speaking a lie, theft, poison preparing, beginning of living in a house, to learn mantra, fixed deeds concerning property, having servants, iron, stone works, sinny deeds, and above all surgery etc. are supposed to be auspicious on Saturday.

SUN, MARS, SATURN are known as cruel planets. Hence, Sun worship by means of SURYA NAMASKAR, GAYTARI MANTRA, JAPA, reciting of ADITYA HRIDAYA STOTRAM. Now use of set is recommended to prevent the evil results of Sun. *Worshipping of Hanuman Ji is best cure for preventing from evil deeds caused by Mars and Saturn* on Tuesday, Saturday, Reciting of HANUMAN KAWACH, BAJRANG BAN, HANUMAN CHALISA, HANUMAN BAHAK, SUNDAR KAND etc. are prescribed.

2. Tithis – There are 15 days in dark fortnight of moon called Krishna Paksha and 15 days in bright moon called *SHUKLA* Paksha. Tithis are of 5 kinds NANDA, BHADRA, JAYA, RIKTA, POORNA.

(a) Nanda Tithi– These are 1-6-11 tithis auspicious for Pleasure deeds, worshipping of GODS, havan, house Construction, Singing, dancing, and all works which produce pleasure happiness. FRIDAY on these tithis Produces *Siddha Yoga* good for marriage and love. In Hindu These tithis are called Padwa, Chhati, Gyaras or *EKADASI*.

(b) Bhadra Tithi- 2, 7, 12, OR DOJE, SAPTMI, BARAS or Dwadasi Tithis are auspicious for marriage, buying vehicles, all the work relating to path (Road, way, Marg), healing etc. Wednesday Produces Siddha Yoga. On these tithis good for festival, marriage, new business, education etc.

(c) Jaya Tithi– There 3-8-13 Teeja, Ashtmi, Teras or Triyodashi auspicious for struggle, conflict, litigation, manufacturing of weapons, Dhwaja Pataka Payment of loans, and evil deeds are Considered auspicious on this tithi though these are not good for society and humanity. Tuesday produces Siddhi Yoga on these tithis, good for competition.

(d) Rikta Tithi- These are 4, 9, 14 CHAUTH, NAVMI, CHAUDAS All cruel deeds by thieves cruel persons, e.g. killing, Poisoning etc. are done on these tithis., For TANTRIK these tithis are important. Saturday Produces Siddha Yoga on these tithis. To minimise the evil effects of these tithis Shri GANESH worship on Chaturthi, DEVI Worships NAVMI and Chaturdashi are prescribed by our rishis as beneficial for having fast. Rikta Tithis are specially prohibited all good deeds as they bring failures, unhappiness, disappointment if important deeds are begun on these tithis.

(e) Poorna Tithis – These are 5-10-15 tithis Panchami, Dasmi, Poonam auspicious for marriage, travel, Peaceful Works, Yagyna, Havan, ANUSHTHAN, UPASNA, VRITA, Satynarayan Worshipping, Meditation. Thursday produces Siddhi Yoga on these tithis.

1, 2, 3, 4, 5 tithis in bright moon after Amavasya are Ominious in dark moon auspicious 6, 7, 8, 9, 10 tithis in bright moon are secondary, in dark moon are secondary 11, 12, 13, 14, 15 tithis in bright moon are auspicious but in dark moon are Ominious.

If nanda tithi falls on Sunday, Tuesday it is Ominius. If Bhadra tithi fall on Monday, Friday it is Ominious. If Jaya falls on Wednesday it is Ominious. If Rikta tithi falls on Thursday it is Ominious. If Poorna falls on Saturday it is Ominious.

To avoid bad results of these tithis with these days DAN, PUNYA, VRITA are Prescribed e.g. if Amavasya falls on Saturday it becomes like a PARVA or Holiday to take sacred bath in GANGA, YAMUNA, NARMADA, SHIPRA, GODAVRI, KAVERI etc.

Significations of Tithis

Tithi	*Name*	*Lord*	*Noun*	*Result*	*Negation*
1	Prtipada (Vriddhi)	Agni	Nanda	Siddhi Dayak	Kushmanda
2	Dwitiya (Sumangala)	Brahma	Bhadra	Karya Sadhini	Katari
3.	Tritiya (Sabala)	Gauri	Jaya	Arogya Dayini	Namak
4.	Chaturthi (Khala)	Ganesh	Rikta	Hani Karak	Til
5.	Panchmi (Shrimati)	Sarda	Poorna	Shubha	Khatai
6.	Shashthi (Keerti)	Kartikeya	Nanda	Ashubha	Tel
7.	Saptmi (Mitra Prada)	Sun	Bhadra	Shubha	Amla
8.	Ashtmi (Balavari)	Shiva	Jaya	Vyadhi Nashini	Nariyala
9.	Navmi (Ugra)	Durga	Rikta	Mrityudayee	Khadoo
10.	Dashmi (Dharmini)	Yama	Poorna	Dhandayak	Parwal
11.	Ekadasi (Nanda)	Vishwa Dev	Nanda	Shubha	Daliya
12.	Dwadashi (Vasobala)	Hari	Bhadra	Sarvasiddhi Da	Masoor
13.	Tryodashi (Jayakara)	Kam	Jaya	Sarva Siddha	Began (Bhata)
14.	Charudashi (Krur)	Shiva	Rikta	Ugra	Shahad
15.	Poornima (Saumya)	Shashi	Poorna	Pushtida	Gambling
30.	Amavasya (Darsha)	Pitra	Poorna	Ashubha	Sexual Deed

NAKSHATRAS : Nakshatras play an important role in Muhurtas. There are 27 Nakshatras, their lords their mouth, their behaving nature, their eyes, shape and probable result may be found from the following Chart.

The above Chart shows generally the Characteristics of Nakshatra and their Shape, number of Stars, which is Visual in the night specially in the dark half of the mouth. Nakshatras give results according to their Devta's tendency. The Mouth of each Nakshatra and behaving nature and movement of eyes is generally seen in the work and conduct of persons born in these particular Nakshatras. So also these Nakshatras result in all our activities such as marketing, business, Education, Marriage, travel, Success, failure etc. is seen. Now we Shall deal with all these Nakshatras falling in a day. Here are some muhurtas for different works in our daily wife.

1. Adhomukh Nakshatra: These are 9 in number, Mool, Kritika, Bharni, POORVA PHALGUN, Ashlesha, Vishakha, Poorva Shada, Poorva Bhadra Pada, Magha, digging of well or digging Neev of house are auspicious.

2. Triyakmuka Nakshatras – These are also 9 in number. These are PunarVasu, Jyeshtha, Hasta, Aswini, Mrigsira, Revti, Chitra, Swati, Anuradha auspicious in buying animals, to begin machinery work, to begin ploughing, to go abroad outside the home.

St. No.	*Nakshatra*	*Lord*	*Mouth*	*Shape*	*Behaving*	*Movement*	*Shape Like*	*No of Stars*	*AUSPICIOUS*
1.	Ashwini	Ashwini Kumar	Obilique	Laghu	Cruel	Slow	Horse	3	AUSPICIOUS
2.	Bharni	Yama	Below	Urga	Ordinary	Medium	Vagina	3	DESTROYER
3.	Kritika	Agni	Below	Mishra	Fixed	Good	Hoof	6	Destruction of work
4.	Rohini	Bhamha	U P	Dhruva	Friendish	Blind	2 Parts	5	SIDDHI
5.	Mrigsir	Chandra	Oblique	Mirdu	Fierce	Slow	Deer	3	AUSPICIOUS
6.	Aridra	Shiva	U P	Teekshna	Moving	Medium	Jewel	1	AUSPICIOUS
7.	Punarvasu	Aditi	Obilique	Char	Immediate	Good	House	4	MEDIUM
8.	Pushya	Guru	U P	Laghu	Fierce	Blind	Arrow	3	AUSPICIOUS
9.	Ashlesha	Sarpa	Below	Teekshna	Cruel	Slow	Round Like Chakra	5	SHOK
10.	Magha	Pitra	Below	Urga	Cruel	Medium	Open House	5	DESTROYER
11.	Poorva Phalgun	Bhaga	Below	Urga	Fixed	Good	Bed	2	DEATH GIVER
12.	Uttra Phalgun	Aryama	U P	Dhruva	Immediate	Bliind	Cot	2	VIDYA
13.	Hasta	Ravi	Obilique	Laghu	Friendish	Slow	Hand	5	LAXMI
14.	Chitra	Vishnu	Obilique	Mirdu	Mourning	Medium	Pearl	1	GOOD GIVER
15.	Swati	Vayu	Obilique	Char	Ordinary	Good	Coral	1	OMINOUS
16.	Vishakha	Indiragini	Below	Mishra	Friendish	Blind	Toran	4	OMINIOUS
17.	Anurdha	Mitra	Obilique	Mirdu	Immediate	Slow	Balisam	4	SAMRIDDHI
18.	Jyeshtha	Indra	Obilique	Teekshna	Fierce	Medium	Kundal	3	CONSUMPTION AND DESTRUCTION
19.	Mool	Rakshash	Below	Teekshna	Fierce	Good	Lion	12	LOSS OF WEALTH
20.	Poorva Shada	Udak	Below	Urga	Cruel	Blind	Bed	4	LOSS
21.	Uttra Shada	Vishwa Dev	U P	Dhruva	Fixed	Good	Elephant	3	INTELLECT GIVER
22.	Shravan	Vishnu	U P	Char	Moving	Good	Vyaktakar	3	GIVER OF HAPPINESS
23.	Dhanishtha	Vasu	U P	Char	Moving	Blind	Vaman	4	WELL WISHER GOOD
24.	Shatbhisha	Varuna	U P	Char	Moving	Slow	Mridang	100	KALYANI
25.	Poorva Bhadradada	Ajaik	Below	Ugra	Cruel	Medium	Circular	2	DEATH GIVER
26.	Uttra Bhadrapaor	Ahirvagh Nyu	U P	Dhruva	Fixed	Good	Twins	2	LAXMI
27.	Rewti	Poosha	Obilique	Mirdu	Friendish	Blind	Mrdiang	32	KAMDA

Note: U.P. means upper month

3. Vrdhwa Nakshatras – These are too 9 in number Aridra, Pushya, Sravan,Uttra Phalgun, Uttrashad, Uttra Bhadrapada, Shatbhisha, Rohini, Dhanishtha. To start work near any religious place Mandapam House, gardening, to sit on throne etc.

4. Dhruva Nakshatras – Rohini, Uttar Phalgun, Uttra Shada, Uttra Bhadrapada these 4 Nakshatras are Dhruva Nakshatras. To put seed in the field to enter a city, Rajya Bhishek, gardening etc are to be done auspicious works in these.

5. Mridu Nakshatras – Mrigsira, Anuradha, Chitra, Rewti these 4 nakshatras are Mridu Nakshatras. To begin friendship, Putting on Clothes, Jewellery, music, Dance and other Manglik Performances are to be taken in these nakshatras.

6. Laghu Nakshatras – Ashwini, Pushya, Hasta, Abhijit (4 Pada of Uttranshada) to begin shop, jewellery, wearing, games, sports, to make medicines, to start faym optician, to start study, technology and kind like branches of knowledge to start journey etc.

7. Teekshna Nakshatras – Aridra, Ashlesha, Jyeshtha, Mool, to get on ghost, to draw, to start any ANUSTIHAN for mantra Sadhna, to find out confidentially all about others jail, assassination etc. may be performed.

8. Char Nakshatras – Punarvasu, Swati, Sravana, Dhanishtha, Shatbhisha, to get pleasure of gardening by means of picnic, to sit on your vehicles, start journeys, to go to hospital etc.

9. Ugra Nakshatras – Bharni, Magha, Poorva Phalgun, Poorva Shada, Poorva Bhadrapada etc. are ugra Nakshatras. In these nakshatras diplomacy, destruction, Poisoning, firing works may be done.

10. Mishra Nakshatras – Kritika, Bharni, Vishakha these 3 are mishra nakshatras some what weak hence seeming to tithis, days etc. should make use of those Nakshatras in different work as usual.

Different Yogas – Now we shall deal with combination of tithis, days, Nakshatras to be auspicious or Ominious. They are as following :-

Mrityu Yoga – If days and tithis are as following then they do not give success but destroys the good results. Hence they should be avoided

मृत्यु योग		दग्धा योग	
Day	Tithis	Dagdhayoga	
		Day	Nakshatra
Sunday	1-6-11	Sunday	Bharni
Monday	2-7-12	Monday	Chitra
Tuesday	1-6-11	Tuesday	Uttrashada
Wednesay	3-8-13	Wednesday	Dhanishtha
Thursday	4-9-14	Thursday	Uttra Phalguna
Friday	2-7-12	Friday	Jyeshtha
Saturday	5-10-15	Saturday	Revti

In DAGDHA tithis as shown in chart above if that particular day falls on that particular Nakshatras then DAGDHA is produced. If work begins then there is fear of firing. Hence they must be avoided.

YAMA GHANTA YOGA – Magha Nakshatra on Sunday Vishakha on Monday, Aridra on Tuesday, Mool on Wednesday, Kritika on Thursday, Rohini on Friday, Hasta on Saturday. There are strictly omitted in beginning business, travel.

SHUBHA AMRIT YOGA. This combination is good

DAY	– Nakshatras
Sunday	– Hasta, Mool, Uttra Phalgun, Uttra Shada, Pushya, Ashwini
Monday	– Sravana, Rohini, Mrigsir, Pushya, Anuradha
Tuesday	– Ashwini, Anuradha, Kritika
Wednesday	– Rohini, Anuradha, Hasta, Kritika, Mrigsir
Thursday	– Rewti, Anuradha, Ashwini, Punarvasu, Pushya.
Friday	– Ashwini, Punarvasu, Sravana, Anuradha, Rewti
Saturday	– Rohini, Shravana.

SAMVART YOGA – On Pratipada Wednesday, On Saptami Sunday are Ominious in good deeds.

JAWALAMUKHI YOGA—Mool On Pratipada, Bharni on Panchmi, Kritika on Ashtmi, Rohini on Navmi, Ashlesha on Dasmi. In these yoga either child dies early or if alive destroys the family.

ADHAM YOGA – This combination produces difficulties in the way of work. Dwadasi on Monday, Ekadasi on Monday, Dasmi on Tuesday, Navmi on Wednesday, Ashtmi on Thursday, Saptmi on Friday, Shasthri on Saturday. Hence they must be avoided.

TRIPATAJ YOGA – These are not auspicious:-

Tithi	*Day*	*Nakshatra*
5	Sunday	Hasta
6	Monday	Mrigsir
7	Tuesday	Ashwini
8	Wednesday	Anuradha
9	Thursday	Pushya Exception.
10	Friday	Revti
11	Saturday	Rohini

VISHA YOGA :- Sunday on Chaturthi, Monday on Shasthi, Tuesday on Saptmi, Wednesday on Dwitiya, Thursday on Ashtmi, Friday, on Navmi, Saturday on Saptmi are poisonous tithis. Hence must be avoided in good deeds.

HUSTASHAN- YOGA – Dwadashi on Sunday,

Ashtmi on Tuesday, Navmi on Thursday, Dashmi on Friday, Ekadashi on Saturday. These are Ominious must be avoided.

SARVARTH SIDDHI YOGA – This is the best yoga and any good work can be done in these days and Nakshatras that will be Successful :-

SUNDAY	–	Hasta, Mool, Uttra Phalgun, Uttar Shada, Uttra Bhadra Pada, Pushya, Ashwini.
MONDAY	–	Sravana, Rohini, Mrigsir, Pushya, Anuradha.
TUESDAY	–	Ashwini, Uttra Bhadra Pada, Kritika, Ashlesha.
WEDNESDAY	–	Rohini, Anuradha, Hasta, Kritika, Mrigsir.
THURSDAY	–	Revti, Anuradha, Aswini, Punarvasu, Pushya.
FRIDAY	–	Revti, Anuradha, Rohini, Punarvasu, Sravana.
SATURDAY	–	Sravana, Rohini, Swati.

RAVI YOGA – This is an important yoga which removes the evils of other combination if any. Count from the Surya Nakshatra in Gochar to moon Nakshatra and 4th, 6th, 9th, 10th, 13th, 20th Nakshatra Produce RAVI YOGA : These are most ominious on which these numbers fall in marriage, Travelling must be Omitted. But if there is Ashwini on Tuesday, Rohini on Saturday, Pushya on Thursday the Yoga is there. Though the combination is under Sarvartha Siddhi Yoga but for marriage and journey not recommended.

Be Cautious about these 14 Nakshatras – In these Nakshatras theft money, mortgaged land, or Property, given on loan money kept underground money is found unreturnable. If there are no other good combinations of days and Tithis. They are Uttra Phalgun, Uttra Shada, Uttra Bhadra Pada, Poorva Phalgun, Poorva Shada, Poorva, Bhadra Pada, Rohini, Vishakha, Kritika, Magha, Aridra, Bharni, Ashlesha and Mool.

There are certain other important Muhurtas useful in our daily life such as Pregnancy, Name Ceremony, Education, Medication, Putting on Clothes, Loans, Opening Shop, Travelling, New House Entry, etc.,

Pregnancy – The natural nights of menses of woman are 16 among them first three nights are called "CHANDALI" and 4, 11, 13, nights are negated. The rest 10 nights are prescribed for combination to get progeny. In 4th night if woman is pregnant the son will be short lived and poor. In 5th night son will be born in 6th night ordinary son will be born. In 7th night son will not be born. In 8th night the son will be devotee of God. In 9TH night Luck will favour. In 10th night Virtuous and wise son will be born. In 11th night unreligious and wicked Son in 12th night good son in 13th night sinny girl in 14th night virtuous grateful son in 15th night husband's devotee girl, and in 16th night the son will be born Kind-hearted, well wisher of all.

For combinations with the wife Monday, Wednesday, Thursday, Friday should be taken. 4, 6, 8, 9, 14, 15, and Amavasya tithis should be avoided. Lagna should be aspected by male planets and 1-4-7-10-5-9- houses should be occupied by benefies. In 3, 6, 10, 11 houses should be malefies. Moon should be in odd विषम Nawamsa. Specially for SON, Moon, Jupiter should be in Odd Navamsa and if these are in even Signs daughters may be born.

Good Nakshatras for Pregnancy – Sravana, Rohini, Hasta, Anuradha, Swati, Uttra Phalgun, Uttra shada, Uttra Bhadrapada, Mool, Shatbisha.

Secondary Nakshatra for Pregnancy – Pushya, Dhanishtha, Mrigsir, Ashwini, Chitra, Punarvasu. Other nakshatras should be avoided.

Name Ceremony – After 10, 11, 12, 20, 22, 27, 100 days after the birth of child in Mrigsir, Punarvasu, Pushya, Uttra Phalgun, Uttrashada, Uttrabhadrapada, Hasta, Chitra, Swati, Anuradha, Jyestha, Dhanishtha, On Sunday, Monday, Wednesday, Thursday, Friday in Taurus, Leo Scorpio, Aquarius, Lagnas in auspicious tithis. Rikta tithis 4-9-14- and other evil condition should be avoided in name ceremony of the newly born child.

Education – Education is the main backbone of life. Hence, education of the child should be started by worshipping Lord Ganesh, Godess Saraswati and the teacher concerned getting reported by the child and Parents. It should be begun on Wednesday, Thursday or Friday. Sunday is Secondary day, Monday makes too intellect dull of the child. Tuesday and Saturday are harmful. Nakshatras are Mrigsir, Aridra, Punarvasa Pushya, Ashlesha, Mool, Hasta, Chitra, Swati, Ashwini, Poorva Phalgun, Poorvashada and Sravaka.

Medication – Revti, Ashwini, Punarvasu, Pushya, Hasta, Chitra, Swati, Sravana, Dhanishtha, Shatbhisha, Anuradha, Mool, Mrigsir, are auspicious with good days and tithis.

Putting on Clothes – If new clothes are put on Sunday they will shortly be useless, on Monday will be wet, on Tuesday will give unhappiness, sadness, Putting on clothes on Wednesday will make wealthy, on Thursday will give knowledge, on Friday friendship will increase, on Saturday disappointment and melancholy, Hence put on clothes on Wednesday, Thursday and Friday only.

Loans and Advances and Their Payments–Debt should not be incurred on Tuesday otherwise it will increase like a disease and it will be difficult to get rid of it. Debt must be Paid On Tuesday and you will see that it will be clear very soon.

Opening a Shop – Monday, Wednesday, Thursday, Friday on 2, 3, 5, 7, 10, 12, 13 tithis in Rohini, Uttra Phalgun, Uttrashada, Uttrabhadra Pada, Pushya, Hasta, Chitra, Revti, Ashwini, Anuradha Nakshatras in

Labhghatis in beneficial Lagnas new shop, new business should be ceremonised.

Travelling – Position of Moon is very important. Moon is 1-5-9-Sings or Rasis abodes in East in 2-6-10 Signs in South, in 3-7-11 in West, in 4-8-12 in North. When moon is in front of you it gives money, aboding in right side gives happiness and wealth. and property. Moon in back side gives Sorrow and trouble in left side loss of Wealth. In the same way dik-shool is also to be kept in mind e.g. on Monday and Saturday dik-shool is in East, on thursday in south on sunday and Friday in west and on Tuesday, Wednesday in North. In DIK-SHOOL Travelling is negated. Dik Shool may be lessen if you travel on Sunday by taking betal Leaf or GHEE. By using Sandal or taking milk on Monday. By eating Gud on Tuesday, by taking TIL on Wednesday by taking Curd on Thursday, by taking barley JAU on Friday, by taking URAD on Saturday. For travelling Ashwini, Punarvasu, Anuradha, Mrigsir, Pushya, Revti, Hasta, Sravana, Dhanishtha Nakshatras are good, 2, 3, 6, 8, 10, 12 tithis are good. 6-8-12-4-9-14 Amavasya, Poornima, and Pratipada of bright Moon (Shukla Paksha) are not auspicious. *Nakshatra Shool,* do not travel in Jyestha Nakshatra to East, in Poorva Bhadrapada to South, in Rohini to West, in Uttra Phalgun to North. The traveller Should not return on 9th day of beginning the journey day.

Newshouse Entry – First of all Put water in a pot and worship Lord GANESH, ISTADEV, NAV GRAHAS, SHODASH MATRKAS, HAVAN for Peaceful Living Prosperity, feeding 9 girls, grass to Cows then enter in the New House. Vaishaka, Jyestha, Magh, Phalguna, in Rohini, Mrigser, Pushya, Anyaradha, Revti, Uttraphalguna, Uttra Shada, Uttra Bhadrapada, Shatbhisha, Swati, Dhanishtha Nakshatras, On MONDAY, WEDNESDAY, THURSDAY, FRIDAY, SATURDAY Omitting 4-9—14 RIKTA tithis, and in fixed Lagnas having benefies, malefies in Kendra, Trikona, 3, 6, 11 houses, No Planet should be in 4, 8, houses.

Panchak Nakshatras – *Dhanishtha Shat the SHOT BHISHA* Poorva Bhadra Pada, Uttra Bhadra Pada, Revti, these 5 Nakshatras are called Panchak. **Using Newthings**, Collection of Wood is prohibited. If a man/woman dies in these Nakshatras then before funeral rites 5 PUTLAS are made of flour and their funeral rite is performed to avoid the ominous evil of PANCHAKAS. If any body dies in Panckas 5 death are Sure in their area.

3

Horary Astrology

Astrology is one of the best, wonderful and useful Sciences which from time immemorial has been the subject of verification and modification based on every event of knowledge in our life. Our great Saints or Maharishis who were the high-minded well wishers of humanity, left behind us the valuable treasure of Astrology for making life and living in the world worthy, meaningful, useful and purposeful our rishis told

"सर्वे भवन्तु सुखिनः सर्वे सन्तु निरामया
सर्वे भद्राणि पश्यन्तु मा कश्चिद् दुख माप्नुयात"

Means all be happy, all be healthy, All see happiness, No body may get trouble.

A Small group of newly educated persons who do not know the basic rudiments of this great science often say that Astrology is nothing more than superstition. These persons who decry astrology showed first of all study Astrology systematically. The definition about astrology as given in our Shastras is quite true.

अप्रत्यक्षाणि शास्त्राणि विवादस्तेषु केवलं
प्रत्यक्षम् ज्योतिष शास्त्रं चन्द्रार्कौ यस्य साक्षिणौ

Means all other sciences are based on hypothecation and deduction based on arguments, reasoning and counter reasoning but astrology is the only science which is perfect and the evidence for this are the Sun and Moon. This means that since this science tells perfectly all about Sun rise, Sun set, Moon rise, eclipses the other derivations of astrological aspersions are true and are based on proper evidence. It is a direct science which is self witnessed and self proved and there is no necessity for further proof about its accuracy and usefulness.

Astrology has many branches of study. Horary Astrology is the most popular branch of astrology. Any type of Question can be answered at any place and at any time. On the basis of Querrychart for the time of Question our wise forefathers have laid down many solid rules, exceptions and other principles for finding out the solution to different problems faced daily by the humanity. Let me give some examples of different problems.

Courtcase – A Question was asked by an advocate friend of mine at Vidisha (M.P.) when Aries was rising on the horizon. The Question was "Will I be able to win the case"?

Acharya Neel Kantha Says in TAJIK NEELKANTHI ''क्रूरा खेचरा लग्नं विवादा पृश्चाशु जयतु विवादं तं'' means malefies in the Lagna give Victory to the Querry Prischak. The Same thing has been said in "BHAVA" PRAKASH" by ACHARYA JIVANATH that if Scorpio Aquarius, Pisces or Cancer happens to be in fourth house the enemy will he defeated and if there are malefies in the fourth house the enemy leaves the battle field. The same thing has been said lay Prathu YASHA, the Son of the great Indian Astrologer Varahmi hir in SHAT PANCHASHIKA"

Date 14-8-1973 at 10 p.m.

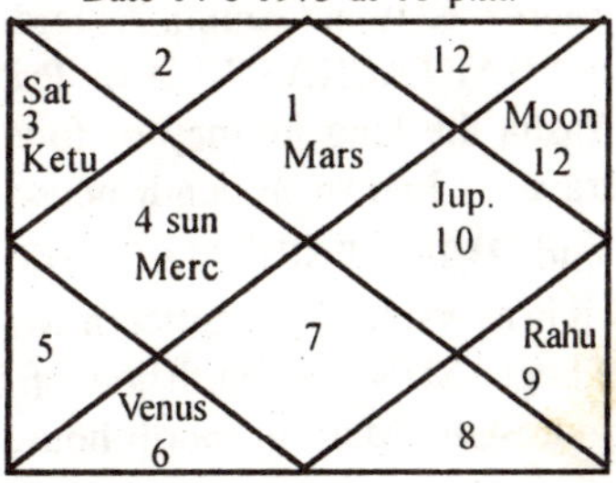

''मेषाणि कुंभ कर्कट रसातले यदा स्थितः
रिपौ पराजयस्तदा चतुष्पदिहि पलायनम्''

Pandit Rudra Mani TRIPATHI says in "Prasna Shiromani" ''तनुनाथ सबलः केन्द्रस्थिते बली पृश्चिकः'' means if lord of Lagna is situated in Kendra i.e. in 1-4-7-10 houses the Querrist will win.

The person who files the suit is called वादी VAADI and the person against whom the suit in filed is called प्रतिवादी PRATIVAADI. The Lagna Presents the Querrist. In such cases, the Seventh house represents Prativaadi. If there are any malefic planets in the Lagna, the Seventh house will be fully aspected by the malefies present in Lagna weakening the seventh house. Malefic means here natural malefics. In the above Example mars, the lord of Lagna is present in Lagna. Mars is a malefies is Strong and hold planet in his own house ARIES. Mars is aspecting the seventh house terribly weakening it. The Seventh lord venus is in debilitation (NEECHA RASI) in Virgo in 6th house (the house of enemy). Thus the Seventh house representing the Prativaadi and his case are both weak. The other malefic planet the SUN is in fourth house in Cancer Sign. The Querrist was told that he will win and really he won the case.

Like this we can easily find out the correct Solutions of many day to day problems like lost things, lost persons, transfer, promotion, Suspension in Service etc. In the Same way when and where profit or less, foreign journey, marriage, children, treatment of diseases.

Foreign Travel : On 26th January 1973 at 7.55 P.M. Mr. Pritam Babu Sharma Lecturer SAMRAT ASHOK TECHNOLOGICAL INSTITUTE VIDISHA (M.P.) Came to me and said that he had no horoscope. He put a Question before me w.f. when will I go abroad for further studies in engineering". At that time Leo Ascendant was rising – Moon in Libra, Mars in Scorpio, Rahu and Venus in Sagittarius, SUN Mercury and Jupiter in Capricorn, Saturn in Taurus, Ketu in Gemini. According to SHAT PACHASHIKA of Prithu Yasha the long journey or foreign travel is known by tenth house as said मध्यात् प्रवासो MADDHYAT PRAVASI. Here the lord of Lagna SUN is in movable Sign Capricorn. Moon too is in movable Sign in Libra. Lord of Lagna SUN is in fourth house from Moon and Moon is in tenth house from SUN. Mars in fourth house is Scorpio, Saturn in tenth house is Taurus. Fourth house indicates स्थान च्युति STHANA CHYUTI or movement from home or residence. The lord of Lagna Sun is with the lord of fifth house Jupiter and Karaka for education mercury. Sixth house is the house of foreign travel. From sixth house in fifth house there is Saturn in friend Sign which means journey will be in connection with education as fifth house denotes education (Tenth house is fifth house from sixth house). Moreover Saturn is an airy planet who is the lord of sixth and seventh houses (movable Signs) indicates that the journey will be through air. Foreign journey yoga is present here—

Date 26-1-1973 at 7.55 p.m.

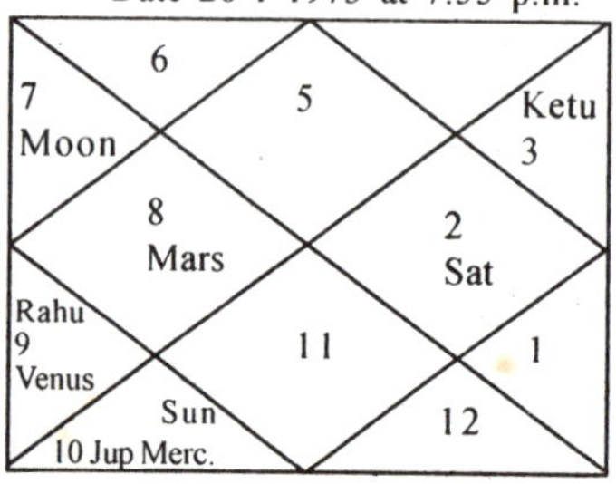

चतुर्थे दशमे वापि यदि सौम्य ग्रहौ भवति
तदा न गमनं क्रूरस्तत्रैव गमनं भवेत्

means if these are benefies in fourth and tenth houses, no travel will take place if malefies are present in fourth and tenth houses then travel is sure. Here Mars and Saturn both malefies are in fourth and tenth houses respectively.

Ascendant in Sheershodoya शीर्षोदय Sign indicates success as said 'शीर्षोदये सिद्धिमुपैति कार्यम्' means if in a Question horoscope there is Sheershodoya Sign then success is Sure.

Now it has been proved that the yoga for foreign travel is present. But when will if commence? Normally the position of ascendant its lord in fixed, movable dual sign indicates about the period of travel by its multiplying the Sign figure by 12, 24, 36 in fixed, movable and dual Signs respectively. Here the ascendant S lord is in Capricorn sign (movable Sign). So we multiply by 24 X 10 Capricorn Sign taking that the journey will start after 240 days. Really Mr. P.B. Sharma Left for England correctly after 240 days from the date of Question on 27th September 1973 from India. Mr. P.B. Sharma a gold medalist in B.E. Postgraduated with honors in machenical engineering from Brimingham Universiy England. After returning from England he worked as professor in Indian Institute of Technology, New Delhi, then worked as Principal of Delhi Engineering College Delhi, then Vice Chancellor RAJIV GANDHI TECHNOLOGICAL UNIVERSITY, BHOPAL (M.P.) INDIA.

TRANSFER On 18-1-1986 Saturday at 05.30 P.M. Mr. S.N. Dubey, Town Inspector of Police, SIRONJ Distt Vidisha. (M.P.) came to me and asked about his transfer. At that time Cancer Lagna was rising with moon and RAHU in Aries, Mars and Ketu in Libra, Saturn in Scorpio, Mercury in Sagittarius, SUN, Venus and Jupiter in Capricorn.

Date 18-1-1986 : 05.30 p.m.

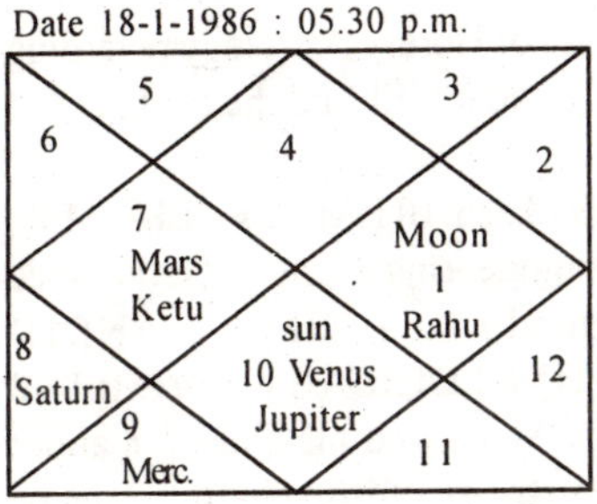

Here Lagna Cancer is MOVABLE (CHAR) Sign. The lord of Lagna Moon too is in movable (Chara) Sign in tenth house in Aries, the house of Profession and Government. The lord of tenth house MAR too is in movable (Chara) Sign in Libra in 4th house aspecting his own Sign Aries. SUN, Venus, Jupiter are also in movable Sign Capricorn in 7th house. Thus the Lagna and Seven planets out of nine were in CHART (movable) Sign. So the transfer was inevitable. In Horary Astrology the position of Lagna and Moon should be Strong. Specially the Moon's Position is very important while calculating results in Horary Astrology.

If lord of lagna aspects the moon or lord of Action or Karya Lord aspects the house of action or Lagna Lord aspects the Karya Lord or they are related either by aspecting each other or being in mutual exchange position by changing Signs of each other. In the present case moon is the lord of Lagna. The lord of action or Lord of tenth house mars too aspects moon. In this way they are aspecting each other. Besides the lord of fourth house Venus aspects the Lagna. Hence Lagna its lord, tenth house its lord, fourth house its lord these three are extremely related to each other by aspect and position.

When there are malifies in fourth and tenth houses transfer of the Querist is Sure. Here mars and Ketu in fourth house and Rahu in tenth house with lagna lord moon are situated. Hence the lagna Lord moon is badly afflicted by malefics in tenth causing soon transfer. Lagna Lord Moon in tenth house aspecting tenth Lord shows that Question is concerned with Profession as tenth house is the house of profession. Tenth Lord Mars aspects Sun. Sun is Karaka for Government. Hence Question is Concerned with transfer in Government Service. Mars is Karaka for Police, Military, Land, House etc. Hence the Querist in Police department. Fourth house means peace or Home so change in place is also concerned with the Question. I told Mr. Dubey that when Mars (Lord of action House) will leave the fourth house transfer order will be received. In fact it was a matter of great wonder that Mr. Dubey got his transfer order on 27-1-1986. He came to me on 28-1-1986 and was surprised to know the accuracy of this great Science Astrology. Mars left the fourth house on 27-1-1986, the date on which he received his transfer order.

Progeny Through Horary Astrology

Here are some experienced examples of Horary Astrology regarding the Question about the birth of children. Reader will find the truthness of ASTROLOGY in these examples—

Example 1 Son Birth: On 25-3-1973 at 5.10 P.M. at Vidisha (M.P.) Mr. P.B. Sharma (Ex-Principal Delhi Engineering College Delhi, Vice Chancellor RAJIV GANDHI TECHNOLOGICAL UNIVERSITY BHOPAL) asked me Question about the birth of child whether son or daughter. The Question was asked in Virgo Lagna. When lord of fifth house, Lord of ascendant, moon are in equal or nearer degrees i.e. in Itthashal yoga इत्थशाल योग the Astrologer should Predict that the wife of the Querrent is pregnant. Here Mercury is the lord of Ascendant in 23 degrees in Aquarius. Lord of fifth house Saturn is in 22 degrees in Taurus, Moon is in Scorpio in 21 degrees. These three planets are in Quadrant position to each other. From Moon Lord of Ascendant Mercury is in Aquarius in 4th house, From mercury Saturn is in Taurus in 4th House. From Saturn moon is also in 7th house. These 3 Planets have Itthashal yoga as 21, 22, 23 degrees are

25.3.1973 : 5.10 p.m.

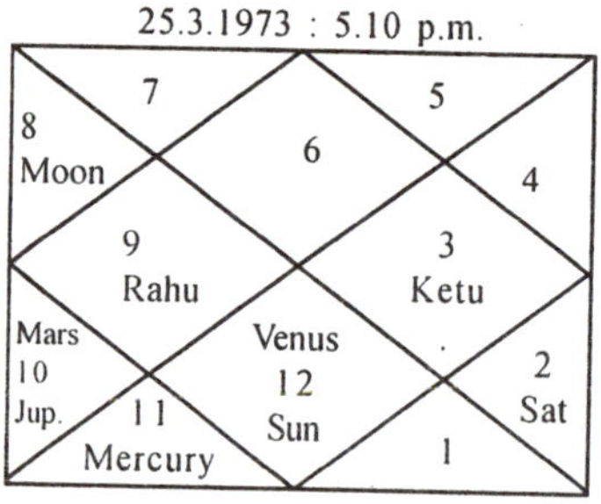

nearer to each other. So it is proved that the wife of the Querrent is Pregnant. JUPITER is PUTRA KARAKA is in fifth house and aspecting the fifth house Lord Saturn. Mars too is known as PUTRA KARAKA who is in exaltation with divine planet Jupiter in fifth house. The Presence of two male planets Jupiter and Mars in fifth house indicate the birth of son. From Moon Sign fifth house is Pisces, Jupiter is lord of the fifth house who is sitting with exalted Mars. The Second and Simple method of finding out son or daughter is that the total of TITHI तिथि PRAHAR प्रहर Day दिन Nakshatra नक्षत्र minus one then divided by Seven, remaining number if विषम Odd then Son, सम even Number then daughter. On 25-3-1973 Tithi was Saptmi 7 Prahar was 4, days was Sunday 1 Number of Nakshatra was 18. 7+4+1+18 added together we get 30-1 we get 29 divided by seven we got remaining number One which is odd विषय. Hence the birth of Son was indicated. Really Birth of Son was gifted to Mr. P.B. Sharma on 7-11-1973 at Bhopal (M.P.) at 8.00 P.M.

Example 2 (Abortion): Question was worked on 30-3-1973 at 2.30 PM at Gyaraspur Distt. Vidisha (M.P.) in Cancer Lagna. Here Lord of Ascendant Moon, Lord of fifth house MARS, Lord of ninth house Jupiter are in seventh house (MARAKA HOUSE) Fifth house is afflicted by lord of Seventh Saturn by aspect. Lord of fifth house Mars, though in exaltation is hemmed in between two malefies Rahu in sixth house in debilitation and the Second Marak Sun. Lord of Lagna is with Mars and Mars aspects the Lagna, Moreover the Lord of Seventh Saturn also aspects the Lagna and fifth house. Hence Lagna, Lagna Lord, Fifth House, fifth lord are in dangerous Position. Jupiter, Lord of ninth is in debilitation in seventh Maraka House. Hence ABORTION will take place. Because from moon too fifth house lord Venus is Cambust with sun and there is Saturn, the Markesh (Second house lord from Moon) Mercury too is being Lord of 12th house is malefic. Thus, Moon, fifth and ninth lords Mars and Jupiter are between RAHU and MERCURY. I hinted the Querent to become Cautious and look after the Pregnant lady seriously. But all was in vain resulting ZERO and abortion took Place on 12-4-1973 after 13 days of Query.

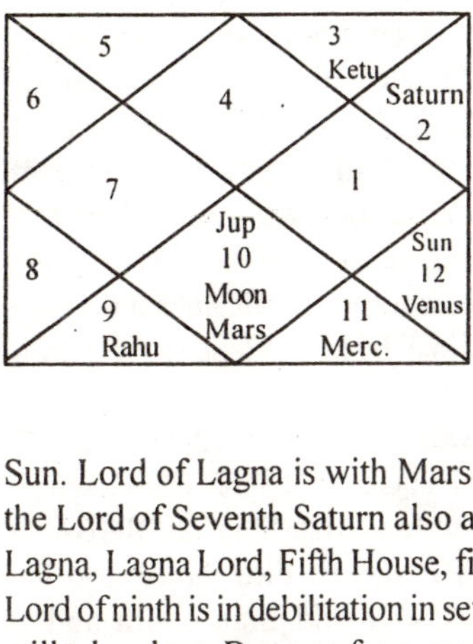

Example 3 Son Birth: Question about Progeny was asked on 8-7-1974 at 5.15 PM. Lagna Sagattarius was rising. Here Lagna is a male sign. The lord of Lagna Jupiter is a male planet and PUTRA KARAKA is in

Aquarius a male sign. In fifth house too there is male sign Aries. Lagna is in first Navamsa. JUPITER, SATURN are connected with benefies. The lord of fifth house Mars though in debilitation is in 8th house but he aspects from there to two natural (benefies Jupiter and Moon. Hence the trinal houses 1, 5, 9 are odd Signs (विषम राशि) and are correlated to each other any how. Jupiter aspects the 9th house and its lord Sun. MERCURY, SATURN, SUN aspect Lagna. From Moon Sign too 5th house is Gemini an odd Sign, its Lord Mercury aspected by Putrakaraka Jupiter. Hence I told the Querent that chances of male-child birth are more. Really a male child was born on 29-11-1974 at 4.15 A.M.

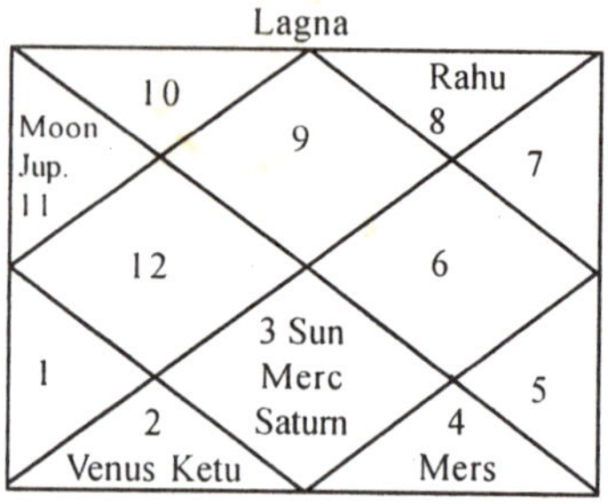

Example 4 Son Birth: Question about Progeny was asked on 24-4-1975 at 10.40 a.m. in Gemini Lagna. Here the three trinal houses 1,5,9, are Gemini, Libra, Aquarius all are male signs. The fifth house, fifth lord Venus both are aspected by male planets i.e. by SUN and MARS. All these conditions indicate that the male child will be born. Hence a male child was born.

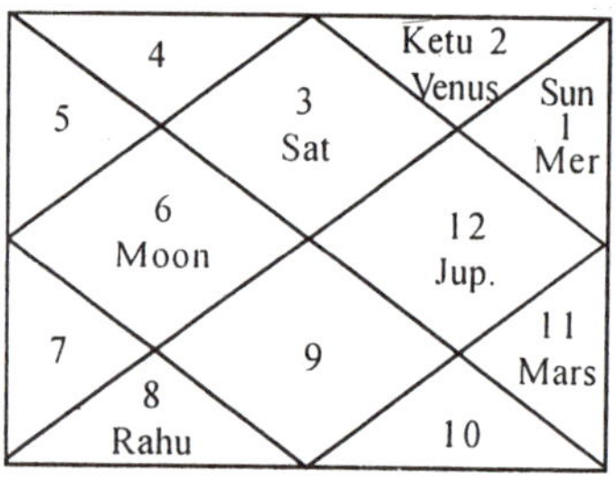

Example 5 Son Birth: Question was asked on 21-12-1973 at 6.15 P.M. in Gemini Lagna. Here Lagna is an odd and Male Sign has DIGBALA STRENGTH. Fifth house too has male and odd Sign Libra and is aspected by male planet Mars. The lord of fifth house Venus is with PUTRA KARAKA JUPITER a male Sign. The period of Pregnancy is known by the position of Venus from Moon. Here Venus is in 3rd house from moon. Hence 3rd month of pregnancy is running. So the male Child be born after 6 months. Really male Child i.e. Son was Born on 17-6-1974 at 4.00 P.M. after 6 months of Query.

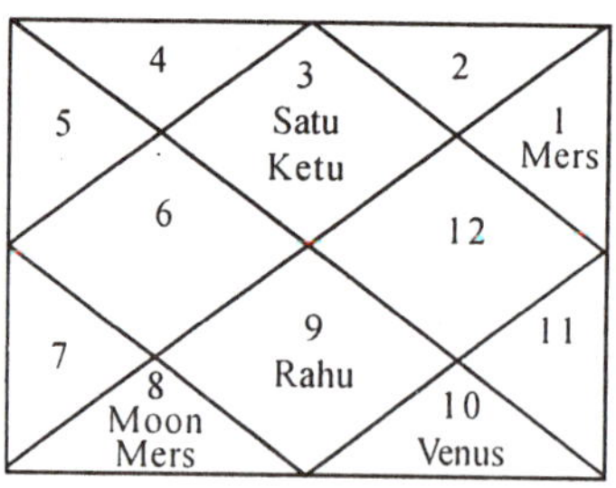

Example-6. Son Birth: Question was put on 19-1-1975 at 9.50 A.M. in PISCES Sign. Here Lagna is Pisces whose Lord is Pútra Karaka Jupiter in male sign in Aquarius. Moon is the Lord of fifth sign aspected by Mars and Saturn who are in male Signs. Moon is in 21 degree Jupiter is in 21 degree Lord of Lagna and Lord of fifth when in nearer degrees have Ithashala yoga इत्थशाल योग which shows that the Lady is pregnant. SUN a male sign too aspects the fifth house, Mars.also aspects the fifth house, its lord. Hence it is Justified that male Child Should be born. Really male Child was born on 21-4-1975 at 2.15 P.M.

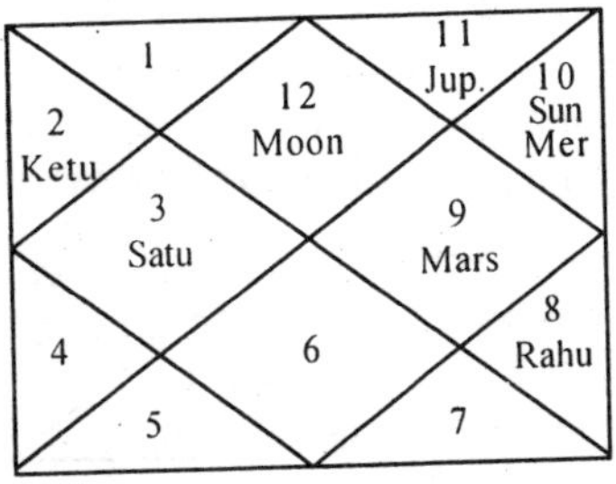

Example7: Son Birth. Question was asked on 11-8-1978 at 10.00 PM. Aries Lagna on odd and Male Sign. Lord of Lagna Mars aspects the Lagna. In fifth house too there is male and odd sign Leo. Moon in odd sign aspects the lagna. From Moon there is an odd and male Sign Aquarius whose Lord Saturn sitting in an odd sign aspects. I told the Querent that when Lord of fifth house Sun will enter the fifth house and will be aspected by moon from eleventh house in Aquarius then there is full possibility of Son Birth. Sun entered in Leo in own Sign on 17-8-1978 and moon was in Aquarius on 18-8-1978 aspecting the fifth Lord SUN. Really on 20-8-1978 at 7.55 A.M. Son was born to the Querent at VIDISHA (M.P.).

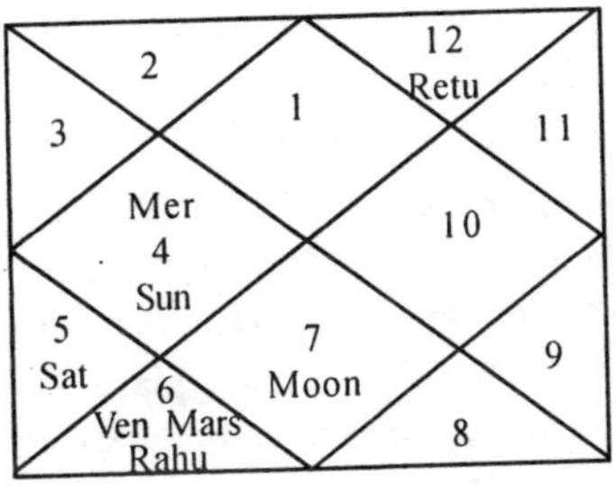

Example 8: Female Birth. Question was asked on 23-8-1978 at 9.00 A.M. in Virgo Lagna. Here RAHU, MARS, VENUS in Virgo Lagna. In Lagna Venus is in debilitation badly afflicted by eighth Lord Mars. Virgo is an even and female Sign. The main trinal Houses, 1,5,9 all are in even and female sign. The lord of Lagna Mercury in Cancer an even Sign aspect the fifth house which is too female Sign. Jupiter too is in female Sign with lord of Lagna aspecting the fifth

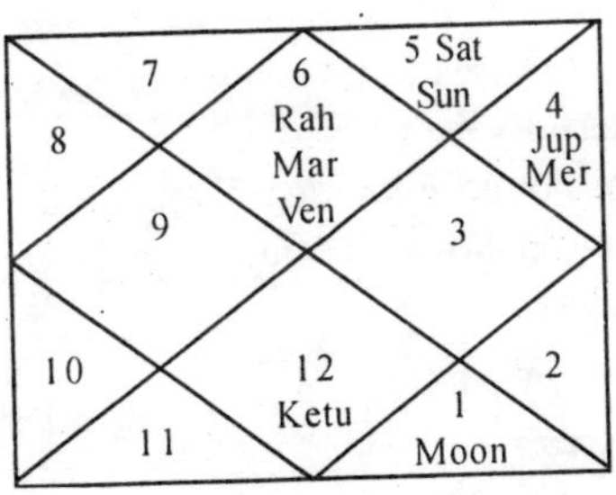

house. Lord of fifth house Saturn though in Leo a male sign but in NAVAMSA the Saturn is in Cancer a female sign. In the Same way Moon though in a male Sign but in NAVAMSA is in Taurus a female Sign. All these things clearly indicate that female child should be born. So female child born on 30-9-1978 at 3.47 P.M.

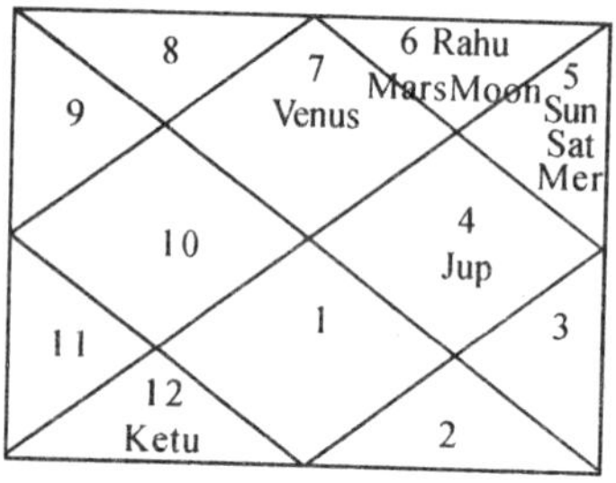

Example 9 Son Birth: Question was asked on 4-9-1978 at 9.20 P.M. in Libra Lagna. Here all trinal House 1,5,9, i.e. 7,11,3 are male signs. Lord of Lagna, fifth and ninth houses Venus, Saturn, Mercury are in male Signs Libra and Leo. Saturn the Lord of fifth house aspects the Lagna, Lagna Lord and fifth house. I told the Querent that when moon will come in fifth house from the lord of fifth house i.e. when moon will be in Sagattarius Sign Son will be born. Really Son was born on 11-9-1978 at 1.10 P.M. When moon was in fifth house from Saturn i.e. in Sagattarius Sign.

Example 10 Female Birth: Question was asked on 12-8-1981 at 1. A.M. It was a typical type of Question which was put after mid night. The general rule in Horary Astrology is that when moon is fifth from the Lord of fifth house delivery takes place. It was Taurus Lagna. The pregnant lady was in trouble as moon is in 8th house aspected by MARS who is lord of 12th and 7th houses. Lord of fifth house Mercury is with two malefies SUN AND RAHU in 3rd house. The three trinal houses 1,5,9 i.e. 2,6,10 are female signs. Jupiter, Saturn too are in female signs. Thus it seems that a female child should be born.

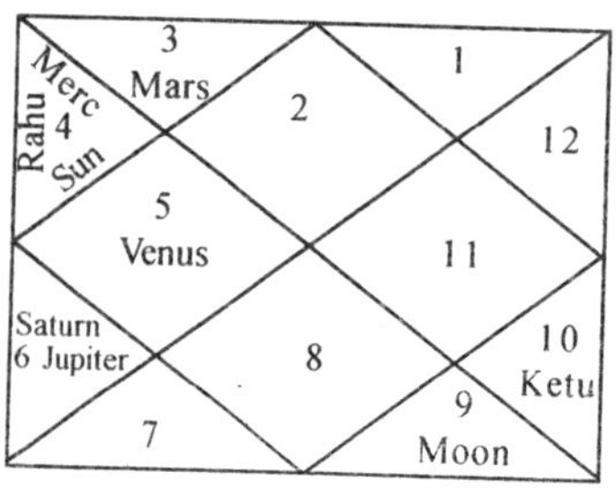

Immediately calculated that delivery should take place in Gemini Lagna because from Gemini the fifth house is Libra whose Lord is Venus and from Venus moon will be fifth. Truly and wonderfully the girl was born on 2.24 am. i.e. after one hour 24 minutes of Query. For benefit of Astrologers and general readers of Astrology I am Quoting Some formulas which I experienced in above examples and found true.

1. यदि प्रच्छयेसस्य स्त्रिया भवेन्मे प्रजा न वा कश्चित्
   लग्नेन्द्वौ सुतपति वा मुथाशील प्रसूतिः स्यात्

Means if the Querent asks what kind of child will be got from his wife then if Lagna, Moon and fifth Lord have muthashila (ittha shala) then Progeny is sure.

2. यदिलग्नेश सुतेशौ पुरूषौ स्यात्तदा सुतो गर्भः

Means if Lords of Lagna and fifth house are in odd Sign and male Sign then Son is in womb (गर्भ)

3. पंचमेशो लग्नेशो विषमक्षर्गतौ यदा।
पुत्र जय प्रदौ झेयौ कन्यानां सम राशि गो।।

Means if Lords of Lagna and fifth house are in odd signs then Son if is even then daughter will be born.

4. वीक्षते पुत्रदः प्रोत्रो युग्म राशौ च दारिकाः
युग्म राशिपते लग्ने यदा तत्र शुभ ग्रहाः

Means if Lord of Lagna in male Sign aspects the lord of fifth house in male sign then Son, if both are in even sign then the daughter will be born.

In this way through Horary Astrology the Question of Progeny Can be answered accurately. If necessary then only the NAVAMSA CHART Should be drawn otherwise not. I hope the write upon will be liked by wise readers as there is hard labour in maintaining these charts experienced by me for the Sake of Research work 25 to 32 years ago.

4

Solar Return Charts: Marriage

Astrology is a wonderful science. Its scope is so wide that there are so many ways to know the future of the Individual. Annual reading is the most popular of them through which the events of the coming year are known. This method of knowing the future of a year is described in TAJIK NEELKANTHI.

To find out the annual ascendant we add the number of the day, ghatis and palas of the birth time in the past year's day, ghatis and palas as given in the Varsha Pravesh Sarini (Solar return table). In adding if the days are more than seven then the total number of days is divided by seven and if the balance is one it is Sunday, two Monday, three Tuesday four Wednesday, five Thursday, six Friday and seven Saturday. Mostly the English dates fall the same as birth date in the month of birth. For example if the birth date is 7th June then the date in annual Chart too will be the 7th June positively.

After this the ascendant for the concerning year should find out by calculation and prepare annual chart with planetary position of that day. The position of the Sun remains the same as that as birth time in degrees. This is because the birth time position of sun when comes to the point of birth time's degrees, ansas, Kalas then the new year starts. In short we can say that the person born in English date of any month will find out the annual chart of the concerning year. On the same date. After this by fixing all the planets in the annual chart in their respective Sign on that date. Then we should find out the Vinishopaka Bala of each planet.

There are five Lords in the annual analysis. The first is the lord of the birth ascendant, the second is the lord of the year, the third is the Lord of the muntha, the fourth is the Lord of trairasis and the fifth is the Lord of the Sign in which Sun is present. Among these five Lords the planet whose Vinishopaka Bala is more and who aspects the ascendant is known as Lord of the year or Varshesha. If a planet does not aspect the ascendant among these five planets then the planet who aspects the ascendant with full strength becomes the lord of the annual ascendant to be considered.

Muntha has specific importance in annual charts in the decision of events as Muntha is regarded as the mother of nine planets in the annual chart.

To know the result of the particular year as found out by the above calculation, we have to see the position of the Lord of the birth ascendant, Lord of the year, and lord of the Muntha. If these three lords have Vinishopaka Strength more than the other planets and are in benefic houses aspected by benefics then generally the coming year is regarded as good and beneficial. If these three Lords are not well placed and are in 6, 8 and 12 houses then the coming year's aspect does not seem good. To know the result of each house we see and think about the position of Lord of that house, the planets in that house the planet, aspecting that house beneficially and maleficially as the case may be.

I am giving here the examples of annual charts for different purposes experienced and found correct by me in the long run of my astrological experiences from four decades. I hope this will help the readers and students of Astrology in general in finding out the truth hidden in this great and secret science of Astrology. I am giving here the example of marriage ceremonies. Whether there is hope of getting married or not in the year concerned. For this we consider the position of Venus, the Karaka for wife, Jupiter the Karaka for husband Seventh house, lord of the seventh house, Muntha and lord of Muntha or Munthesh.

In TAJIK NEELKANTHI it is said that if Jupiter aspects the Mantha sign or Lord of Muntha then marriage ceremony is performed. Secondly if Lord of Seventh house Venus be strong and posited in 7th house having itthaskala yoga with the Lord of the ascendant then the performance of marriage ceremony takes place and the person concerned gets the happiness from wife.

Birth Ascendant

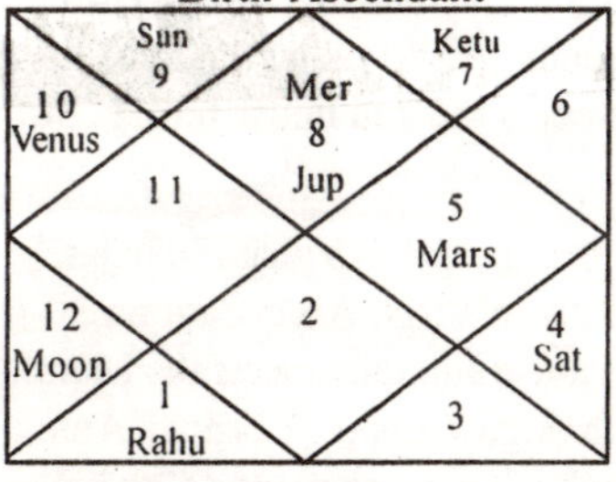

Annual Chart for 26th Year

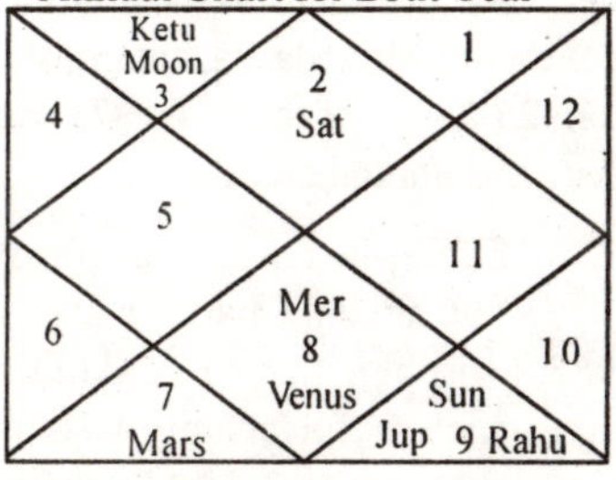

Example 1. Male born on 20-12-1947 Saturday at 53 ghats, 54 Palas.

Jupiter the most benefic planet is placed with Muntha in his own sign. Sagittarius in the annual chart for the 26th year. Ascendant Lord of annual birth chart Venus is with the Lord of Second house (the house of family/Mercury in the 7th house. These two benefics aspect the 26th year annual ascendant Taurus being in 7th house. The Lord of the 9th and 10th houses Saturn, a benefic for Taurus ascendant is also present in the 26th annual ascendant chart.

Mudda Dasha. In annual Chart Mudda Dasha has specific importance. To find out Mudda Dasha we add the number of the past last year and number of birth Star. Then abstract two from the total and divide by nine the balance is the Mudda Dasha of that numbered planet e.g. 1 the Sun, 2 the Moon, 3 Mars;, 4 Rahu, 5 Jupiter, 6 Saturn, 7 Mercury, 8 Ketu, 9 Venus. In this example the last year is 25 and the number of birth star is also 25 (Poorva Bhadrapada) The total is 50-2 = 48 divided by 9 yields a remainder of 3. It means the Mudda Dasha for the 26th year will begin from Mars as following:

Lord of Mudda Dasha	*Duration*	*From*	*to*	
Mars	21 days	20-12-1972	to	9-1-1973
Rahu	1 month 24 days	9-1-1973	to	3-3-1973
Jupiter	1 month 18 days	3-3-1973	to	20-4-1973
Saturn	1 month 27 days	21-4-1973	to	18-6-1973
Mercury	1 month 21 days	19-6-1973	to	10-8-1973
Ketu	21 days	11-8-1973	to	31-8-1973
Venus	2 months	1-9-1973	to	30-10-1973
Sun	18 days	31-10-1973	to	18-11-1973
Moon	1 month	19-11-1973	to	19-12-1973

Rahu is placed with Jupiter in Sagittarius in Sign of Muntha aspecting the 2nd house (house of family) Hence marriage took Place in Rahu Mudda Dasha.

According to Vimshottari Mahadasa. The marriage was performed in Mercury Mahadasha, antardasha of Venus and Prtyautar dasha of Rahu from 26-11-1972 to 29-4-1973. Rahu aspects the 2nd house both in birth chart and annual chart.

Example-2. Male born on 30-6-1961. Friday at 5 ghats 30 palas.

The annual Chart for 25th year falls in Virgo Ascendant on 30-6-1985. Most benefic and Lord of the 7th house Jupiter aspects the Muntha Sign which is fortunately falls in birth Sign Cancer. Lord of Annual ascendant Mercury is also being aspected by Jupiter, the lord of 7th house. Besides the Karaka for wife Venus is also being aspected by Jupiter. The lord of Seventh house of birth Sign Saturn is in 2nd house of annual Chart

Birth Chart

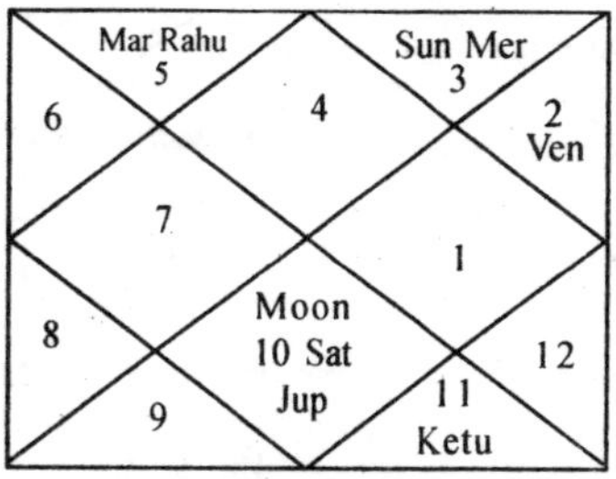

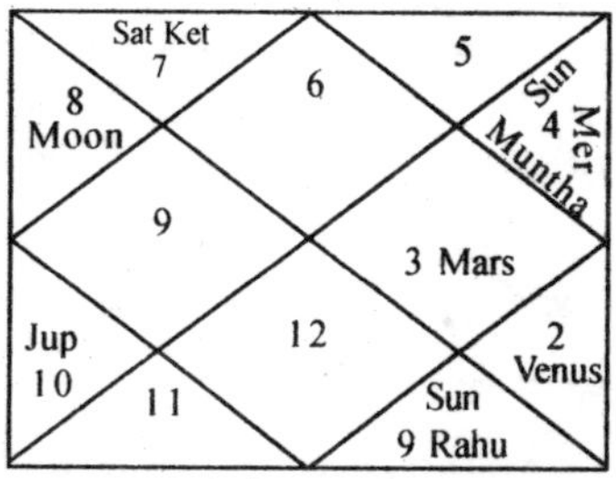

in exaltation in Libra Sign. The native was married in Mudda Dasha of Saturn On 28-6-1986. According to Vimshottari Mahadasha in the period of Rahu Mahadasha, antardasha of Saturn and Pratyantara dasha of Mercury. Here Rahu and Saturn both are Mahadasha and antardasha Lords in 2nd and 7th houses in birth Chart and in 2nd and 8TH houses in annual chart in aspect of Jupiter, the lord of Seventh house of annual chart.

Example 3. Male Born on 8-12-1962 Saturday at 28 ghaits palas married on 28-1-1989 in the age of 27.

Birth Chart 8-12-1962-28 ghaits

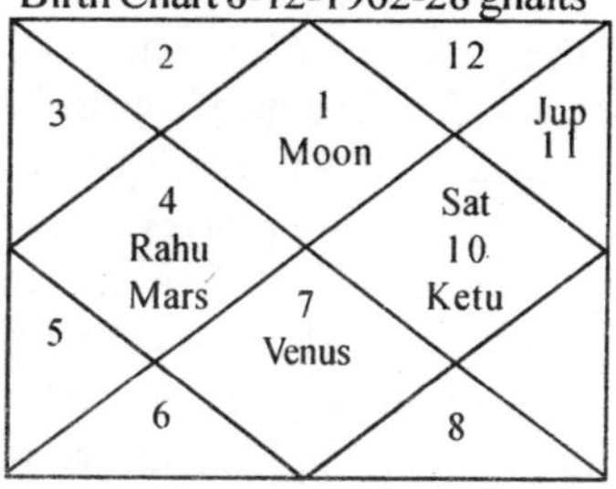

Annual for 27th year

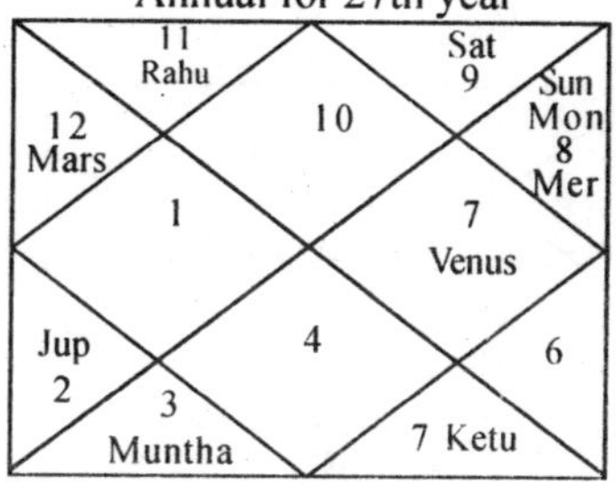

The Birth Ascendant and Annual Chart for 27th year is as following :-

The Lord of MUNTHA MERCURY and Lord of Seventh house moon are in full aspect of Jupiter. Venus the KARAKA for wife and seventh house is in Quadrant in Moola Trikona Sign Libra Lord of Birth Ascendant Mars aspects in birth Lagna and annual Chart to the Lord of seventh house and Karaka for wife Venus. Hence marriage was performed according to the principles described in TAJIK NEELKANTHI.

Example-4. Born on 1-1-1964 Wednesday at 42-27 ghatis and married on 8-3-1985 at the age of 22 in Saturn Mahadasha, antardasha of Saturn.

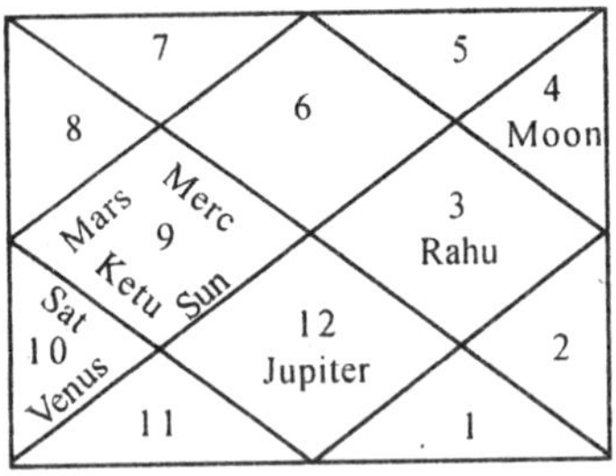

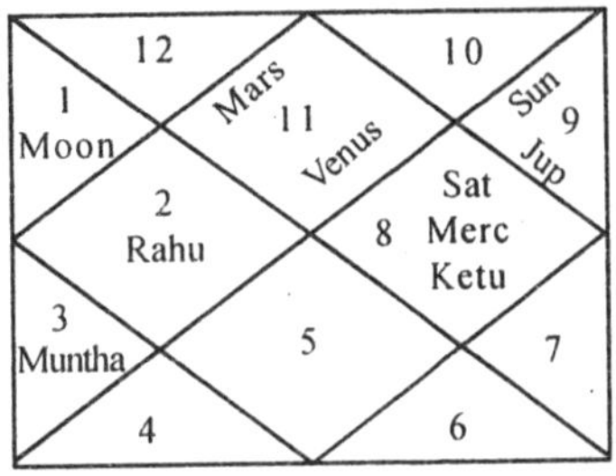

The Muntha Sign Gemini is in full aspect of Jupiter. Jupiter the Lord of 2nd house (family) and Lord of seventh house SUN both are in eleventh house. Thus, Jupiter with Lord of Seventh SUN aspects the Seventh house. Venus too has full aspect On Seventh house Jupiter is Lord of Seventh house in birth ascendant is with the Lord of seventh house SUN of annual Chart. Hence the Position of Muntha is annual Chart aspected by Jupiter guarantees the performance of marriage ceremony in 22nd year.

Truth in Varsha Phala Charts

Here are two examples given below. One is Concerned with the birth of a Son and the other is Concerned with the transfer in government service.

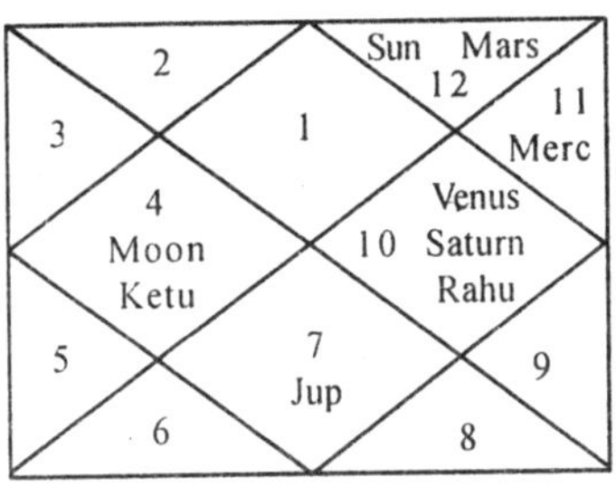

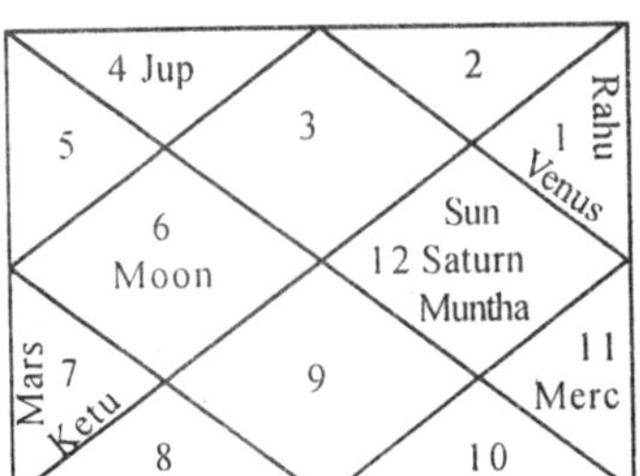

Example 1. This is the horoscope of a person who got his first Son after the birth of 6 girls. Date of birth 26-3-1934 Lagna 0-10-47-14 SUN 11-10-57 Birth place Gyaraspur Distt. Vidisha (M.P.) INDIA. In March 1967 the person asked me that his wife in pregnant and will I get a Son? The person's Varshaphala Chart was prepared for 34th year beginning from 26th March 1967 Monday at 19-40-30.

In the Varsha Kundali for 34th year there is strong Putra Prapti Yoga According to Tajik Neelkanthi Panchama Bhav Phala Verse No. 3 Says that if the rasi in which Jupiter is in radical horoscope is in the fifth in annual Chart (Varsha Lagna) and Mars and Mercury being the Lords of the year are in Putra Bhav, i.e., in 5th house the Yoga gives a Son and the happiness of a Son. In rantha kundli Rasi (Randix) Jupiter is in Libra and Libra in the 5th from Varsha Lagna Mithuna (Gemini). Mars and Mercury are in the 5th and 9th Bhavas respectively. 9th house is 5th from the 5th house. Hence Son birth is Sure. But when will the Son be born? It was definite that the Son birth would be in Some where in July 1967. I told the person that Son would be born. Really the Son was born on 19-7-1967 in Jupiter's Mahadasha antardasha of Mars upto 20-7-1967. According to Vimshottari Mahadasha too is was period of Mercury and antardasha of Jupiter upto 22-1-1968 which Started from 22-10-1965. Jupiter is the Karaka for Son.

Example 2. This is the horoscope of a principal of a Government Junior College. Date of birth 25-3-1926 Thursday. Birth Place Sagar (M.P.) INDIA. The birth Chart is as follows. In March 1968 the person asked me about his transfer. I prepared his Varshaphala Chart (Solar return chart for 43rd year. His 43rd year begins on 25-3-1968.

Birth Chart

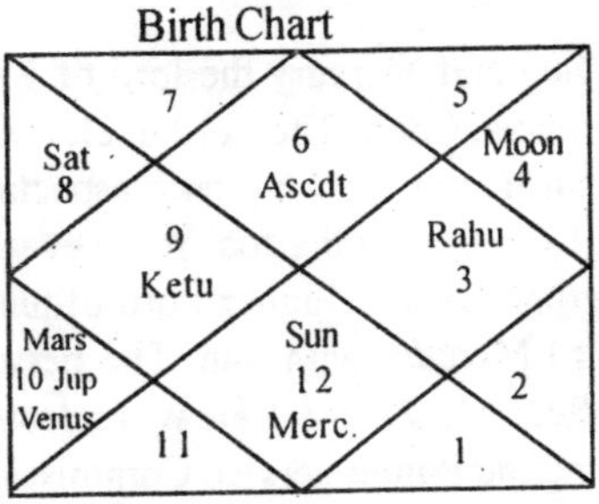

Varsna Kundali

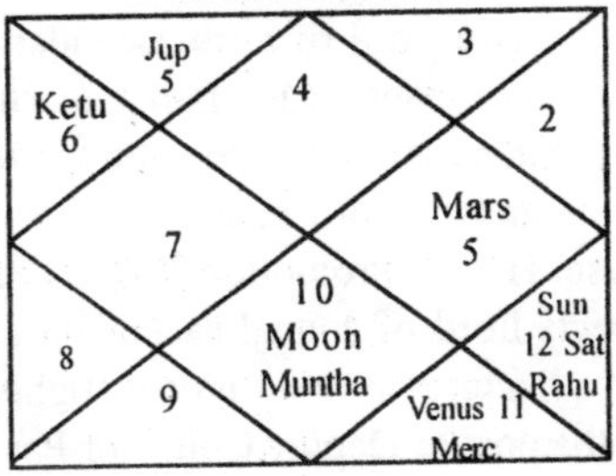

According to TAJIK NEELKANTHI DASAM BHAV PHALA VERSE NO. 1 and 4 Say that if strong lord of the year is in 1st 4th and 7th houses (Centres) transfer and happening of home would result. The person was transferred in his home district, Verse No. 4 Says that if there is Strong Moon in the Sign held by Mars in the birth Chart them transfer and power is result. According to Verse No 1 the Moon is the lord of Lagna and thus Lord of the year too in the Varsha Kundli. The Moon is in the 7th house and according to Verse no 4. the moon is in Capricorn in which Mars is in the radix. Mars is in 5th house in birth Lagna in Capricorn in exaltation and Moon is in Capricorn in Varsha Lagna for 43rd year. Hence, I told him that he will be transferred Some where in May-June but before 8th July definitely. Here I found that Jupiter is responsible for the period of transfer Jupiter's Mudda Dasha is from 21-5-1968 to 8-7-1968. Jupiter is having direct Love sight On the 6th and 10th houses On 6th, 5th Sight and on 10th, 9th sight with strong Mars in the house of Rajya. Jupiter exchanges position with the Sun. Malefics too in 4th and 10th houses in Horary Astrology and in Varsha Phala Charts also Create transfer yoga.

Both of my forecasts came true. My interest in the Study of Astrology increased day by day.

Promotion Yoga – If Lord of Birth Ascendant, Lord of year ascendant, Lord of tenth are strongly Placed in Moola Trikona or Kendras, are with benefics or aspected by benefics there are the indications of promotion.

Male horn on 14-12-1934

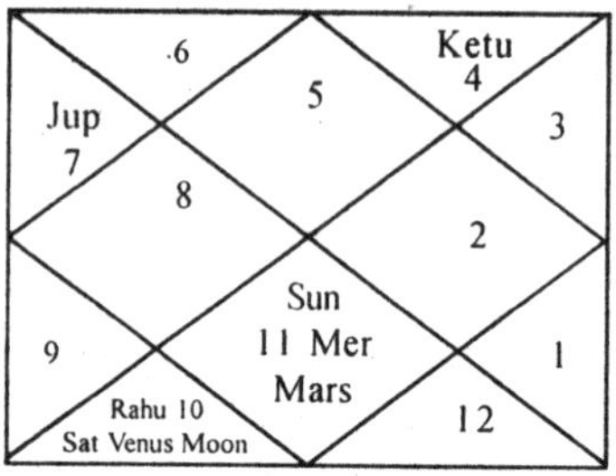

Solar return Chart for 35th year 14-12-1968

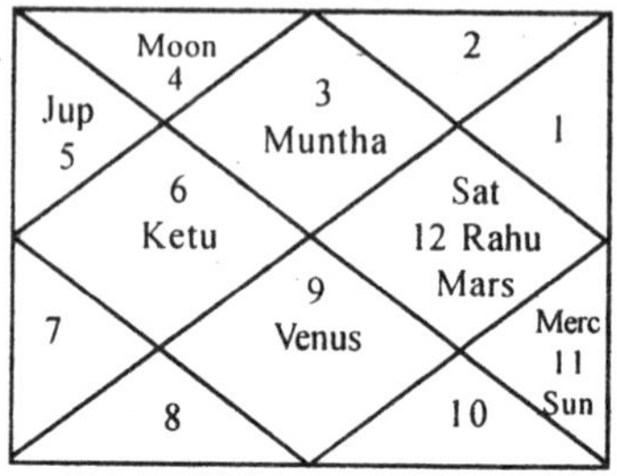

Here Lord of birth ascendant Sun and Mercury the lord of 35th year's ascendant are in ninth house in annual Chart. The Lord of eleventh house (income) Mars is in tenth house. In annual Chart Jupiter is aspecting the ascendant Lord mercury, who is Lord of muntha too, the eleventh house. Hence, Promotion Yoga is Present because Jupiter Lord of tenth aspects Lord of annual ascendant Lord Mercury with Sun. The person was a Lecturer in Government Higher Secondary School. He was selected for the post of Deputy Collector Passing the Public Service Commission examination. He was relieved on 20-12-1968 to join the new post of promotion. Hence there is change in service with better promotion yoga present.

Government Service Yoga - According to TAJIK NEELKANTHI if Lord of the birth Lagna and annual Lagna be in eleventh house (house of income) and Lord of second house of birth be in annual lagna. House of

Birth Chart 8-7-1947

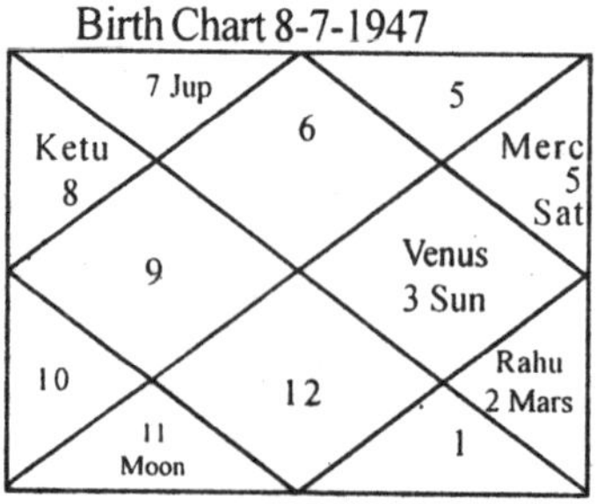

Annual Chart for 24th year

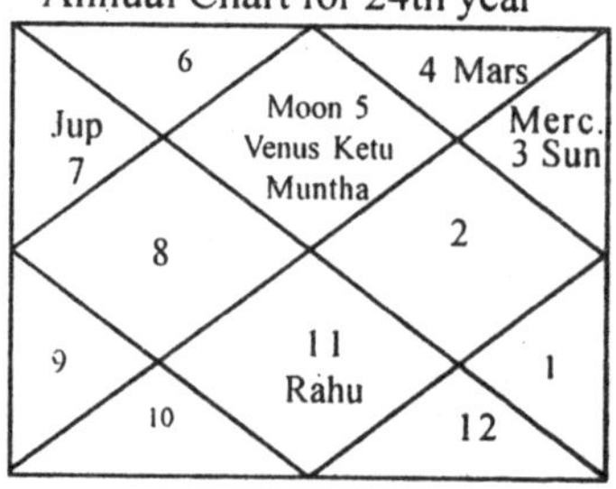

income, i.e., eleventh house aspected by Jupiter, Muntha is in annual lagna then the native in employed in Government Service in that year because for Government Service, the Lord of tenth is the main planet. Hence Lord of tenth should be in tenth, in tenth, eleventh, Lagna, Second or ninth houses. Date of birth 8-7-1947 Wednesday Ishta Kala for 24th year on 8-7-1970 Ishta Kala 11-25-30.

Sun the Lord of 24th year Lagna and Karaka too for Government Service. This placement of SUN in the house of income (eleventh house) Sums up that the source of income will be through Government. The Lord of tenth in annual Chart Venus is with Moon and Muntha in annual Lagna. Mercury being the Lord of Second is with Sun in eleventh house. JUPITER aspects the eleventh house. Muntha is in Lagna and Lord of Muntha SUN is being aspected by benefic Jupiter, who is also Karaka for Leo ascendant. SUN has two Lordships here, Lord of Varsha Lagna, Lord of Muntha. When Muntha is in Varsha Lagna, the native gets happiness through Government. Hence Government Service Yoga is Strong. The native was employed in nationalised Bank Service in November 1970.

Suspension Yoga - JUST opposite to Promotion Yoga Suspension Yoga is known through Solar return Chart. When Lord of birth ascendant,

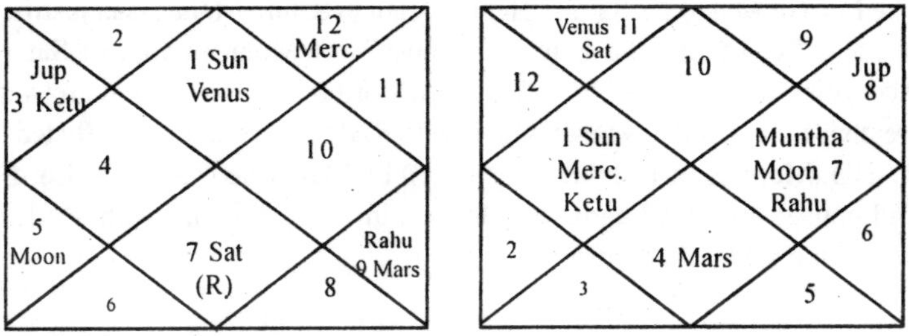

Lord of annual ascendant, and Lord of tenth, Lord of Muntha are being badly afficted by malefics are in weak positions, then suspension yoga is present. For example Date of birth 15-4-1954.

Here Lord of birth ascendant Mars in deliberation (NEECH) in annual Chart in Seventh house aspecting the Varsha Lagna Muntha in 10th house with moon. Rahu malefic combination aspected by Neecha Mars and Lord of eighth house Sun in fourth house is very bad combination for Government Service Muntha when aspected by Sun degrades the position of Person. He was under suspension since 4th July 1995 remained suspended for a long time.

Death Yoga - According to Man Sagri, the planet was being strong aspects the eighth house (the house of death) from its nasal or 22nd Drekkaha of birth Lagna causes death. Birth particular are as following in

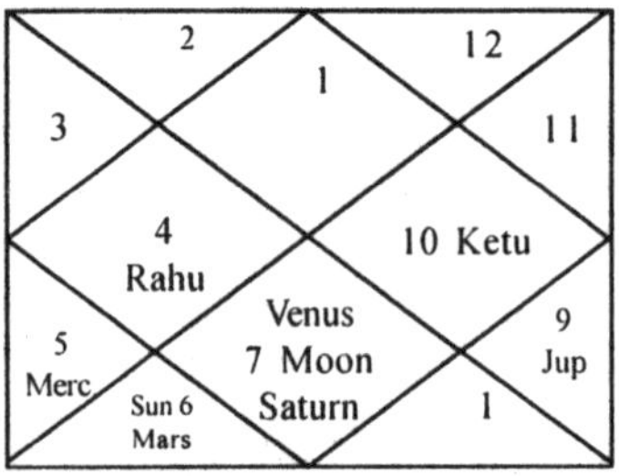

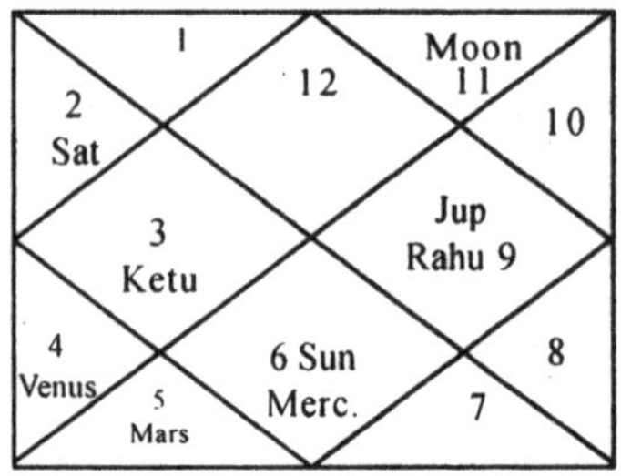

Here Lagna Drekkana is Sagittarius from Sagittarius 22nd Drekkana is Capricorn whose Lord is Saturn who is in Seventh Maraka house in birth Lagna and in annual Chart in 3rd house (eighth to eighth house). The native died on 10th July 1972 in Saturn Mahadasa Moon Antardasha and Mars Prityantardasha. Death falls in Navamṣa Lord of eighth Dasa. Here, birth Lagna is Aries and eighth Lord is Mars who is in Maraka Navamsa. The Lord of Makara is Saturn. Hence Death in Saturn Mahadasah justified. In annual chart Muntha is in 12th house with Moon in sign of Saturn. According to TAJIK NEELKANTHI if Lord of year and moon are weak Death is Sure. Lord of year Jupiter is with RAHU in 10th house afflicted by RAHU. Moon is in 12th house aspected by Mars (the Maraka as Lord of 2nd house). In birth Lagna too Moon is in Seventh house with Markesh Venus and a Malefic Saturn.

5

Professional Astrology

It is very difficult task to an astrologer to judge the Horoscope and find out by which Profession the person will earn livelihood. Before we proceed in this matter we have to remember some rules in finding out the professional ability. According to SARAVALI of KALYAN VERMA :-

Planets in 10th House from Moon

If there is sun in 10th house from moon the person will be active, Progressive. If there is Mars in 10th house from moon the person will be bold, cruel and wishing to live in foreign countries.

If there is Mercury in 10th house from moon the person will be wise, rich, dear to king, famous artist and technician.

If there is Jupiter in 10th house from moon the person will be Virtuous, Secretary, Minister.

If there is Venus in 10th from moon the person will be lucky, dear to king, rich through wife.

If there is Saturn in 10th from moon the person will be poor, ill, unhappy and disturbed.

From Moon 10th House

If there are SUN-MARS	— Active, Astrologer, Logician
If there are SUN-MERCURY	— Businessman, earning by water, Clothes
If there are SUN-JUPITER	— Active, Respected by king, bold, famous.
If there are SUN-VENUS	— Dependent on family, earning through the help of wife
If there are SUN-SATURN	— Servant, Miser, Money by thieves.
If there are MARS-MERCURY	— Bold, earning, by Intellect by enemies

If there are MARS-JUPITER	—	Lucky, Leader of Army, Money by friends
If there are MARS-SATURN	—	Bold, Less intelligent, ill, busy in work
If there are MERCURY-JUPITER	—	Rich, famous, Leader, respect by statesman
If there are MERCURY-VENUS	—	Living like King, Minister, happy with family, friends, Highly Intellectual
If there are MERCURY-SATURN	—	Teacher, writer, famous, potmaker
If there are JUPITER-VENUS	—	Government Servants, teacher, Happy
If there are JUPITER-SATURN	—	Low minded, troubles, behave like old
If there are SATURN-VENUS	—	Doctor, Photographer, Scent merchant
If there are SUN-MARS-MERCURY	—	Lucky, best, giving like a King dear to all.

From Moon in 10th House

If there are SUN, MARS, JUPITER	—	Beautiful, Rich, Victory over Enemies
If there are SUN, MARS, VENUS	—	Cruel, Bold, Clever in taking money of others
If there are SUN, MARS, SATURN	—	Cruel, Fool, Sinner Vicious
If there are SUN, MERCURY,	—	Wise, beautiful, beloved of brothers, Virtuous
If there are SUN, MERCURY, VENUS	—	Virtuous, famous, religions, angerless.
If there are SUN, MERCURY, SATURN	—	Cruel, Vicious, Crush body by gun and fire
If there are SUN, JUPITER, VENUS	—	Beautiful, Rich by Wisdom, Virtuous, religious happy
If there are SUN, JUPITER, SATURN	—	HAVE PATIENT, famous, Loose in character
If there are MARS, MERCURY, JUPITER	—	Big family, wise, Rich, religious
If there are MARS, MERCURY, VENUS	—	Technician, Goldsmith, dear to all Rich by flowers, Scent
If there are MARS, MERCURY, SATURN	—	Idle, low heart, Cruel, Less religious
If there are MARS, JUPITER, VENUS	—	Rich, Brave, devotee to God and Brahmin

If there are Saturn MARS, JUPITER,	— MINISTER, Best but lover of other religions
If there are SUN, JUPITER, VENUS, IN TAURUS or LIBRA	— All every happy
If there are SUN, JUPITER, VENUS, OTHER SIGNS	— Rich but ill.
If there are MERCURY, JUPITER, SATURN	— Writer, Poet, Rich, Servants Journeys.
If there are MERCURY, VENUS, SATURN	— Scientists, Liberal, Living in Foreign lands.
If there are JUPITER, VENUS, SATURN	— Wise, Virtuous, Kind hearted, truth Speaker.
If there are SUN, MARS, MERCURY, JUPITER	— Clever, Doner, Brave, Crushed body.
If there are SUN, MARS, MERCURY, VENUS	— Clever, Writer, Photography flowers.
If there are SUN, MARS, MERCURY, SATURN	— Rich in money by vehicles.
If there are SUN, MERCURY, JUPITER, VENUS	— Farming, Polite, though born in lower caste.
If there are SUN, MERCURY JUPITER, SATURN	— Charming, Cruel and Thug.
If there are SUN, MERCURY, VENUS, SATURN	— Farming, Hard hearted, Speaker.
If there are SUN, JUPITER, VENUS, SATURN	— Many work, living in far lands.
If there are MARS, MERCURY, JUPITER VENUS	— Clever, wise, Victory orer enemies
If there are MARS, MERCURY, VENUS, SATURN	— Wise, Brave, Bigbody
If there are MARS, JUPITER, VENUS, SATURN	— Wise, happy with family and Money.
If there are MERCURY, JUPITER, VENUS, SATURN	— Peaceful, famous, Intelligent

If Malefies in 10th aspected by benefies—Doctor, Priest, Astrologer Cheater From LAGNA AND MOON in 10th which Sign, Planet is there accordingly the persons do that job. Profession according to Lagna and Moon which Sign is in 10th house

ARIES in 10th house—Agriculture, Service, gardener, House Builder.

TAURUS in 10th house—Driver, Business by animals, Birds, Can, Fruits Selling.

GEMINI in 10th house—Pearl, Lord, POTS, Clerk, Accountant Navy, Hotel
CANCER in 10th house—Earning by fire, land, Jewel, Hunting.
LEO in 10th house—Earning by Gold, Silver, Jewels, Agriculture, Cows, Corn.
VIRGO in 10th house—Earning through Vehicles. Jewellary, Scent, Music, Picnic, Writing and General Merchant.
LIBRA in 10th house—Gold Business, Speech, Friends help, Many Businessman, Agriculture, art, milk, Sugarcane.
SCORPIO in 10th house—Rich through Ladies, Agriculture, Thieveness, Government Servant, Businessman of Corn & Iron.
SAGATTARIUS in 10th house—Ministry, Police, Cow, Word, Medical Mathematics.
CAPRICORN in 10th house—Water produced things, garden, chemicals
AQUARIUS in 10th house—Thieve ness, Public Carrier, Firing, Gun making.
PISCES in 10th house—Rich by Ladies, Water Production, Cattle Selling, Pisces in 2, 11 Houses make rich through many ways.

Aspect on Ascendant and Moon of

SUN—Businessman of Water Production
MOON—Businessman of Water Production, Government Service.
MERCURY—Technician, Artist, Wise, Writer, Poet, famous, Respected.
MARS—Police, Military, thieveman, Land, House, Road etc. JUPITER-Religious function, Respected by Government, Judge, Goldsmith, Bank, Treasury, Mandies.
VENUS—Earning through Music, Dance, Film, Photography, Scent, Ladies.
SATURN—Labour, 4th Class Servants, Judges, Leader.

Lagndadhi Yoga : Planets in 6,7,8 houses if they are benefics, they make the person State Minister, Judge, husband of Many Wives.

Businessman : Mercury in 10th house, aspect of benefics on 10th house or Combination of Lord of Ascendant and Lord of 10th house in 1-4-5-7-9-10-11 houses aspected by benefics make the person expert businessman.

Executive Officer with Commanding Power : If Lord of 10th house is a benefic or in with benefic or aspected by benefic or in Navamsa of benefic or in Centre or in 10th house either SUN OR MARS. The person Concerned becomes Executive Officer With Commanding Order Powers. If Rahu is in 10th or Lord of 9th in debilitation sign then the Commanding person becomes Cruel and Hard hearted.

Combination for Government Services : If SUN is in KARAKAMSA LAGNA as ATMA KARAK or Sun be in 1-4-7-10 or Moon in 1-4-7-10-5-9-houses or Lord of 10th in Second house or Jupiter is in 1-4 houses then the person gets Government Services.

Hardware Merchant : If Lord of 6th house be in 3rd house then sells Wood and Stone Material useful in house building, tiles, Cement, bricks, Sand etc.

Navamsa in 10th House of

SUN—Then the person in Salesman, Priest, Speaker, Advocate, teacher, Satire Writer, Representative of M.P., M.L.A. or Public Represents active.
MOON—Jeweller, Farmer, earning through Lady or King, Minister.
MARS—Ordinance Seller, Police, Military, thinking, NAVY, Fireman, Gold smith, Iron man, Sweet Maker, Bakery, Tea, Agricultural Land, Road, House Construction, P.W.D. Agriculture.
MERCURY—Writer, Typing, Photostate, Press Compositor, clerk, Steno, Mathematician, Engineer, Electrical, Mechanical, Poetry, Drama, Teacher, Publisher, Toilet Material.
JUPITER—Pandit, Priest, Preacher, Pilgrimage, Judiciary, Teacher, Minister, Assembly, Parliament Members.
VENUS—Jeweller, Scent, Flower Merchant, Photography, Musician, Dancer, Actor, Actress, Cow Buffaloes Seller etc.
SATURN—Journey, Butcher, Violence, Coolies, Physical Labour, Lower Class Govt. Servants, according to the position of Saturn.

Profession Through Different Combination
SUN MOON MERCURY—Business of Orange Colour clothes.
SUN MERCURY—Textiles.
MOON VENUS—Transport, Navy
MARS MERCURY—Military, Engineer, Machinery Work, Pressman, Brick maker.
SUNMARS VENUS—Executive, Traffic, Police
SUN, JUPITER—Good Doctors
SUN MARS or aspect of Mars On Sun—Surgeon
SUN JUPITER VENUS—LADY Doctor, Expert in NURSING DELIVERY. Specially Jupiter in 10th, Sun in 2nd, Venus in 3rd.

Aspect of Mars and Saturn On Venus but Saturn must be with Sun
GUPTA ROG VISHESHAGYA. If Sun Venus in 6, 8th Houses. Unaffected by other planets.
OPTICIAN – SUN SATURN Combination either in Lagna or 8th Sun Mercury in 5, 9 houses.
DENTIST—SUN, VENUS in 2, 12 houses Separately house
EYE SPECIALIST—Saturn in Lagna, Sun 8th house
EYE, NOSE, THROAT SPECIALIST—Rahu, Venus, Sun, Combination Connected with 9th house.

X Ray Expert Doctor Service in Health Department-SUN, JUPITER Connected with Virgo, Scorpio Sign.

Service in Law Department or Judiciary—MARS with SUN MERCURY and JUPITER.

Some examples are being given here for verification of the above Rules:-

Horoscope of an I.A.S. Officer. Date of birth 14-9-1975 at 12.55 P.M. Sunday at 24.45 N; 78.53E. Lagna Dhanu (Sagattarius). NAKSHATRA. POORVA SHADA first Quarter.

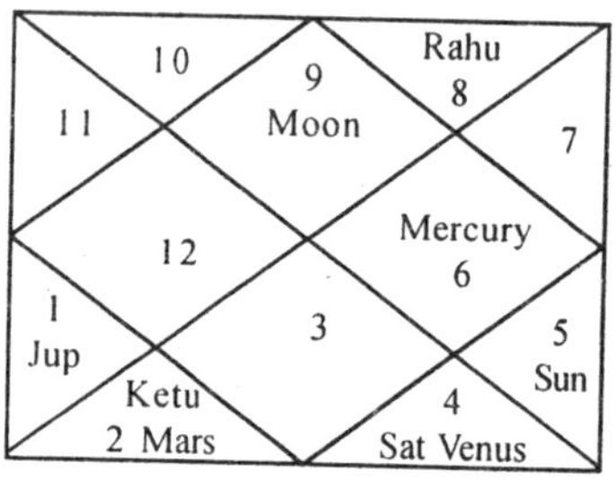

Lagna is Sagattarius whose Lord Jupiter is 5th house aspecting the Lagna, 9th and 11th houses in 10th there is Mercury in Virgo in exaltation. In ninth there is Sun in own Sign. Hence Lagana, 5th, 9th and 10th houses are Strong. Mars the Commanding planet is strong in 6th house with Ketu having Secret power. Mars aspects the Lagna and ninth house and house's Lord Sun. Hence, SUN, MARS, JUPITER are highly connected with each other. The lord of second Saturn is with Venus though in 8th house but aspects the 10th house and its lord mercury. Hence all these combination showing the high executive Commanding power to the Native.

Horoscope of 4 Civil Judges Studied Comparatively are being given here are examples.

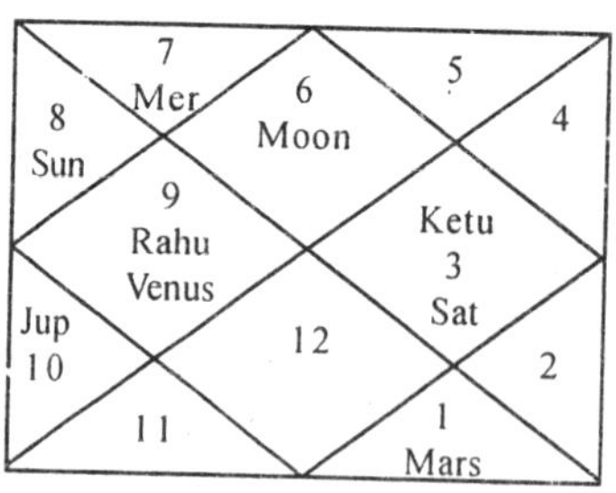

1. Male born on 20-11-1973 Tuesday at 5.15 A.M. at 21.13 N; 76.24E NAKSHATRA UTTRA PHALGUNA 3rd Quarter Lagna Virgo. For Service in Law Department and Judiciary MARS with Sun, Mercury and Jupiter must be related

Here Mars in 8th house in own Sign is strong and aspecting the Mercury in Second, Sun in 3rd Jupiter in 5th aspecting the Lagna and Moon therein and 9th house too. He joined on 20-5-2003 on the post of Civil judge.

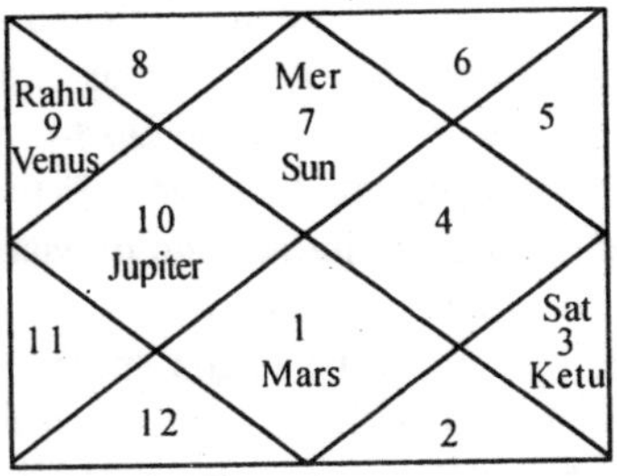

2. Male born On 13-11-1973 at Sun rise at 26.16 N; 78.13E in Libra Lagna.

Here Sun, Mercury, Mars are aspecting each other being in Quadrants. Jupiter also aspects the 10th house and Moon. Mars also aspects the 10th house hence service in Judiciary is verified.

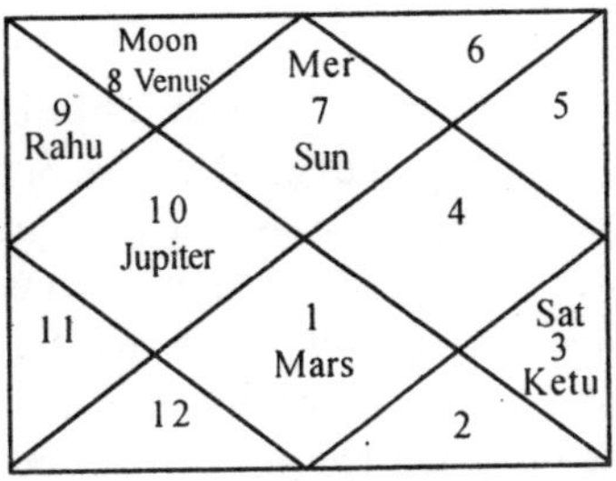

3. Female born on 29-10-1973 Monday Anuradha Nakshatra 4th Quarter born at Sunrise in Libra Lagna. Here too Mars Mercury, Sun are aspecting each other, Jupiter and Mars aspecting the 10th house Mars aspects the Lagna and Moon too. This lady joined as Civil Judge on 20-5-2003.

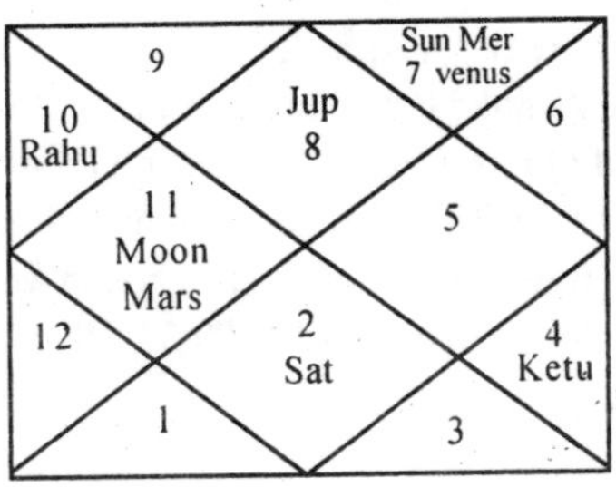

4. Male born on 29-10-1971 at 8.30 A.M at 26.43N 78.13E. Friday at 8.30 A.M. Shat Bhisha first Quarter. Here lord of Lagna Mars is in 4th house with moon aspecting Leo in 10th, 11th houses thus related with Sun and Mercury. Sun Merucury aspect the sixth house where Mars Sign Aries is present Jupiter in Lagna aspecting the 5th and 9th house. This Sun, Mercury, Mars, Moon, Jupiter etc. are in position to allow the Native Civil Judge.

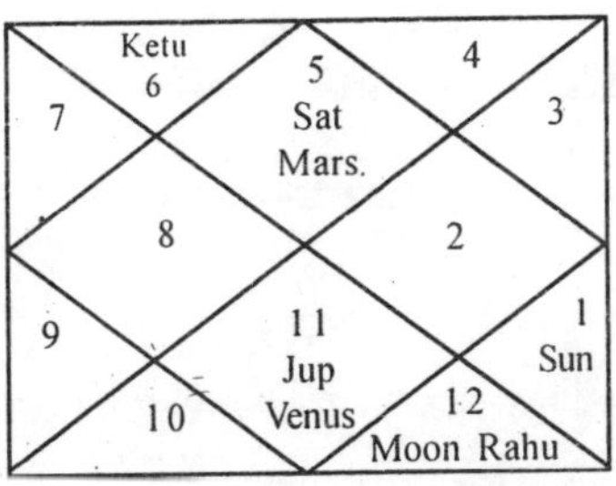

Now the combination for Doctor is to Verity and Judge through the horoscopes of Doctors.

Example 1. This is the horoscope of Dr. Madan Agarwal, District Medical Officer District Hospital Ashok Nagar (M.P.) Born On 16-4-1950 SUNDAY DAY time 2.30 P.M. Revti 2nd Quarter. He is an eye specialist Doctor too. See the combination for eye specialist Doctor and Eye, Nose throat Specialist. SATURN in Lagna and Sun in eighth house make a doctor Eye Specialist. In the same way when Rahu, Venus, Sun combination is connected any how with ninth house then the Doctor is eye, Nose, throat Specialist. Here Saturn in Lagna with Mars. Mars is the Lord of ninth houses in Ninth house there is SUN in the Sign of Mars ARIES in exaltation. JUPITER Being the Lord of eighth house with Venus in Seventh house as Lord of 10th House aspects the Lagna and 11th house. Hence Rahu in Eighth house in Jupiter's Sign PISCES with moon all these planetary position is enough to verify that the native is eye specialist as Saturn is in Lagna Venus aspects the Sign of Sun Leo, Rahu, Venus, Sun Connected with ninth house.

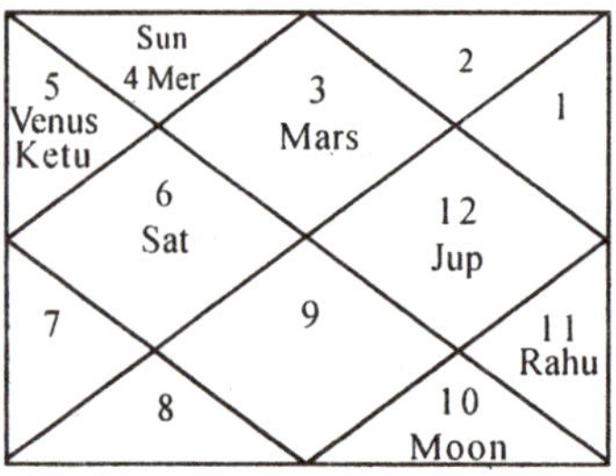

Example 2. Sun Jupiter combination makes good Doctor, Sun Mars combination aspect of Mars Makes Surgeon. SUN Jupiter, Venus Position Specially Jupiter in 10th, Sun in 2nd Venus in 3rd makes a Lady Doctor Expert in Nursing Delivery. See the horoscope of Lady Doctor URMIL Agarwal wife of Dr. Madan Agarwal (Ashok Nagar) in Government Service at District Hospital Ashok Nagar. Born on 19-7-1951 Wednesday Uttra Shada Nakshatra 2nd Quarter at 4.30 A.M. in Gemini Lagna, Mars in Gemini Lagna. Here JUPITER in 10th house in own Sign Pisces, Sun in 2nd House in Cancer Sign with Mercury and Venus in 3rd this combination is making her Lady Doctor Expert in NURSING Delivery.

6

Iron Industry

Below I am giving two example of persons running Iron Industries. Iron is mainly connected with Mars and Saturn. Mars is an fire planet and Sun too but Saturn is an airy planet. Iron is connected with fire and air both.

Example 1. Male born on 13-5-1955 at 6.30 P.M. Uttra Shada 2nd Quarter at 24.36N; 77.43E in Scorpio Lagna. Here Mars is Lord of Lagna Scorpio with Mercury in 7th house and representative of Business. Hence Business of Iron is Proving. SATURN is in 12th house in exaltation aspecting the sixth house where Sun in exaltation in Aries is Present. Aries is the Sign of Mars. Mars aspects 10th house, Lagna, 2nd house these houses are the houses of Profession, Income and Money.

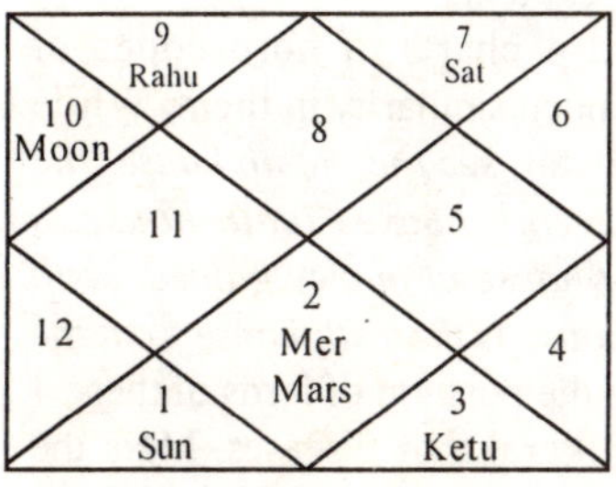

Example 2. Male born on 13-12-1972 Wednesday at 15 ghatis o Palar in Poorva Bhadrapada 2nd Quarter at 24.36N 77.43E. Here Jupiter is in 10th house in own Signs aspecting the second house the house of money, Where there is Sign of Mars Aries. Mars also aspecting the eleventh house (income) Second house (money) and 3rd house where Saturn is Present. Saturn aspecting from 3rd house to ninth house where SUN, MERCURY, VENUS are present and 12th house where Moon is in Sign Aquarius aspected by Saturn. Hence Mars, Saturn, Jupiter, Sun, Venus, Mercury, all these planets are enough proof for Iron Industries.

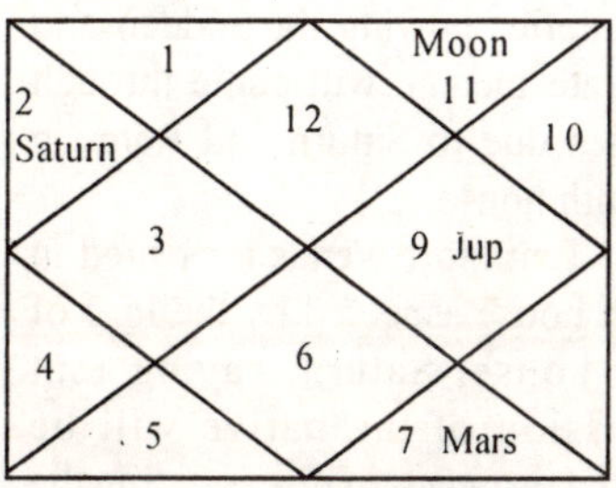

7

Combination for Doctor

I, am interested in the study of great science of Astrology for the last 39 years and have seen and read thousands of horoscopes to find out the truth hidden in astrology.

Astrology is no doubt a great science and our most valuable heritage to guide the human beings. With the help of correctly cast horoscope we can easily find out the future career of man. There are so many combinations found in the astrological texts.

Here one comparatively studied 4 charts of horoscopes of doctors. It is wonderful that there is too much similarity in them. While judging the horoscope for career of a doctor, *see the tenth house, the second house, the sixth house and eleventh house. Tenth house is house of profession, second house is the house of money gained, sixth house is the house of diseases, eleventh house is the sixth house from the sixth house and house of income.* Then see the position of lords of these 4 houses, Saturn the natural malefic and karaka of diseases, Mars the other natural malefic and karaka of surgery and cure. SUN the karaka for Government and profession.

1. This is the horoscope of a *lady* doctor. Sixth house is the sign of Saturn, karaka for diseases. Saturn is posited in eleventh house, the house of income with Rahu, the other great malefic showing the sudden and high rate income will come through diseases due to Saturn and Rahu in eleventh house.

Chart No. 1

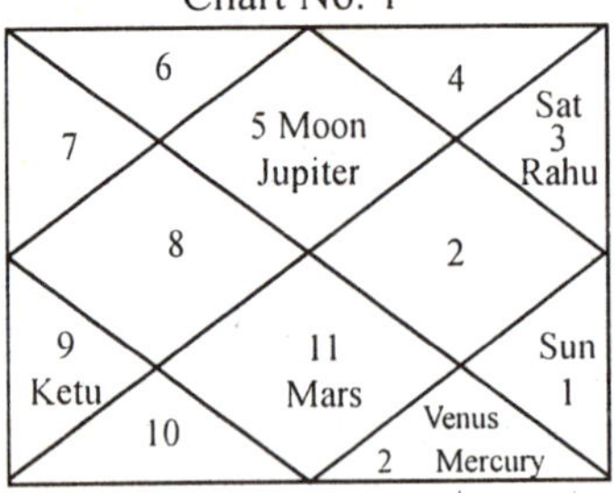

Tenth lord Venus is posited in eighth house aspected by the lord of sixth house, Saturn, saying that profession of the native will be directed by means of diseases. Sun the karaka for government and occupation posited in nineth house in exaltation. The planet of surgery and treatment Mars is in seventh house aspecting the ascendant and having relation with Saturn by occupying Aquarius sign, the sign of Saturn.

2. This is the horoscope of a male doctor. In sixth house Taurus there is Rahu aspecting the sixth lord Venus in vargo tenth house with Mars and Moon. The lord of sixth Venus is in tenth house of profession with Mars, the karaka of surgical matters guaranteeing the fact that the native will be a surgeon. Tenth lord Mercury is in eighth house with karaka of diseases Saturn, Saturn has free aspect on lord of sixth Venus and surgical planet Mars. The second house lord Saturn has also free aspect on his own sign capricorn in second house. The lord of ascendent Jupiter is in eleventh, the house of income whose lord is Venus in tenth house and Venus is the lord of house of diseases, i.e., sixth house.

Chart No. 2

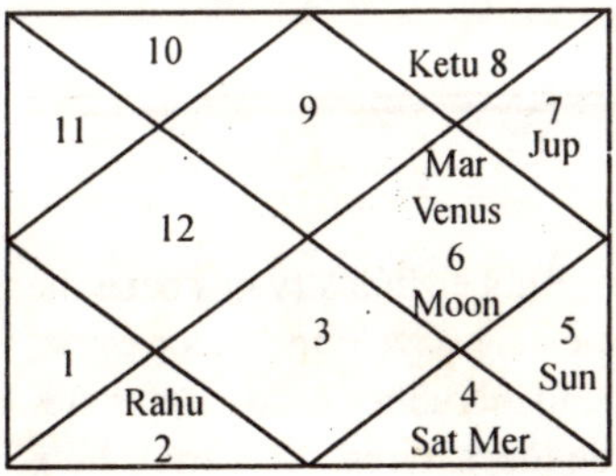

3. This is also the horoscope of a male doctor. Here lord of sixth Jupiter is in ascendant and karaka of diseases Saturn in tenth house having quadrantal aspect manually. Second lord Mars (surgeon) in eighth house with Rahu aspecting the second and eleventh house. Tenth lord Moon in Capricorn aspecting mutually exchanging with Saturn. Karaka for profession Sun is surrounded by Mars and Saturn making the native a surgeon.

Chart No. 3

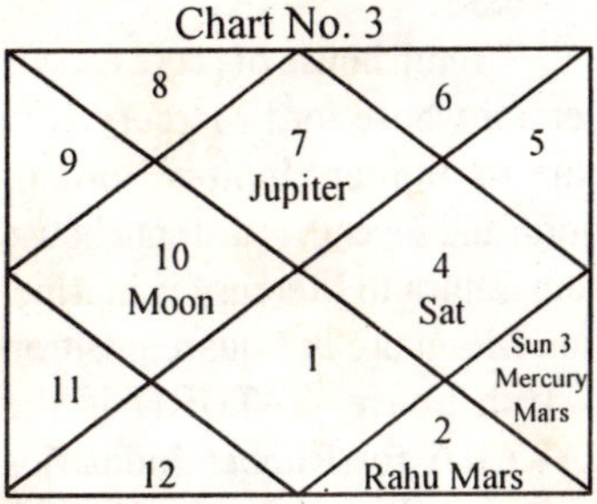

4. In this horoscope, lord of sixth and karaka for diseases is denoting the income through diseases. Saturn is aspected by Mars with SUN karaka for surgery and professions thus indicating an expert surgeon. Lord of second and eleventh Mercury is fully aspected by Saturn, Rahu and Jupiter.

Chart No. 4

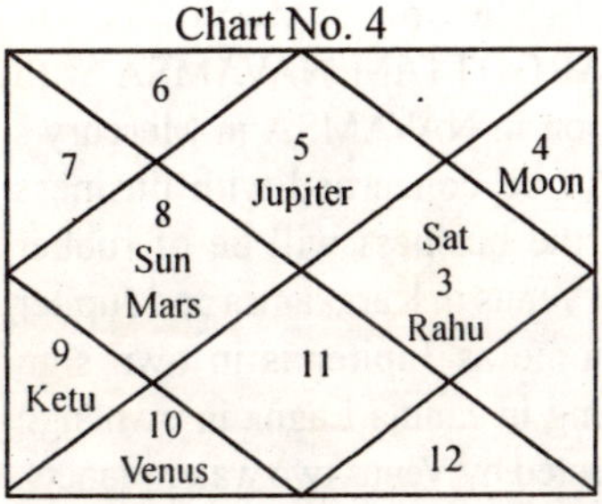

In this way by comparative study we find similarity in case of profession such as engineers, professors, merchants, service private or Government etc.

8

Rubber Industries

Modern age is the age of Industries. Rubber Industry has been the main root of all Industries. All the Vehicles e.g. Cycle to Motor cycle, Bus, Car, Zeep, Truck, Aeroplane etc. depend on rubber. Many Industries are running purely on rubber. Rubber made tubes, tyres, other tools help the mankind all days. In short we can say that without rubber we can not live. It has been essential for our life. How to find in horoscope that there is chance to choose Rubber Industry as profession. Two examples are described here.

Chart 1: Born on Vikram Samvat 2022, Ashwini, Shukla Paksha 15, Sunday, Revti Nakshatra, dated the **11th October 1965, Time of Birth 05:27:45 A.M. Place of Birth 24:36N, 77:43E.**

Birth Chart No. 1

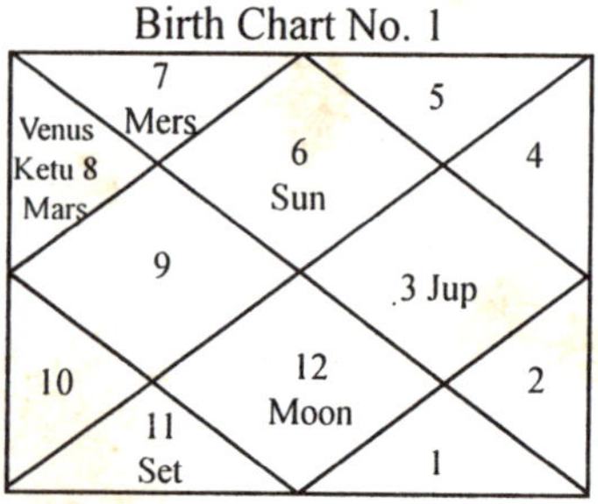

Tenth house of profession is Gemini whose lord Mercury is in trine to Jupiter. Jupiter Lord of fourth and seventh is in Tenth house from Saturn to Mercury is in trine. Sun, Moon are in Square position to 10th house. SATURN is the KARAKA for Rubber Industries posited in Pisces in NAVAMSA with Moon. Moon is in VARGOTTAM NAVAMSA with Saturn Karaka for rubber industries. Moon in NAVAMSA in Mercury's Nakshatra promises that the person will be concerned with business (Mercury's Nakshatra, Moon) and that the business will be of rubber (Saturn with Moon in Pisces) aspected by Venus in Karakamsa and Jupiter in 10th house profession directed at home as Jupiter is in own sign Sagittarius in NAVAMSA. Saturn is strong in Janma Lagna in own sign Aquarius and in Navamsa with Moon aspected by Venus two water planets. Rubber when melted becomes liquid (Here Saturn with water planet Moon in water sign Pisces and aspected by their water planet Venus in KARAKAMSA.

Here ATMAKARAKA is Moon whose mahadasa is running. Hence the rubber Industry of this person is on top in 2000. Saturn came in Taurus aspecting the eleventh house of own sign in Karakamsa.

Chart 2: Born on Vikram Samvat 2026 Vaishakh Shukla 5th Monday Mrigsira Nakshatra, dated the 21st April 1969 at 6:19:20 a.m. Place of birth as above in Chart 2: Here tenth and eleventh houses are in the sign of Saturn, the Karaka for rubber. The lord of Lagna Saturn aspects the tenth house, Jupiter and Ketu too aspects the tenth house both are in Mercury's sign Mercury is with Saturn and Sun in Lagna. Moon is in exaltation in second house (House of wealth) aspected by Jupiter and Ketu.

Birth Chart No. 2

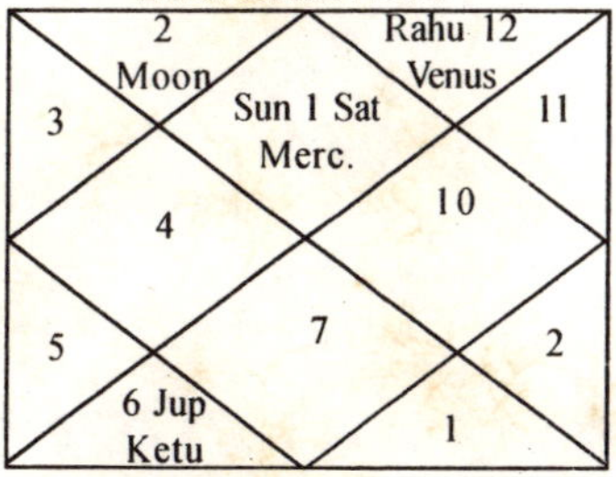

In Karkamsa Mercury is with ATMAKARAKA Moon. Saturn is in trine in 9th house (House of Luck). Saturn's position has been strong in Karkamsa as Saturn aspects the 11th house (House of income) in Karkamsa Lagna.

According to Jaimini Astrology Dual Signs aspect 4-7-10 houses respectively. Here in Karkamsa Lagna 10th house is occupied by Sun in Gemini aspected by Mercury, Moon and Jupiter. Saturn in 9th house aspected by the lord of 9th Venus (Water planet). Jupiter aspects the 11th house in Karkamsa and 10th house in Janma Lagna. Jupiter has been related to saturn in Janma Lagna as he aspects the 10th house (Sign of

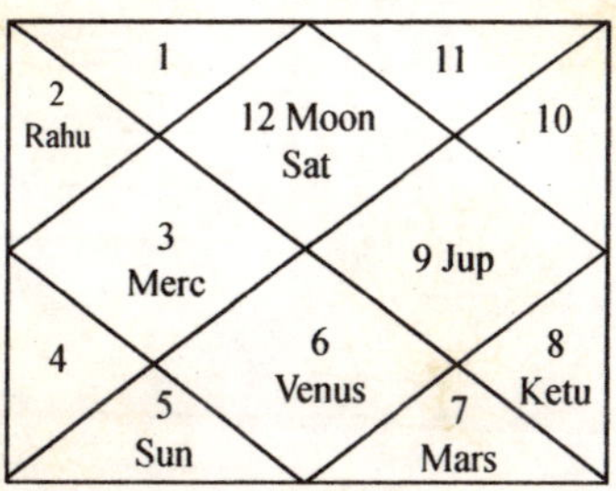

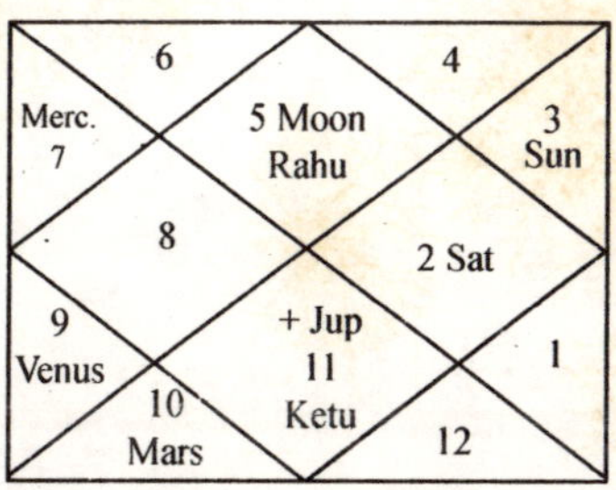

Capricorn) from 6th house Virgo (House of Mercury). Hence Mercury Business, Saturn rubber, are correlated to each other. This person's rubber industry too is Progressing.

Comparison of both the Horoscopes: In both the Horoscopes ATMAKARAKA is Moon and Jupiter Mercury, Saturn are correlated to each other in both horoscopes. Hence the profession of rubber Industry proves itself. In both the Horoscopes the position of Saturn is similar.

9

Essence of Predictive Astrology

Beyond the knowledge of Astrology our ancient Rishis had divine power of prediction. Their lives were spent mostly in the forests and they meditated under trees in open air or in caves. Their lives were guided by strong moral character. They were the master of ethics, Psychology, Philosophy, Astrology and nature. Their necessities were limited to cottage, coin's cloth water vessel and a little food. They applied the laws of morality practically in their lives. They always spoke the truth and had love to all human beings, animals, birds, creatures etc. There was no place for hate, jealousy, lias, corruption in their lives. Purity of heart, brotherly feelings all these pure things made them beloved of the almighty God. Hence, what they said was true unto last as there was no difference in their thinking and action.

They worshipped nature, fire the sun, the moon, the rivers, mountains and felt the presence of ALMIGHTY God every where in every living being. By observing the nature, and planets minutely they experienced certain things that became the rules and regulations of Divine Science of Astrology.

Without thorough knowledge of Predictive Astrology no one can predict correctly. Purity of heart, Simple Living and high thinking, Love to all, belief in HIS HOLINESS the ALMIGHTY GOD are other things necessary for an astrologer. I am going to put some laws of Predictive Astrology which are very essential and base of prediction.

(1) Jupiter, Venus, Moon and Mercury unaffected benefies, they give bad results when they are the ruler of bad evil houses such as 6th, 8th, 12th, houses in Horoscope. They are called natural benefies. While weak moon affected Sinful Mercury, Mars, Rahu and Sun are natural malefies. They produce good results when they are the rulers of good houses such as 1, 4, 7, 10, 5, 9. means land of Squares and triangle KENDRA AND TRIKONA HOUSES.

(2) Any Planet whether malefic or benefic ruling the 5th and 9th houses produce good result. It means the lord of 5th and 9th give more good results when aspected by Jupiter, the Moon or Venus who are natural benefits. The Sun and Mars are powerful in tenth house, Moon and Venus are powerful in fourth house, Mercury and Jupiter in ascendant (Lagna) and Shukra in 7th house.

(3) The planet which in the Same Sign and Same Navamsa is called 'VARGOTTAMA' Planet, Vargottama Planet is as powerful as a planet in his own Sign.

(4) The Planet which is in 8th from his own Sign Weakens his own Sign and thus produces bad results.

(5) The lord of ascendant when resides in another house from his own house or ascendant increases the power of that house e.g. if lord of ascendant is placed in eleventh house then the incame of the native will increase.

(6) Combust Planet is regarded very Weak as he is unable to produce good results. When the moon is 12, Mars 17, Mercury 14, retrograde mercury 12, Jupiter 12, Venus 12, retrograde Venus 11, Shukra 10, Rahu 10, Ketu are 15 degrees far from the Sun they become Combast or powerless. Their result is zero.

(7) The first Nawamsa of movable (Chara) Sign", the fifth Navamsa (नवांश) of fixed (Sthira) Signs, the last or 9TH Navawsa of dual (DwiSwaBHAVA) signs are known as Vargottama Navawsa.

(8) Significater (KARAKAS)—

SUN—Significater or Karaka of 1, 5, 9 houses Soul, father, power, Prestige, Heart, Health.

Moon—KARAKA of 4th house mother, peace, House, Land, mind, intellect, grace of the Administration, Mental power .

Mars—KARAKA of 3, 6, houses, disease, Boldness, enemy, Government Service, Maternal Uncle, Land for agriculture, Police, Military.

Mercury—KARAKA of 4th and 10th houses knowledge, Business, Bank, Electricity, Brothers, Foreign lands, Speech, friend, Manner of work, Mental peace. Jupiter progeny; (Son God, Teacher, Knowledge. Attractive hopeful attitude of mind, inner courage, God gifts, Husband.

Venus—KARAKA of 7th house Wife, Vehicles, Love Ornaments, happiness, luxuray, Scent; All the things of Material world.

SATURN—KARAKA of 6, 8, 10, 12th houses, death, age, Livelihood, Service, democracy, Kindness, Tragedy.

(9) Natural Malefies increase the importance in 3, 6, 11 houses but

they loose the Power of goodness e.g. Jupiter in 6th house in Pandit Jawahar Lal Nehru's horoscope shows the increase of enemy like British Government in India and Pandit Nehru accepted the challenge of enemies and fought bravely for the freedom of India and at last got triumph on British Empire. Malefies in 3, 6, 11 houses are good but they make the house evil and give good results in their Mahdasa and Antardasa.

(10) The lord of the 6th house will give troubles. In the same way lord of 12th houses will be harmful to the house he occupies. Rahu and Ketu are known as Chhayagrahas when alone in Trikona houses 1, 5, 9 will produce good results. In 2, 1-2 houses they will remain silent but in the 8th house they are the worst malefies.

(11) The relation of two planets will be better when they are in one house, in mutual Signs or Exchange is too good, being aspected by each other is generally good but if in Quadrants 1, 4, 7, 10 to each is weak relation.

(12) Kendradipati Dosha—The Planets ruling two Quadrants lose the goodness but if one Quadrant in ascendant Then the goodness in Saved. Lord of Quadrant if in a Quadrant Other than his own the goodness remains safe and loses only one half goodness. If the lord of Quadrant is in his own Quadrant then he does not loose the goodness. If the lord of two Quadrants are with the lord of 5th or 9th the Kendradhipati Dosh gets Cancelled and he gives good results.

(13) Kendradhipati in Trikona and Trikonadhipati in Kendra then both are double powered and they strengthen the power of that house of which they are the lords.

(14) Exchange of lords of 4th and 5th houses is a letter combination but that of the lords of 9th and 10th houses is known as the best Combination resulting in Rajyoga. If a native has these two Combination he will be very lucky. Lords of 4th and 5th if sit in 1, 2, 4, 5, 7, 9, 10 houses then also is the best. The natural relationship of Lords of 5th and 9th houses is not good but the exchange of lord of ascendant with the lords of 5th and 9th houses is ordinary good. From Lord of ascendant, Lord of 4th from Lord of 4th Lord of 7th from Lord of 7th Lord of 10th is more powerful. As against the Lord of 5th, the Lord of 9th is known more powerful. In the Same way from Lord of 3rd, Lord of 6th and from Lord of 6th Lord of 11th is more powerful.

(15) If lord 7th is Jupiter he is the worst Maraka and if lord of seventh is Venus then Venus is Less Maraka than Jupiter. If

7th lord is mercury then mercury is less maraka than Venus. The lords of 2nd and 7th are marakas lord and among them too lord of 2nd is the Stronger maraka than 7th Lord. If any planet is there in 2nd or 7th house then death may take place during the Mahadasa or antardasa of that planet.

(16) If any planet is lord of Lagna and 8th house then being the lord of Lagna the dosha of being lord of 8th is cancelled e.g. Mars in Case of Aries and Scorpio and Venus in case of Libra Lagna. The evil of 8th house is only removed by the lord of the Lagna. The Sun and Moon are kept free from the lordship of 8th house e.g. in case of Sagittarius and Capricorns Lagnas. They are not harmful as lord of 8th to the native.

(17) Cancellation of debilitation- The evil of debilitation of a planet is Cancelled (a) When the lord of Sign is in Quadrant position from Sun or Moon e.g. Jupiter is in debilitation in Capricorn and Shukra is in Quadrant from Sun or Moon. (b) When the debilitated Planet is in Quadrant from the moon or ascendant. (c) When the lord of the Sign of debilitated planet and lord of the exalted Sign are in mutual angles e.g. in Case of Capricorn Sign where Jupiter is in debilitation the lord of this Sign is Saturu and Saturu is exalted in Libra hence when Saturn and Venus are in mutual Quadrant position the debilitation of Jupiter is cancelled. (d) When the planet is in debilitation being the lord of the 8th house. (e) When the lord of the debilitated Sign fully aspects this Sign e.g. in case of Capricorn where Jupiter has got debilitation, the lord of Capricorn Saturn aspects the Sign Capricorn. (f) When the lord of debilitated Sign is in Quadrant in the Sign of debilitated Sign. E.g. when Jupiter is in Capricorn in 11th house and its lord, i.e. Saturn (lord of Capricorn is in Pisces in Pisces Lagna than the cancellation of debilitated Jupiter is known.

(18) Mars, Mercury, Jupiter, Venus, Saturn are the lords of two signs each when they are posited in their own Signs then they give the results of 2nd Sign first and next in which they are posited e.g. if mars is posited in Scorpio then he will give the results of Aries first and of Scorpio Later on. In the Same Way the sign which comes first from the ascendant also gets preference first. These 5 Planets give better result of their moola trikona Signs.

(19) The planet posited in tenth house from any planet or any sign has full control over that Sign or planet from which he is tenth. Whether he sees that planet or Sign or not. This Control is similar to aspecting influence.

(20) When a Planet of two Signs is with the lord 5th or 9th (TRIKONESH) then the Planet gives good result and his KENDRADHIPATI DOSHA is cancelled in this way.

(21) There are two types of combinations of Planets 1, 4, 7, 10, 5, 9, (a) When any Planet is in Quadrant (1, 4, 7, 10) has a relation with lords of 5th, 9th. This combination is Specially good. (b) When any Planet in TRIKONA (5th, 9th) is related to the lord of Quadrants. This combination is less effective than the above mentioned rule (a)

(22) If Saturn in 4th house other than Capricorn, Aquarius, Libra then the old age of the native is trouble some. It means that Saturn in these Signs in fourth house gives good results.

(23) RAHU gives accidental results concerning the house he is in if Posited with lords of 2nd, 11th, then he benefits the Native giving money accidentally unearned too e.g. from lottery or donation or gift or award etc., Ketu–when Ketu is with a Planet who is in his own Sign then Ketu increases the Power of that Planet 4 times Strong. That planet becomes more powerful with Ketu e.g. in the horoscope of Pandit Jawahar Lal Nehru Ketu is in 6th house with Jupiter in Sagittarius.

(24) Venus in 7th either alone or with other planets makes the family life troublesome but if Venus is in own Sign in 7th then the trouble is reduced fifty per cent.

(25) (a) when the lord of 9th is the Sun Luck will rise at the age of 24, the moon 22, mars 28, mercury 32, Jupiter 16, Venus 25, saturn 36, Rahu 42, Ketu in 48 years of age respectively. (b) When Jupiter is in Quadrant from ascendant or the moon the rising Luck will be in middle age, i.e. between 30-40 and if Jupiter is in Sheershoday. Sign Leo, Virgo, Libra, Scorpio, Aquarius then the rising of Luck will be in childhood and if lord of ascendant is in Sheershodaya Signs then the rising will be in middle age 30-40 and when the lord of moon sign is in sheershodaya signs Leo, Virgo, Libra, Scorpio, Aquarices then the rising will be in old age. The above rules are very important and found correct in practical experiences.

(26) Venus gives good result in 6th and 12th houses. In 6th house venus makes a man wealthy but in 12th house more wealthy and happy.

(27) A Planet owing a Quadrant and a trinal position gives the best results. e.g. Saturn for tauras and Libra natives, Mars for Cancer and Leo natives and Venus for Capricorn natives. But Saturn, mars, Venus should not be lords of 3rd, 6th and 11th houses.

Otherwise they will not give good results as mentioned above then what result will they gives in other following Sign. Saturn for Gemini being lord of 8th and 9th houses, Mars for aries being lord of 8th house and ascendant. Mars for scorpio being lord of 6th house too. Venus for Libra being lord of 8th house too in these cases the position of a planet should be Strong in ascendant or it should be aspected by benefies because being lords of 6th and 8th houses they produce much puzzled position as regard the lordship of other house. Many difficulties rise in the way of progress of the native.

(28) KEMADRUMA YOGA – when there is no planet in 2, 12 houses of moon sign then there is Kemadruma Yoga. This Yoga Cancels the Rajyogas and makes one beggar from the position of king. This bad yoga is cancelled only when the moon is aspected by benefies or in with benefies or is with the lord of the Sign in which she is posited.

Besides these there are so many other principles too guiding predictive astrology. Astrology is like an ocean. To find, pearls, jewels, one should study and apply these and other principles sincerely to find out the truth hidden in this great divine science.

10

Female Horoscopy स्त्रीजातक

Mostly in Astrological books and magazines often Male Horoscopy is discussed and described but behind the success of man there is the hand of woman whether she may be mother, wife, sister or daughter. Woman is called Laxmi of the home but from olden times she has been neglected in family, society, literature and nation. So the horoscopes of ladies too are not prepared as the male horoscopes are prepared. President Prime minister, Chief minister, Member of Parliament and Legislative assemblies, Doctor, Engineers, Professor etc. All these if they are male their horoscopes have been analysed by Astrologer but their wives horoscopes have not been analysed. Female horoscopes are prepared only for matching at the time of marriage and the economic condition of the family, children, luck, busines, agriculture, services etc. are analysed only through male Horoscopes.

After thinking seriously on this matter I have studied horoscopes of wives of Professors, Engineers, Doctors, Businessmen, Industrialist, principals, Photographers, musician etc. These studies are made comparatively so that in finding out husbands through their daughter's horoscopes may be guided. Here are 5 Horoscopes of 5 ladies whose husbands are were principals in schools/colleges for comparative studies.

Horoscopes of Wives of Principals (Educationist)

S. No.	*Lagna*	*Sun*	*Moon*	*Mars*	*Mercury*	*Jupiter*	*Venus*	*Saturn*	*Rahu*	*Ketu*	*Nakshatra*
1	12	3	11	8	3	10	2	12	8	2	Poorva Bhadrapada
2	6	6	2	10	6	12	6	1	7	1	Kritika
3	5	4	6	8	4	6	5	6	6	12	Hasta
4	10	4	8	3	4	8	4	11	9	3	Anuradha
5	8	7	12	7	7	12	6	8	2	8	Uttra Bhadrapada

In female Horoscope Jupiter is KARAKA for husband. Hence first of all we think over the position of Jupiter in these Horoscopes.

Jupiter's Position – In Horoscope No. 1 and 4 Jupiter is in 11th house aspecting the seventh house (the house of husband) in horoscope No. 2 Jupiter being lord of seventh in Pisces in own sign is aspecting the Lagna and eleventh house, third house. In horoscopes No. 4 and 5 Jupiter is in 11th and 5th houses and aspecting fifth, ninth and eleventh, Lagna.

Position of Lord of Seventh – Seventh house in female Horoscope is the house of husband and lord of seventh is husband from which husband's character, tendency, habit, colour etc. are known.

Considered – *Horoscopes of Principal's (Educationist) wives* :- In horoscope No. 1 Lord of seventh is mercury and in gemini in own sign in 4th house producing BHADRA YOGA भद्र योग In horoscope No. 2 lord of seventh is Jupiter and is in seventh house in own sign Pisces in Quadrant.

In horoscope No. 3 lord of seventh is Saturn and is with Jupiter and moon house of family, i.e., second house.

In horoscope No. 4 lord of seventh is moon and is in eleventh house with Jupiter.

In horoscope No. 5 lord of seventh is Venus and is in eleventh house debilitated.

Occupation of Husband – The 4th house in the horoscope of female in considered as the house of occupations of husband as it is tenth from the house of husband, i.e., seventh house.

In horoscope No. 1 lord of fourth mercury is in 4th house in Quadrant.

In horoscope No. 2 lord of fourth is Jupiter is in seventh house

In horoscope No. 3 lord of fourth is mars who is aspecting seventh house and is being aspected by lord of seventh Saturn who is in second house.

In horoscope No. 4 lord of 4th is in 6th house aspecting the Lagna and lord of Lagna, 2nd house saturn is also aspecting the 4th house.

In horoscope No. 5 lord of fourth is saturn who is in Lagna and is aspected by Jupiter from 5th house.

Consideration from Moon Sign

In horoscope No. 1 there is sun with mercury in 4th house and is in 5th house from moon. Moon is in 12th house.

In horoscope No. 2 lord of seventh Mars (from moon) is in 9th house in exaltation.

In horoscope No. 3 seventh lord from moon Jupiter is with Saturn, Moon and Rahu.

In horoscope No. 4 seventh lord from Moon is Venus who is in 9th house with Sun and Mercury.

In horoscope No. 5 in seventh house from moon there is Venus in debilitation but aspected by Jupiter, the Karaka for husband.

Conclusion – After studying these 5 horoscopes of wives of principals the conclusion is thus :-

Ladies who are being in Nakshatras of Jupiter, Moon, Sun and Saturn and in seventh house is Jupiter or aspect of Jupiter on seventh house, Lagna, Jupiter – Moon Combination Gaja-Kesuri Yoga, lord of seventh being in Quadrants with Jupiter or aspected by Jupiter, Venus being in Quadrants 1-4-7-10 or in triangles 5-9, being lord of seventh from moon in 5-7-9 houses then woman gets principal, professor, teacher who is wise, handsome and virtuous.

(B) Horoscopes of Engineer's Wives

Modern age is the age of technology, machinery, computer, industrialisation, engineering etc. Hence here are 6 Horoscopes of wives of engineers. Engineering role gives honour, money and fame, happiness now a days.

S. No.	*Lagan*	*Sun*	*Moon*	*Mars*	*Mercury*	*Jupiter*	*Venus*	*Shukar*	*Rahu*	*Ketu*	*Nakshatra*	*Day*
1	12	5	9	5	6	4	5	7	8	2	Uttra Shada	Monday
2	3	5	7	4	6	10	6	5	12	6	Swati	Sunday
3	3	3	3	4	3	6	4	8	7	1	Aridra	
4	3	1	9	10	2	4	3	8	8	2	Poorva Shada	Monday
5	9	3	5	4	3	10	1	10	5	11	Magha	Sunday
6	9	8	3	7	8	5	9	8	9	3		

Horoscopes No. 1 – Lagna Pisces, lord of seventh mercury in 7th house in own sign in exaltation. Mercury being lord of seventh is also the lord of 4th house. From seventh house eleventh house is the 5th house, who is house of income of husband. There in 5th house is Jupiter in exaltation in cancer sign, a water sign. Hence the husband's income sources is water. The husband of this lady in engineer in Irrigation department which is mainly connected with water. In this horoscope 3 planets are in exaltation Jupiter, Mercury and Saturn. Moon is in sagitarius in Quadrant being lord of 5th house (a triangle house) and when lord of triangle, i.e., 5-9 houses is in 1-4-7-10 it becomes double strong by its position.

Horoscope No. 2 – This is the Horoscope of second wife of Divisional engineer. Lord of Lagna mercury is in 4th house in exaltation lord of seventh Jupiter is in 8th house in debilitation but Jupiter is aspecting the 4th house and its lord being in 4th house. Jupiter being lord of seventh in 8th house and in debilitation but in retrogression is giving result of a planet as exalted because a planet in debilitation in retrogression acts as an exalted planet. Moon-Jupiter being mutually in Quadrants creating

Gaja-Kesuri Yoga too (गज केशरी योग). Jupiter is aspecting ten, second house, the house of family and money where Jupiter's exalted sign cancer is being aspected by Jupiter. Mars is in debilitation in 2nd house. Jupiter's aspect on Mars is proving that the female is the wife of a widower (विधुर)

Horoscope No. 3 – Lord of Lagna mercury is with Sun and Moon in his own sign Gemini. Lord of seventh Jupiter is also lord of tenth too is in quadrant from Lagna, lord of Lagna, Sun and Moon in 4th house. Sun, Moon, Mercury, Jupiter's mutual position in Quadrant is important. In 5th house is RAHU in Libra indicates accidentally high income, 8th house being second from seventh house (second house of money) aspected my Venus, Saturn, Mars indicating wealthy combination.

Horoscope No. 4 – Lord of Lagna Mercury in 12th house, Venus in Lagna, Moon in seventh. Lord of seventh in second house in exaltation aspecting fully the tenth house. Seventh house is aspected by lord of fifth house Venus. Lord of 4th house is with Ketu in 12th house aspected by RAHU and SATRUN. In 8th house there is Mars in exaltation aspected by exalted Jupiter. In eleventh house there is exalted Sun thus Jupiter, Sun, Mars 3 planets are exalted Saturn in sixth aspecting mars in 8th house producing VIPREET RAJ YOGA (विपरति राजयोग) which is creating wealth combination.

Horoscope No. 5 – Lord of Lagna Jupiter in debilitation with Saturn lord of money aspecting the 8th house. Lord of 7th mercury is in Gemini own sign with Sun lord of luck (9th house) lord of 4th Jupiter is aspected by lord of 5th mars. Though Mars in 8th house in debilitation but being aspected by Jupiter- Saturn is aspecting the eleventh house (house of income. Thus in 2nd, 5th, 8th houses planets producing good wealth combination.

Horoscope No. 6 – In Scorpio Lagna there are Sun, Mercury, Saturn and Rahu who are aspecting the seventh house. The husband of this lady in engineer in P.W.D. In tenth house Jupiter in Leo is aspecting the second house where his own sign sagittarius is producing wealth-combination. Jupiter's aspect on Venus in 2nd house and on 4th house too is important. All planets are from seventh house to second house producing MALA-YOGA. Planets in Lagna and in 2-12 houses also producing CHHATR-YOGA छत्र योग Venus in second and moon in 8th mutually aspecting are producing daily income yoga.

Conclusion

1. Lord of Lagna are Mars, Mercury, Jupiter or Venus.
2. In seventh house there are Gemini, Vergo, Taurus, Sagittarius.
3. Lord of Lagna, seventh are in own sign, exalted or debilitated.

4. Moon is in Gemini, Leo, Libra and Sagittarius signs.
5. In 7th there is mercury either in own sign or in exaltation.
6. Mercury, Jupiter, Venus either combined or alone are in 1-4-7-10-5-9 houses.

(C) Doctor Husbands and Doctor Wives

Practically I found that tenth, eleventh, second and sixth eight houses. When are connected with Saturn and Mars they produce doctor yoga in a horoscope because Mars is the Karak for violence and surgery and Saturn is Karak for diseases. In ladies horoscopes seventh house, Lord of seventh, karak for seventh house Jupiter for husband and venus for wife, fourth house as house of business of husband and wife as the case may be being tenth house from seventh house and fifth house being eleventh house from seventh house as house of income for husband and wife as the case may be Eighth house being second house from seventh house is known as house of money and wealth for husband wife.

Following are the horoscopes of six ladies whose husbands are doctors.

S. No.	*Lagna*	*Sun*	*Moon*	*Mars*	*Mercury*	*Jupiter*	*Venus*	*Saturn*	*Rahu*	*Ketu*	*Nakshatra*
1	7	7	1	5	7	12	5	6	11	5	
2	11	4	2	6	4	12	3	10	3	9	Kritika
3	4	3	11	12	4	6	2	9	7	1	Dhamisutha
4	5	7	2	9	7	11	7	6	12	6	Mrigsira
5	5	1	5	11	12	5	12	3	3	9	Magha
6	5	12	5	2	12	8	1	9	6	12	Poorva phalgun

Horoscope No. 1 – Here birth Lagna is Libra where Sun-Mercury are present. Sun-Mercury combination makes a native good active in work. Karak for diseases Saturn is in 12th house and is aspecting from there the sixth house (house of diseases) and ninth house (house of luck). In eleventh house there are Venus, Mars and Ketu who are indicating the income will be from surgery connecting with the delivery of ladies (Mars and Venus). In seventh house is Moon in the sign of Mars and Mars is in eleventh house aspecting the second house (house of money and wealth) thus indicating that the lady though a doctor but her husband too is a doctor.

Horoscope No. 2 – Lagna Aquarius, lord of Lagna Saturn, lord of seventh sun in 6th house with lord of 5th house mercury. In 8th house is mars, in second house is Jupiter who are mutually aspecting each other. Moon the lord of sixth house (house of diseases) is in 4th house in exaltation which is indicating that the husband of this lady is a Doctor because occupation of the husband is connected with diseases. Lord of 4th venus is in 5th house with Raku aspecting the eleventh house. From seventh house sixth house is 12th house where ROGAKARAK Saturn is present aspecting the house of diseases, i.e., sixth house. Hence husband has been connected with diseases, i.e., husband is a Doctor.

Horoscope No. 3 – This is the horoscope of a lady lecturer whoset husband is Doctor. Lagna is cancer, lord of seventh in sixth house being retrograded aspecting the ninth house where Mars is present. Lord of 4th Venus in eleventh house, Rahu is in fourth house aspected by mars from 9th house. Moon is in Aquarius in 8th house being second house from 7th house is the house of money and wealth. The moon is also aspecting the second house in the horoscope which is the house of family and money and wealth.

Horoscope No. 4 – This is the horoscope of a lady-teacher whose husband is a Doctor Lagna is Leo, Lord of seventh Saturn is in 2nd house (house of money and wealth). Mars is in 5th house aspecting the eleventh house (house of income) Lord of 4th is Mars. Here 7th, 8th, 2nd, 4th and 5th houses are concerned with Saturn and Mars. Hence husband of this lady is a doctor is proved here.

Horoscope No. 5 – In this horoscope Lord of seventh the Saturn is in 11th house with RAHU. Mars in seventh house aspecting the 10th and 2nd houses. Lord of fifth Jupiter in Lagna with moon aspected by Saturn and Mars is proving that the husband of this lady in a Doctor. The lady too is a Doctor herself.

Horoscope No. 6 – This is the horoscope of a lady Doctor Lagna Leo, Saturn in 5th, Mars in 10th, Jupiter in 8th Mars is fully aspecting lord of seventh Saturn and Jupiter lord of 5th and 8th houses. Hence it is proved here that the husband of this lady Doctor too is a Doctor himself.

(D) Eighth House in Female Horoscope

Eighth house is important in female horoscope because this house shows the luck of female, happiness of husband and her family life. In eighth house Mars in a female horoscope is indicator of widow. Hence while matching the Horoscopes of boys and girls care showed be taken.

1. In 8th house if there is sun aspected by malefics then trouble and sufferings in family, husbands health is not good and if Mars aspects the 8th house death of her husband too may take place.
2. Moon in 8th house aspected by Mars and Rahu or Combination of Moon, Mars and Rahu in 8th house then abortion or delivery by operation may be done.
3. In 8th house Moon- Saturn combination is had death may occur of mother and newly born child.

4. Mercury in 8th gives fruit according to the lord of sign in which mercury is situated or with planet combines or aspected by gives fruit accordingly.
5. Jupiter in 8th combined or aspected by malefics widow after 40 years of age.
6. Venus in 8th widow in old age.
7. If venus in 8th is aspected by weak moon death of husband and wife may occur soon after the death of any one.
8. Saturn in 8th widow after giving birth to 3 children.
9. Rahu in 8th aspected by malefics in a female horoscope causes death of the husband after settlement of marriage but before the performance of marriage.
10. Rahu in 8th with malefics as Sun, Mars, Saturn weak moon widow before the delivery of child.
11. Rahu alone in 8th house death of male progeny but if aspected by Jupiter then survives.
12. Ketu in 8th aspected by malefics death of husband may take place in Mahadasa or Antardasa of that planet who aspects the RAHU.

(E) When and How Marriage will be Performed?

1. Find out the NAVAMSHA of Lagna, then see that the lord of Navamsha is in which sign. Hence when in GOCHAR गोचर, i.e., in current period Moon. Rahu or Jupiter come in that sign. Marriage will be performed.
2. When Jupiter comes in Gochar गोचर in the birth sign of Venus or Lord of seventh.
3. If mercury is strong in seventh marriage will be in near relation early.
4. Add the Degrees of Lord of Lagna and seventh house then in that sign when Jupiter comes in GOCHAR MARRIAGE will be performed.
5. If lord of Lagna is with lord of fourth house marriage will be with the girl who lives in the house of his mother.
6. Add Degrees of Moon and Lord of seventh then in that added sign when Jupiter will come marriage will be performed.
7. Add the Degrees of Lord of Lagna, Lord of second house, lord of sun occupied sign. If Jupiter is in GOCHAR in that sign then when sun will come in that sign then in that month marriage will take place.
8. If there is RAHU in seventh and lord of seventh is in 5-9 houses then family life will be happy.
9. If lord of 8th house be in third house and lord of second aspects the lord of third and lord of second and third be in 5-9 houses then the native has sexual contact with other ladies and wife of such native too may have sexual contact with other persons.

10. If lord of third house from moon is in seventh house from Lagna aspected by lord of third house then too person has contact with pros.
11. If lords of second and third houses are in 5-9 house with Venus aspected by Jupiter the native has sexual contact with other ladies.
12. If lord of third house is in seventh house aspects Jupiter or is aspected by Jupiter and lord of seventh Mercury aspects Venus then the person have contact with old ladies.
13. If lord of fifth, lord of third are in fifth house then the person has contact with handsome ladies.
14. If Jupiter or lord of tenth is in fifth house and lord of eleventh is in 4th house with Rahu then the native marries once.
15. The native marries 3 times when SATURN, VENUS and Lord of sevnth are in eleventh house, lord of eleventh in second house aspected by Venus. Secondly if lord of eleventh is not alone, lord of seventh is in second house, venus in eleventh house.
16. The native marries four times when malefics are in 2nd house, Venus with lord of eleventh Saturn and moon in seventh house to each other secondly lord of 2-7-11 houses from moon are in eleventh house from venus.
17. The native marries many times when lord of 8th in seventh, Moon in eleventh with lord of second house. Eleventh house is responsible for more than one marriage venus in cancer, virgo, sagittarius, Gemini (Except Pisces) marries more than one time.
18. Malefics in seventh house, lord of seventh with malefics, make the female corrupt. Secondly venus and lord of eleventh are in seventh, lord of seventh in fourth house with lord of third house.
19. Moon in 6-8 houses, Malefics in Lagna or seventh house make the female widow in 8th year after marriage if not aspected by benefics.

(F) Happy Married Life

1. Lord of seventh and venus are in own house or in friend's house or in exaltation, lord of second house in exaltation.
2. If benefics in seventh, Venus with benefics, lord of seventh in tenth house wife will be devotee to husband.
3. Venus in 9th in good position, lord of third in friend's sign Jupiter related with seventh house.
4. Lord of 2-7-11 be in good position. Benefics in 2-7-11 make the family life happy.
5. Mercury is prince in planet and when connected with seventh house or lord of seventh marries early.

6. Lord of seventh in exaltation and from there in seventh house is moon and Jupiter lord of second, third houses is well, soon and happy marriage.
7. If lords of second and third are in one friend's sign then happy married life.
8. If lords of second, seventh are in 4th house with venus and Jupiter is related with seventh house then happy marriage.
9. Lord of second in second and mercury, venus aspect the seventh house then wife in devoted to husband and is wise.
10. Lord of seventh in 5-9 houses aspected by moon, Lord of second in exaltation then wife is beautiful, virtuous and devoted to husband. After married good collection of wealth, money, land and ornaments.
11. If lord of seventh in fifth house with benefics, and in second house too are benefics then beautiful wife who is virtuous devoted to husband. Wealthy after marriage.
12. If Jupiter or free moon aspects the Venus then one marriage which is helpful in bringing money, honour, happiness and wealth.
13. Venus alone, Lord of second exalted with Lord of seventh both aspecting the fourth house, Lucky, beautiful wife.
14. Lords of second and seventh combined in angle and triangle then only one marriage.
15. Benefics in seventh house from moon bring happiness through marriage.

(G) Short-lived Wife

1. Wife is short lived if lord of seventh is in 6-8-12 houses.
2. If lord of seventh is in eleventh house in fixed or dual sign with benefics then wife is devoted to husband. But if there is moving sign चरराष्ि in eleventh house then wife is short-lived.

(H) Relation with Many Ladies

1. In Virgo Lagna Moon Saturn are in 1-4-7-10 or 5-9 houses, Venus in Taurus in ninth house.
2. Venus is weak, Moon Saturn are strong.
3. Jupiter in 5th, Moon in 11th, Saturn mercury combined in 1-4-7-10-5-9 houses.
4. If lord of seventh in moving sign then 2 marriages in fixed sign one marriage, in dual sign keep one kept separate from wife.

(I) Chances of no Marriage

1. Venus, Lords of second, seventh in evil houses 3-6-8-12 on seventh no aspect of Jupiter.

2. Moon-Jupiter in 6-8-12 houses and either moon in debilitation or Jupiter in Caprican in debilitation. It means that Jupiter-moon in Scorpio or Capricorn in 6-8-12 houses denial of marriage.
3. Death of wife soon just after marriage if SUN-JUPITER aspect the Lagna or seventh house being combined.
4. If the Lord of the sign occupied by Venus is in 6-8-12 houses wife dies.
5. Sun, Moon, Mars, Jupiter, Venus in one sign are combined.
6. Sun, Moon, Mercury, Venus, Saturn are in odd sign विषम राशि
7. When sun moon mercury Venus Saturn are in 1-3-5-7-9-11 Signs and Jupiter have relation with seventh house too then No marriage. Lord of seventh aspects these planets then no marriage and the native lives too far from home.

(J) Late Marriages

1. Lord of seventh house is in 2-6-12 houses from 7th house, malefic with Lord of seventh or in seventh house.
2. when from Lagna or moon there is Jupiter or Saturn in seventh house.
3. Lord of seventh with Jupiter Saturn.
4. Venus with Jupiter or Saturn.
5. Venus aspected by Saturn and Mars.
6. In seventh house when there is SUN-MARS combination or Moon-Mars combination.

(K) Character of Female

Character of female is known through Trishamsha. We have to find out trishamsha of Lagna and Moon. Sun and moon have no Trishamsha. Trishamsha Chart is given below :

Degrees	1	3	5	7	9	11	2	4	6	8	10	12	Degrees
	5	1	1	1	1	1	2	2	2	2	2	2	5
	10	11	11	11	11	11	6	6	6	6	6	6	10
	18	9	9	9	9	9	12	12	12	12	12	12	18
	25	3	3	3	3	3	10	10	10	10	10	10	25
	30	7	7	7	7	7	8	8	8	8	8	8	30

Result is as following

Lagna/Moon	*In Trishamsha of*	*Result*
Aries/Scorpio	1-8	Bad Conduct
Aries/Scorpio	2-7	Corrupt
Aries/Scorpio	3-6	Dirty
Aries/Scorpio	10-11	Maid Servant
Aries/Scorpio	9-12	Virtuous

Taurus-Libra	1-8	Quarrelsome
Taurus-Libra	2-7	Beautiful, Husband wife
Taurus-Libra	3-6	Expert in Art/Music
Taurus-Libra	10-11	Do Second Marriage
Taurus-Libra	9-12	Good Character.
Gemini-Virgo	1-8	Mother of son
Gemini-Virgo	2-7	Good Clothe and ornaments
Gemini-Virgo	3-6	Brave and Bold
Gemini-Virgo	10-11	Common gender, Sinful Dead Children, Widow
Gemini-Virgo	9-12	Devoted to Husband
Cancer	1-8	Moon aspected by malefics corrupt
Cancer	2-7	Specially Sex-sufferer
Cancer	3-6	Expert in Handicraft, Faithful
Cancer	9-12	No more age, Less sons.
Leo	1-8	Male type nature, Wicked
Leo	2-7	Love with Lower Person, Killer of Husband
Leo	3-6	Wicked, Male type Nature, Quarrel
some		
Leo	10-11	Sad, Troubled
Leo	9-12	Virtuous, married with high seated person.
Sagitariue Pisces	1-8	Big Family, Fames
Sagitariue Pisces	2-7	Wealthy, Clothes, Ornaments, Valuable, Good sons
Sagitariue Pisces	3-6	Good Character, Honourable.
Sagitariue Pisces	10-11	Poor.
Sagitariue Pisces	9-12	Wealth, Clothes, ornaments Valuable.
Capricorn Aquariaus	1-8	Full of Sadness, Shocked
Capricorn Aquariaus	2-7	No Progeny But fair behaviour
Capricorn Aquariaus	3-6	Highly Intellectual but cunning and wicked.
Capricorn Aquariaus	10-11	Unlucky
Capricorn Aquariaus	9-12	Good Conduct and Behaviour According to family.

According to Author of JATAK PARIJAT जातक पारिजात Add Degrees, Minutes, Seconds of Lagna and Moon. say that from TRISHAMSHA.

Importance and utility of Astrology

Astrology is a mystic utility science. It is the branch of Vedas who informs us about the changes in nature controlled by 9 planets. In finding out the conclusion labour, time and control over mind is necessary. It is said about Astrology

अप्रत्यक्षाणी शास्त्राणि विवादस्तेषु केवलं
प्रत्यक्षं ज्योतिषं शास्त्र चन्द्रार्कौ यस्य साक्षिषौ

Means in other subjects there is dispute but Astrology is a direct science whose witnesses are Sun and Moon. 24 hours of day and night have been divided in 12 signs in the form of Ascendant (Lagna) from the beginning of sunrise till the sunrise of next day.

From time immemorial India has been the birth place of Astrology and from India went to other old countries as China, Japan, Egypt, Arabian countries and Persia etc. 18 Rishis are called the director of Astrology who are Surya, Pitamah, Vyas, Vashishtha, Atri, Parashar, Kashyap, Narad, Garg, Marichi, Muni, Angira, Lomash, Polish, Chyawan, Yavan, Bhrigu, Shownak. Their books are called Samhitas which are proved scientifically and are true guide.

Acharya Varahmihir was one of the nine jewels of Emperor Vikramaditya of Ujjain. He for the first time collected all the principles of these 18 Acharyas and wrote Vrihajjatak वृहज्जातक. After Varahmihir Arya Bhatta, Bhattatpala, Kalyan Verma, Bhaskaracharya, Arya Bhatta second enlarged Astrology for the welfare of human beings. Sarawal, साराताली of Kalyan Verma, Lilavati लीलावती of Bhaskaracharya, Veej ganit, Siddhanta Shiromaki, Karan Kutuhal, Arya Bhattiya, Maha Siddhanta are the valuable books. Then Sheeghra Vodh शीघ्रवोध by Kashinath Lagnachandrika, Vrihadyavan by Yavana Charya, Mukurta Chintamani by Ram Daivagya, Jatakalankar by Ganesh Daivagya, Khetu Kantak by Rahim, Jataka Bharam by Dhundhiraj, Jajir Neelkanthi by Neelkanath, Prashna Bhushan by Jeevnath Jha, Prashna Shiromani by Rudramani, Phala Deepika by Mautreshwar, Jatak Parijat by Vaidyanath, Uttara Kalamrit by Kalidasa, Jatak Tatwa by Mahadev Pathak, etc wrote in Sanskrit. Varahmihir's son Prithuyasha wrote Shatpanchashika. Whose translation in Sanskrit by Bhattatpala was done. In 18-19 centuries Param Hansa, Sitkantha, Kriparam, Fateh Singh, King Shambha Singh of Suthaliya, Laxmi Narayan Tripathi of Nar Singh Garh etc wrote books on Astrology. Thus Indian Astrology is the valuable cultural heritage of us.

Sun rounds 12 signs in 12 months. When Sun transits from one sign to other sign it is called Samkranti संक्रति. There are 12 signs Aries, Taurus, Gemini, Cancer, Leo, Virgo, Libra, Scorpio, Sagittarius, Capricorn,

Aquarius, Pisces. Their lords are Mars of Aries, Scorpio, Venus of Taurus and Libra, Mercury of Gemini and Virgo, Jupiter of Sagittarius and Pisces, Saturn of Capricorn and Aquarius, Sun of Leo and Moon of Cancer. There are 27 Nakshatra. One sign consists of 2 ¼ signs. One Nakshatra has 4 quarters on the basis of quarter name is introduced and future, past and present is described. One sign has 9 quarters in this way 27 x 4 = 108 quarters are composed of 12 signs.

Moon, Mercury, Jupiter and Venus are benefics and Sun, Mars, Saturn and Rahu, Ketu are malefics. The first house of horoscope is called 'Tanu' second 'Dhan' third 'Sahaj' Fourth Mother, Property, happiness, Fifth progeny and mind, intellect, education etc. Sixth enemy, debt, disease, seventh 'spouse' eighth Age and Death, ninth 'Dharma' Tenth 'Karma' Eleventh 'Income' twelfth 'Expenditure'.

In 12 houses of Horoscope are called the alcode of 'Kalpurush'. One of 12th houses may be Ascendant or Lagna. First house and Aries indicate 'Head' second house and Taurus 'Face' Third house and Gemini Soldier, Teeth, Ear, Lungs, Throat, Fourth house and Cancer Heart, Lungs, Fifth and Leo stomach, backbone, sixth house and Virgo Intestines, Seventh house and Lebra sex organs eighth house and Scorpio vterus, ninth house and Sagittarius Tenth house and Capricorn knees, right eye, Eleventh and Aquarius upper part of leg below knees, Twelth and Pisces lower part of feet.

Planets aspects the house and planets. All the planets have 7th aspect on each other, besides the following planets have two more aspects other then 7th e.g. Mars aspects 4-7-8 houses from his seat Jupiter aspects 5-7-9 houses from his sitting place Saturn aspects 3-7-10 houses from his sitting place Rahu and Ketu aspect 5-7-9 houses in retrogressive from their seat.

For judging a horoscope if any house has benefics in if it will give good result. 6-8-12 houses are called evil houses planets in them, lords of 6-8-12 houses are called evil houses planets in them, lords of 6-8-12 will sit where there will be had influence. 1-4-7-10 houses are called squadrands, 5-9 houses are called TRIKON houses they give good results. Besides planet are friends, enemies to each other according to their nature. 5 kinds of TATWA are found in planets e.g.

Sun – Mars – Fire – Moon – Venus – Water
Saturn – Rahu – Air – Mercury – Earth , Jupiter – Sky

In the same way signs are as following –

1-5-9	Fire	3-7-11	Air
2-6-10	Earth	4-8-12	Water

Signs are of 3 Kinds :

1-4-7-10	Moving or Chara
2-5-8-11	Fixed or Sthira
3-6-9-12	Dual or Duiswa Bhava

27 Nakhatras are Asuwini, Bharmi, Kritika, Rohini, Mrigsira, Aridra, Punarvara, Pushya, Ashllsha, Magha, Poorva, Phalguna, Uttra Pholguna, Hasta, Chitra, Swati, Vishakha, Anu Radha, Jyeshtha, Mool, Poorva Shada, Uttra Shada, Sravaus, Dhanishtha, Shatbhisna, Poorva Bhadra Pada, Uttra Bhudrapada and Revti.

11

How to perform Marriage Ceremony

In India among Hindus marriage ceremony is known as pure and lovely bondage of two souls approved by Seven surroundings of GOD FIRE to live harmoniously and happily throughout the whole life adjusting themselves. But alas! It is shameful on our part that we do not care for the importance of chosen period for this ceremony experienced and given us by great rishis and avoid it knowingly. We see that while Horoscope matching of bride and bridegroom we go to the Astrologer for asking the time of Tilak Ceremony fulling godi of bride and at last the most important selection of Lagna of marriage for seven surroundings round the God FIRE by means of doing a yagna (Havan) is performed under the direction of Pandit who must be learned in vedas, Puranas etc.

First of all bridgegroom Party should engage the bride in Uttrashada, Swati, Sravana, Poorva Bhadrapada, Poorvashada, Poorva Phalgun, Anuradha, Dhanishtha, Kritika or in the Nakshatras of marriage which are Rohini, Mrigsira, Magha, Uttra Phalguna, Hasta, Swatis, Anuradha, Mool, Uttra Shada, Uttra Bhadrapada, Revti etc. Tithis should be all except 4,9,14,30 leaving aside Bhadradi doshas. The days should be Monday, Wednesday, Thursday, Friday. According to Electional Astrology the fixed time or Muhurta should not be neglected. Now a days the Modern lighted Hindu Persons think this cultural function as superstition and knowingly, jump and dance for a long time. The selected Muhurta thus leaves behind and the marriage ceremony is not celebrated in fixed time which results in widowhood, family conflicts, divorce, maladjustment, sickness, no issues etc. and Astrologers are abused for this wrong timely celebration of such as must important function of life, i.e., Marriages who is responsible for this? No doubt we all are responsible for this who knowingly Neglect our culture due to mal-influence of Western culture in our lives.

The marriage ceremony should be celebrated when SUN is in ARIES, TAURUS, GEMINI, SCORPIO, CAPRICORN and AQUARIUS Signs. At the time of marriage the Sun should be 3, 6, 10, 11 from the birth sign of bride and when the Sun is 1,2,5,7,9, from the birth sign of bride is called RED WORSHIP (लाल पूजा) by worshipping the SUN. The Red Worship should only be allowed in emergencies. Only for person born in Libra sign SUN WORSHIP is not bad as they are married after worshipping the SUN GOD because SUN in Libra is called NEECHA (debilitation). Hence to remove this DOSHA. Red Worship is necessary to Libra born persons.

JUPITER of the bridegroom should be 2,5,7,9,11 from her birth sign in transit and when Jupiter is in 1,3,6,10 from the birth sign of the bride groom it is called YELLOW WORSHIP (पीली पूजा) by worshipping Jupiter. The Sun and Jupiter from their birth Signs as well as Moon should not be 4,8,12 at the time of marriage. Moon should be 1,2,3.5,6,7,9,10,11 from the birth Signs of both the bride and bridegroom.

If the Son or daughter is the first issue then the birth month, birth Nakshatra, birth tithi should be Omitted. In the same way for the first issue either the bride or bridegroom. Jyeshtha month should be omitted because 3 Jyesthas (Bride, Bridegroom, Jyeshtha Month) is called TRI KHALA DOSHA which is harmful to both parties.

In a home within 6 month's of Son's marriage the daughter should not be married. When marriage is settled and if any death occurs in either side of male or female within 3 peedhis e.g. grandfather (दादा) grandmother (दादी) maternal father (नाना) maternal mother (नानी) then in emergency the marriage ceremony may be celebrated after a month.

Horoscope Matching — In Horoscope Matching keep in mind the following things—

1. The Varna of girl should not be superior to the boy.
2. When enemy 'YONI' is indicated it should be omitted as they are mutually enemies.
3. When both have the same gana that is very good increasing love. Rakshasa and Manushya gana results in death and Rakshasa and Devgana are struggle some hence should be omitted.
4. 6, 8, Signs are death giver 5-9 Signs harmful to Progeny, 2-12 Signs give poverty Hence should be Omitted. Only 6-8 are allowed when their lords are friends. This is called Preeti Khadashtaka.
5. When Lords of both Signs are friends gana dosha is cancelled.
6. When both are born in the Same Nadi that is not admissible. If both have Madhya Nadi death may occur. Hence it should be cancelled. NADI DOSHA is cancelled when birth Nakhatra of both is the Same but CHARAN or Quarter are different. From olden times it is said that NADI DOSHA. For Brahmins, VARNA DOSHA for Kshatriya, GANA DOSHA for Vaishyas, Yoni Dosha for Shudras is admissible.

Hence while matching the horoscopes for 4 Varnas this thing should be kept in mind.

If guna's matching 19 to 27 are medium more than 27 are very good.

7. Nakshatras of both should not be 1,3,5,7 to each other. There are 3 groups of Nakshatras. If bride and bridegroom's Nakshatras fall in the same group that is very acuspicious. These are as following:-
    1. Revti, Ashwini, Bharmi, Kritika, Rohini, Mrigsira.
    2. Aridsa, Punarvasa, Pushya, Ashlesha, Magha, Poorva Phalguna, Uttra Phalguna, Hasta, Chitra, Swati and Vishakha.
    3. Anuradha, Jyeshtha, Mool, Poorva Shada, Uttra Shada, Shravan Dhanistha, Shatbhisha, Poorva Bhadrapada, Uttar Bhadra Pada when bride and bridegroom are of first group the bridegroom is dear to bride. When both are of 2nd group they love naturally to each other, when they are of 3rd group the bride is dear to bride groom.
8. Gandanta Doshas-The last 48 Minutes of Jyestha, Revti, Ashelsha Should be omitted. This is called Nakshatra gandanta Dosha. The last 12 minutes of Cancer, Scorpio, Pisces Ascendantas, the starting 12 minutes of Aries, Leo, Sagittarius should be omitted. This is Called Lagna Gandanta Dosha. The last 24 minutes of Poorna Tithis 5-10-15 Starting 24 minutes of Nanda Tithis 1-6-11 should be omitted. Thus these 3 gandanta doshas are unauspicious hence to be omitted.
9. Kartari Dosha-Malefics directional in 12th house and retrograded in 2nd house is Papa Kartari Yoga which gives death, Poverty, melancholy hence to be omitted.
10. The combination of Moon with Mercury and Jupiter is good.
11. From birth Lagna, Moon Sign 8th sign to be decided as marriage Lagna is unauspicious. Only then 8th Sign is allowed when there is friendship in their Lords.
12. According to Astrological texts following are called VISHAGHATIS which are to be omitted in marriage Lagna:—30 to 34 ghatis of Revti, Magha Nakshatra, 40 to 44 GHATIS of Rohini, 18 to 22 ghatis of Uttar Phalguna, 14 to 18 ghatis of Mrigsira and Swati, 24 to 28 ghatis of Uttra Shada, 21 to 25 ghatis of Hasta 10 to 14 ghatis of Anuradha, 56 to 60 ghatis of Mool.
13. Nakshatra Vedha according to Panchshalaka Chakra and Saptashalaka Chakra should be omitted.
14. Libra, Scorpio Sagittarius Lagnas are deaf in day after midday. Capricorn is deaf at night. Aries, Taurus and Leo are blind in day, Gemini, Cancer and Virgo are blind in night. Aquarius in day, and Pisces are lame during Sunrise and Sunset. If there is deaf Lagna during the time of marriage then poverty if day blind then widowhood,

if night blind then death of Progeny. If lame Lagna then loss of wealth is indicated. If these malefics Lagnas are aspected by their Lords then they are beneficial. Hence while deciding marriage Lagna the abovementioned things should be considered.

15. If marriage takes place in Navamsa of Sagittarius Pisces, Gemini, Virgo, Libra the girl will be equal to Sati (सति) or Pati Vrita.
16. Last Navamsa should be Omitted. Only Vargottama Last Navamsa is admissible.
17. Saturn in 12th Mars in 10th, Venus in 3rd, Moon in any malefic Lagna, Lord of Lagna, Venus, Moon in 6th, 8th any Planet in 7th Mars in 8th should not be in marriage Lagna.
18. Good combination for marriage Lagna is the position Mercury, Jupiter, Venus in Kendras, 1-4-7-10 or Trikona 5-9 Sun or Moon in 11, Vargottama Lagna Cancel all the doshas.
19. Godhuli Vela is the best for marriage Lagna but there are some rules for GODHULI Velá Lagna—In Cold days i.e. in November to February at Sunset time when Sun set is half round it is GODHULI. In Summer days when Sunset is full it is GODHULI on Thursday after Sunset, On Saturday being Sun in the Sky is good GODHULI.
20. Moon in 1-6-8 kills the bride, Moon in 1-7-8 kills the bridegroom Moón in 1-2-3 is very good.
21. Pat, Vyatipat, Dagdha titihi, Combustion of Moon, Venus and Jupiter, tithi Kshaya, Tithi Vriddhi, Bhadra,Sanskranti, Lata Vedha, Yama, Upagrahe etc. all these doshas should be considered so that the life of new couple may be healthy, wealthy, happy throughout with long life.
22. Mars in 1, 4, 7, 8, 12 produces KUJA DOSHA or Mangli Dosha and the horoscope is called Manglik. Both of the horoscopes should be mangalik for future's guidance.
23. KUJA DOSHA is Cancelled—
    1. When Jupiter and Venus are strong in Lagna.
    2. When Mars is Combust, Neecha, retrograded.
    3. When Saturn is posited strongly in 4-7-8-12 houses.
    4. Jupiter, Moon are in 4-7 houses.
    5. Mars for Cancer and Leo Lagna is auspicious.
    6. When Mars is aspected by benefic Jupiter.
    7. When Lord of Lagna and Seventh, Jupiter, Venus are in Strong position.
    8. When Mars is in 8th and Jupiter is in 9th house.

Mars of bride and Venus of bridegroom

1. From Venus of bridegroom Mars of bride muse be in Quadrant in 1-4-7-10.

2. If Moon of bride will be 6-8-12 from the Venus of Bridegroom there will be no Sexual attraction hence it is Seen that in such a position a most beautiful girl fails in getting love of her husband.
3. When Mars is with Jupiter or Moon Kuja Dosha is cancelled.
4. When Mars is in Aries and Scorpio Lagnas then there is no Kuja Dosha.
5. When Mars is in Gemini or Virgo in 4th house then No Kuja Dosha.
6. When Mars is in Cancer or.Capricorn in 7th house No Kuja Dosha.
7. When Mars is in Sagittarius, Pisces, in 8th houses No Kuja Dosha.
8. when Mars is in Taurus or Libra in 12th house No. Kuja Dosha.
9. SATURN in 1-7-11 Cancel the Kuja Dosha. Hence, Position of Mars should be considered seriously. There is no question of fear from KUJA DOSHA. Readers are requested to experience the position of Planets mentioned above in Connection with KUJA DOSHA.

12

Jaimini Astrology

There are so many systems of future prediction in Indian Astrology. Among them Jaimini system of prediction is wonderful and peculiar as it differs in some way from the most popular system of Parashar. In practical life the rules of Jaimini system are very near to truth. Besides it is somewhat hard and difficult to understand. It requires more mental labour. As Rashis aspect each other in this system and not the planets. The Astrologer has to prescribe different cases in this system. The Planets who are in highest degrees are very important but they loose their importance in Parashar System e.g. Any planet between 25° to 30° will be most important in Jaimini but in Parashar System it will be known as oldest or weak planet.

Aspects : The first and most peculiar thing in this system is the aspect of signs (with Planet therein) to other signs (with Planets therein). The moveable signs, aspect signs and planets in 5,8,11 houses, the fixed signs aspect signs in 3,6,9 houses and dual sign aspect sign in 4,7.10 houses. For example :-

Signs	**Aspecting Signs**
ARIES (Moveable)	Leo, Scorpio, Aquarius
CANCER (Moveable)	Scorpio, Aquarius, Taurus
LIBRA (Moveable)	Aquarius, Taurus, Leo
CAPRICORN (Moveable)	Taurus, Leo, Scorpio
TAURUS (Fixed)	Cancer, Libra, Capricorn
LEO (Fixed)	Libra, Capricorn, Aries
SCORPIO (Fixed)	Capricorn, Aries, Cancer
AQUARIUS (Fixed)	Aries, Cancer, Libra
GEMINI (Dual)	Virgo, Sagittarius, Pisces
VIRGO (Dual)	Sagittarius, Pisces, Gemini

SAGITTARIUS (Dual)	Pisces, Gemini, Virgo
PISCES (Dual)	Gemini, Virgo, Sagittarius

These aspects are to be kept in mind seriously. In parashar system not signs but planets aspects; planets each other e.g. Each Planet aspects planet/ planets in seventh house. Besides Mars aspects 4,8 houses, Jupiter aspects 5,9 houses, Saturn aspects 3,10 houses. But in Jaimini System 12 signs aspect 3,3 sign altogether. This System of aspecting signs by sign is really peculiar in Jaimini System. Hence it must be remembered well in mind to grasp this theory.

Argala : The second thing in this system in Argala. Argala means barrier as on roads, custom posts are seen. Argalas control the movement of carriers. In Jaimini Astrology argalas are 2,4,11 houses the Sign of aspect. If any Planet in any sign aspects any Planet/Planets in 2,4, 11 houses it is called Argala. In this way each sign has its own argalas in 2,4, 11 houses.

To know opposite planets for Argala Karaka Planets, in 3, 10, 12 houses are known as opposite or enemy Planets. When there are maximum 3 planets in these houses than that house is barrier for the planets who aspect these houses. According to Jaimini system Saturn, Mars, Mercury Jupiter, Venus, Moon and Sun are strong in progressive way. Sun is the most strong Planet and Saturn in the lowest strong Planet in this system of Jaimini Astrology.

When we consider Argalas for a particular sign than the Planets who aspect this particular sign then in 5th house from the aspecting planet when there are Planets in 5th and 9th houses then this planet will be known as Argala Karaka Planet.

Karaka Planets : In Jaimini Astrology the planet who has more degrees is known as Atmakaraka then in lesser degrees-AMATYA KARAKA, BHARATRA KARAKA, MATRA KARAKA, PUTRA KARAKA, GYATI KARAKA and in the last DAR KARAKA. The importance of ATMAKARAKA is more than Ascendant in Jaimini Astrology. If two planets have equal degrees, then both of them will be known as ATMA KARAKA. In such a position one Karaka may be Rahu otherwise not. Atma Karaka Planet plays important role in future construction of man. If Atmakaraka is strong then its fruit will be seen in successful future life; if weak then the person concerned will get trouble in its Mahadasa, Antardasa etc.

For purpose of relations Mars is the Karaka for sister, brothers of wife, brother and mother. Mercury is the Karaka for maternal uncle maternal aunt, other caste fellows, ladies equal to mother rank, i.e., aunt TAI, CHACHI, BUA etc. Jupiter is the Karaka for grandmother and grandfather DAD A, DADI, NANA, NANI etc. Venus is the Karaka for wife, beloved ladies 'PREMIKA' etc. while Saturn is the Karaka for Son.

Pada Lagna or Aarudha Lagna : According to Jaimini PADA LAGNA too has important role in prediction made from the Rasis. How far is lord of Lagna or any house from Lagna or that particular houses are posited, where the counting stops that house is the PADA of Lagna or that house e.g. if there is Cancer Lagna and lord of Cancer moon is in 12th house then count from the 12th house, the XIth house will be 12th house from 12th house. There is exception about fourth house that is if lord of fourth house is in fourth house then there is no necessity of Counting from fourth house but the fourth house will be PADA of 4th house. In the same way if lord of any house is posited in 7th house from his own house then the PADA of 7th house will be tenth house. In such a case seventh house or Lagna will not be known as PADA.

Varnadarasi : As for prediction knowledge of KARKASAS, Lagna, Padalagna is necessary so the knowledge of VARNADA rasi a VARNADA LAGNA is also necessary. To find out Varnada Lagna first of all put one place the sign, degrees, minutes of ascendant. Then know the HORA LAGNA. To know the Hora Lagna multiply by 2 the birth time (ISHTAKALA) sign, degrees and minutes then divide it by 5, then balance must be multiplied by 30 and divide it by 5. Then again the balance must be multiplied by 30 and divide it by 5 the result will be degrees then again multiplied by 60,60 divide two times by 5,5 they will be kalas and Viklas.

All this must be added in Sun's Sign, degrees, Kalas, Viklas the result will be HORA LAGNA.

The other method is to multiply the birth ghatis, palas, into 12 and add the result in Sun's Sign, ghatis, Palas. At sunrise the Hora Lagna will be that in which Sign. Sun in posited. Then after sunrise by one hour the Hora Lagna will be sign wise.

If Janma Lagna plus Hora Lagna is in odd sign this total is VARNADA LAGNA. But if the total is in even sign then substract the total from 12, the balance will be VARNADA LAGNA. Remember Varnada Lagna is always in odd sign. So if total is even sign then by substracting it from 12 we prepare in odd sign.

Karakamsa : The Navamsa in which Atmakaraka Planet (Planet of highest degree) falls is called Karkamsa. According to Jaimini Rishi if Atmakaraka falls in Aries the native gets trouble from rats, cats and other animals.

If it falls in Taurus the native gets happiness from quadruped (four feet animals) such as COW, OX, Buffalo, Horse etc., and he is a merchant too.

If it falls in gemini there is possibility of itches and skin diseases and increasing of fatness.

If it falls in Cancer there in fear from water and possibility of Leprosy.

If it falls in Leo there is fear of biting by dogs and cats.

If it falls in Virgo the native suffers from itch, skin diseases, and fear from fire.

If it falls in Libra the man is a great merchant.

If it falls in Scorpio there is fear from water and snakebite.

The man gets mother's milk little.

If it falls in Sagittarius there is fear of falling from high Place, Vehicles, trees etc.

If is falls in Capricorn there is trouble from birds, skin diseases, tumors etc.

If it falls in Aquarius the man is religious by nature and helps the people by doing good deeds such as digging wells, tubewell etc.

If is falls in Pisces the man is pious, virtuous, religious and gets salvation. (Moksha)

If Atmakaraka Planet in under the aspect of benefic it decrease the fruit of sins and under malefics aspect lessons the fruit of good deeds.

Planets in Karkamsa and Profession

If there is Sun in navamsa of Atmakaraka, i.e., in Karkamsa the person performs government jobs.

If there in full Moon or Venus aspected by Venus free Moon the person is happy, wise and earns money by means of knowledge and intellect. He gets all the things and uses them.

If there is mars the person in Chemist, Fighter with arms and earn money by fire work, i.e., he is Engineer, Engine Driver, Goldsmith, Black Smith, Confectioner etc. He is also Atomic Engineer, Bakery Man, Brick Maker etc.

If there is Mercury the person is cloth merchant, merchant of other daily use things, Politician, Artists, well versed in human behaviour.

If there is Jupiter the person is just and religious minded, learned in Vedas, Religion, Philosophy, duty full, Judge, Yagnik etc.

If there is Venus the person holds higher position in government and has many wives, long lived and happy.

If there in Saturn the person is famous in his profession. He is famous in Society, State and even in world and plays important roll in his life.

If there is Rahu in karkamsa the person prepares arms for battle, earns money by thief, sceptic medical poison, Specialist in making engines and external affairs.

If there is Ketu the person is merchant of elephants, busy in mystic works as C.I.D. and has thief mentality, mysterious in all his works. If Ketu is in karkamsa lagna and is aspected by malefics the man suffers from ear diseases his ears are cut. If aspected by Venus well-versed in religious activities or he leaves too world becomes SANYASI. Such Ketu aspected by mercury and Saturn the person is unable to give birth of Children, aspected by Mercury and Venus the person repeats one talk again and again or he is son of Devdasi, Veshya or such woman has many husbands.

Such Ketu aspected only by Saturn or with other planets the man is Saint or TAPASWI or Servant. If only Saturn aspects, then the person is not SANYASI but DHONGI SANYASI.

According to Parashar if Ketu is in Karkamsa is aspected by Sun and Venus the person is Government Servant.

Sun and Rahu with Atmakaraka

If there are Sun and Rahu in Karkamsa the man dies from Snake bite and if such Sun and Rahu are aspected by benefics the man survives. And if such Sun and Rahu have no relation with malefics but only with benefics the man becomes doctor of Poison. In such position he has no fear of snake bite. If such Sun and Rahu are aspected only by mars, then the man fires his own house or gives fire to others. But if such mars is aspected by Venus then the result of house firing is cancelled and only fire can he given as donation. If such Rahu and Sun are only aspected by Jupiter the own house of the man relieves from burning by fire and neighbouring house is burn.

If in Karkamasa GULIKA is with Atmakaraka then the person kills others by poison or is died or killed by poison. And if Gulika is with Atmakaraka and is aspected by moon the person is thief or his money is stolen by thieves. If Gulika is with Atmakaraka and is aspected only by Mercury then the person's Hydroceles are big.

GULIKA in Karkamsa

on	I	II	III	IV	V	VI	VII	VIII
Sunday	Sun	Moon	Mars	Mer	Jup	Ven	Sat	Gulika
Monday	Moon	Mars	Mer	Jup	Ven	Sat.	Gulika	Sun
Tuesday	Mars	Mer	Jup	Ven	Sat	Gulika	Sun	Moon
Wed.	Mer	Jup	Ven	Sat	Gulika	Sun	Moon	Mars
Thursday	Jup	Ven	Sat	Gulika	Sun	Moon	Mars	Mer
Friday	Ven	Sat	Gulika	Sun	Moon	Mars	Mer	Jup
Saturday	Sat	Gulika	Sun	Moon	Mars	Mer	Jup	Ven

1 1/2 Hours each from Sunset at Night

Sunday	Jup	Ven	Sat	Gulika	Sun	Moon	Mar	Mer
Monday	Ven	Sat	Gulika	Sun	Moon	Mar	Mer	Jup
Tuesday	Sat	Gulika	Sun	Moon	Mar	Mer	Jup	Ven
Wed.	Sun	Moon	Mar	Mer	Jup	Ven	Sat	Gulika
Thursday	Moon	Mar	Mer	Jup	Ven	Sat	Gulika	Sun
Friday	Mar	Mer	Jup	Ven	Sat	Gulika	Sun	Moon
Saturday	Mer	Jup	Ven	Sat	Gulika	Sun	Moon	Mar

Karkamsa and Occupation: If Atmakaraka in Karkamsa is aspected by Sun and Venus the person is Government Servant. If from Karkamsa in third house there are malefics the man is brave and not afraid of anything. But on the other-hand if there are malefics in 3rd and 6th houses the man is farmer or earns his money through agriculture.

Gulika in Karkamsa : GULIKA in called the part of Saturn. It is not mandi. The 24 hours of day and night are divided in 8, 8 parts. In day is in counted by day lord white in night it is counted by 5th from day lord, e.g., 8 parts of day contains 1 1/2 hours each from Sunrise.

Karkamsa and Fourth House : If there is moon in fourth house or aspect the fourth house in Karkamsa Lagna the man intercourses sexually his wife for first time in open air under the sky. If there are Venus and moon in fourth house or both aspect the fourth house the person is owner of a big building like palace. If there is any planet in exaltation sign in fourth house then too the owner has a building like palace. If Saturn and Rahu are in fourth house or aspect it the owner has a home made of stones. If mars and Ketu are in fourth house or aspect it the person has a house made of bricks. If there is Sun or Sun aspects the fourth house the person makes a cottage of grass, leaves, wooden things. But if there is mercury alone or aspects the fourth house the person has no house of his own lives in the rented house unaspected by other planets the man sleeps down in the sky in open air but he can have his own house only after marriage.

If there is Jupiter and moon in 7th house or aspect the seventh house in Karkamsa Lagna the man marries with the most beautiful lady. If there is Rahu in 7th house or aspects the 7th house the man marries with widow. If there is Saturn in 7th house or aspects the 7th house the man marries with elder lady Mars in Seventh or aspects the seventh house in Karkamsa the man marries with a handicapped lady. If there is Sun in seventh house or aspects the seventh house the man marries with a domestic handicapped lady. If there is Mercury in seventh or aspects the sevanth house the man marries with a lady expert in music and fine arts.

Karkamsa and Ninth house: In Karkamsa in ninth house if there are benefic or benefics aspect the ninth house the person is religious, truth speaking and devotee of his teachers. On the other hand if there are malefics or malefics aspect the ninth house the person is liar, dishonest and has no respect for teachers. If there are Saturn and Rahu in 9th house or aspect the 9th house the person is athiest and goes against his parents and teachers. In the same way if Sun and Jupiter are in 9th house or aspect the 9th house the person does not believe in teachers. He is some what proudy. If there is only Jupiter in 9th house and aspects the man is mentally absorbed in other's women. If there is Rahu in 9th or aspects the 9th house the man spends money openhanded in desire of other's ladies.

Karkamsa and Tenth House: In Karkamsa Lagna in tenth house if there in Mercury or aspects mercury the man is very famous in his profession or business. If benefics other than mercury aspect the tenth house the person in strong in decision and perform his business nicely.

If there is sun aspected only by Jupiter the person performs his business by having milky animals like cows, buffaloes, goat etc.

Karkamsa and Twelth House: If there are benefics in Karkamsa in 12th house the person goes to heaven after death. If there is Ketu he gets salvation (MOKSHA) specially in Cancer or Pisces signs. If there are malefics other than Ketu and 12th house is aspected by malefics then the person may not go to heaven and does not get salvation (MOKSA).

If there are sun and Ketu in 12th house in Karkamsa the man is devotee of Lord Shiva. Ketu with moon devotee of Gauri, Ketu with Venus devotee of LAXMI, Ketu with Mars of Kartikeya Swamy, Ketu with Saturn and. Mercury devotee of Lord VISHNU, Ketu with Jupiter devotee of SHIVA PARWATI. If there is Rahu devotee of Mahakali and Durga. If Ketu alone is there devotee of Lord GANESH and Kartikeya Swamy. If there is Saturn in sign of malefics then man is devotee of Yakshini, Pishachini, Dakini and Bhairav.

Karkamsa and Trikona Houses: If in Karkamsa Lagna there are 2 planets in 5th and 9th Trikona houses, i.e., one, one malefics in 5th and 9th houses each. Then the person uses Mantra or he is MANTRIC, TANTRIK, YANTRIC. If malefics aspects 5, 9 houses them the person commands BHUTA PRETA or GHOSTS but if benefits aspect then the person is well wisher of others.

If in Karkamsa Lagna there are Venus and moon or Venus aspects Moon in Karkamsa Lagna then the Person prepares chemicals and drugs. If mercury aspects the moon the person is Doctor.

Diseases Known Through Karkamsa: If there is moon in fourth house in Karkamsa and Venues aspects the man suffers from white spot or white leprosy. If mars aspects such moon the Leprosy is Produced from blood bile combination.

If Ketu or Rahu and Mars in fourth and fifth houses the person suffers from T.B. and if moon aspects such Rahu T.B. will surely be to the man.

Karkasma and Fourth, Fifth Houses: If only mars is in fourth or fifth house in Karkamsa Lagna the man suffers from wounds. If there is Ketu in fourth and fifth houses the person suffers from Dysentry, Dropsy or other water diseases. If there are GULIKA and RAHU in fourth, fifth houses the man suffers from diseases e.g. biting by Dogs, Monkey, Rats and Snakes etc.

If there is Saturn in fourth house in Karkamsa Lagna the person is expert in using bow and arrow and other arms. If there is Ketu in fourth house in Karkamsa Lagna the man is expert in watch making. If there is mercury in fourth house in Karkamsa Lagna the person is Spiritually Strong or DANDADHARI SANNYASI, If there is Rahu alone in fourth house the person is Ironic machine maker. If there is sun in fourth house in Karkamsa Lagna the man is expert in using swords. If there is mars in fifth house in Karkamsa the man is expert in using Bhala.

Karkamsa and Author : Fifth House : If there are Jupiter, moon in Karkamsa in 5th house the Man is author. If there are Venus and moon the moon is author of second grade. If there are mercury and moon the man is author of third rank. If there is Venus alone the man is expert in verses making and speech and knows poetry well. If there is only Jupiter the man is wise and have knowledge of many subjects but not expert in speech besides he is also expert in Vedas and Grammar. If there is Saturn alone the man fears of Speaking before the gentry. If there is mercury the Man is expert, in MIMANSA SHASTRA. If there is mars alone the man is wise in law and logic. If there is moon the man is Singer, Literary, expert in SANKHYA SHASTRA. If there is Sun alone the man is expert in Music and VEDANTA. If there is Ketu man is mathematician, Astrologer or Computer person.......)

Now we give examples of truth found in Jaimini Astrology. Example-1, When Karkamsa is in Leo there is fear of biting by cats and dogs. Here Karkamsa is leo and dog bit this man in 1961. When there is Venus in Karkamsa Lagna Jaimni Says :-

"राजकीयः कामिनः शतेन्द्रियाश्च राज्याधिकारी स्त्रीसुखा दीर्घायुः"

Means the man is Government official, huge happiness of women, living with happiness for about a hundred years and long-lived. When there in Moon in seventh house of Karkamsa the wife is beautiful and when there is Mercury in 7th house the wife is knowing art. Here both Moon and Mercury are in 7th house of Karkamsa Lagna the wife was beautiful and art knowing.

Ketu in 12th house of Karkamsa gives salvation or Moksha. Here is Ketu in 12th house; the man will get salvation or Moksha. Now we consider some things from PADALAGNA, UPPADA and PADA of 7th house.

Pada Lagna - Here lord of Libra Lagna, Mars is in 6th house hence 6th house from Mars, i.e., Virgo will be Pada Lagna as following: Hence eleventh house is Cancer. Cancer is aspected by Scorpio-Saturn, Aquarius-Jupiter. Hence eleventh house is aspected by Saturn and Jupiter. Hence the person is rich. The 12th house Leo is aspected by Aries-Mars, Capricorn-Sun, Mercury, Venus hence expenditure too is not less.

Pada of 7th house - Now see the PADA of Seventh house. From birth Lagna there is Taurus in seventh house whose lord Venus is in ninth house from Seventh house, hence Pada Lagna, Pada of Seventh house in the same Virgo. When Pada of seventh house falls in 1,4,7,10 or 5,9 houses the man is rich. Here Pada of seventh house is in first house of Pada Lagna. Hence the man is rich and has friendship with wife. They love to each other mutually.

Now we consider some things from UPPADA, i.e., Pada of 12th house from Lagna. Here lord of 12th house Venus is in 4th house from 12th house. Hence Capricorn where Venus in there is UPPADA because when lord of particular house falls in 4th house from that house, the 4th house becomes Pada of that house.

Jaimini says that when they're in aspect or position of benefics in second house from uppada, the wife of the man beautiful. Here Jupiter is in second house from UPPADA. In the same way benefics in UPPADA too give the same result as above. Here Venus, Mercury two benefics are in UPPADA. Hence the wife in beautiful.

CHARA RASIDASA - As we have mentioned that in Jaimini Astrology aspect of Rashis in important so the Dasa System is important. There are many Dasa Systems in Jaimini Astrology among them Chara Rashi Dasa System is first. In odd sign Lagna we count from left to right and years of Rashis are to be taken in account with the position of Lord of that sign. In even signs coming will be right to left. In this way each Rashi Dasa will be different in different sign. The Astrologer must be careful in finding our the years of Dasas' of Rashis.

But there is exception in Taurus and Scorpio signs and Leo and Aquarius. In Taurus and Scorpio the counting will be left to right and in Leo and Aquarius right to left. Dasa years are as following: when Lord of

Sign is in second house then one year in third house two years, in fourth house 3 years. In own sign the years will be 12 year. If Planet is in exaltation one year should be added and if in debilitation then one year should be minus. Counting should be from Lagna e.g.

In odd signs 1-3-5-7-9-11 (Right to Left)
In even signs 2-4-6-8-11 (Left to right) But
In Leo signs 5-4-3-2-1-12-11-10-9-8-7-6
In Aquarius 11-10-9-8-7-6-5-4-3-2-1-12
In Taurus 2-3-4-5-6-7-8-9-10-11-12-1
In Scorpio 8-9-10-11-12-1 -2-3-4-5-6-7

Here in the example of Scorpio is being given so the Dasa years for every sign will be follows:

Birth Lagna : 22-1-1927

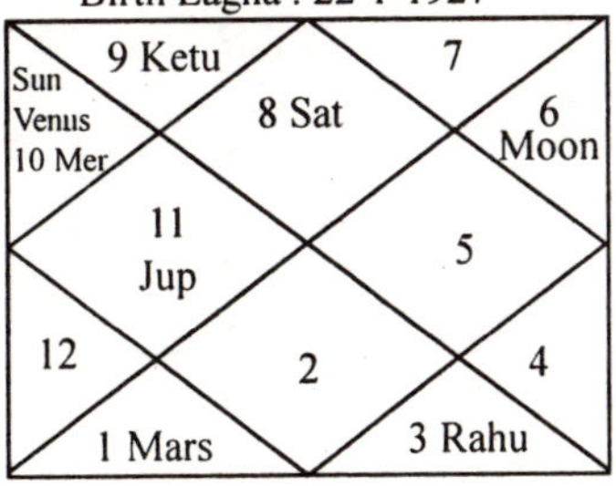

Karkams : Atmakaraka-Mars

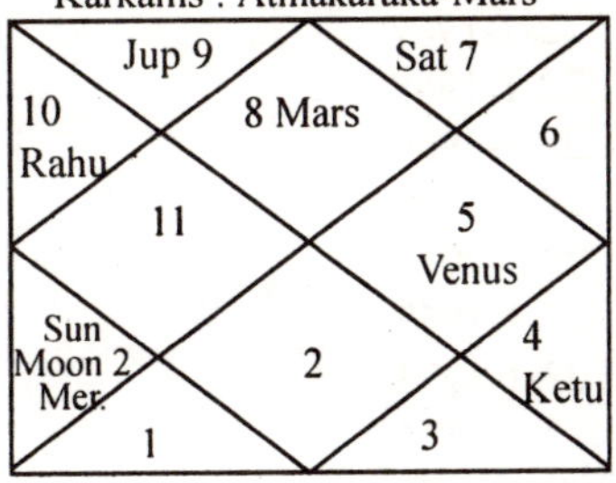

Main events	*From Dasa of birth*	*Rashi*	*Years*
	22-1-1939	8	12
	22-1-1942	9	3
Marriage, Son, birth, Service in State Bank	22-1-1953	10	11
Dog bite in 1961, Promotion	22-1-1963	11	10
Death of Father	22-1-1975	12	12
	22-1-1987	1	12
	22-1-1996	2	9
Death of wife and Death of Mother on 24-4-99	22-1-2004	3	8
		4	2
		5	6
		6	
		7	

In Karkamsa Lagna Pitri Karaka Sun is in Pisces in eighth. Hence father expired on 30/31-8-1966. According to Jaimini "रवि शुक्रयो प्राणी जनक:" means Sun and Venus are STHIRA KARAKA of Father. Here Venus is in sign of Sun i.e. Leo in Karkamsa. Death of father is known through the Sign occupied by Pitriakaraka. Here Pisces sign in Karkamsa in owned by Jupiter. Death of father is indicated in TRIKONA RASI. Dasa of sign occupied by Pitri Karaka. TRIKONA RASIS from PISCES are 12-4-8 sign. Hence the Death of father in Pisces Dasa is justified. Now we prepare Antar Dasa chart of PISCES Dasa for 12 years.

From 22-1-1963 to	*Antar Dasa years*	*Rashi*
22-1-1964	1	12
22-1-1965	1	1
22-1-1966	1	2
22-1-1967	1	3
22-1-1968	1	4
22-1-1969	1	5
22-1-1970	1	6
22-1-1971	1	7
22-1-1972	1	8
22-1-1973	1	9
22-1-1974	1	10
22-1-1975	1	11

Father expired in Antar Dasa of Mercury i.e. Mithuna sign, Gemini in eighth sign from birth sign Scorpio. (Gemini)

Now See Prityantar Dasa chart for Antar Dasa of Gemini

From 22-1-1996 to	*Antar Prityantar Dasa Days*	*Rashi*
21-2-1966	30	3
22-3-1966	30	4
21-4-1966	30	5
22-5-1966	30	6
21-6-1966	30	7
22-7-1966	30	8
21-8-1966	30	9
22-9-1966	30	10
21-10-1966	30	11
22-11-1966	30	12
21-12-1966	30	12

Death of father occurred in Prityantar of Capricorn, i.e., eighth sign from Gemini in birth Lagna, i.e., Capricorn where Pitriakaraka Sun and Venus and Antar Dasa Rashi Lord Mercury are present.

Now prepare Sookshma Rashi Dasa chart to find out two correct day of death. Divide 30 days by 12 Rashi we get $2\frac{1}{2}$ days.per Sookshma Rashi Dasa for each Rashi Dasa.

From 22-8-1966 to 24-8-1966	Sookshma Dasa Days	Rashi
26/8/1966	$2\frac{1}{2}$	10
28/8/1966	$2\frac{1}{2}$	11
31/8/1966	$2\frac{1}{2}$	12
	$2\frac{1}{2}$	1
	$2\frac{1}{2}$	2
	$2\frac{1}{2}$	3
	$2\frac{1}{2}$	4
	$2\frac{1}{2}$	5
	$2\frac{1}{2}$	6
	$2\frac{1}{2}$	7
	$2\frac{1}{2}$	8
	$2\frac{1}{2}$	9
	$2\frac{1}{2}$	10

Now we conclude that death of father occurred in PISCES Rashi Dasa, Gemini's antardasa, Capricorn's Prityantar Dasa and Aries Sookshma Dasa. See the position of Aries. Aries is the eight sign from Moon sign

Virgo in birth Lagna. In Navamsa chart too Aries is in eighth sign aspected by Mars and Saturn. Saturn is Prityantar Dasa Lord. In Karkamsa Lagna both Saturn and Mars are in eighth sign from PISCES -SUN.

In Gemini Rashi Dasa the wife and the mother died on 20-3-1997 and 24-4-99 respectively : In Gemini Astrology it is said about the death of wife. गुरु शूले कलत्रस्य where Jupiter is in birth Lagna then from Jupiter's sign in TRIKONA RASI Dasa, i.e., 1-5-9 Rashi Dasas the death of wife occurs. Here Jupiter is in Aquarius and from Aquarius 11-3-7 signs are TRIKONA (1-5-9) signs. From 21-1-1996 to 21-1-2004 Gemini Rashi Dasa is running. Hence in Gemini sign Dasa death of wife occurred. Now see the Anatardasa Chakra of Gemini Rashi Dasa. Gemini Dasa is for 8 years. Hence 8 months are prescribed for each Antar Dasa sign as following:

From 22-1-1996 to	*Antar Dasa months*	*Rashi*
22.9.1996	8	03
22.5.1997	8	04
22.1.1998	8	05
22.9.1998	8	06
22.5.1999	8	07
22.1.2000	8	08
22.9.2000	8	09
22.5.2001	8	10
22.1.2002	8	11
22.9.2002	8	12
22.5.2003	8	1
22.1.2004	8	2

See that Gemini is eighth sign from birth Lagna Scorpio and second to seventh house sign Taurus, i.e., Maraka Sign. Death of wife occurred in Antardasa of Cancer Rashi Dasa in Gemini Rashi Dasa. From Gemini Cancer is second sign, i.e., again a maraka sign. See the Navamsa Chakra where Cancer is in eighth house from Lord of seventh house Jupiter who is in Sagittarius and in Cancer sign there is Ketu.

Now see the Prityantar Dasa of Cancer antardasa Rashi 8 months=240 days divided by 12 we get 20 days Prityantar Dasa period for each sign:

From 22-9-1996 to	*Antar Dasa months*	*Rasi*
12.10.1996	20	04
01.11.1996	20	05
21.11.1996	20	06
09.12.1996	20	07
29.12.1996	20	08
18.01.1997	20	09
10.02.1997	20	10
02.03.1997	20	11
22.03.1997	20	12
10.04.1997	20	01
01.05.1997	20	02
21.05.1997	20	03

So In Prityantar Rashi Dasa of PISCES in antardasa of Cancer Rashi Dasa and Main Rashi Dasa of Gemini wife died as PISCES is in 8th house ofKarkamsa Lagna. From Moon sign Virgo Pisces is the sign of seventh house (the house of wife).

Now see that mother died in Libra antardasa. Fourth house is the house of mother where Aquarius sign is Present. From Aquarius TRIKONA Rashis are Gemini and Libra.

Hence mother's death in Libra Rashi antardasa in main Rashi. Chart Rashi Dasa of Gemini is justified as Gemini and Libra both Rashi are 5-9 to Aquarius Rashi.

Now See the Prityantar Dasa Chart of Libra Rashi Antardasa

From 22-9-1998 to	*Days months*	*Rashi*
10.10.1998	20	07
30.10.1998	20	08
20.11.1998	20	09
10.12.1998	20	10
30.12.1998	20	11
20.01.1998	20	12
10.02.1999	20	01
02.03.1999	20	02
22.03.1999	20	03
12.04.1999	20	04
02.05.1999	20	05
22.05.1999	20	06

Mother expired on 24-4-99, i.e., in Prityantar Dasa of Leo. Here see that according to Jaimini aspect Leo is aspected by 3 sign-Planets.

ARIES MARS (CHARA RASHI) 5th
aspect on Leo
LIBRA (Sign in 12th house) 11th
aspect on Leo
Capricorn - SUN MERCURY VENUS
- 8th aspect on Leo

Sun is the lord of tenth house - 7th house from 4th house hence Maraka house, Mercury is the lord of 11th house, i.e., 8th house from 4th house and Venus is lord of 12th house.

According to Vimshottari Dasa of Parashar Sun Maha Dasa was in balance for 2 years 6 months 19 days i.e. upto 11-8-1929 then 11 -8-29 to 10-8-39 Moon Mahadasa

11-8-39 to 10-8-46 Mars Mahadasa 11-8-46 to 10-8-64 Rahu Mahadasa 11-8-64 to 10-8-80 Jupiter Mahadasa 11-8-80 to 10-8-99 Saturn Mahadasa 11-8-99 onwards Mercury Mahadasa

Father expired on 30/31-8-1966 in Jupiter Mahadasa antardasa of Jupiter. Wife and mother both expired in Saturn Mahadasa antardasa of Jupiter i.e. from 29-1-96 to 11-8-99. See the Position of Jupiter in fourth house in Aquarius a sign of Saturn. Saturn and Jupiter both aspect tenth house, The house of father. Saturn is in inimical sign aspecting inimical sign.

Birth Lagna 14-06-1908

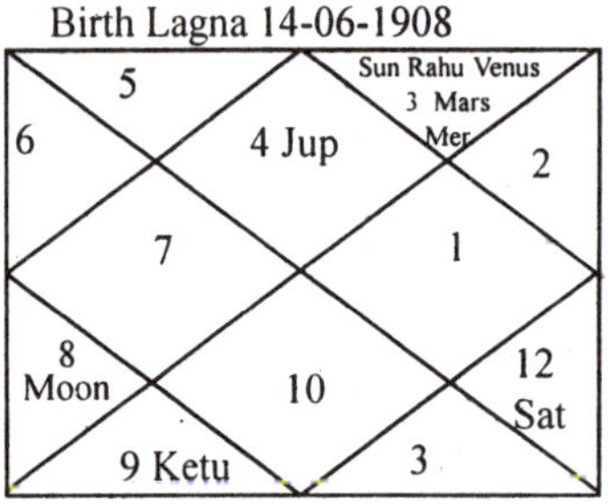

Example - 2 Male born on 14-6-1908 Ishta Kala 8 ghatis 16 Palas. Jyeshta Nakshatra 3rd Quarter.

Planetry Position: Sun-Gem; Mon-Sco; Mar-Gem; Mer-Gem; Jup-Can; Ven-Gem; Sat-Pis; Rahu(R)-Gem.

Atmakaraka-Venus; Amatya Karaka-Moon; Bhratrakaraka-Mercury; Matrakaraka - Mars; Putra Karaka - Jupiter; Gyatikaraka - Saturn; Dasakaraka - Sun.

From the 11th house of AARUDHA LAGNA the economic condition is known. Here Scorpio-Moon aspects the 11th house. Moon is in debilitation. Hence, due to NEECHA aspects on 11th house economic condition was poor. Sign Aries, Cancer-Jupiter, Libra aspects the 12th house of Pada Lagna, i.e., Aquarius sign and 5 planets in 12th house of birth Lagna, too, show more expenditure than income.

Mother expired on 15-12-1938; Father expired on 23-9-1939. The first wife expired in June last week in 1942. Second marriage took place in 1943 at the age of 35 with the younger sister of first wife.

In Uppada Lagna (Pada Lagna of 12th house) when there is Mercury in 2nd house in own sign the wife of the native expires. Here is Mercury in 2nd house in Gemini. Hence truely the first wife expired early. Malefics too in 2nd house of Uppada Lagna destroys wife. In Gemini in 2nd house from Uppada Lagna SUN, MARS, RAHU 3 Malefics are present.

Secondly when Gemini falls in 2nd house of Uppada Lagna man marries more than once. According to this rule of Gemini this man married second time.

UPPADA LAGNA is the Pada Lagna of 12th house. There is Gemini-Mercury in 12th house from Lagna. Hence 12th house from Gemini will be in Taurus sign in llth house of birth lagna. In the same way by the position of Lord of particular house in a particular house may be counted from his own sign to the position of planet. So Pada lagna of each house may be found and results of that particular house may be gained.

According to Jaimini if there is Moon in the seventh house in Uppada Lagna the person is blessed with a son. In this example Moon is in 7th house of Pada Lagna so only one son was born who is still living. This is hundred per cent true and correct. In the same way if there is Jupiter in 3rd house of Uppada Lagna the person has many brothes. This is again also true. He had five brothers including himself. Readers may experience the truth of Jaimini Astrology.

In Jaimini Astrology there are many Dasa systems one of them is CHARA DASA which has been analysed in Jaimini Astrology -II article. Now we come to see and judge the other Dasa system " STHIRA RASHI DASA" of Jaimini Astrology generally CHARA RASHI DASA and STHIRA RASHI DASA indicate the periods of death of wife, parents, other relations accurately. In Sthira Dasa years are fixed for Chara Rasi - 7 years; for Sthira Rashi- 8 years and for dual (DWISWABHAVA) Rashi - 9 years by Maharishi Jaimini. To decide from which Rashi Dasa should begin, see which Rashi in strong among all 12 Rasis in Horoscope. The sign which has more planet in stronger than others to which have less or no planets therein. In the present example 'Gemini' is the strongest of all the rasis. Hence we start Sthira Rasi Dasa from left to right as Gemini is an odd sign.

Mercury is in own house with his friend Sun, Venus, Rahu. Venus is in Vargottama Navamsa. Mars too is in Gemini. Thus being 5 planets in Gemini it has been strongest of all. In Jaimini Astrology Sthira Rasi is stronger than chara, DWISWABHAVA (Dual) Rasi is stronger than Sthira. Hence Dual sign is stronger than Sthira and chara Rasis. So Gemini being dual too is strong.

Gemini Rasi Dasa Table (Main Dasa)

From Date of birth 15-06-1908 to	*Years*	*Sign*
15.06.1917	9	03
15.06.1924	7	04
15.06.1932	8	05
15.06.1941	9	06
15.06.1948	7	07
15.06.1956	8	08
15.06.1965	9	09
15.06.1972	7	10
15.06.1980	8	11
15.06.1989	9	12

According to Maharishi Jaimini if Sun-Mercury combine in 12th house in Gemini then in 3rd or 5th Rasi Dasa death of parents occurs. Here from birth Lagna 3rd Rasi is Virgo and parents died in Virgo Dasa. Thus truth of Jaimini Astrology is true.

In Trikona Rasi Dasa from matrakaraka death of wife occurs. Here Mars is Matrakaraka according to Jaimini system and Mars is in Gemini and from Gemini trikona Rasis are Gemini-Libra-Aquarius or 3-7-11 Rasis. First wife expired in 1942 in Libra Rashi. Now let us see the antardasa chart of Virgo and Libra Rasis in which death of parents and wife occured. Death of self occured on 23-7-1982 in Pisces Dasa.

Antar Dasa chart of Main Virgo Rasi Dasa

Antar Dasa of Virgo started from 15.06.1932 to 15.06.1941 from 15.06.1932	*Antar Dasa Months*	*Sign*
15.03.1933	9	06
15.12.1933	9	07
15.09.1934	9	08
15.06.1935	9	09
15.03.1936	9	10
15.12.1936	9	11
15.09.1937	9	12
15.06.1938	9	01
*15.03.1939	9	02
**15.12.1939.	9	03
15.09.1940	9	04
15.06.1941	9	05

*Death of Mother on 15-12-1938 in Taurus antardasa.

**Death of Father on 23-9-1939 in Gemini antardasa.

Taurus is 8th sign from 4th house (house of mother) in birth Lagna and seventh from Moon, 12th from Matrakaraka Mars. Father expired in Gemini Antar - Gemini is 3rd from 10th house (House of father) and 8th from 8th house from 10th house, i.e., 5th house in birth Lagna. See the Navamsa chart where Taurus is in 9th house and Gemini is in 10th house. Taurus is 12th house from position of Venus in Navamsa chart and Gemini is 12th from Cancer (Moon sign, Naisargik karaka for mother and third from Mars) Jaimini Matrakaraka.

Now we see Prityantar Dasa. Dasa chart of Taurus and Gemini for clear justification of death of parents. Antar Dasa period 9 months. 9x30 =270-M2 = 221/2 days for each Prityantar.

Virgo-Main-Taurus-Antar Capricorn-Priyantar

Prityantar Dasa remained wef 15.6.1938 to 15.3.1939 From 15.6.1938	*Prityantar Period in Days*	*Sign*
7.7.1938	$22\frac{1}{2}$	2
30.7.1938	$22\frac{1}{2}$	3
23.8.1938	$22\frac{1}{2}$	4
16.9.1938	$22\frac{1}{2}$	5
8.10.1938	$22\frac{1}{2}$	6
31.10.1938	$22\frac{1}{2}$	7
22.11.1938	$22\frac{1}{2}$	8
14.12.1938	$22\frac{1}{2}$	9
8.1.1939	$22\frac{1}{2}$	10
30.1.1939	$22\frac{1}{2}$	11
21.2.1938	$22\frac{1}{2}$	12
15.3.1938	$22\frac{1}{2}$	1

Mother expired in Rasi Dasa VIRGO Antardasa TAURUS PRITYANTAR CAPRICORN. These three Rasis are TRIKONA RASIS Mutually.

Virgo Main-Gemini Antar
Aqauarius-Prityantar

Prityantar w.e.f. 15.3.1939 to 15.9.40 From 15.3.1939	*Prityantar Dasa*	*Sign*
17.4.1939	$22\frac{1}{2}$	3
1.5.1939	$22\frac{1}{2}$	4
23.5.1939	$22\frac{1}{2}$	5
15.6.1939	$22\frac{1}{2}$	6
7.7.1939	$22\frac{1}{2}$	7
30.7.1939	$22\frac{1}{2}$	8
22:8.1939	$22\frac{1}{2}$	9
14.9.1939	$22\frac{1}{2}$	10
6.4.1939	$22\frac{1}{2}$	11
29.10.1939	$22\frac{1}{2}$	12
22.11.1939	$22\frac{1}{2}$	1
15.121939	$22\frac{1}{2}$	2

Father expired in Main Dasa GEMINI Prityantar Aquarius, Aquarius Sign in 12th sign from 9th Sign (PISCES) and eleventh to Aries.

FIRST wife expired in Main Dasa Libra-antardasa Scorpio

15.6.1941 to 15.6.1948 From 15.6.1941	*Prityantar Dasa Dasa of Libra Months*	*Sign*
15.1.1942	7	7
15.8.1942	7	8
15.3.1939	7	9
15.10.1943	7	10
15.5.1944	7	11
15.12.1944	7	12
15.7.1945	7	1
15.2.1946	7	2
15.9.1946	7	3
15.4.1947	7	4
15.11.1947	7	5
15.6.1948	7	6

Main Libra antar Prityantar Dasa Cancer

From 15.1.1942	*Prityantar Dasa Days*	*Sign*
2.2.1942	$17\frac{1}{2}$	8
20.2.1942	$17\frac{1}{2}$	9
10.3.1942	$17\frac{1}{2}$	10
27.3.1942	$17\frac{1}{2}$	11
14.4.1942	$17\frac{1}{2}$	12
2.5.1942	$17\frac{1}{2}$	1
20.5.1942	$17\frac{1}{2}$	2
7.6.1942	$17\frac{1}{2}$	3
25.6.1942	$17\frac{1}{2}$	4
12.7.1942	$17\frac{1}{2}$	5
29.7.1942	$17\frac{1}{2}$	6
15.8.1942	$17\frac{1}{2}$	7

Wife Expired in Libra Main, Scorpio antar, Cancer Prityantar Dasa in Last week of June 1942.

Death of self occurred in Main PISCES DASA. Now we see the antardasa chart of PISCES Rasi as following:

15.6.1980 to 15.6.1989 From 15.6.1980	*Antar Dasa Months*	*Sign*
15.3.1981	9	12
15.12.1981	9	1
15.9.1982	9	2
	9	3
	9	4
	9	5
	9	6
	9	7
	9	8
	9	9
	9	10
		11

Death occurred on 23.7.1982 in Taurus antar. Now look as the Prityantar Dasa of Taurus antar.

From 15.12.1981	*Prityantar Dasa Days*	*Sign*
6.1.1982	$22\frac{1}{2}$	2
28.1.1982	$22\frac{1}{2}$	3
20.2.1982	$22\frac{1}{2}$	4
12.3.1982	$22\frac{1}{2}$	5
5.4.1982	$22\frac{1}{2}$	6
27.4.1982	$22\frac{1}{2}$	7
20.5.1982	$22\frac{1}{2}$	8

13.6.1982	$22\frac{1}{2}$	9
5.7.1982	$22\frac{1}{2}$	10
27.7.1982	$22\frac{1}{2}$	11

Death occurred in Main Rasi Dasa of Pisces, Antar dasa of Taurus, Prityantar dasa of Aquarius.

In birth Lagna in Pisces there is Saturn lord of 8th house Taurus is aspected by Cancer-Jupiter, Libra, Capricorn, sign according to Jaimini aspects. According to Parashari Saturn aspects Taurus and Jupiter aspects Saturn lord of Capricorn and Aquarius.

According to Vimshottri Mahadasa Mercury Mahadasa was at balance 7 years 7 months 19 days. Duing Venus Mahadasa Parents' and wife's deaths occured. During Rahu Mahadasa Mars antar from 9-6-1982 to 27-6-1983, Native himself expired. Rahu-Mars are together in 12th house in birth Lagna.

KARKAMSA AND RASI DASAS IN JAIMINI ASTROLOGY

In Jaimini Astrology Atmakaraka is that planet which has the highest degree among other planets and in which Navamsa that planet is posited is known as Karkamsa. Hence Atmakaraka is the main planet according to Jaimini Rishi.

In Navamsa chart its position in 12 houses are as follows :-

First house : - Good health, handsome, attractive personality.

Second house :- Good nature, wealthy, honourable.

Third house :- If malefics then good, brave deeds are done. If benefic then moraly sensitiveness.

Fourth house :- Popular, feels happiness in public deeds.

Fifth house :- Good logic, wise, man of minister rank.

Sixth house :- If malefic defeats enemy if benefic then coward.

Seventh house :- Lover of beautiful ladies, sexy, travelling.

Eighth house :- Art of living well sicky and afraid.

Ninth house :- Lucky, rise in public life soon, Fame in good deeds.

Tenth house :- Most honourable, world famous.

Eleventh house :- High income in life from many sources, but greedy.

Twelfth house :- Expensive, good or bad action according to benefic and malefic.

In Jaimini Astrology there are many Dasas Chara Dasa is the first Dasa. There are some rules of Chara Dasa which are as follows :-

In Jaimini Astrology Rasis aspect each other and not the planets as in Parashari System. Planets only aspect with Rasis.

Taurus, Cancer, Libra, Sagittarius, Pisces Dasas generally give good results. Gemini, Virgo give good result in case of education, service, marriage, promotion, progeny etc. But these rasis should not be in 6, 8, 12 houses or connected with the lords of 6, 8, 12 houses.

On the other hand, Aries, Leo, Scorpio, Capricorn, Aquarius give bad results as they are the rasis of malefics. In these rasi Dasas main events like money loss, depression, litigation, travels in service, occupation and sudden transfer, insomnia, break in education, death of parents unhappy life are generally seen.

If there is Ketu in Scorpio, the Scorpio dasa goes most trouble some. Rahu too placed with rasi Dasa gives bad results. The person may be deprived of houses, property, may be transferred to a far distant place, may go far from parents and birthplace.

Exceptionally sometimes Ketu in Scorpio gives beneficial results too. Rahu in Aquarius in Aquarius Dasa too gives good results. But antar Dasa of Scorpio-Ketu is seen troublesome In other rasis Ketu gives generally beneficial results.

From Ascendant 6, 8,12 rasi Dasas are generally bad. Moon-Venus in Second house from rasi Dasa is beneficial in case of money matters and education. But on the other hand if Moon Venus are in 12th house of Dasa rasi then loss of money is indicated. In second house Rahu from Rasi Dasa deprives of money, trouble in Service, occupation, suspension, degradation, fine, loss of money heavy expenditure, trouble to parents etc like bad results are experienced.

Mars and Ketu in 12th house from Rasi Dasa give fire accident when Dasa- Rasis between 2 malefics then imprisonment (jail), loss of money be the result and if Dasa rasi lord too is in bad position then sudden accident or even death is indicated.

Marriage According to Jaimini is Performed When

(1) In which Rasi Dasa Darakaraka, Ketu, Venus are posited in that rasi dasa, antar dasa marriage is possible.

(2) In rasi dasa of lagna or PADA LAGNA.

(3) In seventh Rasi Dasa from Atmakaraka.

(4) In rasi dasa of UPPADA too marriage is possible.

(5) In rasi dasa of Darakaraka,Dara- PADA.

For Service, Occupation, Promotion

(1) In which Rasi Sun and Venus are posited in dasa of that rasi.

(2) In 5, 9 rasi dasal from Venus. Jupiter Moon or 5, 9 rasis aspected by these planets.

(3) In 10th rasi dasa or when lord of tenth in posited in that rasi Dasa.

(4) In any rasi Dasa from where in 10th house are with benefics or aspect by benefics.

In Jaimini Astrology Rasis Aspect as Follows :-

CHARA RASIS - Aries, Cancer, Libra, Capricorn rasis aspect 5, 8, 11 rasis from them.

STHIRA RASIS - Taurus, Leo, Scorpio, Aquarius aspect 3, 6, 9 rasis from them.

DWISWABHAVA RASIS :- Gemini, Virgo, Sagattarius, Pisces aspect 4,7, 10 rasis from them.

In Jaimini Astrology Rasi Dasas for CHARAS. Dasas are not fixed Parashari for planets, that they are to be fixed according to the position of lord of each rasis far from them.

Generally results of Jaimini Astrology are wonderful and nearer to truth than any other system of Astrology.

13

Reliablity of Vimshottari Mahadasa System

Vamshottari Mahadasa System is the most reliable Dasa System Propounded by the great Maharishi Parashar in Indian Astrology. In this system the total average age of human being is recognised 120 years as Sun—16 Years, Moon 10 Years, Mars-7 Years, Rahu-18 Years, Jupiter-16 Years, Saturn-19 Years, Mercury-17 Years, Ketu-7 Years, Venus-20 Years. This system is based on birth Nakshatra of the Native e.g.
Born in Kritika, Uttra Phulgun, Uttra Shada get SUN MAHADASHA-6
Born in Rohini, Hasta, Sravan get MOON MAHADASHA-10
Born in Mrigsir, Chitra, Dhanishtha get MARS MAHADASHA-7
Born in Aridra, Swati, Shat Bhisha get RAHU MAHADASHA-18
Born in Punarvasu, Vishakha, Poorva Bhadrapada get JUPITER MAHADASHA-16
Born in Pushya, Anuradha, Uttra Bhadra pada get SATURN MAHADASHA-19
Born in Ashlesha, Jyeshtha, Revti get MERCURY MAHADASHA-17
Born in Magha, Mool, Ashwini get KETU MAHADASHA-7
Born in Poorva Phulgun, Poorva Shada, Bharmi get VENUS MAHADASHA-20

Total 120 Years

Before discussing the Mahadasha analysis of different Planets we should understand and keep in mind the following things. JEEVANATH in BHAVA KUTUHAL says that Planets in odd Signs

1-3-5-7-9-11 from 0° to 6° are said to be in Balyawastha
1-3-5-7-9-11 from 7° to 12° are said to be in Kumarawastha
1-3-5-7-9-11 from 13° to 18° are said to be in Yuvavastha
1-3-5-7-9-11 from 19° to 24° are said to be in Vriddhawastha
1-3-5-7-9-11 from 25° to 30° are said to be in Mritawastha.

Planets in even sign 2-4-6-8-10-12 are to be understood in opposite order. Any Planet whether benefic or malefic gives normally good or bad results in Balyawastha. Half good or bad in Kumarawastha, Fully good or bad in Yuvawastha, but towards results in Vriddhawastha and zero results in Mritawstha. Planets are divided in 8 kinds as following:-

1. A Planet in Exaltation is in DEETAWASTHA the best of all the position in respect of effects in Mahadasha and antardasha. Its results are success in every field of life, defeat of enemies, going on Pilgrimages, genuninners, name, fame, lands, and all comforts and Luxuries in life. Planets in Exaltation are—SUN in Aries, MOON in Taurus, MARS in Capricorn, Mercury in Virgo, Jupiter in Cancer, VENUS in Pisces, SATURN in Librra. RAHU Iin Taurus, GEMINI, VIRGO gives like exaltation results. KETU in Scorpio, Sagittarius, Pisces gives like exaltation results.

2. A Planet in own sign is said to be in SWASTHAWASTHA. The results of such Dasa are wisdom, benefit, defeat of enemies, kind. hearted men, fame, noble deeds, recognition by king or State Government. Own signs are as following For Sun, Leo, For Moon Cancer, For Mars Aries and Scorpio. For Mercury Gemini and Virgo, For Jupiter Sagittarius and Pisces. For Venus Taurus and Libra, For Saturn Capricorn and Aquarius.

3. A Planet in Sign of friends is known as in HARSHAWASTHA which gives happiness with friends, Sons, family and relatives. One will be religious, rich, wise, and will have knowledge of the results of other persons actions.

4. A Planet in SHUBHA VARGAs is to be in SHANTAWASTHA results are native will enjoy peaceful life, will have elders, live like kings, will have servants, be wise have literary instinct, be rich and devoid of disturbances of any kind.

5. UDIT Planet is known to be in ATISATWASTHA will be praised among wise man, will be healthy, wealthy and beautiful in appearance, garlanded and worshipped being head of the public institution, will speak sweet, pure and true words.

6. A COMBUST Planet is known to be in LUPTAWASTHA Planets are Combust or ASTA when they are for from Sun as following:- Moon by 12°, Mars by 17° Mercury by 13° Retrograded Mercury by 12°, Jupiter by 11°, Venus by 8° Combust Planet is considered as weak and the results are devoid of good deeds, defeated by enemies, fond of other's money and women, wondering uselessly in dirty, bad places. Will have sickness and disturbances of mind. He will have no success will be idle and Sinful.

7. Planet in debilitation is Said to be in DEENAWASTHA which makes the man weak in mind. He will suffer through kings, be deroid of god values, fond of others money and women and be in frustrations etc.

8. A Planet in a malefic sign or inimical sign is known to be in PEEDITAWASTHA. As a result one will be Sicky will suffer from many diseases, be unhappy, unrest and very idle, greedy and will suffer mentally.

The strength of BHAVA and Planet Plays important role in knowing the results of Mahadasha and antardasha. Besides these things the following should also be noted.

SATURN- As Maraka among all maraka planets, Saturn is more malefic planet. Saturn gives death in his own Mahadasha or antardasha as the case may be Lords .of 5th house and ninth house these are always beneficial whether malefics or benefic. The ninth house and its Lord are the most beneficial as ninth house is the house of fate and divine grace.

Lord is of 3,6,11 houses are always malefics whether they are natural malefics, or benefics. But Saturn as Lord of 11th for Pisces Lagna RASI in beneficial. Kalidas in Uttar Kalamrit Says "Saturn in PISCES, Libra and Sagittarius Lagnas gives wealth. I have experienced that when Saturn transists in 11th house to these. Ascendants then it is beneficial and becomes yoga Karak.

Lord of Quadrants : Benefics as Lords of 1-4-7-10 houses do not give good results, they always give bad results. The Moon, Mercury, Jupiter, Venus as benefics owening Kendras suffer from KENDRADHIPATI DOSHAS. Hence they give bad results.

RAHU-KETU: They give results of that Planet with whom they are or according to the Lord of house where they are. If with malefics they are malefics, if with benefics they are somewhat benefics.

LIFE SPAN: JEEVA NATH in BHAV KUTUHAL Says that if Lord of ascendant is the enemy of the Sun then Short life is indicated if Sam (सम) then middle life and if in friend's Sign Long life, if neutral Sign middle life but if enemy's Sign then short life is indicated. There are some rules which should be followed while predicting according to VIMSHOTTARI MAHA DASA.

Parmochcha or Highly Exalted Planets : The Sun upto 10° in Aries Moon upto 3° in Taurus, Mars upto 28° in Capricorn, Mercury upto 15° in Virgo, Jupiter upto 5° in Cancer, Venus upto 27° in Pisces, Saturn upto 20° in Libra. These Planets according to their position give good results in their Mahadasha Exalted Planets should not be in 6-8-12 houses or any way connected with Lords of Trika houses i.e., 6-8-12 houses.

Aarohi or Ascending Planets : One Sign behind exalted Sign is called Aarohi or ascending Planets. e.g. Sun in Pisces, Moon in Aries, Mars in Sagittarius, Mercury in Leo, Jupiter in Gemini, Venus in Aquarius, Saturn in Virgo, Rahu in Taurus, Ketu in Scorpio. Thus position of Planets increases the economic and material happiness, silver, gold, land rise in business etc.

Awarohi or Descending Planets : A Sign a head of exaltation Sign is called Awarohi e.g. Sun in Taurus, Moon in Gemini, Mars in Aquarius,

Mercury in Libra, Jupiter in Leo, Venus in Aries, Saturn in Scorpio, Rahu in Cancer, Ketu in Capricorn. Mahadasha of Planets in these Signs gives diseases troubles, mental disturbances, fatigue Loss of Position, of health, of wealth etc.

Debilitated Planets: Mahadasha antardasha of debilitated planets brings loss of health, wealth and happiness. SUN in Libra, Moon in Scorpio, Mars in Cancer, Mercury in Pisces, Jupiter in Capricorn, Venus in Virgo, Saturn in Aries, Rahu in Sagittarius, Ketu in Gemini are debilitated (NEECH) But retrograde-cum debilitated planets give good results as they are equal to exalted planet.

Param neech or highly debilitated Planets: Just opposite to highly exalted degrees are Param neech degrees. The results are loss of position, Suspension or degradation in Service, Business, father's illness or death, unhappiness, mother's illness or death, mental disturbances, loss of money, income, illness to brothers, fear of fire and thieves, loss of health to maternal uncle, elders, wife, nervousness, unexpected accidents are according to occupation of the planets in different houses.

Moola Trikona Planets: Sun upto 20° in Leo, Moon upto 4°, in Taurus, Mars upto 12° in Aries, Mercury from 15° to 25° in Virgo, Jupiter in Sagittarius upto 10°, Venus upto 20° in Libra, Saturn upto 20° in Aquarius, Rahu upto 15° in Aquarius are said to be in Mool Trikona Position. Their Mahada of Antardasha is beneficial as regards monetary benefit and increase in Luck. According to BHAVARTHA RATNAKAR Taurus is exaltation Sign of Rahu, Gemini, Cancer are Mool trikon Signs, Virgo is own Sign and exalted too. For Ketu Pisces is own Sign, Libra is friends Sign, Aquarius and Scorpio are exaltation Signs of Ketu Sagittarius and Capricorn are Mool trikon Signs for Ketu.

Planets in Own Signs: When Mars in Aries, Scorpio, Moon in Cancer, Sun in Leo, Mercury in Gemini and Virgo, Jupiter in Sagittarius and Pisces, Venus in Taurus and Libra, Saturn in Capricorn and Aquarius. Then they promote education, living standard, fame, service, business and victory in their Mahadasha/antardasha. Planets in 1-5-9-10-11 houses play very important role in Promoting life and happiness. Planets in quadrants direct the native to go to foreign Countries in their Dasas. Dasas of Lords of evil houses 6-8-12 or of those placed in these houses or with their Lords, make relations by aspect or mutual exchange are troublesome and dangerous. They threaten the native life-span and happiness.

According to Phala Deepika 20/22

"वर्गोत्तमांशरूथ्ढ दशा शुभप्रदा मिश्रैव सा चास्तमिते च नचिगे
मृत्यु व्यय राशि दशापहारयोस्तत्र स्थितस्यास्यशुंभ फल भवेत्

Which means Planets in Vargottama Navamsa is beneficial, but if that Planet be in debilitation or Combust then mixed result is got. In Mahadasha of any one of Lords of 6-8-12 and antardasha of the other, the result is bad. In the same way the mahadasha of a Planet in 6-8-12 houses and antardasha of any other planet in 6-8-12 is also bad.

In PHALA DEEPIKA 20/20 MANTRESHWAR Says—

क्रूर ग्रहस्यैव दशापहारे त्रिपचसप्तर्सपसेर्विपाके तथैव
जन्माष्टमवाक्ष भुक्तौ चोरत्तर पीड़ां लभते ऽरिदुंख

This means that in the Mahadasha of Cruel planet and in the antardasha of Lord of 3-5-7. Nakshatras from birth Nakshatra, then the native's condition is very sad by sufferings due to thieves, enemie. Again in PHALA DEEPIKA 20/23 it is said—

शनैश्चतुर्थी च गुरोस्तु षष्ठी दशा
कुजाद्यार्येदि पंचमी सा कष्ट
भवेद्वारम वसान भाग स्थितस्म

दुःस्थानं पलेस्तथैव च means Dasa of Saturn in 4th, Jupiter in 6th, Mars and Rahu in 5th house that of a Planet in the last degree and that of Lords of 6-8-12 are very troublesome and painful.

The results of the Mahadasha, antardasha, and Pratyantardasha are exhaustively discussed in Phala Deepika JATAK PARIJAT, JATAK TATWA, Shundhanshu Hora Prakasa, SARAVALI, BRIHAT JATAK, Satya Jatkam and other books as LAGHU PARASHARI, JAT KA LANKAR, MAN SAGRI, JATKABHARAN and many many more books.

Often Prediction go wrong when made in haste without pondering over the strength, position, Sign of Planets. Hence we have to correctly measure the strength of the house and planet carefully in the light of the rules propoinded by great seers of Astrology.

Now I will give practical examples of Horoscope with events and dates occurred in certain Mahadasha/antardashas. Everybody wants to know about his future life. So I myself too was eager to know about my future. But I am unlucky in this matter as I have not got my horoscope. So to begin with I put my case study before some learned Astrologers and wise readers. I have in record horoscopes of my father, Uncles Brothers, their families, my wife, my children and other relatives.

I was born in a very poor family of SANADHYA BRAHMIN in a small village MAHANA 15 K.M. from ASHOKNAGAR (M.P.). My date of birth according to High School certificate is 30th December 1934. My father expired on 23-9-1939 and my mother expired before nine months of the date of death of my father, i.e., on 15-12-1938. My elder brothers brought me up with love and care So I could not feel parentless though I have to face a lot of difficulties and troubles to have my studies regular. Due to this Non-availability of my horoscope I began to learn Astrology since 1963. With the help of finger and thumb Prints and previous events My horoscope was prepared by an Astrologer of Maharashtra who fixed my date of birth 20th March 1934 at 9.30 A.M. But I am not satisfied with this Horoscope.

So I am presenting here the horoscope of my wife Smt. Kamla Devi Sharma born on 30-6-1937 at Ishta GHATIS 47 PALAS 22 in Poorva BHADRA PADA NAKSHATRA at AshokNagar (M.P.) Balane of Jupiter Mahadasha 12 years 5 months 26 days Planetary position is as following—

	Sign	*Degree*	*Kalas*	*Nakshatra*	*Charan*
Ascendant	11	20	02	REVTI	2
SUN	02	13	40	ARIDRA	3
MOON	10	23	30	POORVA BHADRA PADA	2
MARS	06	29	0	VISHAKHA	3
MERCURY	02	07	01	ARIDRA	1
JUPITER(R)	09	03	21	UTTRASHADA	3
VENUS	0	29	40	KRITIKA	1
SATURN	11	08	32	UTTRA BHADRAPADA	2
RAHU	07	21	3	ANURADHA	4
KETU	01	21	3	ROHINI	4

Here Lord of Lagna Jupiter and Lord of eleventh Saturn are in mutual exchange. Jupiter is in Nakshatra of Sun and Saturn is in Nakshatra of own. Mercury is in Nakshatra of Rahu in own sign is in 4th house producing BHADRA YOGA SUN- Mercury combination is also important. The Seventh house (house of husband) has been aspected by Lagna Lord Jupiter, Saturn and Ketu. Sun with Seventh Lord Mercury aspects the tenth house (house of Profession and fame, prestige)

According to BHAVA KUTUHAL 15/23

शुभग्रहा: प्रयच्छन्ति व्ययस्था विपुलं घनं Here Moon in 12th house is not bad because benefics or benefic aspected Planet in 12th house gives more money.

According to BHAVARTHA RATNAKAR

चतुर्थेस्सोम सुतो ज्योतिष शास्त्र विथारद: This means Mercury in 4th house makes the native expert in Astrology. Though this not applying to the native but applying on her husband (myself)

In PHALIT VIKAS RAMYATNA OJHA Says—

शुभा व्ययस्था द्रविणं सुखं च कुर्युन कुर्वन्ति रिपुद्गमच

Means benefics in 12th house give money and happiness. Here Moon is in 12th house

लाभस्थे हिमगौ सुरेन्द्र सचिवे सद्वस्त्र कान्ता सुखं
विद्यावान्सद्यौ भवेतु मनुजो राजधिराजर्चित:

Means Moon or Jupiter in eleventh house makes the native wear good clothes, happiness of Spouse, wise, wealthy, worshipped by the king. Here Jupiter is in 11th house in debilitation in retrogression and has changed Sign with lord of eleventh Saturn. Saturn in Pisces Ascendant this cancelled debilitation of Jupiter.

According to Jain muni Rishi:

If Lord of Ascendant and 8th house are in movable Sign or

If Saturn in Dual Sign and Moon in fixed Sign or

If Hora Ascendant in dual and Moon in fixed Sign. In these 3 cases Long life is assured.

According to PHALIT VIKAS of Ramyatna Ojha If there is relation between Lord of Ascendant and Lord of eleventh then the native does pious deeds, be long lived, noble, rich and wise.

RAMANUJACHARYA in BHAVARTHA RATNAKAR Says

Mercury and SUN in a Quadrant, trine or in eleventh house make the person mathematician.

Ketu in 3rd house is Yoga Karak and gives beneficial results. Here ketu is in 3rd house. In man Sagari the following statement is given:—

विद्वानो राजमान्य: सेवाशील प्रियंवदा
यशस्वाच स्थिर द्रव्यो बुध सूर्य समागते

Sun-Mercury Combination makes the native wise, recongnised by the Government, service to others, Sweet Speaker, famous and wealthy. Sun-Mercury are in 4th house.

एकादशस्थतनुप सुजीवित सुत समन्वित विदिसन्
तेजं फलितं कुरुते पुरूषं बलिनां सुवाहनै युक्तिम्

This means if Lord of ascendant is in eleventh house the native lives happily with Sons is famous, genius, strong, have vehicles. Here Jupiter Lord of ascendant is in eleventh house:

तुर्यगते तुर्यपतौ पितरि रक्षंतिपाघाय मानकर:
विदित: पितृलाभ करो भवति सुघर्मा सुखी धनप

This means 4th Lord in 4th house makes the native rewarded by king, famous, beneficial to father, religious, happy and rich. Here Mercury is Lord of 4th house is in 4th house in Gemini: सूर्य मित्र गृहे ख्यात: शास्त्रज्ञ: स्वस्थ: सौहृद: means Sun in friends house makes the native famous, perfect in Shastras, healthy and kind hearted.

मानोजितार्थ सहितो माता तदराक्षिणी भवेत्सुखिनी
दीर्घायुमातृ सुखी पुरूषो लाभस्थितो

If the Lord of the tenth house is in eleventh house the native earns money with respect, is rich, secured by mother, Long Lived. Mother is long lived and makes the native happy. Mother of my wife died on 24-4-1999 at the age of 97 years.

BHAVARTHA RATNAKAR Says—

कर्मकारक देवेन्द्र पूज्यस्थ यदि विद्यते
संबंध कर्मनाथेन सत्कर्म निरतां भवेत्

If Karma Karak Jupiter has relation with Lord of tenth house the native does pious deeds. Here Jupiter is the Lord tenth house and in posited in eleventh house. Hence here Lord of Karma. BHAVA is Jupiter. The Lord of eleventh house Saturn sitting in Lagna in Jupiter's Sign aspects the tenth house. Hence Lord of Lagna, 10th house Jupiter has been related by aspect of Saturn on 10th house and having mutual exchange of Sign. For Pisces Ascendant Jupiter, Mars and Moon are Yogakaraka being Lord of Ascendant, tenth house-Jupiter, fifth house Lord-Moon, ninth house Lord-Mars. Saturn is also karaka for Pisces ascendant born natives. BHAVARTHA RATNAKAR Says—

राज्य लाभाधिपत्योश्च संबंधो यदि विद्यते
लाभाधिप दशाकाले राजयोगो भविष्यति

This means that if Lord of tenth and eleventh are related and there is Lord of eleventh's Mahadasa then Rajya Yoga is arisen.

Saturn is the Lord of eleventh being in Ascendant has relation with Jupiter In SATURN MAHADASHA following events occurred.

Saturn Mahadasha from 26-12-1949 to 26-121968

Antardasa	*From*	*to* *Main events occurred during this period*
SATURN	26-12-49 to 29-12-52	Husband Passed High School in 1951 Marriage on 18-19 February 1952

MERCURY	30-12-52 to 8-9-55	First Poem of husband published in VIRARJUN (Weekly) New Delhi 9-12-1951 Husband Passed Inter and B.A. Examination
KETU	9-9-55 to 11-10-56	Husband came in Government Service on 12-3-1956
VENUS	12-10-56 to 17-12-59	Husband Passed M.A. Ist daughter born on 31-3-57
SUN		18-12-59 to 29-11-60 Husband Passed B.Ed. Promoted as H.M. MIDDLE SCHOOL
MOON	30-11-60 to 29-6-62	Son born on 30-6-61 Promoted as Lecturer On 7-7-61 Land for house bought on 23-10-1961
MARS		30-6-62 to 8-8-63 2nd Son born on 21-4-1963
RAHU		9-8-63 to 14-6-66 Ist half was better than second half.
JUPITER	15-6-66 to 26-12-68	Father of the native expired on 31-8-1966 More Interest in Astrology rose.

Marriage held on 18-19 Feb. 1952 when Moon was in Anuradha Nakshatra (Saturn's Nakshatra) Jupiter was in Hasta nakshatra (Moon's Nakshatra), Saturn was in Revti Nakshatra (Mercury's Nakshatra). It means Saturn was in Pisces, Jupiter in Virgo, Moon in Scorpio.

In Saturn Mercury Husband Passed Inter in 1953 and B.A. in 1955 Mercury is Lord of 4th and 7th houses. Mercury is Karak for education and as 7th Lord Karak for Husband.

In Saturn-Ketu Husband came in Government Service on 12-3-1956 as Graduate Teacher. Ketu in 3rd house is Yoga Karak aspecting the 9th house the house of Luck.

In Saturn-Venus Husband Passed M.A. Examination in 1957

First daughter Sharda born on 31-3-1957

In Saturn-Sun Husband Passed B.Ed. Examination in 1960 Promoted as Head Master in Government Middle School.

In Saturn-Moon- This was the golden period of Life. Ist son Rakesh born on 30-6-1961. Promoted as Lecturer in Government Higher Secondary School on 7-7-1961. Land bought for house construction on 23-10-1961. Arrears of Revised Pay Scale Received in February 1962. This was due to the fact that Lord of 5th house Moon is related to Saturn being in Moola Trikona Sign of Saturn Aquarius and Moon is in trinal position to 4th house (House of Land, Property, Happiness) SATURN as dasa Lord being Lord of eleventh has relation with 10th Lord Jupiter by mutual exchange of Signs. Saturn in Pisces and Jupiter in Capricorn. In Saturn-Mars 2nd Son ADITYA was born on 21-4-1963.

Pandit Ram yatna Ojha in Phalit Vikas says that Dasa of Lord of eleventh and Planet seated therein is troublesome to Parents. Hence on 31-8-1966. Father of the native died in Saturn-Jupiter period.

Mercury Mahadasha 26-12-1968 to 26-12-1985

In Mercury-Mercury antar w.e.f. 26-12-1968 to 23-5-1971. On 13-2-69 Last issue BHARTI was born. This period was well to husband. He was transferred to VIDISHA (M.P.) Ist Radio Broad Cast on AIR BHOPAL in December 1969. Ist Astrological Article was published in the Astrological magazine in July 1969 Published from Bangalore. He was the founder-secretary of the VIDISHA JILA HINDI SAHITYA SAMMELAN. The Literary Activities developed due to the fact that Mahadasha of 4th Lord Mercury and its antardasa was running.

In Mercury-Ketu: W.e.f. 24-5-1971 to 20-5-1972. This was not good period. The native fell ill. This was because Ketu is in 12th house to Dasa Lord Mercury.

In Mercury Venus w.e.f. 21-5-1972 to 20-3-1975. Venus as Lord of 3rd and 8th house. Hence this period was not good. Such Period of Sun (Lord of 6th) Moon (Lord of 5th) Mars (Lord of second) and Rahu were trouble some. Though marriage of daughter was held on on 27-11 1978 in Antar dasa of Rahu. The daughter was ill and took long time in treatment. In Mercury Jupiter w.e.f. 12-1-1981 to 7-4-1983. This period was good. The husband (myself was promoted at Principal Government Higher school On 25-3-1982. In July 1982 the eldest brother Shri Narayan Prasad (of husband) expired on 23-7-1982. Husband too was in grip of Dengu fever in October 1982. Eleventh house is the house of elder brother and there is Jupiter. From Dasa Nath Mercury, Jupiter is in 8th house hence death of eldest brother of husband justified. Mercury-Saturn period gave mixed results.

Ketu Mahadasha w.e.f. 26-12-1985 to 26-12-1992

Though Ketu in 3rd house is recognised as yoga karak. In Ketu Mahadasa mixed result was experienced.

In Ketu-Ketu-20-12-85 to 23-5-86 – Mixed Result

In Ketu-Venus 24-5-86 to 23-7-87- Marriage of elder Son Rakesh in June 1986. Son-in-Law fell ill.

In Ketu-Sun-24-7-87 to 29-11-87 Birth of grand Son Deepesh on 14-8-1987.

In Ketu-Moon-30-11-87 to 29-6-88 generally tension making period.

In Ketu-Mars-30-6-88 to 26-11-88- Husband's elder brother DAMODAR PRASAD expired on 23-9-88. On 3-11-1988 Son-in-Law Ajay Sharma expired due to failing of Kidney transplantation. Mars and Ketu are in 6-8 Position.

In Ketu-Rahu w.e.f. 27-11-88 to 14-12-89-Mixed Result.

In Ketu-Jupiter 15-12-89 to 20-11-90. Pilgrimage due to aspect of Ketu on 9th house and 11th house where Jupiter is seated.

In Ketu-Saturn from 21-11-90 to 29-11-91 Marriage of 2nd Son ADITYA on 17-2-1991.

In Ketu-Mercury from 30-11-91 to 26-12-92. This was good period to husband for ritual deeds. A NATIONAL ASTROLOGICAL CONFERENCE was held at Sironj (Distt. Vidisna) on 19-20 January 1992 which was appreciated through out India.

VENUS MAHADASA w.e.f 26-12-1992 to 26-12-2012

Antardasha in Venus Mahadasha is as following:-

Venus Mahadasha Venus Antardasha w.e.f. 26-12-1992 to 26-4-1996

Pratyantar Dasa in Venus-Venus period—

Venus Mahadasha Venus Antar-Party antar of Venus-26-12-1992 to 16-7-1993-Generally Good.

VENUS-VENUS-SUN-17-7-1993 to 16-9-1993-Ordinary.

VENUS-VENUS-MOON-17-9-1993 to 26-12-1983-Expenser.

VENUS-VENUS-MARS-27-12-1993 to 6-3-1994-Husband, wife both ill

VENUS-VENUS-RAHU-7-3-1994 to 6-9-1994-Generally Good

VENUS-VENUS-JUPITER-7-9-1994 to 16-2-1995-Ist book Published in Hindi released by Jagadguru Shankara Charya Swami Nischhala Nand Saraswati of Puri ओंकारलाल शर्मा प्रमद जीवन और काव्य संपादक - डा० श्यामसुन्दर 'सुमन' मथुरा Retirement of Husband on 31-12-1994 from the Post of Principal Government Girls Higher Secondary School, SIRONJ (Distt. Vidisha) M.P. Death of elder brother's wife on 12-1-1995 as Jupiter is seated in 11th house (House & elder brother) VENUS is lady Planet. Venus is Karak for Poetry too.

VENUS-VENUS-SATURN w.e.f. 17-2-1995 to 16-8-1995. Expense in House construction.

VENUS-VENUS-MERCURY w.e.f. 27-8-1995 to 16-2-1996-Marriage of 2nd daughter BHARTI on 27-11-1995.

VENUS-VENUS-KETU w.e.f. 17-2-1996 to 26-4-1996 Generally good.

BHAVARTHA RATNA KAR SAYS-

रंध्र भाग्याधिपस्योश्च संबंधो यदि विद्यते
अपरमाधिपतेदीये योगमादिशेत

This means that if the Lords of eighth and ninth houses have relation either by aspect, Combination or Mutual exchange of signs then in the Dasa of Lord of eighth *Moga* is fulfilled. Here Venus is the Lord of eighth house and is in Aries aspected by Lord of ninth and second house Mars who is giver of money and luck. Hence in Venus-Venus the Husband of the native (myself) retired and got money from pension payment in Venus-Venus-Saturn period as Saturn is too Lord of eleventh (Income). Venus is a benefic is in 2nd house (House of Family). Hence in this period marriage of 2nd daughter Bharti was ceremonised.

In VENUS-SUN Partyantar Dasa w.e.f. 26-4-1996 to 26-4-1997. VENUS-SUN-SUN 26-4-1996 to 14-5-1996 –Ordinary good.

VENUS-SUN-MOON-15-5-1996 to 14-6-1996-Ordinary or good result.

VENUS-SUN-MARS-15-6-1996 to 5-7-1996- Problematic Period.

VENUS-SUN-RAHU-6-7-1996 to 29-8-1996-Disturbances.

VENUS-SUN-JUPITER-30-8-1996 to 17-10-1996-Mixed Results

VENUS-SUN-SATURN-18-10-1996 to 14-12-1996-Sickness to husband and wife both.

VENUS-SUN-MERCURY-15-12-1996 to 5-2-1997-Some how good.

VENUS-SUN-KETU-6-2-1997 to 26-2-1997-Mental Worries.

VENUS-SUN-VENUS-27-2-1997 to 26-4-1997-Elder brother's wife of the native expired on 20-3-1996. w.e.f. 26-4-1997 to 26-12-1998 in Venus Mahadasha Antardasha of moon was running. This was the most important period to the husband (myself) of the Native because I wrote 2 Books in this Period JAI PARASHURAM (EPIC in Hindi) and MEDICAL ASTROLOGY in English. Awarded with GOLD MEDAL and Ph.D. (Astrology) Degree from the Open International University, Colombo (Sri Lanka). In Venus Mahadasha MARS Antardasha RAHU Pratyantardasha w.e.f. 20-1-1999 to 23-3-1999 Attack of Paralysis on me on 22-2-1999 at 10 P.M. was occurred but by the grace of ALMIGHTY GOD LORD PARASHURAM. It could not do any harm to my health except some weakness and tablets of B.P. are being taken by me since 25-2-1999 till now on Doctor's advice for safty and security of health. In Venus-Mars-Jupiter Pratyantar w.e.f. 23-3-1999 to 20-5-1999 the mother of the native (My mother in Law) died on 24-4-1999 at the age of 97. Good results too received-In Venus-Mars-Jupiter Pratyantar My elder Son Rakesh made a house at Vidisha (M.P.) House entry ceremony was performed. Jagadguru Shankara Charya Swami Swaroopa Nand Saraswati released my Hindi epic Book "JAI PARASHURAM" on 21-4-1999. In Venus-Mars-Saturn Deputy Director Mr. Bhandarkar of DOOR DARSHAN BHOPAL Came with his team at ASHOKNAGAR at my house to take interview in connection with poet Shri Krishna Saral and Astrology. My elder brother MADHO PRASAD RAJORIA expired on 23-12-2000 in Venus-Rahu-Jupiter w.e.f. 8-5-2000 to 2-1-2001. The nephew of my wife Kamla Devi Sharma Dr. Suresh Sharma expired on 20-12-2000 during the period.

In Venus-Rahu-Sun w.e.f. 29-7-2002 to 23-9-2002 My elder brother Liladhar Rajoria aged 88 fell on the flour and bone fracture on upper part of Buttock.

In Venus-Jupiter-Jupiter younger Son ADITYA SHARMA made the house at VIDISHA. Entry in the house was ceremonied in may 2003. In Venus-Jupiter-Saturn w.e.f. 4-7-2003 to 6-12-2003 my wife Kamla Devi became serious ill 21-30 October 2003. Now Venus-Jupiter antar is running till 26-10-2005.

Five Children Born to us

1. Daughter Sharda born on 31-3-1957 B.A., B.Ed. married to Ajay Sharma on 27-11-1978 widow on 3-11-1988. Donated a Kidney to save life of her husband in Jaslok Hospital Bombay in May 1986. Now teacher in Saraswati Shishu Mandir ASHOK NAGAR (M.P.)
2. Daughter born on 17-8-1959 expired on 4-5-1963.
3. Ist Son Rakesh Born on 30-6-1961 Diploma in Civil Engineering married on 28-6-1986 with Rajni. Grandson born Deepesh born on 14-8-1987. Grand daughter MADHVI born on 14-1-1990.
4. 2nd son ADTIYA born on 21-4-1963 Diploma in Photographer married on 17-2-1991 with SUNITA. Grand Daughter Yashi born on 11-7-1992.
5. Daughter BHARTI born on 13-2-1969 M.A., B.Ed, married on 27-11-1995 with Shailesh Sharma Serving in Central excise. Grand Son Naman born on 27-2-2000; GRAND Daughter Surabhi born on 7-8-2001.

14

Birth in Mool Nakshatras

Ashlesha, Jyeshtha, Mool these are major Mools and Ashwini, Magha, Revti these are minor Mool. The Lord of Ashwini, Magha and Mool is Ketu, Revti, Jyeshtha, Aslesha's 15 Lord is Mercury. God of Ashwini is Ashwini Kumar, of Magha Pitra, of Mool is Rakshasa of Revti is Poosha, of Ashlesha is Serpant, of Jyeshtha is Indra. Natives born in Mool Nakshatras suffer in one way or the other because they committed sins in Previous life. Hence their activities are not good and Shanti after 27 days in Major Mools and after 12 days and minor Mools is suggested.

If Birth in Ashada, Bhadrapada in Ashwini, Magha Nakshatras and 2,5,8,11 fixed Lagnas, they reside in heaven. *Sravan, Kartika, Chaitra Poosha in 3,6,9,12 dual Lagnas Mools reside in Land (BHUMI)* and in Phalgun, Margsheersha Vaishakha, Jyeshtha in 1,4,7,10 moving Lagnas Mools reside in Patal. Residence of Mools in Land is not good. The last two ghatis (48 minutes) of Revti, Ashlesha, Jyeshtha, and in beginning of Ashwini, Magha, Mools 2 ghatis (48 minutes) are called ganda Mool, not considered good in birth and marriage of the native. In marriages seven rounds must not be committed, in last 48 minutes of Revti and in beginning of Magha, Mools 48 minutes must be avoided as marriages are performed in Revti, Magha, Mool Nakshatras. Hence they must be avoided as they are harmful. Kalyan Verma in SARAVALI says.

जातो न जीवति नरो मातुरपथ्यो भवेत्स्वकुल हन्ता।
यदि जीवति गण्डान्ते बहुगज सुरगो भवेद् भूपः''

Those in gandant Mools are not good for mother, self and family. As they destroys the own family but if they alive then acquire elephants, houses and become kings. Vaidya Nath Says in *JATAK PARIJAT* 9/48

दिवाजातस्तु पितरं रात्रिजो जननी तथा
आत्मानं सन्ध्योर्हन्ति नास्ति गण्डे विपर्ययः''

Birth in day in first Quarter of Mool Nakshatra is bad to father, in night in second Quarter bad to mother, at evening morning twilight bad to self. Vaidya Nath says again

ऋक्षस्यान्ते भवेद्रात्रावादौ यदि दिने तथा।

सन्ध्यासु ऋर्क्षसन्धौ तु तदेतर यदि दिने तथा''

Birth in last Ashlesh, Jyeshtha in night is called ganda dosha (गंडदोष) at evening in Last of Cancer, Scorpio, Pisces Lagnas, in beginning of Leo, Sagittarius, Aries is called Riksha Sandhi Ganda ऋक्ष सांधि गंड These are not auspicious. By examples the matter is made more clear.

Example-1. *Female* born on 5-5-1959 Tuesday at 10.00 A.M. Revti Nakshatra 2nd Quarter. Lagna Gemini. Balance of Mercury Mahadasha. 10 years 7 months 12 days.

Birth Lagna

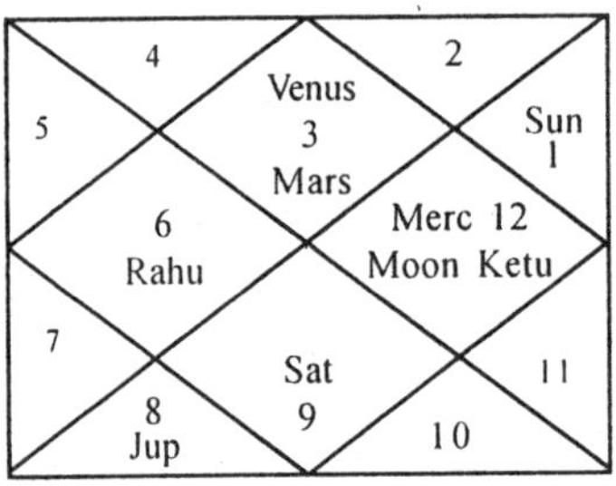

Navamsha

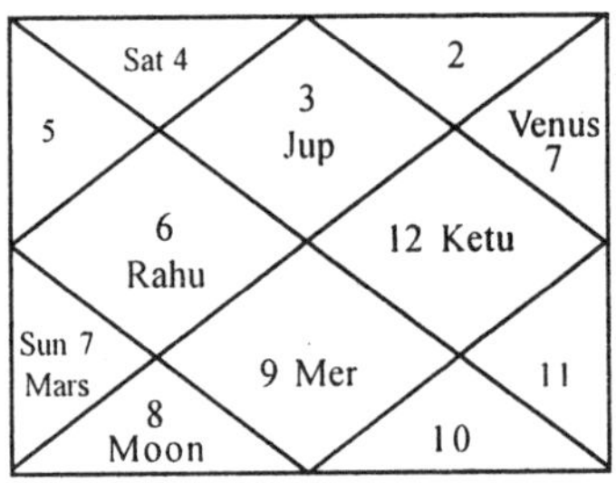

Lagna Gemini is in Vargottama Navamsa. Jupiter and Saturn both are retrograded. Lord of 6, 8, 12 houses (evil house) i.e. Lord 6th Mars in Lagna, Lord of eighth in Seventh, Lord of 12th Venus in Lagna and a benefic Jupiter in Sixth afflicted the Lagna and the 7th house. All the Quadrants 1-4-7-10 are occupied by malefics. The Lord of Lagna Mercury is debilitated in 10th house with Ketu and Moon. In Navamsa Jupiter and Mercury on one hand and Venus and Mars on the other hand exchange their Sign. The Moon in Navamsa is in debilitation in 6th house. Hence No Pleasure of marriage and sexual enjoyment. The Native got married in 1974 but after a short time the husband married other beloved woman without her consult. Now she is in Government Service Living with his father. VENUS, MARS, combination in Lagna and exchange of Venus and Mars in their Signs destroyed her married Life. Lord of Lagna and Lord of Revti Nakshatra Mercury also destroyed his married Life as Mercury is in debilitation under Malefic influence.

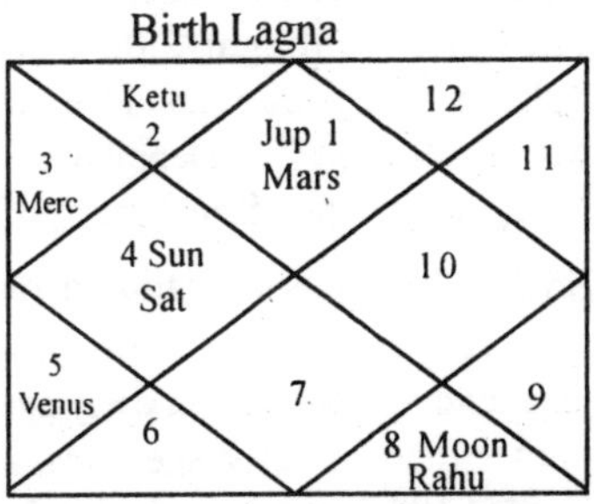

EXAMPLE-2. Male born on 19-7-1975 Saturday after mid night at 0.20 A.M. Jyestha 2nd Quarter. Balance of Mercury 10 years 4 months 15 days. Vaidya Nath in JATAK PARIJAT 10/66-68 Says

"सुखेशे त्रिके पितृसुखमल्पम्"

means if Lord of 4th house Peace and Happiness is less due to 4th house Lord Moon being in Neecha Sign in 8th house with malefic Rahu and also aspect of Mars. SATURN too aspects the Lagna. If Lord of 10th is in fourth house early death of father is indicated Saturn Lord of 10th is in 4th house with Lord of 5th Sun and a great enemy of Saturn. Sun is the Lord of 8th house from 10th house. Lord of 8th and 12th Mars and Jupiter in Lagna also made the native devoid of happiness of father.

EXAMPLE-3. Female born on 2-7-1966 Saturday at 5.25 a.m. Moola Nakshatra 3rd Quarter Lagna Gemini. Balance of Ketu 3 Years 4 Months 17 days.

In Birth Lagna tenth house is occupied by the Lord of eighth Saturn. Lord of 6th house, Mars is in Lagna. Moon in 6th house debilitated. SATURN and RAHU enemies of Putrakrak SUN and Jupiter. Rahu aspects

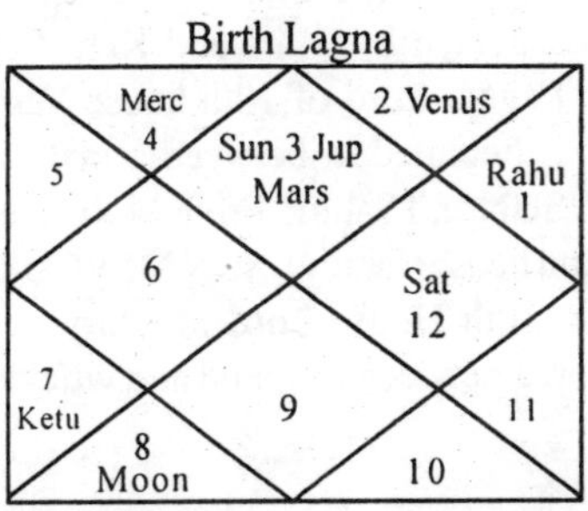

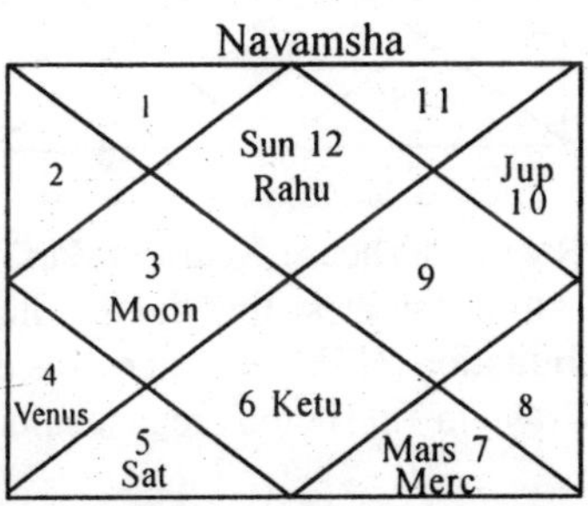

the 5th house, whose Lord is Venus in 12th house. Father of this native expired in April 1970 in Venus Mahadasha antradasha of Venus. She has not been married till now as 7th house is afflicted by Mars and Saturn's aspect on 7th house. More over RAHU too aspects the Seventh house. In Navamsa two malefics SUN (Lord of 6th) and Rahu are in Lagna. The Karaka for father, Lord of 10th Jupiter is in debilitation. Jupiter is also the Lord of Navamsa Lagna. Hence loss of father in early age and living unmarried is Justified. Malefics in 6, 7, 8 houses too are responsible.

Example-4. Male born Vikram Samvat 1997 Sravan Krishna 7 Friday birth after midnight 2.00 A.M. Ashwini Nakshatra Second Quarter Mantreshwar in Phal Deepika Says 19/26 भवति गुरू वियोगो वान्धवार्ति मनोरूक In venus Mahadasha old and respectable persons like teacher or parents die in early age. Father died in early age because Lord of 10th Saturn is in debilitaion (Neecha). Thus Saturn being weak aspects the tenth house. The Lord of 4th Moon and Lord of 12th Jupiter are with Saturn. Lord of 8th Mars with Lord of 6th Mercury are in 4th houses and aspecting too tenth house. In this way 10th house from Lagna and Moon are aspected by 4 malefics Saturn, Mars, Mercury, Rahu on 25-11-1995 Mother too died in the of 56. Father diod in Mohadasha of Venus casting maraka for Aries Lagna.

Birth Lagna

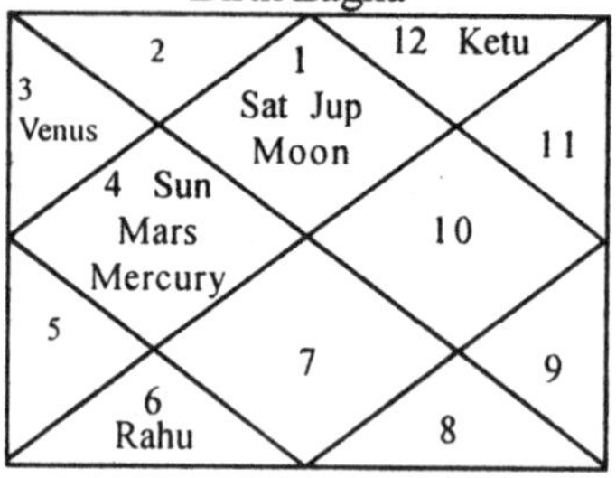

Example-5. Male born on 28-3-1943 Sunday Mool Nakshatra 4th Quarter after midnight at 2.00 A.M. Father of this native died early, got married with great difficulty. Because there is RAHU in 7th aspected by Mars and Ketu from Lagna. Lord of 10th house Venus is hemmed in between 2 malefics SUN and Saturn. From Moon there is Rahu in 8th house, Ketu and Mars in 2nd house (family), SUN MERCURY in 4th house aspecting due the house. 10th House Lord Mercury is in debilitation (NEECH). There was divorce between husband and wife due to Rahu in 7th He took renunciation.

Birth Lagna

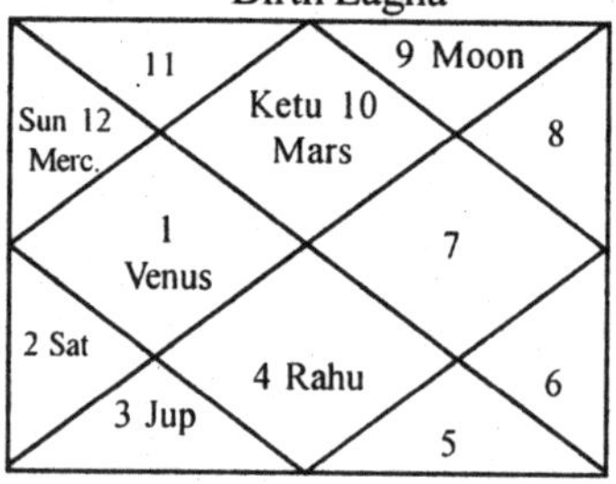

Example-6. Female born on 27-5-1955 Friday Ashlesha Nakshatra 2nd Quarter in Cancer Lagna. This is the Horoscope Birth Lagna of wife of Native of Example 5 (See above). Now if it seems that Jupiter Moon Combination in Cancer Lagna While Jupiter is in exaltation,

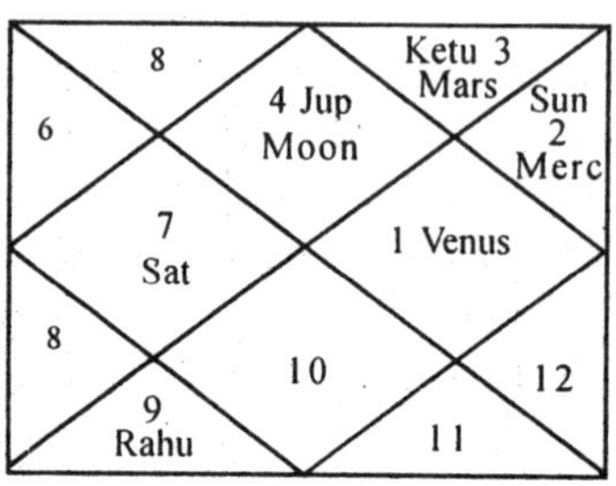

Moon in own Sign are strong but in result zero. Because the Lord of Seventh house. Saturn is in exaltation in 4th house retrograded but in Navamsa is in debilitation (NEECHA). Hence it has been powerless and unable to give sexual pleasure. Jupiter in Leo Navamsa, Moon in MAKARA NAVAMSA. Mars from 12th house aspects the seventh house. Debilitated (NEECHA) RAHU aspects the Main Yoga Karaka Mars for Cancer Lagna. Hence No happiness of married life and separation became necessary.

Example 7. Female born on 20-10-1974 Sunday after mid night at 1.00 A.M. in Moola third Quarter in Cancer Lagna. Father of this girl died of drowning in water before 45 days of her birth. When crossing a river. He wanted to go to the other side of the river to take Bilwa Pattaries for worshipping of Lord Shiva. Though the river was small. There was no sign of flood when he entered into the water but while in the middle of river floods struck suddenly and he was drowned. Even his dead body could not be found. Mahadev Pathak in "JATAK TATWA" Says that if Sun and Mars are in 10th house the father dies before the birth of Child. The Sun from 4th house and Mars from 3rd house aspects the 10th houses From Moon sign there are Mars and debilitated (NEECHA) Venus in Virgo in the 10th house. The Moon is badly afflicted by the debilitated RAHU in sixth house in Sagittarius aspected by 7th and 8th Lord Saturn. Jupiter as Lord of sixth house is in 8th house in Aquarius in 12th from the 9th house. Sun and Venus both are in debilitation (Neecha) in 4th and 3rd respectively.

Birth Lagna

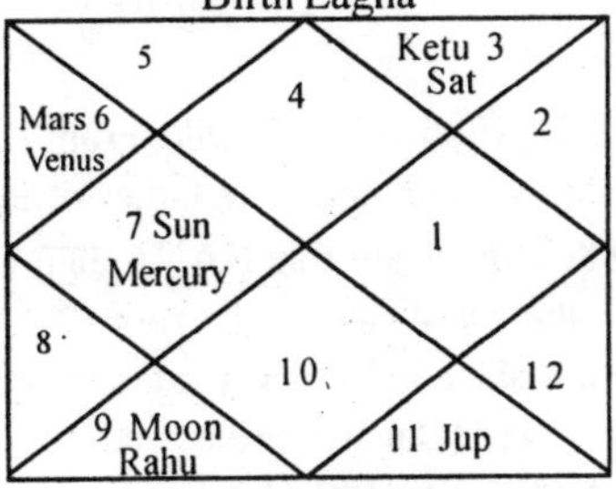

Example-8. Male born on 21-10-1955 Tuesday Mool Nakshatra first Quarter in Libra Lagna. Mother of this boy died early giving birth to this only one child. Lord of 4th Saturn in Lagna in exaltation (UCHCHA) with his great enemy Sun debilitated in Lagna with Lord of eighth house Venus. From Moon the fourth house is Pisces aspected by Mars and Mercury. Mercury being the Lord of 12th is not auspicious. Mother died in Ketu Mahadasha, a Planet in 8th house. Thus the fourth house from Moon is aspected by malefics. Moon is being aspected by Saturn and Mars.

Birth Lagna

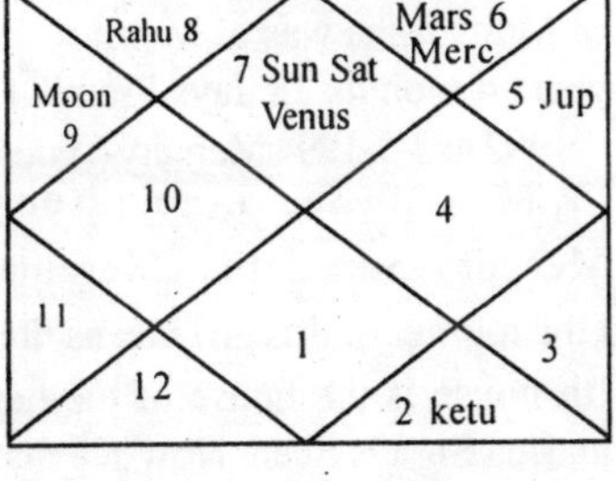

Example-9. Female born on 28-10-1984 Libra Lagna at 7.30 A.M. Jyestha Nakshatra 4th Quarter Sunday.

Birth Lagna

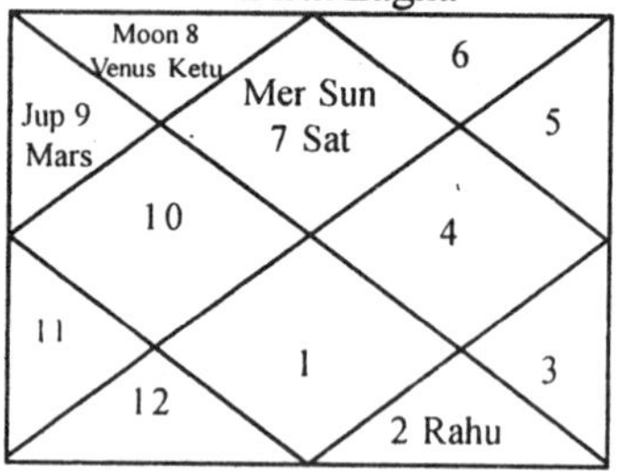

Planetary Position as following:-

SUN-6-10-52	SATURN-6-24-0
MOON-7-27-10	RAHU-1-4-53
MARS-8-26-8	KETU-7-4-53
MERCURY-6-23-1	Balance of Mercury
JUPITER-8-16-36	2 years 1 month 15 days

Mercury Mahadasha was w.e.f. 28-10-1984 to 13-12-1986. From 13-12-1986 to 13-12-1993 Ketu Mahadasha was running. The father of the mother of this female died on 23-9-1988. This means that NANA नाना of this girl Jyeshtha Born Child died when she was 4 years old. From 13-12-1986 Ketu was running and this event took place in Ketu Mahadasa Surya Antardasha. i.e. w.e.f. 10-7-1988 to 16-11-1988 'Day was Friday and Lagna was Scorpio. Now see the horoscope. Fourth house is the house of mother and mother's father house means 10th house from 4th house i.e. in Libra Sign there are SUN SAT and Mercury. From this house in 2nd House Ketu is posited who is Lord of Mahadasha Sun is in 12th house from Ketu badly afflicted by Saturn a great enemy of SUN in debilitation. Venus is in Scorpio and It was Friday whose Lord Venus is with Ketu and death was in Scorpio Lagna where Ketu and Venus both are present.

Example-10. Female born on 11-7-1992 Saturday at 10.7 P.M. in Aquarius Lagna Jyeshtha Nakshatra 2nd Quarter. The father of the mother of this girl it means NANA नाना died on 23-6-1994 at the age of about 2 years. Balance of Mahadasha was of Mercury 12 years 4 months 28 days From 11-7-1992 to 3-3-1994 Mercury-Venus. From 4-3-1994 to 9-1-1995 Mercury-Sun. In Mercury Mahadasha Sun antardasha the father of the mother of this girl means नाना NANA.died early See the horoscope 4th house is the house of mother From 4th house 10th house is where Aquarius Sign is Seen. Now see that

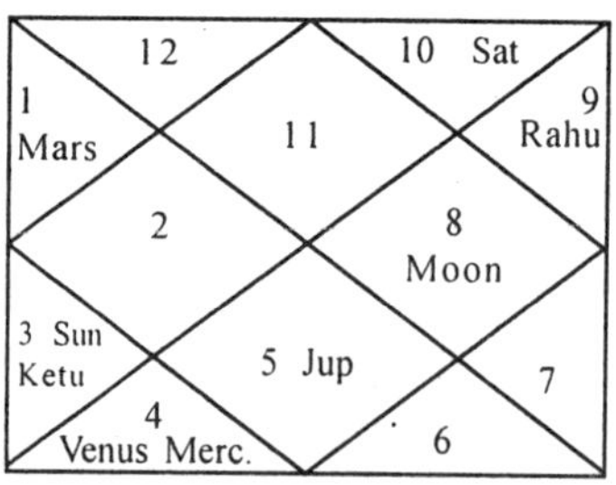

Aquarius Sign became the sign of NANA नाना of this girl. Mercury is Lord of the 8th house which is in 6th house means Lord of evil house Present in evil house, the Sun is in 12th house from Mercury. Hence in Mercury Mahadasha Sun antar the father of the mother of this girl died.

Birth Lagna

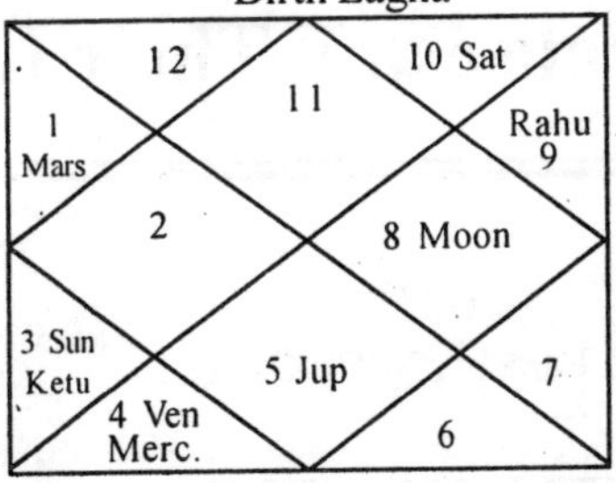

Now compare both horoscopes No 9 and 10. Both girls are born in JYESHTHA NAKSHATRA. NANA नाना of both girls expired inearly age before completing the age of 5 years.

In example No. 9 death of Nana happened in Ketu-Sun. Sun is in 12th house from Ketu.

In example No. 10 death of NANA happened in Mercury-Sun. Sun is in 12th house from Mercury.

15

Evil House and Their Lords

The great Sage Parashar पाराशर Says-

"लाभस्तृतीयो रन्ध्रश्च षष्ठभावो व्ययस्तथा
एषां योगेन यो भावस्तस्य नाशो भवेद् ध्रुवम्"

Means whatever Bhavas are related to the house of income (i.e. eleventh) third, eighth, sixth and twelfth are definitely destroyed. The Lords of 3, 6, 8, 11 and 12 Bhavas give sinful results, they are malefic. पतयास्त्रि षड़ायानां यदि पापफल प्रदा: It is clear by this verse. Besides the second and Seventh houses are also Marak or Killers as Parashar Says- अष्टमायुष स्थान मुच्यते Eighth house is the house of Life Span and another house of life Span is the third house. From the eighth house and third houses the seventh and Second houses are the twelfth houses respectively. Hence the 2nd and 7th house are marakas.

In this way the evil houses in a horoscope are 3, 6, 8, 11, 2 and 7 houses. Whenever their Lords Combine, aspect with Lords of other houses they totally give evil results. How these houses and their Lords affect other houses is made clear by giving examples experienced by me.

Example-1. Male born on 2nd November 1941 at 1.30 A.M in Cancer Lagna Dhanishtha Nakshatra 4th Quarter with a balance of Mars 1 year 5 months 15 days. Planetary Position is as following:-

Birth Lagna

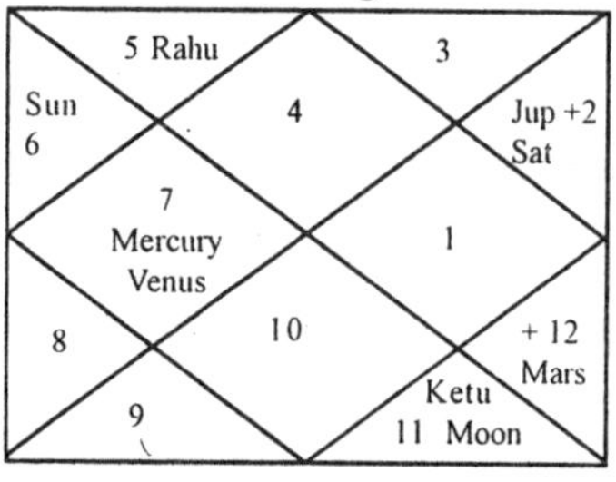

SUN-5-14-11; MOON-10-4-10; MARS; 11-24-18 (Retrograded) MERCURY-6-7-7; JUPITER-1-29-0; VENUS-6-29-3; SATUN-1-5-6 (Retrograded) RAHU-4-28-45; KETU-10-28-45.

This is the Horoscope of a person who is fighting for the last 38 years. His Life has become the second name of struggle. His forefathers migrated from Rajasthan to Madhya Pradesh some 70 or 80 years ago. His father and uncle lived together in a joint family till 1966 with ownership of 50 Buses and 12 Cinemas. In March 1966 after the nationalisation of Buses the family had to be separated and struggle began. The Native got half a part of the house and a Cinema in a city, the rest house was under Uncle's ownership with 2 Cinemas. The native lived with 3 brothers and parents. In 1967 elder brother separated from the family. On 16th January 1968 Father expired. Due to heavy burden of family the Talkies was given on rent while the loans increased. The younger brother worked with towering Talkies. The Native Being B.E., M.Sc. went outside for service to fulfill the requirements of the family. After 4 years, the Talkies on hire was under his possession in1978. The younger brother too separated and started a New Talkies in another town. His Talkies had to close down soon as case was executed in Supreme Court. The case was fought for 3 years and order of the Court passed in 1982. In 1983 after repairing the Talkies was again started. All was going well but on 3rd September 1984 the younger brother died of heart attack leaving behind his wife, three sons, 2 daughters. Three Marriages (one of the Native's daughter, 2 of younger brother's daughters) were performed on December 21, 1987; January 20, 1990, December 12, 1990 respectively. Now 3 boys (2 of the native and one of the brother and one daughter of younger brother are still due for marriage. Meanwhile the mother expired at the age of 96. Since then due to economic pressure loan increased upto 20 lakhs.

The native wants to sell the 4 storied Talkies and a towering Talkies both of Rs. 60-70 Lacks in value. But None is ready to buy at this price. Since 1-3-2000 Talkies are closed. On 16.11.2000 A customer was ready. He took all the materials and made the Cinema useless. On 10-3-2001 His partner died and the matter of selling cancelled. About 5 Lacks Loss occurred. During this period in the recovery of Income Tax the house behind Cinema in which he used to live with his family and the Shops in front of Cinema sold. Now one boys lives in a House of rent, the other in Cinema on upper storey and wife lives in office of the Cinema. Once again on 16-11-2002 the matter of selling Cinema has been settled but it is also to be broken. For the Last 3-4 years the family is in great trouble. Both boys are unemployed. Anyhow Living hand to mouth.

The native has mental tension, B.P. Swelling in Knees due to water according to Doctors, The wife of the native is also sick.

Sage Parashar Says about Cancer Lagna:-

भार्गवेन्दुसुतौ पापौ भूसुगुरवौ शुभौ।
एक एव ग्रहः साक्षात् भूसुतो योग कारकः।।
निहन्ता रविजोन्ये तु पापिनो मारकान्द्वयाः।
कर्क लग्नाद्भवस्यैवं फंलान्युक्तानि सुरिभिः।।

Means for those born in Cancer Lagna Venus and Mercury as Lord of 11,12,3 are malefics. Jupiter and Mars are benefics. Mars is special benefic being Lord of 5th and 10th houses. Saturn Sun etc are malefics and marakas. Jupiter being Lord of 6th is not beneficial. Here Jupiter as Lord of sixth house in eleventh house in Taurus Sign from sixth to sixth Sign and an inimical sign has become more malefic being in an evil house lost the beneficial Quality. Saturn being Lord of Seventh and eighth retrograded Rasi in eleventh house (house of income made the native wondering here and there in search of occupation on and business.

Most of the events of struggle, tension occurred in Jupiter Mahadasha. In the Present Case Dasa of Jupiter is that of VIPATTARA विपत्तारा प्रत्यरीशौ वधभेशस्तथैवच। मारका जातके प्रोक्ता: काल विदर्मनीषिभि:।। means the Lord of VIPAT, Pratyari and VADHA TARAS are called Marakas in Astrology. Division of family, Separation of brother, expiry of father, mother, younger brother, Court cases etc all occurred in Jupiter Mahadasha w.e.f. 17-4-1961 to 17-4-1977.

From 17-4-1977 to 17-4-1996 Saturn Mahadasha and From 17-4-1996 to 17-4-2013 Mercury Mahadasha running. The Lord of Lagna Moon is in eighth house with Ketu in the sign of Saturn who is Lord of Seventh and eighth houses which are marakas. Here the Moon's position is also the worst and Moon is aspected by RAHU from another Maraka house.

Though natural benefic Venus and Mercury both being the Lords of 4th-11th and 3rd-12th posited in 4th house are aspected by Vakri Mars, the Lord of 5th and 10th houses Killed the happiness. Mars though only benefic for Cancer Lagna is in 9th house of Luck in the sign of Jupiter but Mars is retrograded and is in the 12th house from 10th house, house of business. RAHU in 2nd in inimical Sign divided the family and interrupted the financial position. Only Sun, i.e., maraka Lord too is in 3rd well place, But only Sun could do nothing. The Lords of 3rd and 11th posited in 4th house aspected by Ketu from 8th house are also killing the happiness of the native.

In NAVAMSA Chart the Lord of birth Lagna. Moon is in debilitation (Neecha) in 2nd house, and wealth. Jupiter being Lord of 6th in Birth Lagna and Lord of 3rd and 6th in NAVAMSA is in 12th house. Mars and Saturn Combination in 5th house arose tension and B.P. to the native. Only Sun Lord of 11th is in exaltation but his sign is aspected by Saturn and Mars (Lord of 2,7) and RAHU could not give beneficial results. Lord of NAVAMSA Venus is in the sign of Lord of 12th house Mercury aspected by Mercury and Neecha-Rahu from 3rd house.

NAVAMSHA

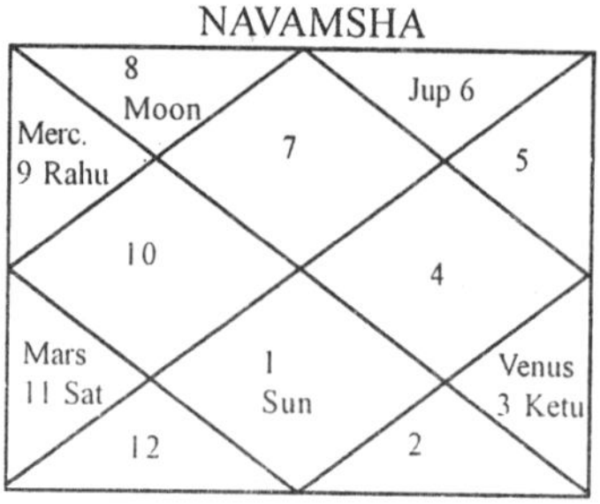

Thus we see that the Lords of 3,6,8,11,12,2,7 afflict badly the future of native and there is no hope for getting happiness because Lord of 12th from birth Lagna and Navamsa both, the Mercury's Mahadasha is running. Hence there are no chances of getting rid of troubles to the native.

Chart-2

Male born on October 6, 1955 at 8.35 P.M. in Taurus Lagna with a balance of Moon 1 Year 1 Month 6 Days Rohini 4th Quart with the following Planetary Position—

SUN-5-18-12; MOON-1-21-44; MARS-5-1-2; MERCURY-5-22-00; JUPITER-4-1-45; VENUS-5-27-30; SATURN-6-22-57; RAHU-7-26-12; KETU-1-26-12

BIRTH LAGNA

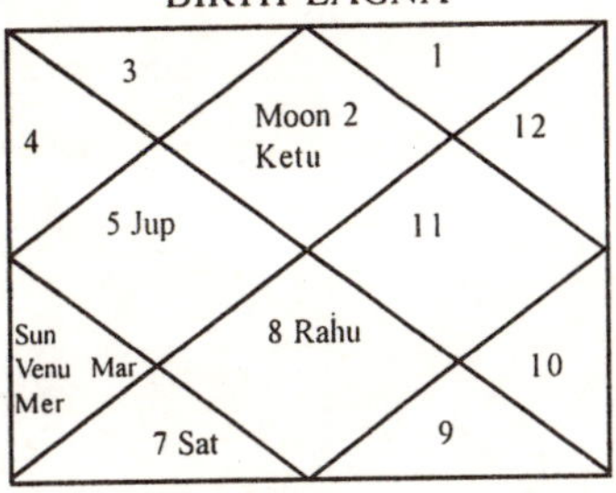

NAVAMSHA

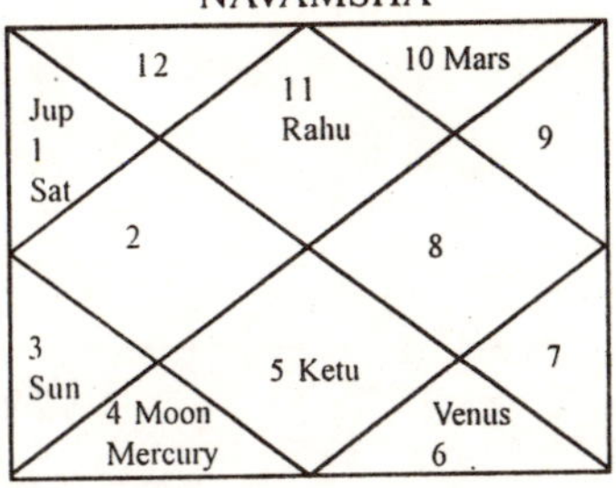

The Native of this Horoscope was in Government Service but being fond of own business left the Government Service. For Sometime he sold milk keeping Buffaloes them for sometime took agency work in food products. After that taking loan from the bank started a mill in 1992. All was going well since 1993 but all of a Sudden in August 1995 the loan increased due to fall in Prices he had to stop the mill. The person from whom he took loan began to trouble him. By Court Case he had to remain in jail in September 1995 for 15 days. Now he is puzzled about future course and cannot decide. Divorced his first wife for some family difficulties, got married second time.

See the position of Jupiter, the Lord of 8th and 11th being in 4th house in friendly Sign disturbed him when Jupiter transited in 8th house in Sagittarius. The Lord of Lagna Venus in debilitation (Neecha Rasi) hemmed between 3 malefics Sun, Mars, Saturn and Rahu. Exalted Moon being the Lord of 3rd with Ketu made him to do as he desired without thinking about future. Saturn the Lord of 9th and 10th being in 6th house in exaltation increased Loan on high level. Besides here is Kala-Sharpa कालसर्प योग too as all the planets between Rahu and Ketu. In Navamsa too there is

Rahu in Aquarius Lagna. The Lord of 9th and 10th houses Saturn exalted in birth is in Neecha Navamsa in 3rd house with 8th Lord Jupiter. Jupiter has been marak being Lord of second house in Navamsa Venus the Lord of Lagna is in Neecha Rasi in Lagna-Chart and in Navamsa too in Neecha Rasi getting the lowest position. Mars being the Lord of 12th house in Birth Lagna has fallen in 12th house in NAVAMSA in exaltation indicating high expenses. Moon with Lord of 8th Mercury did nothing except putting the native in the hell of High loans and giving less in business. This happened during Mahadasha of Jupiter and antardasha of Rahu w.e.f. 18-6-1995 to 12-11-1997. From 12-11-1997 Saturn Mahadasa is running and he is still wondering here and there doing nothing with the fear of loans as Saturn in exaltation in house of loan and in debilitation in 3rd house in Navamsa discouraging him.

16

Indian Religion Philosophy and Astrology

In Indian Philosophy knowledge is purposeful, i.e., Perfection of human life through knowledge. To gain perfection we try to understand the life and action of the world's people, Pray the GOD, meditate and do yogabhyas and Pranayama. This process of Praying the GOD for the welfare of human beings of the world is running from time immemorial since the existence of the UNIVERSE.

This UNIVERSE consists of five elements Fire, Water, Air and Sky Earth. In every thing these five elements are present whether it may be movable or immovable.

UNITY in DIVERSITY is the main Principle of Indian Culture and Civilization. Though the tendencies, inclinations of Science and Philosophy are similar but their scope is different. Science is related to the materialistic or outer side while Philosophy is related to the Spiritualistic or inner side of humanity.

VEDANTA (वेदान्त) is the Soul of Indian Philosophy. The IRON of Vedanta has been accepted by all the great thinkers as Kant, Shopenhover, GOTHE MAXMULLAR etc.

"अहंब्रह्मस्मि I am the ALMIGHTY GOD or BRAHMA. तत्वमसि or thou art the same सोहमस्म I am HE etc. are the Sutras of Vedas, the mother of Indian Religion and Philosophy.

Curiosity is the mother of knowledge and wisdom. When man in early days thought WHO AM I? What is this UNIVERSE? Who is the Controller of this world? What are the Stars, Sun and Moon? Can I know myself? These Questions are still to be answered.

In Vedas, Puranas, UPNISHADAS Our ancient seers of wisdom told that this world is full of lives. Nature is full of Mysteries. Nobody can boldly say that he has known the mysteries of Nature in full. Science Invented so many things wonderful in nature but the mystery of Nature is still to be discovered.

Science begins with UNITY to DIVERSITY while Philosophy begins from DIVERSITY to UNITY. This is the main difference between science and Philosophy. Thus unity among Diversity is the main Characteristics of Indian Philosophy. Spiritual thinking is over going (ऊर्ध्वगामी) while materialistic or Scientific thinking is down going (अर्ध्वगामी) that is why there is dissatisfaction, troubles, struggle, poverty among the countries or mostly in materialistic world of the western countries.

In reality Indian Philosophy is great. In western countries life is struggle for existence and survival of the fittest in the end (DARWIN) But we Indian do not stay here but go on ahead where trouble and happiness, Profit and loss, fame and defame, good and bad, friend and enemy, are equal. As our motto is "KNOW THY SELF" or Self Realisation is the goal of Indian religion and Philosophy.

In BHAGWAT GITA LORD KRISHNA Says to ARJUN वासुदेवः सर्वमिति स महात्मा सुदुर्लभः This world is VASUDEV (GOD) and the Saint who knows God is difficult to find. In ईशावास्योपनिष्द् (ESHAVASYOPNISHADA) the Rishi said "ईशावास्यमिदं सर्वं" Means this all the world is the abode of GOD. GOD IS OMNI PRESENT. He lives every where; every time, in everything of the world. In other words we can say UNIVERSE is the form of GOD. This world whom we see, hear, think, Percept is nothing but GOD. Our motto is "वसुधैव कुटुम्बकम्" The whole world is our family. My home is the whole world. The great Saint Poet TULSIDAS Said in RAM CHARIT MANAS कहहु सो कहाँ जहाँ प्रभुनाही Tell me where there is not GOD. These are the highlighted thoughts of Indian Wisdom and Philosophy. Ram Left the Kindom of Ayoddhya for keeping the words of his father Dash Ratha, Gautam Buddha and Mahavir Swami too left the kingdom for what & for Perfection, For Knowledge, for self Realisation. For removing the troubles of People. There is space for every body in our heart. Hence the great Sage told—

सर्वो भवन्तु सुखिनः सर्वे सन्तु निरामगा।
सर्वो भद्राणि पश्यन्तु मा कश्चिद् दुखमाप्नुययात्।।

Means all be happy, all be healthy, we wished welfare of all, Nobody be troubled, I translated this in Hindi—

सब सुखी हों, सब निरोगी, सबका हो कल्याण
कोई भी न दुख पावे हे मेरे भगवान!

Indian Philosophy realized and Said", एकं सद्विप्रा बहुघा वदन्ति नेह नानास्ति किंचन" "He is one vipras Say often and again the sage said", I am one and second is none. Lord Krishna too said in Bhagwat Gita Thou art born my Light's Part "The other great Hindi Poet JAYA SHANKAR PRASAD said" हमे जाना है जग के पार means we have to go beyond this materialistic world.

The modern materialism Says that Religion is the Opium for Indians. But that is not true. The English word Religion is not enough to indentity Bhartiya Dharma. DHARMA or DUTY is the means and not the end. The end is Self-Realisation. Bhartiya Dharma or SANATAN DHARMA forewards towards perfection, spiriualism and not towards materialism. It is not limited only to worshipping of deities only. Though the modern materialism of western civilisation is attacking seriously to harm the Indian Culture, Indian Philosophy, and the Indian Culture. But our motto is "सत्यमेव जयते नानृतम्" Truth always triumphs and not the false. This attack is timely and we Indian will not leave the path shown by our great seers of culture. Though our literature, our art, our music, our standard of life everything is going now-a-days in the lines of Western Civilisation that is not only harmful but destructive too. Even then we hope that the day is not far when the whole world will have to go on the path of Indian Philosophy, the path of peace, of sacrifice, of brotherhood.

The Evil minded Western Civilisation is eating our cultural heritage and trying to destroy if finally. Hence, AWAKE BE PREPARED to fight against any kind of evil. For us knowledge is power and not the wealth. Character is the main and important capital of our nation. After Independence India developed well in the field of Science and Technology. Industrialisation and the material standard of living of Indian too increased but on the cost of character. Hence morality is diminishing day by day.

We cannot think of body without Soul शरीरमाद्यं रवलु धर्मसाधनं means the body is the means to get the DHARMA or Self Realisation. We mean religion a virtuous pure life full of inner morality. There is no salvation without the knowledge of TRUTH. Hence MAHATMA GANDHI Said "TRUTH IS GOD".

Nature is the store of energy. Without knowing nature we cannot be powerful. Nature is our friend Hence Swami Vivekananda Said, Energy, we want only energy and that can be gained through Self-control, Self-endurance, Self-Reliance and Self-Realisation. One who controls the mind controls the nature. Our Rishis were great Scientists who saw, studied and perceived the nature.

Without perceiving the nature we cannot go ahead in the way of perfection. And what is ASTROLOGY? It is the study of nature. The

Curiosity to know the nature gave birth to ASTROLOGY. Hence the birth of Astrology is the great event in the History of Human World. Astrology is a great wonderful science full of natural knowledge outside and inside both.

Astrology is said the clear eye of GOD VEDAS वेदस्य निर्मल चक्षु ज्योतिष शास्त्रमनुत्तम्'' In six parts of Vedas or Vedanga ज्योतिष or Astrology is यथा शिखा मयूरानां नागानां मणयो यथा Shikha of Mayur or Pearl among serpants. Vedas are the source of all the sciences, all the knowledge in Indian Philosophy. In other words Vedas are the poetry of Nature. Among Nature GOD SUN is the most important. Without Sun we cannot think of life on earth. In Rig Veda there is Prayer of SUN GOD or SAVITA and that is known as Gayatri Mantra. ''ॐ भूभुर्वः स्व त्तसवितुर्वरेण्यं भर्गो देवस्य धीमहि धियो यो नः प्रचोदयात्'' Oh GOD SUN thou art master of earth, world, heaven, thou art the best among GODS guide our intelligence towards good deeds, hour, day, night, fortnight, months, year, all are due to SUN. Therefore RISHI Prays the Weather, Sun पश्येम शरदः शतं जीवेम् शरदः शतम् Live for hundred years and see the Sun for hundred years.

The Sun rotates one round in a year rising and setting of SUN is the base of our day and night. The month is determined by Moon. The difference of Moon from the Sun 12° is known as tithi.

In the way of sky the movement of SUN among Constellation is marked by 12 divisions known as 12 signs. The solar year of Hindus begins when the Sun rises in the east in first degree of Aries. Thus in ASTROLOGY we study the business of SOLAR SYSTEM. The Signals of great energy i.e. divine power are studied in Astrology through intuition, perception, experience and movements of Planets. All the Planets act according to the WILL of TIME GOD (कालपुरूष) so it is said truly in Astrology कालाधीनं जगत्सर्वं The whole universe is in the control of Time. The Planets determine the fruits of good and evil deeds of human beings. The Role of Planets is clear in the following verse:-

ग्रहा राज्यं प्रयच्छन्ति ग्रहा राज्यं हंरति च।
ग्रहैर्व्याप्तमिदं सर्वं त्रैलोक्य सचराचरम्।।

means Planets give power make king to someone and deprive others of Powers. The Planets are involved in doing their duties in this world of Past, Present and future above the earth and down the earth. In giving fruits of deeds the theory of cause and effect is applied in Astrology. Through Astrology forecast of future is possible. When will it rain? Who will win? etc are answered in Astrology. The Planetary position of the birth of Child is the key to know all about the Past, Present and future.

In Astrology there is remedy of evil effects of Planets. The nature is not in our control, hence we cannot check any incident from happening but through the knowledge of Astrology we can lessen the evil effects of Planets to some extent.

ACHARYA VARAHAMIHIR in his great work वृहत्संहिता VRIHAT SAMHITA remembered 18 names of founders of Astrology SUN, PITAMAHA, VYAS, VASHISHTYA, ATRI, PARASHAR, CHYVAN NARAD, GARG, MARICHI, MUNI, ANGIRA, LO MASH, PULASTYA, KASHYAP, SHAUNAK, BHRIGU and YAVAN. They wrote big volumes known as Samhita after their names. Most of these volumes are not available. BHATTOTPALA, the first Commentator of VARAHA MIHIR's work has Quoted Some of these Acharyas. Parashar's Roll is the most important of all in the field of Indian Astrology. Another RISHI JAIMINI is also important and famous for his SUTRAS. Though there is some difference in applying the aspects and dasas methods in Jamini Astrology even then Jaimini is also remarkable in applying timing of events.

From India Astrological Knowledge reached Arab, Egypt, and China. With the spreading of Buddhism religion in sixth Century, many books on Astrology were written. A Chinese Buddha Tantric HWANSANG was sent to India to learn Astrology. In Arabian Countries many Indian books on Astrology were translated in Arabic Language. In the period of Mansoor Khalifa an Astrologer Ibn al adamin and Bulkh ke Abu Masher has referred in their books about those Indian Pandits who learned Astrology. In century Mohammed Ibn Ibrahim al Fazudi got Bramha Sphuta Sidhants Khand Khadyak translated with the help of Hindu Pandits.

During the period of Islamic attack on India Astrology flourished Arab and reached again in India in New form Pandit Neel Kantha translated TAJIK Neelkanthi in Sanskrit during Mughal empire time. In Jain religion too the study of Astrology was compulsory to Jain Sadhus. Though Jainism opposed the Vedic religion due to Karma Kand even then Jains accepted Hindu Astrology. In 3rd century Bhadra Bahu was the great Astrologer.

In this way we can say that this process of Astrology developed in India like other sciences Astrology and Ayurveda both subjects of Vedanga are human centred and hence their knowledge is honourable and useful to men. A doctor well versed in Ayurveda if also has knowledge of Astrology can say by reading the horoscope what disease is due to what Planet's evil effect and can Cure in a more easy way. How long a man will suffer from a particular disease can be known to a doctor expert in Astrology too. He may cure the diseases at ease through the Lord of Lagna and Moon's position. Sixth house and in Lord's Position in a natal chart he can treat easily.

In ancient days knowledge of gems was so developed that it was possible to cure the diseases with the help of gems wearing a ring. Mathematics and Astrology too have deep relations chemistry too developed with Ayurveda without hard work and endurance we are unable to know the secrets of nature. Thus, Astrology, Ayurveda are deeply related and lucky in finding out the secrets of Nature.

If there were not truth in Astrology then this science would have been dropped in Ocean of forgetting. But there is utility to human beings of Astrology. Hence this science is developing more and more day by day without the recognition of Government. Every statesman, Politician, Administrator, Criticise Astrology but take advice secretly from renowned Astrologers. Ayurveda.Cares for the healthy mind in a sound body Astrology studies the effect of constellations and prepares man for doing his duties well. Though the man of today landed on Moon but more people of the world are hungry, thirsty and exploited by the rich even in democratic Government. Then what is the necessity for man to find out the Planetary surface in the SKY? By spending Crores of dollars. Men are hungry, un educated, unemployed have no money for clothes, for medicines for building houses and on the other hand scientists are preparing Atom Bombs, Neutron Bombs, to destroy the humanity. What is the use of Such Kind of destructive Scientific knowledge? Hence philosophy, religion, Astrology, Astronomy, Ayurveda, Palmistry, Numerology etc. should be studied more and more for the welfare of man kind.

The misuse of films by their producers is increasing Vices among the infants and youths of today, virtues, truth, Politeness, honesty all are crying as there is no place for them. Corruption on high level is destroying the humanity. We Indians from the olden times thought always for the welfare of humanity सर्वभूत हिते रत: has been our motto. So we should try to follow our great cultural heritage Past and Present guide the future. Philosophy, Astrology we should prepare ourselves to save the human race from the evil effects of blind materialism. Peace and Prosperity through our great cultural heritage must be top priority of today. Then and then alone we may save ourselves from evil spirits heavily entering in our daily lives by western materialistic civilisation.

SONS OF INDIA AWAKE?
GO on the way of Truth.
Boldly fight against vices .
For India's Paradise Sake.

17

Our Health and Astrology

According to Astrology Planets and Nakshatras, Signs deal with our bodily requirements. According to Ayurveda there are 3 main doshas VAT, PITT, Cough. These are called TRIDOSHA त्रिदोष: SUN and MARS. represent bile or Pitta in our body, Venus and Moon wind and Cough, Saturn and RAHU wind, Mercury Nerves and 3 doshas Vat, Pitt and Cough. Human body is the Symbol of KAL-PURUSHA. Each Sign is corresponded to certain parts of human body, e.g.

ARIES—Head
TARUS—Face
GEMINI—Throat, Bronchit Region
CANCER—Lungs and Heart
LEO—Heart and Belly
VIRGO—Navel
LIBRA—Intestines
SCORPIO—Sex Organ
SAGITTARIUS-Thigh's
CAPRICORN—Knees
AQUARIUS—Calves
PISCES—Feet

Planets too represent in our body-
SUN—Soul
MOON—Mind
MARS-Vitality
MERCURY—Nervous System
JUPITER—Heart
VENUS—Sex Organs
SATURN—Feet

27 Stellers abode in the body as following:-

KRITIKA—Head
ROHINI—Forehead
MRIGSIR—Eye Brows
ARIDRA—Eyes
PUNARVASU—Nose
PUSHYA—Face
ASLESHA—Ears
MAGHA—Lips
POORVA PHALGUNA—Right Hand
UTTRA PHALGUNA—Left Hand
HASTA—Fingers
CHITRA—Neck
SWATI—Chest
VISHAKHA—Breast
ANURADHA—Stomach-Upper
JYESHTHA—Stomach-Lower
MOOL-Womb
POORVA SHADA—Back
UTTRA SHADA—Back Bone
SHRAVAN—Waist
DHANISTHA—Anus
SHAT BHISHA—Right Thigh
POORVA BHADRAPAD—Left Thigh
UTTRA BHADRA PADA—Pindli
REVTI—Ankle
ASHWINI—Upper Part of Feet
BHARNI—Lower Part of Feet

When there are malefics in different Sign and Nakshatras they Produce many diseases in the human body. There are 3 kinds of diseases—

1. Natural diseases—They are caused by natural powers such as Heavy rain. Flood, Fire, Flood, Storm, Bus, Train, Air Ships accidents, Earthquake etc.

2. Seasonal Diseases—Caused by Heat, Cold, Rains such as Malaria, Cholera, Pneumonia, Plague, Seasonal fevers etc.

3. External Diseases—Caused by Spirits, Planets, Persons, fighting, Attack etc.

Besides there are 3 kinds of diseases more which are caused by—

1. Physical—Such as Pain in any part of the body Eczima, Itches, Tumours etc.

2. Psychological—These produce mental troubles such as love, hate, angermen, happiness, mental pressure. They affect the mind internally and externally.

3. Based on Circumstances—Such as due to change in Climate, Dust, Dirtyness etc.

Ayurveda has given importance for three things more for our healthy life (1) Food (2) Sleep (3) Mental Control Improper food produce deficiency or weakness in the body so, milk, fruits, green vegetables must be taken in our food daily and they must be fresh. As you will eat So will be your mind. Sleeping is very necessary for our healthy life. As we charge Battery so power is charged in our body through balanced sleep.

Early to bed and Early to rise
makes a man healthy, wealthy and wise.

This apherism is totally true. Hence we must wake up early in the morning and sleep too early so that there may be balance in our body, health and mind. It is said "Sound mind in a sound body".

Thirdly mental control too is necessary so it is also truly said "Health is Wealth". Hence study of medical science and cure diseases with knowledge of Astrology is extremely useful and essential.

Generally all diseases are caused by interruption in blood circulation and this is due to indigestion. Planet Play an important role when they are weak, debilitated, combust, in enemies house or aspected by malefics or with them. What result do the weak planet give is given in the following lines:-

SUN—When Sun is weak, debilitated, in enemies house or aspected by malefics it causes trouble in heart, eye, lungs, fractures in bones. It is bilious by nature so becomes the cause of indigestion, Sun is hot by nature.

MOON—When Moon becomes malefic or warming causes diseases with blood, cold, cough, veneral diseases, nose inflammations, headache etc.

MARS—When Mars is weak, it causes fever, Small Pox Swelling, Jaundices, blood pressure, menstrual disorder in ladies etc.

MERCURY—Due to weak mercury all diseases caused by Nerves, Skins itches, eczema etc. Whole Nervous System is controlled by Mercury and all disorders of Vata, Pitta, and Cough are due to weak Mercury.

JUPITER—When Jupiter is weak it causes diseases of fatness, Diabetes Jupiter's both Sign Sagittarius and Pisces when are occupied by malefics these diseases may harm the body and health.

VENUS—Diseases of Semen, Sore throats, eye's diseases when SUN, MOON, VENUS, SATURN are in 2-12 houses from Lagna or Moon.

SATURN—Muscular troubles, Cold, melancholy, epileply, fistula, deafness, troubles in legs, feet, Paralysis, rheumatic troubles etc. are due to weakness of Saturn.

RAHU—Epilepsy, Pox, Suicide, Lepresy, Pain in the body, where is RAHU is seated in Horoscope or in which Nakshatra Rahu is posited the part of the body represented by RAHU (Sign and Nakshatra) external Spirits. Accidental diseases occurred in incidents suddenly occurred are due to RAHU.

KETU—Mysterious Pain in the Part of the body, diseases the cause of which cannot be known, diseases by curse of spirits, deities, by unknown signs done in previous life. Ketu causes secret diseases.

Salt and Signs

Each Sign has salt of different kinds. Lack of which Produces deficiency in the body. Sea water contains Sodium chloride, magnesium, calcium and Potassium Salt. These Salts are in our blood in the same ratio as in Sea water. If these Salts are unbalanced diseases caused by Moon as cold, Cough, mental Unhappiness, epilepsy are the result. So see the nature of Sign in 6th house, Planet in 6th house, Position of Lord of 6th house aspect of Planets on 6th house and its Lord. In fixed Signs 2,5,8,11 Girvilitary and glandular System disturb. In dual Signs 3,6,9,12 Liver dusturbance, disorder of nerves. In Cardinal Sign 1-4-7-10 disturbances in renal circulation, stomach, kidney, skin etc. will be affected. Salts found in Signs is described here as following:-

ARIES—There are 4 kinds of Salt in our blood in the form of water. The Salt found in Aries is Potassium Phosphate. Its lack produces jealousy, feelings of revenge, lying, headache, irritability and insomnia. When any Planet transits in this sign the chemical ground of understanding and material expression in body affected. Which expresses the above mentioned things in behavious of the man. Hence when any Planet affects this Sign Aries by adverse aspect mental energy is surely wasted in expression by means of above mentioned change in the feelings and behaviou of man. Hence, in this position the person should take in his food Lettuce, Cawliflower, Spinach, olives, unrected potatoes, Onions, Cucumber, Cabbage, Lima, Beams, Walnuts and Apples.

TAURUS—Lord of Taurus a Planet of emotions and mind seeks to reach in equilibrium position through planets in transit in this Sign. As this Sign rules over the mouth. Hence when emotion are affected headly by occupation or transit Jealousy goes deep and deep. As the cell salt of Aries is Potassium Phosphate so the Cell salt of this Sign is Sulphate of Soda. This Salt makes the water supply regular, when water supply is disturbed the position of equilibrium will also be affected and disturbs the balance of lower brain, Liver, pancreas, spleen and inter cellular tissues. Hence when there is Planet in Taurus or aspects Taurus it will increase Carbonate Cleaus waste in the blood. So in this position food should take in food celery sprouts, carrots, spinach, asparagus, apple, fig, peaches, beets, turnips, cheese, almonds, coconut, should be taken to regularize the equilibrium position.

GEMINI—The medicinal Salt of Gemini is Potassium Chloride it maintains the weight of the body. If this salt lacks than the body is thin. Gemini is atleast affected by Sex Problems. When we see fear, hate, nervousness apprehension, or dread it is sure that Potassium Chloride Salt is being affected and disturbed so the result is Constipation, Gonorrhoea. The native of this Sign should take in food celery, Carrot, spinach, Lettuce, Tomatoes, Barley, Watermelon etc.

CANCER—The Salt prescribed for Cancer is Fluoride of lime. This gives elasticity to tissues. Cancerions are over sensitive hence sometimes their mental balance is disturbed, when adversely aspected by malefics this will shock his mind. Hence negligence of loved ones is the result and the native suffers from tumours, Cancer, Varycose Veins, fear, dread, suspicion. The food should be taken with milk, cabbage, lettuce, water berries, and pumpkin.

LEO—Leo is Concerned with heart Centre of Circulatory System. Leo is the Symbol of strength, Courage and Life. Phosphate of magnesia is the cell salt of Leo. It helps in flexibility of bones and elasticity to muscles and tissues. It neutralizes the waste acids which would tend to destroy tinny tissues. Over exertion, over excitement should be avoided otherwise the heart will be weak and fever, liver congestion, kidney, spleen, spinal doctorates. For Leo native Spinach, Lettuce, almonds, Cucumber, barley, walnut, fig, wheat should be taken in food. Lack of Salt produces Cramps, Sperms, Cough etc.

VIRGO—Its Salt is Potassium Sulphate. The salt's work is to get out the poisonous waste matter and its lack produces constipation, dandruft, Eczema, Catarrh, pleurisy, Pneumonia etc. To fulfill lack of this salt spinach, Cawliflower, Cucumber, Lettuce, Cabbage, Tomatoes, Celery, Onion etc. In spite of cooking food raw vegetables are useful and health making. Hence raw vegetables and fruits are recommended for Virgo people.

LIBRA—Sodium phosphate is the salt of this Sign when transiting any Planet in this Sign aspected by Venus body becomes unable to absorb this salt and kidney gets disturbed. Rivalry in business, envy, Jealousy, fluids of Nerves Liver, brain etc are affected so to remove this disturbance Rice, Peas, Cawliflower, Cucumber, blue berries, cherries, strawberries, black figs, walnuts, wheat bread, almonds, coconut should be taken in food.

SCORPIO—Sulphate of lime salt is the cell salt of this Sign. Its action is to get out impurities either through kidneys or through skin, bowels. Scorpion generally are too much fond of sexual delights. Secret types of diseases usual to Scorpions are internal and deep seated Cancer. Hence precautions in food is necessary. Red Cabbage, Onion, asparagus, goose berries, blue barries, straw barries coconut should be taken.

SAGITTARIUS—Silica is the Cell Salt of this Sign its lack in the body makes the person pessimistic. Broken nails early baldness, broken teeth, T.B. Cancer diseases can enter in the body Spinach, Carrots, Cucumber's peal, Almonds, Walnut, Wheat, Barley should be taken in food.

CAPRICORN—Calcium Phosphate is the Cell Salt of this Sign. Which helps in building new bones. Lack of this Salt causes constipation, Storegraval and pimples. Nose diseases ear diseases are the results when Saturn Lord of this Sign aspect adversely in transit Planets in this Sign Red Cabbage, Onion, Lemons, Spinach, Turnips, Lettuce, asparagus, cawliflower, upper part of Potatoes, Prunes, data, pears, walnuts, almonds and wheat bread should be taken in food.

AQUARIUS—Sodium Chloride is the Cell Salt of this Sign. It distributes water in the body. When lacking dryness, nerve ends, are unable to function. Hence blood strength is affected. Intense nervousness, desire for safety food. Hence celery, spirits, asparagus, Cucumber, Strawberries, turnip, oatmeal, almonds, coconut should be taken in food.

PISCES—Phosphate of iron helps in building nervecells. Its lack lead to anemia, open air in very necessary to Pisces born persons. Iron needs oxygen as a career. Ripen and the Sunlight food is to be taken as they have lot of iron. Lettuce, Spinach, Carrots, berries, Red Cabbage, Strawberries, Onion, ripe olives should be taken in food.

Causes of Diseases

HEART ATTACK—Lagna, its Lord, 4th and 5th houses, their Lords, Sun, Moon when are afflicted by malefics or by Lords of 6-8-12 houses in any way either by combination, occupation or by aspect heart trouble is sure. Sun represents heart, Moon represents mind. Heart is Centre of Vitality and longevity. The work of heart is to supply strength through purifying blood circulation to all parts of the body and strength the brain through Nervous System.

BRAIN HEMORRHAGE—Nervous System enclosed in Skull is called Brain and Brain is inside the head. The head is studied through ARIES Sign its Lord Mars, Sun the controller of brain, Lord of Lagna, Moon Sign, 6th house its Lord, sixth to sixth house, i.e., eleventh house.

PARALYSIS—When Lagna, Sun, Moon and Mercury are under malefic affliction and Saturn, Rahu aspect the Lagna Lord the disease of Paralysis attacks the native. 6-8-12 Houses, their Lords, Planets in 6-8-12 Houses should also be considered.

KIDNEY TROUBLE—In our body liver and kidney these two glands are very important part in abdomen Liver is a gland by which bile is secreted while kidney is a pair of glands in abdomen which excrete urine. Kidney is disturbed when the salt indicated by Libra, i.e., Sodium Phosphate is not absorbed. Lord of Libra is Venus and Venus is concerned with URINE. So when Libra is afflicted by malefics and Venus is adversely aspected by malefic or is with malefics kidney gets disturbed and stops working being out of order. When 6th house is aspected by Karak of diseases Saturn and Lord of 6th house has any connection with Jupiter too kidney troubles increases. Irregularities in taking flood at proper time in Proper Quantity, exhausting work, insomnia, melancholy, loss of appetite are the main causes so when this disease increases blood turn into water and dialysis becomes necessary.

EYE DISEASE—When Venus is with malefics in second house the Person is one eyed or has small eyes.

DUMB—When Venus is in second NAVAMSA with malefics in second house then the person is Dumb.

HESITATING SPEECH—When Venus is in third house in third NAVAMSA the Person's speech is not clear or he speaks by gaps.

DEFECTIVE EYES—When SUN, SATURN, RAHU are in 2nd house and Lord of 2nd house is Combust or with malefics or does not aspect the second house the person's right eye is defective. In the same way when SUN, RAHU are in 12th house Lord of 12th house is combust or with Saturn, has no aspect on 12th house then left eye is defective.

BLINDNESS—Person born in Leo Lagna with SUN, MOON there aspected by Saturn, Mars then the person is blind but if benefics as Jupiter, Venus, Mercury aspect the Lagna the person has small eyes.

BLIND BY LEFT EYE—Sun, Moon in 12th house.

NIGHT BLINDNESS—Mercury, Venus in 6-8-12 evil houses.

BIRTH BLINDNESS—VENUS, SUN, Lord of Lagna are in 6-8-12 houses.

SHORT EYED—When in 12th house are Venus-Mars with Moon.

EAR DISEASE—Venus Mars in 2, 12 houses.

DYSENTRY—VENUS MARS in 7th house combined and malefics SUN, SATURN, RAHU, KETU, weak Moon aspect them.

DISEASES IN SECRET PLACES—7th house is the House of Sex organs and 8th house is the house of anus. Venus is the indicator of Sex organs So when Venus in 7th or 8th diseases of Semen, Urine, Diabetes are there.

DISEASES IN MOUTH—When Moon with Mars in Lagna the person is like a dumb and if Lord of 6th with Mercury in Lagna he cannot speak clearly. Rahu in 2nd produces teeth disease. When birth Ascendants are Aries, Taurus, Sagittarius, and malefics are in them teeth are not well settled. RAHU Ketu in 6th and 8th houses person suffers from teeth trouble.

LEPROSY—Moon in Lagna, Sun in 7th Mars and Saturn in 2nd and 12th denote Leprosy. Persons born in Cancer, Scorpio, Pisces, Capricorn, Virgo and Malefics aspect 5th, 9th houses the person suffers from Leprosy.

FEVER—Sun in 6th, 8th houses.

INJURY—Mars and Ketu in 6th and 8th houses.

URINARY, SEX DISEASES—Venus in 6th and 8th houses.

T.B.—Jupiter in 6th, 8th houses, Saturn in 6th, 8th.

GOITRE—Saturn in 6th, 8th houses.

LIVER SPLEEN—Moon is 6th and 8th houses.

DIABETES—Jupiter typed people are more prone to this disease as they are fond of Carbohydrates with glycogen. People born on Thursday in Sagittarius, Pisces Signs of Jupiter afflicted are prone to this disease. The main Planet Jupiter afflicted by malefics either with them or aspected by them may causes diabetes. Sugar in blood increases due to Conversion of Carbohydrates with sugar in intestine. Hence Carbohydrates should be checked and not to be allowed to increase sugar in blood.

APPENDICITIS—When some sort of tumour is formed in the colon and pain ensures from stomach that is known simply as appendicitis. The tumour or gilti is removed by means of surgical operation.

RENAL DISEASES—Mars in 7th house with or aspected by malefics the patient will suffer from urinary diseases. Formation of Stone which stops the urine from coming out.

SWELLING—When Jupiter and Venus are in 6th house aspected by malefics then Swelling gives trouble to the person.

ASTHMA—When Mars and Saturn aspect the Lagna then the disease of asthma is produced. Generally when moon and Venus are in 3-6-11 houses or in watery Signs birth in January or February then Person's nature is windy and coughy and they are prone to cold, cough, Lungs diseases , T.B. etc.

EPILEPSY—It is the disease of nervous system Near wells, rivers, dam, kund etc. Water attracts the victim and then there is foam in mouth, giddinees, and the Victim fall down in water. Planet Moon, Venus Play an important role in causing this disease.

PILES—Piles is of 2 kinds. 1. Bloody 2. Constipated. In bloody Piles blood passes through anus. When wind and bile cough are disturbed they make moles inside the rectum. These males are the root of constipated piles. This disease is due to intake of Spices, oil and salt in food. Wine, lack of proper sleep at night, disturbance of liver etc.

ASTROLOGICAL REMEDIAL MEASURES

1. SUN—If native is suffering set back in business, Government Service, Occupation and having problem from bile (Pitta), fever, stomach, heart, epilepsy, Skin diseases then the native is suffering from the ill effects of SUN. The Following remedial measures are prescribed to lessen the sufferings from SUN.

(as Recitation of 7000 Japam of Surya Mantra Om Ghrini Suryay Namah. ॐ घृणि सर्याय नमः

(b) Donation of Red things like Red clothes, Copper, Oval ruby, saffron, gud, Red flowers, Red fruits etc.

(c) In Ravi-Pushya yoga wear golden ring of Ruby 5-6 Rattis in Gold in Anamika Ring.

2. MOON—When diseases are due to Moon such as cold, Cough, Lungs, nose, eyes, blood, dysentery, disturbance in occupation mental disturbances, anxiety etc are due to Moon.

(a) Recitation Moon Mantra ॐ सोमाय नमः "Om Somay Namah" 11000.

(b) Donate white clothes, white sandal, silver, Sugar, Milk, Ghee, Curd, Pearl etc.

(c) Wear pearl Ring in Silver on Monday

(d) Worship Lord Shiva with Om Namah Shivay Mantra. ॐ नमः शिवाय

3. MARS—If there is fear, lack of courage, fear of accident fractures, wound, blood, diseases, struggle, conflict in life useless discussion, Blood Pressure, Progeny trouble these are due to Mars. Mars may be weak, Combust, in an enemy's Sign, afflicted by malefic etc then.

(a) Recitation of Mars Mantra Om Angarkay Namah. ॐ अंगारकाय नमः Angarkay 10000 times.

(b)Wear Coral in Gold ring in Anamika. The Coral's weight should be 4,5, Rattis.

(c) Donate Coral, Land, Wheat, Gud, Red Sandal, Red clothes, Copper, Gold, Safforn, musk, Red Fruits, Red Sweets.

(d) Feed wheat bread with gur to red dogs on Tuesday Read Hanuman Chalisa, Hanuman Kavach, Hanuman Bahuk Worship Hanuman with Sindur and Ghee on Tuesday.

(4) *MERCURY*—If there is nervousnees, obstacles in daily life, opposition to friends, loss in business, Skin Diseases Loss of Memory etc. there sufferings are due to weak Position of Mercury. Then:

(a) Recitation of Mercury Mantra ऊँ बुं बुधाय नम: Om Bum Budhay Namah 17000 times.

(b) Worship Lord GANESH with Durba and Laddu. Have fast On Wednesday and on GANESH CHATURTHI.

(c) Donate green clothes, Ghee elephant teeth, emerald, camphor, books, flowers and fruits feed small girls.

(d) Wear emerald in Golden ring in Little finger 4 to 6 Rattis.

(5) *JUPITER*—Sufferings from Diabetes, Liver, fever, Cough and Brain, Heart disease, disturbance in Service, marriage, Son birth etc. These are due to Jupiter

(a) Japa of Jupiter Mantra Om Brim Brihaspatye Namah ऊँ बृं बृहस्पतये नम: reciting it 19000 times.

(b) Wear Pukhraj in 4-5- Rattis in golden ring in first finger.

(c) Have fast on Thursday. Donate yellow clothes, fruits, flowers, Pukhraj, Haldi, Horse, honey, book, salt, Sugar, land, umbrella etc.

(6) *VENUS*—If there is loss of wife's and family's happiness, property, diseases in hidden parts of the body, Hydrocele, gonorrhea, etc, these are due to Venus. Venus is karak of wife of sweetness in life and music, of vehicle, of poetry, of property and so many worldly things. Hence when Venus is weak, Neecha, combust in an inimical house or aspected by the malefics then to remove all these weakness do the following things :

(a) Japa of Venus Manta. ऊँ शुं शुक्राय नम: Om Shum Shukray Namah 20000 times reciting.

(b) Wear diamond 2 to 7 rattis in middle finger in gold. Real diamond is very dear and rarely available. Hence American Diamond can also be used.

(c) Donation of white sandal, rice, clothes, flower, fruits, silver, ghee, gold, curd, scented clothes, papers, books, sugar, cow, land, feeding the little girls with Kheer.

7. SATURN

If there is melancholy, loss of dignity, wealth, rheumatism, mental trouble, fever, paralysis, dyspepsia, disturbance due to wind. Sade sati Dhaiya gastric trouble, indisgestion. All these things are due to Saturn. sweak position. Hence

(a) Saturn is the main planet of disease. It is the Karaka of diseases. Hence Japa of Saturn mantra. ऊँ शं शनेय नम: Om Sham Shanye Namah reciting 23[illegible] times with Havan

(b) Wear Blue Sapphire either in gold or silver ring of 1.25 to 5 Rattis. Care should be taken before wearing the ring. Sapphire is costly, wear in middle finger ring prepared from Nal of a black horse. It is easily available.

(c) Donate blue, black things as iron, oil, clothes, flowers, sesame, urad (उडद), Til (तिल). Donate oil on every Saturday, black shoe, black umbrella, black woolen clothes.

8. *RAHU*

Accidental diseases, epilepsy, gastric problem, trouble by spirits, small pox, blood disturbance and many other diseases are caused by RAHU. Hence getting rid of troubles due to RAHU :

(a) Do 18000 Japa of RAHU mantra ॐ रां राहवे नमः Om Ram Rahwe Namah

(b) Wear zircon 3, 6, 9 rattis in five metal's ring.

(c) Donate seven corn, wheat, gram, rice, jwar, Bazra, makka, Udad, Moong, Tuwar, Masoor, etc. blue clothes, black flowers, oil sesame, Til, black shoes, black umbrella etc. Rahu acts as Saturn and most strong Malefic.

9. KETU

Ketu is known as unseen planet having unseen power hence Ketu gives such kind of diseases which are out of control of doctors. Ketu is Karaka of hidden, sudden, mysterious diseases. Ketu is also a Karaka planet for Moksha (Salvation), divine power and divine curse.

(a) Do 18000 Japa of ॐ कें केतवे नमः Om Kem Ketwe Namah.

(b) Wear Cat's eye 5, 7 Rattis in 5 metals ring.

(c) Donate white clothes, black flowers, black sesesame, oil, iron. Ketu acts as Mars.

In serious cases 125000 Japa of Maha Mrityhujaya Mantra (महा मत्युंजय मंत्र) Shatakshara Gayatri Mantra (शताक्षरा गायत्री मंत्र) Ram Raksha Stotra (राम रक्षा स्तोत्र) Panch Mukhi Hanuman Kavach (पचंमुखी हनुमान कवच) Shri Gajendra Mokshavali (ॐ श्री गजेन्द्र मोक्षावली). Patha (पाठ) of these stotra or Book is beneficial.

Yogasans (योगासन)

Nowadays Swami Ram Dev Ji Maharaj doing well in Kankhal (Haridwar) by establishing पतंजलि योग पीठ (Patanjali yoga peeta) and exercising yogasana pranayama in Bhatinda, Amravati, Hyderabad, New Delhi thousands and lacs of people are taking part in camps for 7 days in Swami Ram Dev's Pranayama and Yoga Shivirs. Pranayama is simple system of keeping good health, strengthening Digestive system and keeping away from many diseases. Here are some simple and useful Asans for our daily use :

Diseases	Asan
Leucorrhoea	Naukasan, Bhujangasan, Sarvan Gasan, Dhanurasan
Gastric Trouble	Muktasan, Vajrasan, Triphala should be taken Daily
Insomnia	Sarvangasan, Vajrasan
Rheumatism	Pawan Muktasan, Sarvangasan Maha Yogaraj Gugghal
Hysteria	Sarvangasan, Bhujangasan
Diabetes	Karela juice is the best medicine-Sarvangasan, Dhanurasan
Heart Attack	No smoking, No wine, No Tambakoo, Avoid Anger. Sound sleep is necessary Arjunarishta, Ashwagandharishta use of Lahsun, Shavasan is very useful in Heart trouble.
Cold and Cough	Shavasan
Asthma	Shavasan
Headache	Sheershasan, Sarvangasan
Stomach Pain	Padmasan, Siddha San, Vajrasan
Anemia	Vajrasan
Liver Trouble	Halasan, dhanurasan
Kidney Trouble	Bhujangasan

Use Ayurvedic Medicines in Place of Allopathic medicines. As Ayurvedic medicines do not harm in any way and cut the root of disease slowly. Here some famous Ayurvedic Medicines are recommended for various diseases.

Name of Medicine	*Useful in*
Triphala Churna	Indigestion, Gastric Trouble
Ashwagandharishta	Heart Trouble, Weakness
Arjunarishta	Heart Trouble, Weakness
Dashmoolarishta	After delivery for ladies.
Sitopaladi Churna	Cold, Cough, Fever, T.B.
Abhyarishta	Long Constipation and Piles
Yoga Raj Guggal	Paralysis; spleen and Liver trouble.
Liv 52 Tablets	Liver troubles, Indigestion.
Sanjeevni	Cold, Cough Fever
Amlant Vati	Acidity
Amritarishta	Fevers of Long time.
Godanti	Cold Cough, headache flu, Malaria etc.
Brahmi Rasayan	Improvement of Health
Chyauan Prash	Improvement of Health
Loha Sav	Improvement of Health
Draksha Sav	Improvement of Health
Vasant Malti	Cough Fever

Chandra Prabhavati	Renal diseases.
Makradhwaj	Cold, bronchitis, old fever Strengthen Heart and health.
Tribhuvan Keerti Ras	Cough and wind fever Pneumonia Cold fever etc.
Gasex	Gas Trouble
Abana	To Control B.P.

N.B. For Details: Read my Book "Medical Astrology" Published by Gyan publishing House, New Delhi-2.

18

Sun-Mercury Yoga

My wife and 3 children have Sun-Mercury Yoga in their horoscopes. It is wonderful that on the birth date of my wife on her 24th birthday my first Son Rakesh was born on the same birthday i.e. as 30th June 1961. My first Son's birth brought luck in my life as I was promoted as Lecturer in Government Higher Secondary School on 7-7-1961, bought a plot for house Construction on 23-10-1961 and got arrear of revised pay scale in February 1962. As per the Horoscope of my IInd son my life is long:- 'लाभस्थौ यदि दीर्घायुर्योगवल पिता" Here Lord of eleventh is Venus and is in 9th house with Lord of ninth house Jupiter, Lord of Lagna Moon, father is Long lived. Hence my (father's life is long) Now I am about 70 years old.

Birth Lagna IInd Son

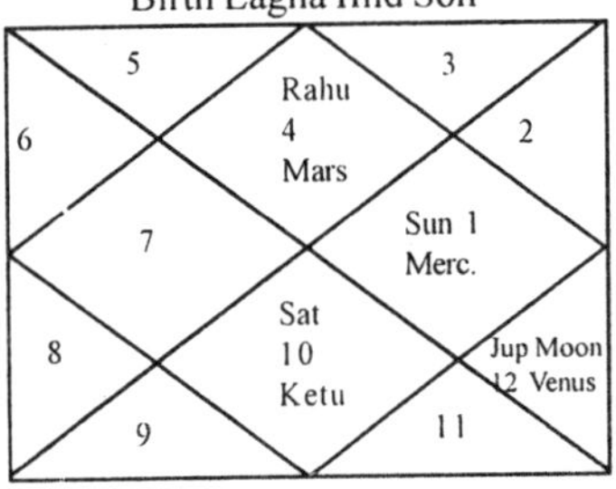

In the same way चतुर्थेशश्चन्द्रमाश्च भाग्ये राज्येथ लाभगेपंचमेति स्थितो मातु: दीर्घायुषं भवेत् If Lord of fourth house and Moon are Combined in 9, 10 or 6 houses the mother is long lived. The Lord of fourth Venus is with Moon in ninth house and with Jupiter more. In this way my wife Smt. Kamla Devi and Mother of this boy of mine is too long lived. भाग्याधीशो लाभगे वा लाभेशो भाग्यमादिशेत्" Means if Lord of ninth be in eleventh or Lord of eleventh be in ninth house or they are related by combination or aspect the native is Lucky. Here Lord of eleventh Venus is with ninth Lord in ninth house. So is the combination or aspect of eleventh Lord and ninth Lord is in the Horoscope of my Ist Son Rakesh:-

Here Lord of ninth Jupiter being in seventh house aspect the eleventh Lord Venus in eleventh house. In both these Horoscopes there is Sun-Mercury yoga. In IInd Son's Horoscope in 10th house and in Ist Son's horoscope is in 12th house as shown above.

Birth Lagna Rakesh

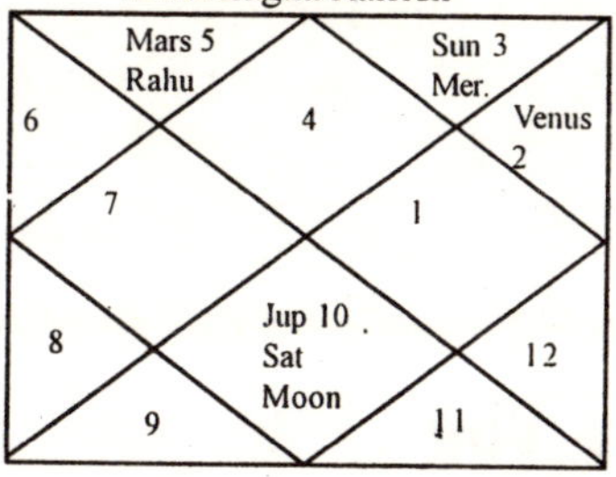

यद् भावकारको लग्नाद्व्यये तिष्ठति चेद्यदि।
तस्य भावस्य सर्वस्य भाग्ययोग उदीरित।।

Means if Karak of any house is in twelfth house from Lagna then the native is Lucky in that house related matter. In the Horoscope of my Ist Son Rakesh there is Sun in Gemini in 12TH house. Sun is the Karaka of father. Hence at the birth time of my Ist Son Rakesh I was promoted as Lecturer had bought land for house, got money due to arrear of revised pay scale. In the horoscope of my wife too there is Moon in twelfth house Karak for mother and 4TH house property. Hence the mother of my wife lived for 97 years old and expired on 24-4-1999. I bought land for House Construction on 23-10-1961.

पितृकारक भावश्च भाग्यमानेश्वरोपि वा
उभौ तौ व्ययौस्थिता पितृभाग्य मुदीरितम्

Means father of the native is lucky if Karak for father Sun is in twelfth house with Lord of ninth houses. In the Horoscope of my first Son Rakesh Sun is in 12th house

"सूर्य मेषं गते चैव पितृभाग्य मुदीरितम्'

Means Sun in Aries rises the luck of father. Sun is in Aries in tenth house in the Horoscope of my second Son ADITYA

"व्ययेश भाग्येश शशि सूर्याचसंस्थिति व्यये
पितृस्तु भाग्योगश्च व्यये देवेज्य रि:पुयौ"

Means if Lord of ninth, twelfth and Sun are in 12th house then father is lucky. If Lord of twelfth and Jupiter are in twelfth house the same is the result.

In this way without my horoscope I used to see and think about my future through the Horoscopes of my wife and children.

19

Sun-Rahu Yog

Generally Moon-Rahu combination is Raj-yog-karak Sun-Rahu combination also produce Raj-yoga but when this yoga is in Aries, Capricorn, Aquarius, Leo, Libra, Sagittarius, it produces Raj-yoga. Sun-Rahu combination in Aries with Saturn produces Raj-Bhang Yoga. Otherwise in other signs this yoga makes the native to leave the world and convert in Sanyasa Yoga.

In the horoscope of Yeshwant Rao Chauhan, there is Sun-Rahu-Mercury combination in first house in Aquarius Lagna. In 12th house Jupiter, in second house Venus in exaltation in 10th house is Scorpio whose Lord Mars is in 5th house in Gemini aspected by Rahu. Shri Yeshwant Rao Chauhan was the Chief Minister of Maharashtra and later on defence Minister and finance Minister of India.

In the horoscope of Karl Marx there is Sun-Rahu yoga in Aries in third house. Karl Marx had Aquarius Lagna in which in 4th house there was Mercury in Taurus being lord of 5th house aspecting the tenth house. Lord of tenth Mars is in 6th house in debilitation (Neecha). Hence he could not part in Government, but in 3rd house with Sun-Rahu there is Moon too. Hence his thoughts are recognised in the world.

Christ too had Sun-Rahu combination. In Stalin's horoscope there is Sun-Rahu combination in 3rd house in Sagittarius. Rahu in Sagittarius is in Neecha sign debilitated. Hence he was dictator, i.e., this Rahu made him some what Neecha in tendency. In his Libra Lagna is Mercury who was aspected by Jupiter being in 5th house. So in his life time he was any how recognised as honourable. Mars is in Aries in seventh house aspecting the tenth house where cancer sign is present (Neecha sign for Mars). So after his death he was opposed and his dead body was dug from the earth ground.

Sun-Rahu combination in 4th house lack of mother's happiness, wandering in far off lands in search of happiness, lack of parent's happiness and lack of happiness of mother-in-law and father-in-law, but if there is Sun-Rahu yoga in Libra in 4th house with Mars it produces acquring land through cunning men. The native becomes hard and cruel in nature.

In the horoscope of Chaitanya Mahaprabhu Sun-Rahu combination in 5th house in Aquarius sign. In fourth house Mars is in exaltation, in seventh Venus in Aries, Moon Ketu combination in 11th house. From Moon in 7th house Sun-Rahu yoga makes indifference from worldly and family happiness. In second house Saturn in Scorpio too producing such in indifference men. Jupiter aspects 9th house.

Sant Tukdoji too was born in Libra Lagna in which Jupiter, Venus, Mars and Ketu and in seventh house Sun-Rahu-Saturn combination is present. Saturn in Neecha sign with Sun-Rahu too makes indifference to native from all worldly happiness.

Chandra Shekhar Azad had Sun-Rahu-Mars-Moon combination in 8th house. Moon-Mars yoga in 8th house denotes unnatural death.

In Netaji Subhash Chandra Bose's horoscope there is Sun-Rahu-Mercury combination in tenth house in Capricorn. Lord of tenth Saturn is in 8th house in Scorpio in inimical sign. Hence Netaji got world fame but could not get Administrative power's happiness.

Teepu Sultan had Sun-Rahu in 12th house. In Godse Nathu Ram's horoscope there is defame yoga due to Saturn in Neecha in 11th and Sun-Rahu-Mercury in 12th house in Taurus.

In this way Sun-Rahu combination is less important than Moon-Rahu combination.

20

Kuldeepak Yog

The native who gives name and fame to parents, family, state and native is known as Kul Deepak. In Astrological text books it is said thus :-

शत्रु स्थाने यदा जीवो लाभ स्थाने शशि भवेत्
गृहमध्ये स जातश्च विख्यात: कुलदीपक:-1

Jupiter in sixth, Moon in eleventh makes man famous Kul-Deepak

सहजेच यदा जीवो लाभस्थान च चन्द्रमा
स राजा गृह मध्यस्थ: विख्यात: कुलदीपक-2

Jupiter in 3rd, Moon in eleventh man is famous, Kul-Deepak

शुक्र: यस्य बुधो यस्य केन्द्रे बृहस्पति:
दशमे अंगारको स जात: कुलदीपक:-3

Venus, Mercury, Jupiter in 1-4-7-10 Mars in 10th is Kul-Deepak

एक: पापो यदा लग्ने चापैको च रसातले
जायते च द्विनाली स्यात्स: जात: कुल दीपक: -4

One malefic in Lagna, One malefic in 4th have NALI in Kul-Deepak

मृगपति वृष कन्या कर्कटस्थे च राहौ
भवति विपुल लक्ष्मी राज राजाधिपो वा-5

Rahu in Leo, Taurus, Virgo, Cancer gives wealth and Kingdom

हय गज नर नौका मेदिनी मण्डिलश्च
स भवति कुल दीपो राहु तुंगी नराणां-6

Rahu in Exaltation gives horses, elephants, servants, lord of lord etc. and man is Kul-Deepak

सिंह लग्ने यदा भौमे पंचमे च निशाकर:
व्यय स्थाने यदा राहु स जात: कुलदीपक:

Mars in Leo Lagna, Moon in fifth house, Rahu in 12th house makes a man Kul-Deepak.

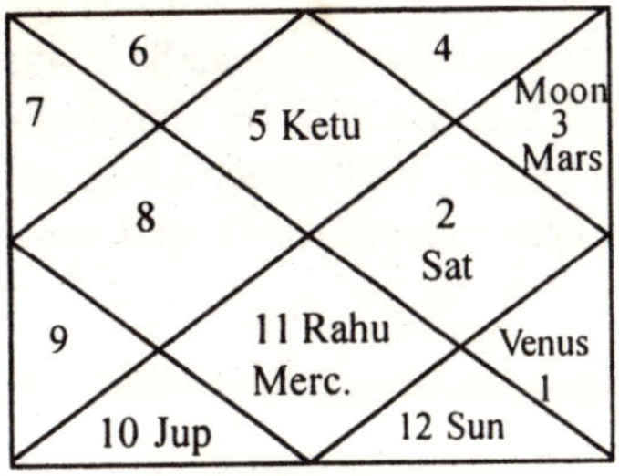

Examples : Horoscope of general Manek Shaw : According to verse No. 1 Jupiter is in 6th house in Capricorn aspecting the tenth and 12th and 2nd house. Moon in eleventh in Gemini with Mars produced Kul-Deepak yoga.

Horoscope of Chaitanya Mahaprabhu

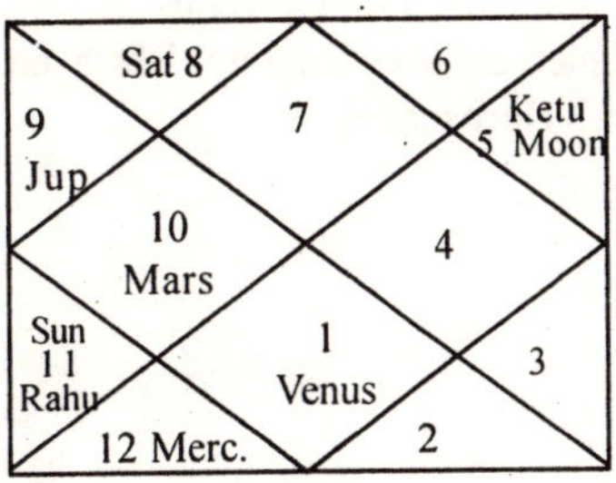

According to Verse No. 2 Jupiter in 3rd in own sign, Moon in Leo in this horoscope produced Kul Deepak yoga.

Horoscope of Sardar Ballabh Bhai Patel

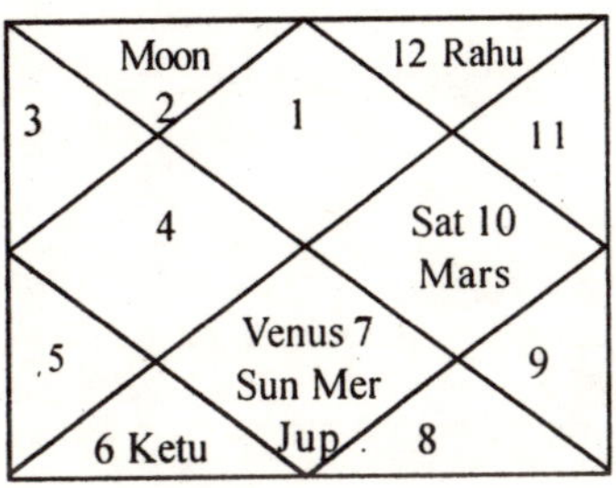

According to Verse No. 3 benefic mercury Jupiter and venus in 7th house in Quadrant and Mars in 10th in exaltation formed Kul Deepak yoga in Loh Purush Sardar Patel's horoscope. Mars in 10th in exaltation made him Kul Deepak.

Horoscope of Akbar the King Emperor

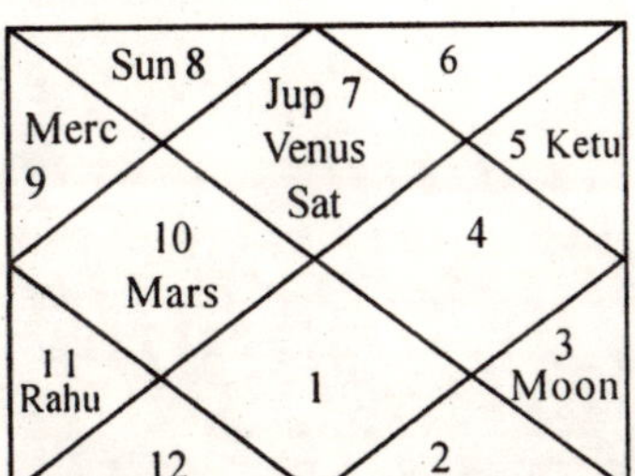

Horoscope of Atal Behari Vajpayee

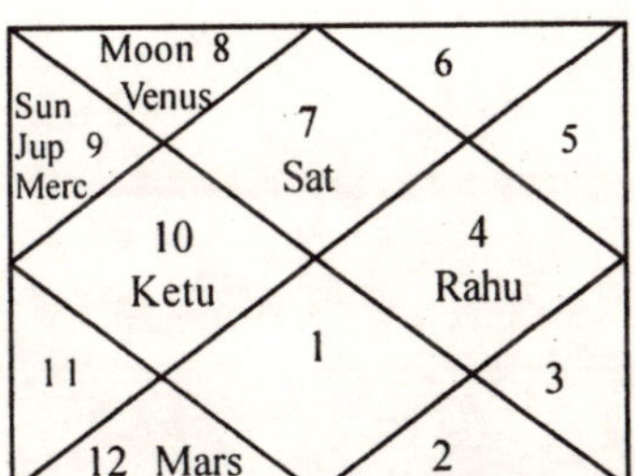

According to Verse No. 4 one malefic in Lagna one malefic in 4th house. Here in Akbars Horoscope in Lagna Saturn and in 4th Mars Both malefic are Present. In the same way in Atal Behari, Vaj Payees, Horoscope Saturn in Lagna and Ketu in 4th both malefics produced Kul Deepak yoga in both horoscopes.

Birth Chart of Bhagwan Ram

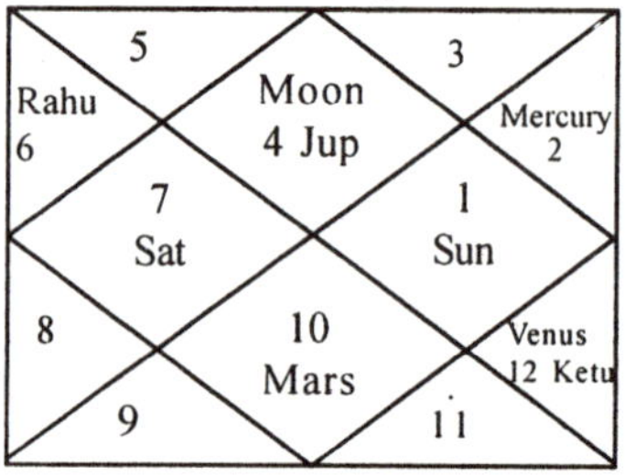

In Bhagwan Ram's Horoscope Rahu is in Virgo in 3rd house. Sun, Moon, Mars, Jupiter, Venus, Saturn 6 Planets are in exaltation in Bhagwan Ram's Horoscope.

21

Neecha and Neechabhilashi Grahas

Debilitated and Desirous of debilitation planets generally some times give good results. Modern age is 'Kaliyuga' कलियुग and Tamoguna तमोगुण is a head every where.

The world famous palmist, Astrologer, Numerologist Cheiro's horoscope is a good example of Neecha planets. Cheiro was born in scorpio Lagna with Mars in Neecha sign Cancer. His tenth lord Sun is also in Neecha sign with Saturn in 12th house. His lord of second house Jupiter too is in Neecha sign in third house. In this way there are 3 planets in Neecha sign in his horoscopes Sun, Mars and Jupiter are Neecha. Saturn and Rahu are exalted. Moon as lord of ninth house is in tenth house in Leo. Lord of Lagna Mars is in Neecha sign in 9th house and has full aspect on 2 other Neecha planets Sun and Jupiter. Due to these Neecha planets position Cheiro become famous Astrologer, Numerologist of the world. Though these 3 Neech planets have Neecha-Bhanga Yoga too as their lords (Lord of Neecha Sign) are in Quadrand as moon in 10th, Saturn is in 10th from Jupiter and with Neecha Sun there is exalted Saturn producing Neecha Bhanga Yoga in Quandrant from Neecha Sun. Though in his horoscope Lords of 8-12 houses Mercury and Venus are in Lagna. The 8-12 lords have lost their evil effects due to being in inimical sign Scorpio, the sign of a military general mars.

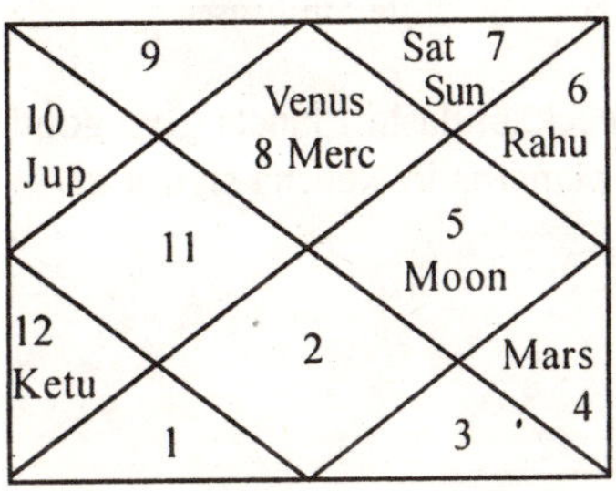

Raj Gopalachari has Jupiter in neecha Rasi in his horoscope. In Mahatma Gandhi's horoscope Sun in Virgo in 12th house is Neecha Bhilashi going towards, Neecha sign Libra. In Pandit Jawaharlal Nehru's horoscope Jupiter is in 6th house in Sagittarius is Neecha Bhilashi. In the horoscope of Lok-Nayak Jai Prakash Narain, Lord of tenth Mars is in Neecha sign and Lord of 9th Jupiter is in Capricorn in Neecha sign.

In the horoscope of Dr. Radha Krishnan Venus is in Neecha sign in Virgo Lagna. In V.V. Giri's horoscope too moon is in 12th house in Scorpio in Neecha sign.

In the horoscope of Dr. Sampoorna Nand Jupiter is in Sagittarius Neecha Bhilashi. In Sardar Patel's horoscope Sun is in Neecha sign in 7th house. In Prithvi Raj Chauhan's horoscopes Jupiter is in Neecha sign in tenth house. In the horoscope of Saint Poet Kabirdas there is Mercury in Neecha sign in eleventh house. The following persons have Neecha sign in houses as indicated below :

Name	*Neecha sign posited Planet*	*House in which posited*
Arvind Ghosh	Mars in Cancer	In 11the house
Ranjit Singh	Venus in Virgo	In 3rd house
Chhatrapati Shivaji	Mercury in Pisces	In 8th house
Gen. Manek Shaw	Jupiter in Capricorn	In 6th house
Charan Singh	Jupiter in Capricorn	In 11th house
Laxmi Bai	Mars in Cancer	In 10th house
Tulsidas	Mars in Cancer	In 10th house
Mansingh Dacoit	Venus in Virgo	In 11th house
Sheikh Muzib	Mercury in Pisces	In 5th house
Yeshwant Rao	Jupiter in Capricorn	In 12th house
Karl Chauhan Marx	Mars in Cancer	In 6th house
Swami Ram Tirtha	Venus in Virgo	In 7th house
Satya Sai Baba	Jupiter in Capricorn	In 3rd house
Arjun Singh	Sun in Libra	In 5th house

Thus it seemahat Neecha and Neechabhilashi Planets give good results. It is said that when retrograded planet is in Neecha sign it gives result like planet in exaltation.

22

Kal- Sarpa Yog

Astrology is the Divine light offered by the Almighty God to human beings so that they may remove kindrances produced by malefic planets in the Horoscope of a native. Though Astrology is like a deep ocean even then anybody can get knowledge through going deeply in water and get some drops of nectar of this divine knowledge.

We see in everyday life that in a family due to poverty or other cause marriage cannot be performed of the young girl, someone has no progeny, and if children are born they are not alive but die. There are so many diseases which are out of catch of Doctors, After absolute labour the money collection is not possible, there is restlessness in home in the family. Young boys and girls are not getting employment after getting even honours in master's degree. Somebody is in loss in profession, somebody is being suffered by his Boss, In this way there are so many causes due to which human life has been a hell. What are the reasons of all these difficulties? Can they be solved with the help of Astrology?

Astrology is a noble trial to remove all the difficulties by reading the Horoscopes and finding in them the causes of these difficulties.

When all the planets are in one side of Rahu and Ketu or all the planets are surrounded by Rahu and Ketu or in other words when all the planets are between Rahu and Ketu. This combination is called *'Kal-Sarpa'* Yog. This is not good but produced hindrances in the way of progress, action and make the native disappointed.

When there is *kal-sarpa* yog in the Horoscope of the native, then the native sees snakes in dream and are afraid of snakes. Rahu is the Head of the snake and Ketu is the tail of snake.

Rahu and Ketu are Chhaya graha. They are not independent planet. It is said that birth Star of Rahu is Bharni and birth star of Ketu is Ashlekha. Bharni's lord or God is kal (काल) Ashlekha's lord of God is Snake or Sarpa (सर्प).

Rahu gives the result like saturn, wherever will Rahu be or with any planet than Rahu will give result of that planet and Saturn. Saturn has the Quality of Spiritual thinking and to move after thinking of Loss or profit for a long time. Hence Saturn is called 'Move Slow" or शनै: चर.

Rahu is exalted in Gemini, debilitated in Sagittarius and his own house is 'Virgo'. Saturn, Mercury, Venus are his friends, Sun, Moon, Mars are his enemies. Jupiter is neutral. Ketu has the Qualities of Mars so Marsand Venus are friends of Ketu and Sun, Saturn, Rahu are his enemies. Moon, Mercury, Jupiter are neutral.

Kal-Sarpa Yog make the life of the native struggle some, there are delay and hindrances in the way of Progress. The native is Physically, mentally, economically troubled. I am giving here an example of a person who has kal-sarpa yog in the Horoscope born on 12-8-1947 at 2.00 a.m. in taurus lagna. This native is educated upto VIIIth class and was married at the age of 22, a danghter was born but unfortunately the wife and daughter both died within a year.

Any how he got job in Malaria department but due to Laziness, Physical and mental weakness could not serve more. Now he is alive but doing nothing being dependent on others. This is the effect of *kal-sarpa* yog in his horoscope.

IInd example of *Kalsarpa* yog. Born on 9-1-1898 in Capricorn Lagna Vishakha 1st Charan. He was not more educated but due to moon jupiter combination was wise and devotee of God. He was a priest in a temple. Married at the age 29 and could hardly enjoyed married only for 15 years 4 sons one daughter took birth among them 2 sons died in early childhood and his wife died at his 45 years of age. Mars in debilitation in seventh house could not give him more pleasure of wife. In the last time he was suffered from stone diseases and died in February 1963 at the age of 65.

Due to *kal-sarpa* yog the following hindrances came in the way of the native:

1. He cannot get proper education.
2. Delay in marriage
3. Struggle with life partner or mother-in-law.
4. No birth of progeny or son
5. No result after hardwork.
6. Physical and Mental weakness.
7. Incurable diseases.

Kal-sarpa yog native are different from ordinary persons. Theis yog also gives positive results not only negaitves. Hence to say that the native who has *kal-sarpa* yog will always suffer is not correct. The main thing is that *kal-sarpa-yog* natives live for others. They suffer for others too and have sympathetic view. Rahu-Ketu in 4-8-12 houses is negative and the results will be in Mahadasha of Rahu or autardasha of Rahu in other planets Mahadasha.

When *Kal-sarpa* Yog is positive and in transit when Rahu comes at natal position it gives very good positive results for the whole 18 years of Rahu Mahadasha. It is also seen that if with kal-sarpa yog in the Horoscope of well wealthy persons there is sun-moon combination or equal degrees angular position then in their Rahu Mahadasha period they destroy all the wealth and property and due to previous birth's vice and evil deeds done by their forefathers they have to suffer with poverty.

Snake is the symbol of wealth. All the wealth of the world is in the control of snakes. Wherethere is hidden wealth in land, field or house there snakes are found to save that property and wealth.

Rahu in 2-4-5-6-7-12 houses gives negative results and loss in any way and in 1-3-9-11 houses gives positive results and gives the native wife, Son, wealth and property.

Rahu in 1-4-5-7-9-10 houses and 6-8-12 houses produces kalsarpa yog. Saturn in 8th house from Rahu also produces kal sarpa yog. From Moon too Rahu or Ketu in 8th house produces kal-sarpa yog. Whatever the planetary position is but the native is born in *'Sarpa'* Yoni then it produces *kal sarpa* yog persons born in Kritika and Rohini Nakshatras have sarpa yoni. In the same way persons born in 'अ' Vargas or in 'ट' Vargas also suffer from Sarpa Dosha.

In 12 signs there are 12 kinds of each sign kal-sarpa yog in this way 12 x 12 = 144 kinds of kalsarpayog will be there. Main kalsarpa yog are of 12 kinds.

1. *Anant Kal-sarpa yog :* When Rahu is in Lagna and Ketu is in VIIth house and other planets are on the either side of them but within the area surrounded by Rahu-Ketu due to this yog mental restlessness, wicked tendency, cruelty, insincerity, Liar-speaking. He has to make a hard struggle to get peace and prestige, property and profession. Marriage life also suffers.

2. *Kulik Kal-Sarpa-Yog :* If there is Rahu in IInd and Ketu in VIIIth house then this yog is produced. Due to this yog the health of the native produces. His economical condition suffers too does not remain good. There is more expenses than income. The Native speaks hard, family struggle and defame in every work, conflicts with life partners, enemies are the results.

3. *Vasuki Kal-Sarpa Yog :* When there is Rahu in 3rd and Ketu in 9th house it forms vasuki kalsarpa-yog. Troubles from younger brothers, sisters or other family members, friends are made. Many difficulties in the

way of service, profession, hindrances in rising luck, trouble in foreign country, no faith in religion, less due to careless in low documents.

4. *Shankha Pal Kal-Sarpa Yog :* Rahu in 4th Ketu in 10th form this yog. Due to this yog troubles from mother, Vehicle, Servants, movable and immovable property, ups and downs in Service and Profession, Financial loss, obstalces in getting proper education etc.

5. *Padam Kal-Sarpa Yog :* Rahu-Ketu in 5-11 houses respectively form this yog. Due to this yog lack of progeny. If progeny is there then children live far or separate from the parents in old days. Loss due to secret enemies, secret diseases, no cure at time, may be jail, character of wife in Suspicious, Friends become insincere, Loss through gambling or speculation, Hand may be wounded.

6. *Maha Padam Kal Sarpa Yog :* Rahu Ketu in 6-12 houses form this yog. unsuccess in love affairs, divorce or death of the life partners Native's Character becomes suspicious. mind is always disappointed, defeated by enemies are the general results of this yog.

7. *Takshak Kal Sarpa Yog :* Rahu-Ketu in 7-1 houses produce this yog. Due to this yog loss in partnership and married life. Restlessness at home. Money given to others do not return. Enemies increase, disease in Secret parts of body are the results of his yog.

8. *Karkotak Kal-Sarpa Yog :* In 8-2 houses Rahu-ketu from this yog. Due to this yog hindraces break the rising luck. Suspension or degradation in Service, No profit from paternal property. Loss in Business, Profession, Death may occur due to long illness, accidental blow of arms, sudden or poisonous death. Loss due to insincerity of friends.

9. *Shankhanad Kalsarpa Yog :* Rahu in 9th ketu in 3rd forms shankhanad kalsarpa yog. In this yog luck does not favour. Trouble from Government, No happiness of father, Loss in business-profession, Not in good books of officers. The native has to face challenges of struggle to gain happiness.

10. *Ghatak Kal-arpa Yog :* Rahu in 10th ketu in 4th house forms Ghatak Kalsarpa Yog. Unexpected difficulties in service and profession, being possibility of profit, loss is in direct way. Progeny is ill, maternal grand parents, paternal grand parents may die. Separation from parents due to their death also may occur.

11. *Vishakta Kal-sarpa yog :* Rahu in eleventh, Ketu in fifth house produces this kalsarpa yog. due to this yog. native has to live far from birth place, dispute with elder brother, life strugglesome native suffers from eyedisease, heart trouble, insomnia etc. life ends mystically.

12. *Sheshnag Kal-sarpa Yog :* Rahu in 12th Ketu in 6th house make this yog. Due to this yog fear of enemies, defeat infight, life long bad name, surgery of eye, name and fame after death is sure.

EXAMPLE OF KAL-SARPA YOGA in Important Horoscopes

Independent India : India become free on 15-8-1947 Night 0.02 a.m. after 12. This is Anant kal-sarpayog. The main Characteristics of this yog is no peace in mind, cruelty, wicked tendency, insincerity speaking a lie etc. Rahu is in Lagna Rahu is called *"Vidharmy"* विधर्मी Vichchhed Karak विच्छेदकारक and most powerful Diplomate sitting in friends sign. So India was divided in 2 parts 1. India 2. Pakistan. Due to this Rahu English Language, English culture and civilization, Christianity is increasing day by day. Hindi though National Language but could not get its own place. In 2nd House mars a fiery planet of struggle, fight with neighbour, e.g., case of kashmir is not solved. On Boundary daily firing is due to this mars there is no solution till now and violence is still going on.

In 3rd house Sun, Moon, Mercury, Venus, Saturn 5 Planet are combined. Sun in Cancer opposes own family members makes the persons drinking wine, envy and jealous of Parents and we are seeing in present that in India National congress party, the president is not of our country. This is due to this sun in cancer. Moon and saturn, moon and Mercury, moon and Venus these all are female planets and opposite each others. Sun in cancer in feminine sign denotes that in future ladies will command Government in India. Male will be weaker and weaker. Sun is the lord of 4th house, the mother, land and public, peace, property, profession every is gone in 12th house to 4th house, i.e., in 3rd house. Sun and Saturn in one house are inimical Sun-Government, Saturn public hence both are puzzled. There is no peace in country. Leaders and politicans are too much selfish, corruption in going on top. How can we say that we are citizen of a free country. Reservation and satisfaction of minorities are poisonous to the future of the country. Name is Democracy but in real sense No Democracy.

Jupiter in 6th house in inimical sign being lord of 8th and 11th is seated. Loan on country is increasing day by day Jupiter is the karak of law, education, religion spiritualism. Everything has been turned in to foreign effect. Law and Edùcation, Wisdom and Spirituality, Religion and culture all are changed, doing nothing good to the country in real sense. This all is the result of Anant Kal Sarpa Yog in India's Horoscope.

Pandit Jawaharlal Nehru: The first Prime Minister of India. Born on 14-11-1989 at 11.30 p.m. at Allahabad.

In this horoscope there is Sheshnag *kal-sarpa* yog beginning from the 12th house to 6th house. He went to England for education so that he might be barrister. He became barrister But seeing the condition of our country and countrymen he came in politics and under the Truth and Ahimsa movement started by Mahatma Gandhi he joined Indian national congress. He went for jail many times. He sacrificed his everything for the freedom of India. He was devoid of his family, wife and son. But due to this kal-sarpa yog. He fought bravely with the British empire enemies of the country due to jupiter ketu in 6th house and got trimph at last and sworn in as P.M. on 15-8-1947. He lived for others and met with China Prime Minister chow En Lai in 1955 and campromised with him on *"Panchsheel"* and *"Hindi Chini Bhai Bhai"* Slogan But that insincere, unreliable friend become cruel enemy and attacked on India on 20-10-1962. Pandit Jawahar Lal Nehru was very kind-hearned true man hence he could not bear this sorrow agressive blow and breathed his last on 27th May 1964 by brain Haemorrhage.

Queen of Lyrics Lata Mangeshkar

Born on 8-9-192 at 9:55 p.m. at Indore

This is also Sheshnag kal-sarpa Yog. She lived unmarried for her younger brothers and sisters and devoted whole heartedly Lyrical music by her sweet songs all over the world. Jupiter, Venus in Kendra, Saturn in 8th aspecting the second house of speech and its lord Mercury and tenth house. Venus too have full aspect on 10th house. Jupiter aspects on 5th house to Sun and Mercury and 9th house, the sign of saturn. One thing here is remarkable that all the planets are bounded not by Rahu. Ketu but by Rahu Saturn. As Rahu aspects Saturn too. So this world famous Bharat Ratna Lady Lata Mangeshkar will live for ever. Acharya Rajneesh who said himself "Bhagwan Rajneesh too have Vasuki kal sarpa yog in his horoscope. He was a great oratar, writer, philosopher, student of all world religious, writer of "संभोग से समाधि" was professor of Logic in Jabalpur. But due to some characteristic suspense left the service. Delivered lecture on philosophy of Mahavir swamy and the public called him Bhagwan Rajneesh. He went to America and opened a Vast Ashram in Toronto (Canada) but the government of that country removed him. He came to India and in Poona Goregaon Park opened Osho Ashram. He earned a lot did not marry. See his horoscope :

Rahu in 9th Ketu in 3rd house produced Vasuki kal-sarpa yog. Due to this Yog he wondered in India, America then again in India delivered lectures in Sweet-Short style and become world-wide famous. He was a materialistic saint. But could not do for himself. His osho Ashram is in India.

Ramayan Katha Kar Murari Bapu also has this Yog. Born on 25-9-1946. Rahu in 9th ketu in 3rd producing Shankha Nad kal sarpa Yog. Exalted with sun moon produced "Bhadra Yog" Jupiter Venus in second house of speech made him sweet music singer of Ramkatha. Sat in 11th made him simple not earning but sacrificing for others.

Hence Kal Sarpa Yog is not totally bad. It makes the native to struggle hard and face difficulties. Hence those who have kal sarpa Yog in their horoscopes should not be disappointed but should try to take advantages of struggles and sacrifices made by them.

REMEDIAL MEASURES

1. Go to Triyam Keshwar (यंबकेश्वर) (Nasik) and do there Shanti for getting rid of Kalsarpa Dosha

2. Devote Lord Shiv by Abhishek on Monday by Rudrashtadhyayi "रूद्राष्टाध्यायी"

3. Give baths to silver shiv having snake on head and take that water daily.

4. Om namah Shivay ॐ नमः शिवाय JAP 108 times daily

5. Wear Gomed गोमेद in Silver in Middle Finger

6. Wear ring of Snake idol

7. Jap of Rahu Om Ram Rahway namah ॐ राहवे नमः

8. If with kal- sarpa Yog there are other yogas such as moon rahu, sun-rahu, moon-ketu, sun-ketu than wear cat's eye in silver in middle finger.

9. Donation of Rahu as Til, Oil, Black Cloth, iron made pot, coconut, etc.

10. Take Gau mutra गोमूत्र a spoon daily.

N.B. When there is kalsarpayog in the Horoscope and with this yog there is SATURN-SUN, SATURN-MARS, SUN-RAHU or KETU such type of native taken birth in struggle and education, service, profession, marriage, progeny etc. are not performed without difficulties. Family members, friends, neighbourer all deceit such type of natives.

KALAMRIT YOG कालामृत योग

Rahu gives good result from 0 to 20 degrees and from 21 to 30 degrees gives mixed result. If Rahu is in 1-3-5-7-9-11 houses in female signs such as Taurus, Cancer, Virgo, Scorpio, Capricorn, Pisces. It gives good result. If Rahu-Ketu are on Birth stars they give good results. If Rahu-Ketu are in 2-5-11 houses aspected by benefics it will give progeny. Rahu in 8th house makes a native briber. The native earns too much money by bribery and doing No. 2 Jobs.

If Rahu is in 6th house and jupiter is in 1-4-7-10 houses. This Yog is called Laxmi Yog this gives good result a happy, peaceful and distinguished life.

Rahu in 1-3-6-11 houses aspected by benefics give good result.

If ketu is from Lagna to 6th house and there is kalsarpa Yog then this Ketu gives good result and turns the bad result of kalsarpa yog into good results. This is called *kalamrit Yog*. Kalamrit Yog destroys the bad result of kal-sarpa Yog.

Hence while judging the horoscope the Astrologer should carefully judge the kalasarpa Yog and should not take decision suddenly.

23

Sadanta Jatah Kulnashkari

सदंत जातः कुलनाशकारी

A Child born with teeth in his month either in upper or lower Jaw is not considered auspicious astrologically because such child is regarded as killer and destroyer of Parents and family as said in Classics texts in Sanskrit "सदंत जातः कुलनाश कारी" means child born with teeth destroys all his family. The great Poet and Saint, devotee of Ram Tulsidass too was born with 32 teeth in her mouth and spoke "RAM" So he was called (राम बोल) RAMBOLA. The Parents of Tulsidas died in his early life as he was born in ABHUKTA MOOL NAKSHATRA अभुक्त मूल नक्षत्र with 32 teeth in his mouth.

Teeth appeared in the mouth of one month old child are harmful to the child himself. If teeth appeared in mouth of two month old child they are harmful to the brothers of the born child. If teeth appeared in month of 3 months old child they are bad to the sisters of born child 6 months old child's appearing of teeth is harmful to elder brother of child. In six months appearing of teeth in mouth are harmful to the Pandit who performs the Jat Karma of Child. Teeth appearing in Seventh month to 12th months are auspicious.

In any family where child is born with teeth in upper jaws there is Struggle Jealousy, Quarrels, Sufferings to Parents, Mental disturbances to mother. Father or both, death of either mother or father is the result.

If the child is born in Chitra, Vishakha, Hasta Nakshatra with teeth in mouth father dies before the birth of the child. If Saturn or Mars are even in one degree or Virgo rasi or Navamsa is Gemini or Virgo the Child's birth is with teeth in two month. If Saturn is in retrogression in Aries or Scorpio and Mars is in dual rasi i.e. in Gemini, Virgo, Sagittarius, Pisces and aspects the Saturn or Saturn aspects both rasis of Mars Aries or Scorpio. In the Horoscope of two great poet Tulsidas. Saturn is in Virgo aspecting the Scorpio Sign, the Second Sign of Mars.

I am giving here an example of a child born with teeth in his mouth as a proof of the saying Male born on 27th September in 1987 in a town

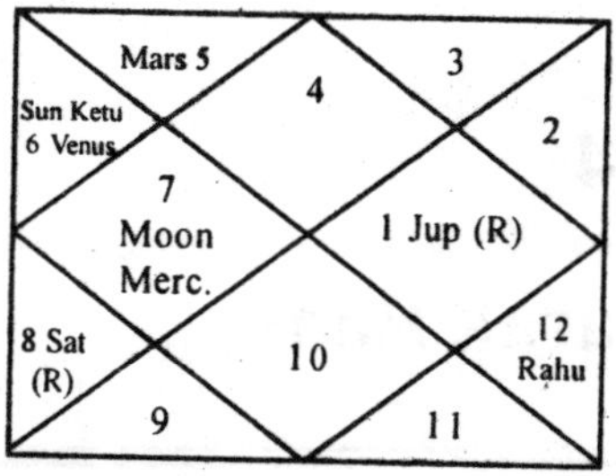

near GWALIOR at 2.10 PM in Vishakha Nakshatra first Quarter in Cancer Lagna on 11.5.1986 Marriage was performed and on 20-6-1987 the father of child died Mars is in fixed Sign Leo. Mars aspects the Saturn in Scorpio. SATURN too has full aspect on MARS. Hence MARS and Saturn are aspecting each other SATURN is in 5th house is in retrogression. Child born with teeth in upper Jaw. In 9th House (BHAGYA BHAVA) there is Rahu and lord of ninth in 10th house Jupiter is in retrogression too aspects Moon (Lord of Lagna) and Mercury (Lord of 12th house). The father of the child was assassinated by his enemy on 20-6-1987 before the birth of two child. MARS from second house aspects the 9th House Pisces whose Lord Jupiter is in 10th house in retrogression. After the birth of the child there was struggle, jealousy in the family on both sides of mother and father. Mother lost mental balance.

24

Rajyogakarak Rahu

Rahu is a chhaya graha. He gives the result of the owner of the house in which he is at the time to birth. Generally it has been seen that Rahu in tenth house in Aries, Libra, Taurus, Scorpio, Gemini, Sagutarius, Cancer, Leo, Virgo, Pisces, Capricorn and Aquarius is far better if he is alone. The Karaka of tenth house is Sun. Sun in tenth house gives rise in profession, promotion and fame to father and self and if in politics then world wide fame for example in chart No. 1 in the horoscope of Mahatma Gandhi Rahu is posited in tenth house in Cancer between Jupiter and Moon. There is Panch Mahapurusha Yoga "Malavya Yoga" due to VENUS in Lagna Libra. Venus is with Mercury Lord of 9th house, the house of religion and God. Rahu in Cancer alone in tenth house between Jupiter and Moon two benefies made him great man and world fame in the field of freedom struggle of India and religion. He was benevolent, kind hearted and devotee of God and Motherland, the depressed. The lord of fouth house Saturn in Scorpio in an inimical sign, aspects the fourth house Saturn in Scorpio in an inimical sign, aspects the fourth house his own sign. Thus fourth house is aspected by Saturn and Rahu which shows that India was badly affected by British Empire, as two malefics Rahu and Saturn are connected here with the fourth house, the house of Motherland. Jupiter aspects the Lagna and Moon. Thus Mahatma Gandhi was highly spiritual minded and a great politician too, but this Rahu kept him far from any political post as President or Prime Minister, but gave him fame in the world. He was the greatest orator Simple and high thinking which he showed in his words and action, Chart No. 2 position of Rahu in tenth house in Virgo in the horoscope of the first President of

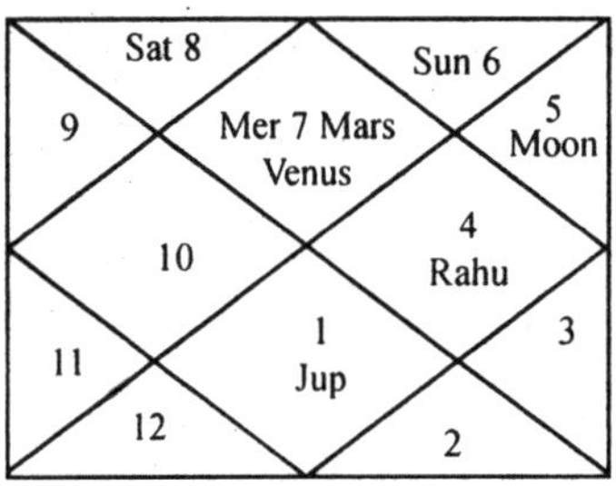

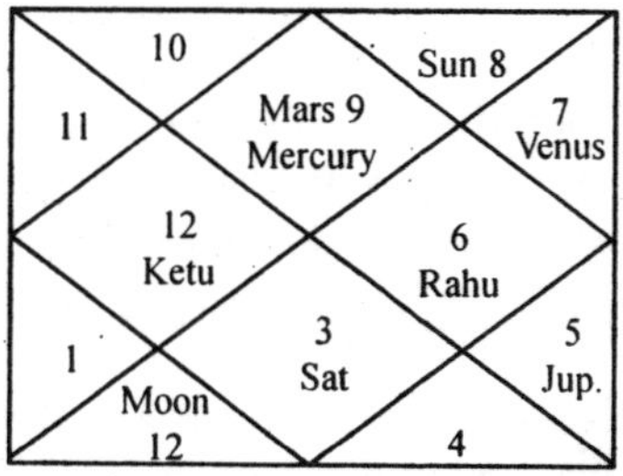

India. Dr. Rajendra Prasad. Dr. Rajendra Prasad was the true follower of Mahatma Gandhi really a great man by heart and action Politeness, Simplicity, Devotion to the nation, Love to his country men was the main characteristic of his life. Rahu is tenth between Jupiter and Venus, in the sign of Mercury made him a great politician, but religious and noble minded too. Saturn in a Quadrant made him very kind hearted. A great benefic and lord of Lagna Jupiter aspects the Lagna, Lord of tenth Mercury and lord of fifth Mars. The position of Rahu alongwith Jupiter, Mars and Mercury is strong.

Birth Lagna

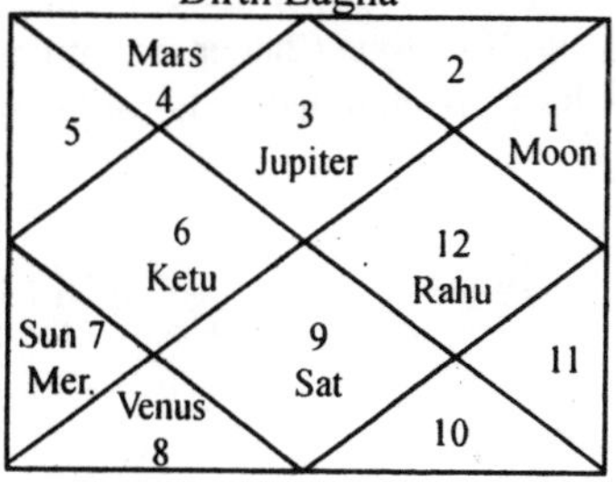

CHART NO. 3 : Horoscope of Shri Arjun Singh, the Cabinet Minister for Human Resources and Development has also Rahu in tenth house posited lonely. The significator of Rahu Jupiter is posited in Lagna aspected by the lord of ninth Saturn. Rahu in Gochara is Pisces. When Jupiter came in Cancer he became the union minister in 2004 again.

CHART NO. 4: Horoscope of Shri Atal Bihari Bajpai, Ex P.M. and a great politician, an orator, Statesmen, Poet this Rahu in tenth house in Cancer alone. The benefic Saturn for Tula Lagna aspects Rahu. Hence when 1977 Saturn was in Leo aspecting the Lagna and Rahu in Virgo, Leo, Cancer, he was the foreign Minister of India more successful in his career. Rahu also aspects the Moon, the owner of tenth house. He became P.M. of India when Saturn was in Taurus, Gemini. Rahu in cancer made him P.M.

Birth Lagna

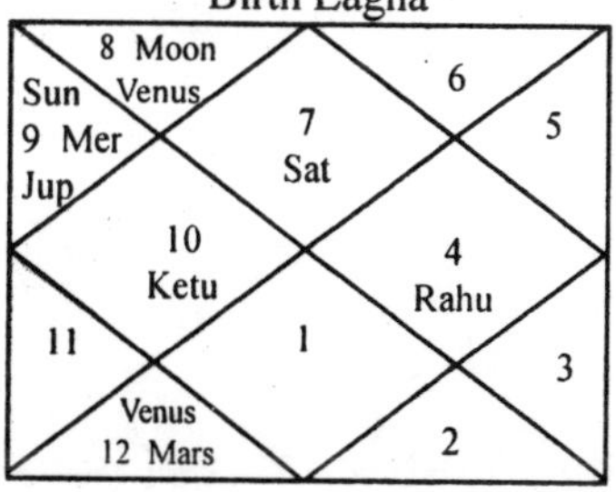

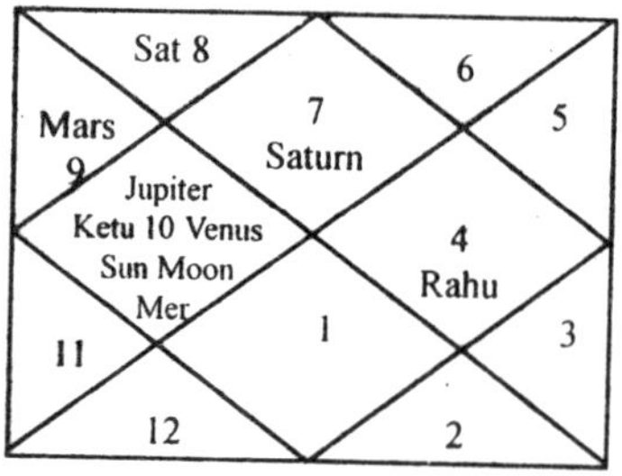

CHART NO. 5 : Horoscope of Shri Shiv Charan Mathur, the Ex-Chief Minister of Rajasthan born in Guna District of Madhya Pradesh. Rahu in Cancer alone aspected by six planets, the Karaka of tenth SUN. The owner of tenth Moon, three benefics Mercury, Jupiter, Venus and Ketu. This is a peculiar horoscope having six planets in a sign in a quadrant. This position shows the position of support by the people for him as the lord of fourth house Saturn also aspects the fourth house. Hence fourth house has been strong by the position of six planets therin and aspects of Rahu and Saturn too.

Ravindra Nath Tagore, Jai Prakash Narain, Choudhary Charan Singh, Ram Krishna Param Hansa, Hari Singh Gaur, N.G. Ram Chandran, Antuley, Netaji Subhash Chandra Bose also have Rahu in tenth in their horoscopes.

25

Rahu in the Tenth House

Rahu is called a malefic planet. In astrology it is known as Chaaya graha or a shadow planet. In the present age, ie., in Kaliyuga Rahu plays an important role in making a man a politician, educationist, Engineer, Doctor, Leader, Photographer, Film hero and heroin. It bestows with the nature of the lord of the house which it occupies or the ones which are the fifth and the nineth houses as the case may be. It is said that Rahu is the enemy of the sun and the moon. Generally it gives good results in the upachaya houses 3rd 6th, 10th, 11th houses counted from the ascendant. Rahu generally gives benefic or favourable results while occupying Aries. Taurus, Gemini, Cancer, Virgo, Sagittarius and Capricorn. It is said to give malefic or at least mixed results while in Leo, Libra, Scorpio, Aquarius and Pisces. Rahu is known as the Karaka for Cancer and Leo ascendants. Rahu further gives benefic and good results while occupying the quadrants or the trines alongwith their lords. It makes a man very clever, quick-witted, strong and is aspected by Venus or Jupiter. But while in Scorpio or Aries and with Mars and (or Saturn) it makes the native adventurous, risk taking bold and cunning.

Rahu gives invariably extraordinarily good results while in the tenth house - if it is alone or with benefics and if the tenth house is of Venus or Jupiter. I have seen that Rahu Dasa improves the career of the native and opens up tremendous opportunities. For example Rahu made Rajiv Gandhi, Prime Minister of India, during its Dasa. Simultaneously Rahu gave misfortune too - his mother was assassinated. This proves Rahu is capable of giving both benefic and malefic results simultaneously especially while in the tenth house.

Here are some examples of horoscopes in which Rahu is in the tenth house. These are selected charts of great men, leaders, saints and politicians of our country. Tenth house is the house of name, fame, work, occupation, profession, avocation, source of earning, degree of one's attainment, ups and downs in one's career life. Hence the position of Rahu becomes very important in a man's life and part of it.

1. In the horoscope of Mahatma Gandhi Rahu is in Cancer, the tenth house. Rahu is Karaka for Cancer. Jupiter has square aspect on Rahu from the seventh house. The lord of the nineth. Mercury is situated in the Lagna. Rahu keeps under its control both the house and its lord. Rahu made Mahatma Gandhi Vishwa Vandya or internationally worshipped. The other factors too played a very important role, in Gandhi's horoscope to make his strict follower of truth and non-violence. Venus in Libra Lagna too. Jupiter in the seventh house aspects the moon also. Mutual aspect between Jupiter and Venus creates Chaamara yoga, Rahu made Mahatma Gandhi fight strongly the mightiest power in the world, the British and succeed in freeing the mother land from the clutches of slavery.

2. In the horoscope of Lok Nayak, Jay Prakash Narayan, Rahu is in tenth in Aries and the Lord of the tenth, Mars is in the Lagna. Here too Rahu is in square position from Jupiter who is in the seventh house. Jupiter is the lord of the nineth house also. In this case too Rahu is very strong and has made the late leader second to none in Indian politics though after no mean amount of suffering.

3. In the horoscope of Ravindra Nath Tagore. Rahu is in tenth house in Sagittarius being aspected by the lord of the trine, Mars. The nineth house, Scorpio is aspected by the greatest benefic Jupiter the lord of the ascendant and the tenth house who is in exaltation in Cancer - the fifth house from the ascendant.

4. In the horoscope of the late Dr. Rajendra Prasad, Rahu is in the tenth house, in Virgo having Jupiter in the nineth and Venus in the eleventh. The lord of the first trine, i.e., the lord of the fifth house is in the Lagna having square aspect with Ruhu who is in the tenth house.

5. In the horoscope of Ramkrishna Parama Hamsa, Rahu is in Scorpio, the tenth house. Jupiter has full aspect on the Lagna, the Sun and the Moon. The lord of the nineth, Venus which is in exaltation in second house, is in Trine to Rahu.

6. In the horoscope of Jain Muni, Vidyananda, Rahu is in the tenth house, in Cancer being in Square position both from the lords of the fifth and the nineth house and the ascendant lord.

In most of these cases it can be seen as stated in Vaidya Nath Dixit Jataka Parijatam that Rahu is in Cancer with a strong planet in its quadrant causing Raja Yoga.

The above examples show that Rahu in the tenth makes a person famous in the world if it is in square position from the lords of the fifth and the nineth houses and/or the ascendant lord and the exalted planet. There are many other examples of horoscopes having Rahu in the 10th house. Such natives Sir Harisingh Gaur, Dr. Jagadish Chandra Bose, Rana

Ranjit singh Choudhry, Charansingh, Atal Bihari Bajpai, Thakar Arjun singh etc. are great people of recent times who have proved to be great in their own way.

Horoscopes: 1: Ascendant : Libra, Sun in Virgo, Moon in Leg, Mercury, Venus and Mars in Libra, Saturn in Scorpio, Jupiter in Aries, Rahu in Cancer and Ketu, in. Capricorn.

2: Ascendant : Cancer, Sun and Venus in Virgo, Mars in Cancer, Saturn in Sagittarius. Moon and Jupiter in Capricorn, Rahu in Aries and Mercury and Ketu in Libra.

3: Ascendant : Pisces, Moon in Pisces, Sun, Mercury and Venus in Aries, Mars and Ketu in Gemini, Jupiter in Cancer, Saturn in Leo and Rahu in Sagittarius.

4: Ascendant : Sagittarius with Mars and Mercury. Sun in Scorpio, Venus in Libra, Saturn in Gemini, Jupiter in Leo, Moon in Taurus, Rahu in Virgo and Ketu in Pisces.

5: Ascendant : Aquarius, Sun, Moon, Mars and Mercury in Aquarius, Venus in Pisces, Ketu in Taurus, Jupiter in Gemini, Saturn in Libra and Rahu in Scorpio.

6: Ascendant : Libra. Saturn in Libra, Jupiter in Sagittarius, Ketu in Capricorn, Sun, Moon, Mercury, Venus in Aries, Mars in Taurus, Rahu in Cancer.

26

Raj-Yog
राजयोग

In old text books of Astrology Raj-yog is described by means of kings, Emperors, Mahamantri, Amatya, Senapati, etc. But in modern times all over the world is democracy hence there old Raj-Yogs now has been related to President, Prime minister, Chief minister, M.L.A, M.P, Governor etc.

According to BHAV-KUTUHAL भावकुतूहल if lord of ninth is in 5th house and lord of fifth house is in 9th house then the person with pearls is the lord of land or earth :-

नवम भावपतिस्तनयालये सुतपर्तिनवमे यदि जन्मिन:
अति विचित्र मणिब्रजमण्डिलो वसुमती विभूतां स नरो ब्रजेत्

In the same way lord of tenth in fifth and lord of fifth in tenth aspected by a lord of 5-9 houses, the person becomes sure a king :-

कर्माधिष्ठा: सुतस्थाने सुतेशा कर्मगो यदा
त्रिकोणपतिमा हण्टो राजा भवति निश्चितम्

Lord of tenth, Lagna, fourth, fifth among these any one planet being strong with lord of ninth or aspected by lord of ninth the person becomes a king:

राज्यलग्नप वाहनेश्च सुतपा धर्मालय स्वामिना
संयुक्ता यदि वीक्षिताश्च बलिनो राजा भवेन्मानव:

For Raj-yog tenth house, lord of tenth house, planet in tenth house, Exchange of Lords of ninth and tenth houses or mutually aspecting being in fourth and tenth houses and the Quadrant houses 1-4-7-10 and Triangle houses 5-9 must be strong either by occupation, exchange, or in friend's house or in own sign or in exaltation. Besides Jupiter, Venus, Moon, Mercury, Sun Saturn must be strong correlated with 1-4-7-10 and 5-9 houses.

Birth Chart 1

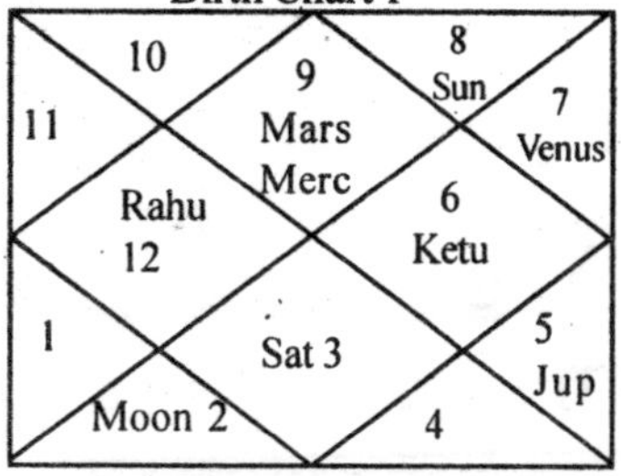

For example :

1. Horoscope of Dr. Rajendra Prasad. The first president of India. Here lords of 5th and 10th combined in Lagna aspected by Jupiter and Saturn. Jupiter as lord of Lagna and Saturn as lord of 2-3 houses. In eleventh venus in own sign too is strong.

Birth Chart 2

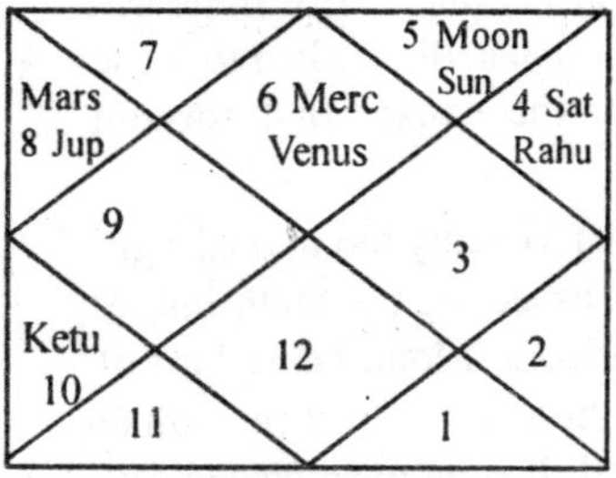

2. Dr. Radha Krishnan. The second President of India. Here the lords of ninth and tenth combined in Lagna aspected by lord of 5th Saturn. Jupiter aspects 7-9-11 houses. Mars too aspects 9-10 houses.

Birth Chart 3

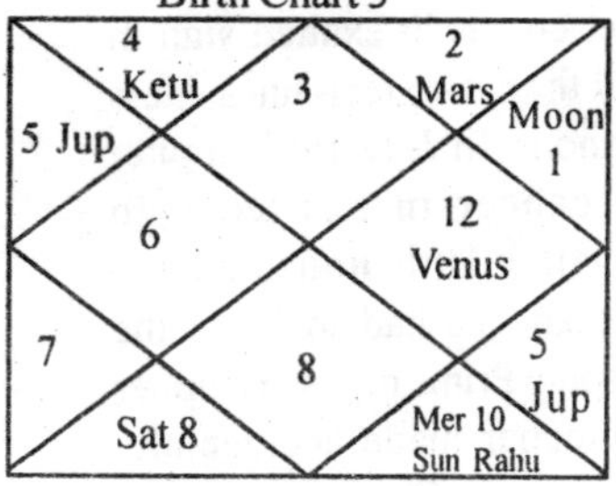

3. Horoscope of Zakir Husain. In the expresident Zakir Husain's horoscope lord of fifth venus in 10th exulted. Lord of 10th Jupiter aspects 9th house and Moon Saturn aspects lord of 10th Jupiter. Thus 9-10 lords have been related by aspect.

Birth Chart 4

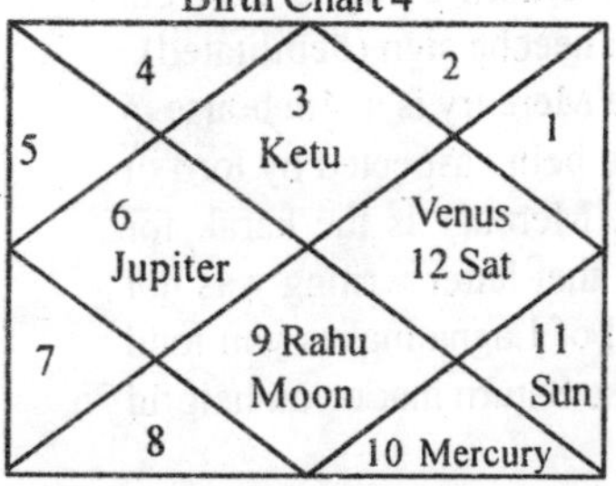

4. Horoscope of George Washington. In the first president of U.S.A. George Washington's horoscope. Lord of ninth and 10th are mutually aspecting each other. Lord of fifth venus in 10th house with lord of 9th Saturn. Thus created strong Raj-yog.

27

Raj-Bhang Yog

राज भंग योग

In August 1990 in first week deputy Prime minister of India Mr. Devilal and Pakistan's Prime minister Mrs. Benazir Bhutto had to loose their post and power. Now see what are the causes that formed ***RAJ-BHANG YOGA राज भंग योग.***

Lagna Gemini Dual Sign, lord of Lagna Mercury too in dual sign, though in exaltation in 4th house with Sun aspecting the tenth house. Lord of tenth Jupiter is in 8th house in capricorn. Moon being lord of second house is in 6th house debilitated. It is an experienced fact that when any planet is in debilitation in birth Lagna in any house, then when that planet comes in exalted sign in GOCHAR the native feels uneasiness and dishonour. In July 1990 Jupiter came in cancer in exalted sign aspecting the 10th house in his horoscope and he had to loose the post of Deputy Prime minister. Jupiter in cancer with Ketu aspected by Rahu in Gochar made accidentally suddenly this position.

Birthchart-Devi Lal

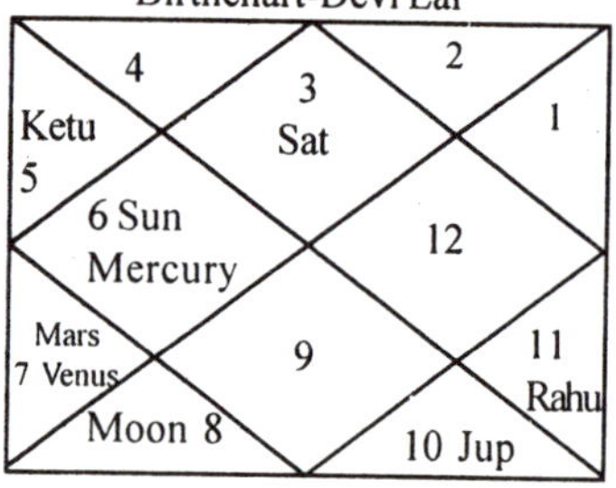

For Raj-Bhang yoga 8th house, Lord of 8th, 11th house and lord of 11th house are responsible. In his horoscope Saturn being lord of 8th aspects the 10th house. The lord of tenth is in neecha sign (debilitated).

Though in his horoscope Lord of Lagna Mercury is in 4th house in exalted own sign aspecting the 10th house and being aspected by lord of 10th house Jupiter producing Bhardra-Yoga. Mercury is the karak for writing hence letter writing produced dispute that letter writing was not true but false. Mercury in own sign being lord of Lagna makes you loud speaker. Saturn in Lagna aspects the 10th house Saturn made you helpful for villagers and their supporter.

In the horoscope of Benagir Bhutto too lord of tenth is in 8th house with Ketu aspected by Rahu. In this way in both horoscope the lord of tenth is in 8th house the lord of 12th house mars aspects the tenth house.

Horoscope of Benazir Bhutto Mrs. Benazir Bhutto was dismissed on 6-8-90 in Moon-Eclipse yoga on 6-8-90 there was Saturn in the horoscope of Benazir Bhutto Saturn was retrograded. Saturn is Markesh to sagittarius Lagna and is in tenth house retrograded. Hence retrogression of Saturn in her birth Lagna, Moon Rahu combination in second house. In fifth house lord of eleventh venus is situated. In 8th house Mercury Ketu combination and lord of Lagna Jupiter's presence in 6th house aspecting the 12th house (Expense House) all these circumstance in Gochar are telling the story of loosing power in Government in both the Horoscope.

Birth Lagni Benazir Bhutto

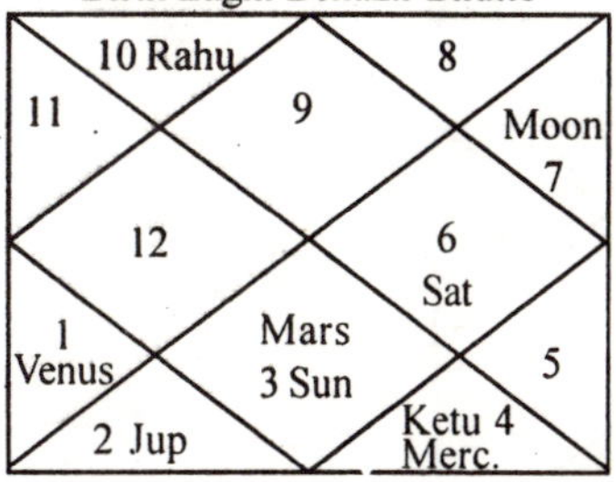

It has been concluded that if lord of tenth house (Government) is in 8th house and is aspected by the lords of eleventh and twelfth houses then RAJ-BHANG YOGA राजभंग योग is sure.

ANTAR of VENUS in SATURN MAHADASA

I have experienced that Venus antardasa in Saturn Mahadasa make the politicians far from chair or in words produces *RAJ-BHANG YOGA* who had to leave the chair of prime minister of India e.g., in case of Mrs. Indira Gandhi, the ExPrime Minister of India on 22-3-1977. When Venus antar was running in Saturn Mahadasa w.e.f. 21-2-1977 to 21-4-1980. For Verification we have to Study the Horoscope of Late Prime Minister Mrs. Indira Gandhi.

Horoscope of Indira Gandhi
Example-1

Born on 19-11-1917 at 11.11 P.M. at Allahabad. Vikram Samvat 1974 Kartik Shukla 5 Monday 30/6 Uttra Shada Nakshatra 55/52 Gand Yoga 52/58 Vava Karan 30/6. Birth Lagna Cancer.

Birth Lagna

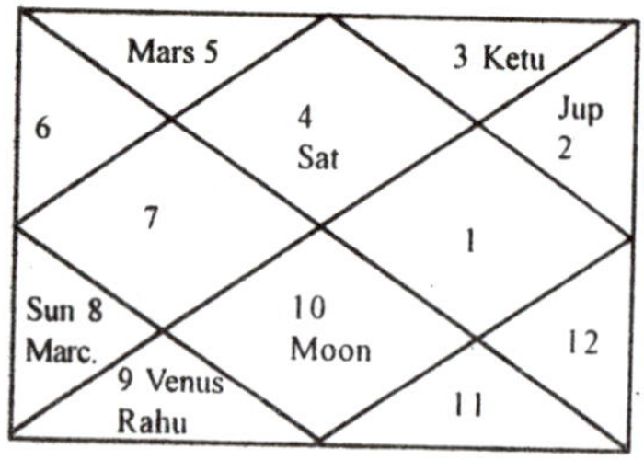

Moon Lagna

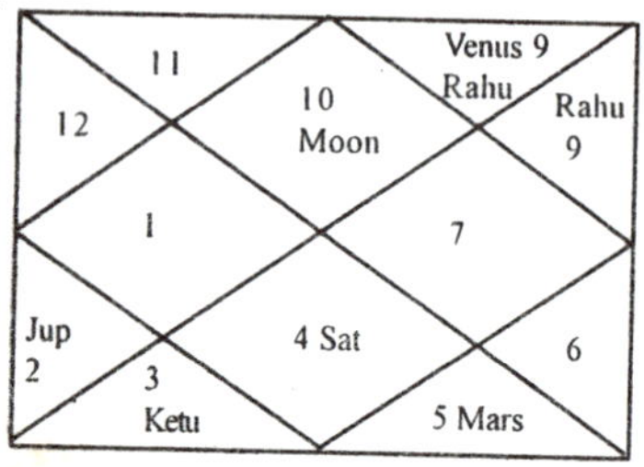

Karkausa-Capricorn, Atmakarak-Saturn

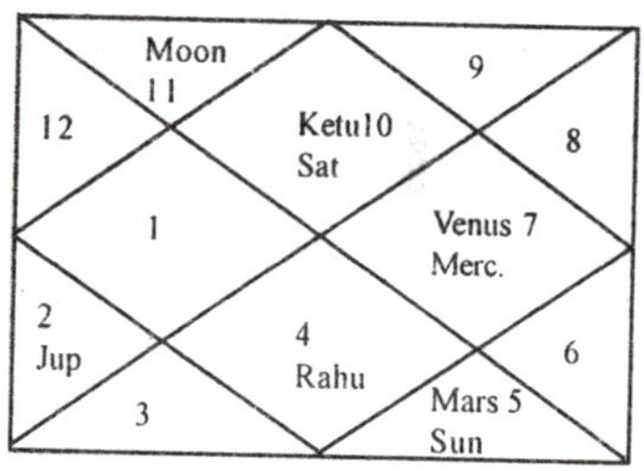

Mars is in vargottama Navamsa Jupiter too is in vargottama Navamsa.

Planetary Position is as following:

Planet	*Sign*	*Degree*	*Kala*	*Nakshatra*	*Charan*
LAGNA	3	27	13	Ashlekha	4
SUN	7	4	8	Anuradha	1
MOON	9	5	37	Uttra Shada	2
MARS	4	16	23	Poorva Phalguna	1
MERCURY	7	13	15	Anuradha	3
JUPITER +	1	15	1	Rohini	2 R.
VENUS	8	21	0	Poorva Shada	3
SATURN	3	21	47	Ashlekha	2
RAHU	8	10	33	Mool	4
KETU	2	10	33	Aridra	2

VIMSHOTTARI MAHADASA

SUN—19-11-1917 to 30-4-1919

MOON—1-5-1919 to 30-4-1929

MARS—1-5-1929 to 30-4-1936

RAHU—1-5-1936 to 30-4-1954

JUPITER—1-5-1954 to 30-4-1970

SATURN—1-5-1970 to 30-4-1989

In the Horoscope of Mrs. Indira Gandhi 3 Planets are in Mutual exchanges of Signs—

SUN—MARS (SUN IN SCORPIO, MARS IN LEO)

JUPITER—VENUS (JUPITER IN TAURUS VENUS IN SAGITTARIUS)

SATURN—MOON (SATURN IN CANCER, MOON IN CAPRICORN)

She was elected Congress President in 1959 in Mercury antar Jupiter Mahadasa.

Death of father—in Venus antar Jupiter Mahadasa.

Minister for Information antar Jupiter Mahadasa.

Prime Minister 30-8-1963 to 30-12-1966

In Moon antar Jupiter Mahadasa Again Prime Minister in March 1967, In Mars antar Jupier Mahadasa.

Division in Congress RAHU Antar Jupiter Mahadasa.

SATURN MAHADASA

30-4-1970 to 3-5-1973 P.M. on 18-3-1971 SATURN ANTAR

(21-2-1977 to 21-4-1980) Resigned from P.M. on 22-3-1977 Venus Antar

Again Prime Minister on 14-1-1980: Venus Antar in Saturn Mahadasa.

Assassinated on 31-10-1984 in Sun Antar Saturn Mahadasa.

The Period of Venus in SATURN MAHADASA

Because Saturn is in Ashlekha Nakshatra whose Lord is Mercury Lord of 12th house, 3rd, house and Venus is in own Nakshatra Poorva Shada Venus is in SAGITTARIUS in JUPITER. Sign hence, Venus Anatar proved fatal.

Example-2

Dig Vijay Singh

Recently last year the ex-Chief Minister of Madhya Pradesh had to leave the Chair of C.M. in Venus Antar in Saturn Mahadasa. Born on 28-2-1947 at 8.00 A.M. at Indore in

PISCES LAGNA

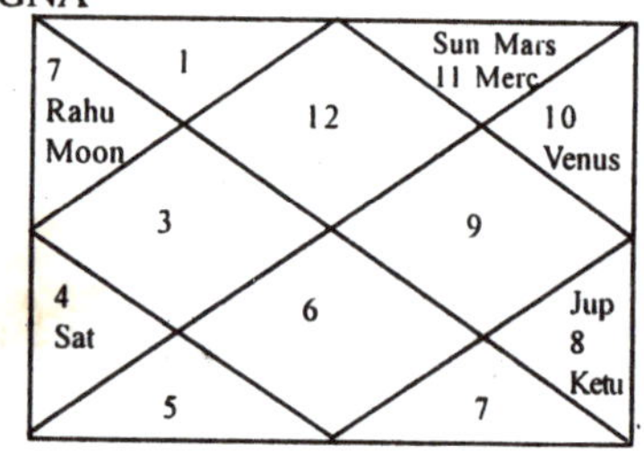

MOON LAGNA

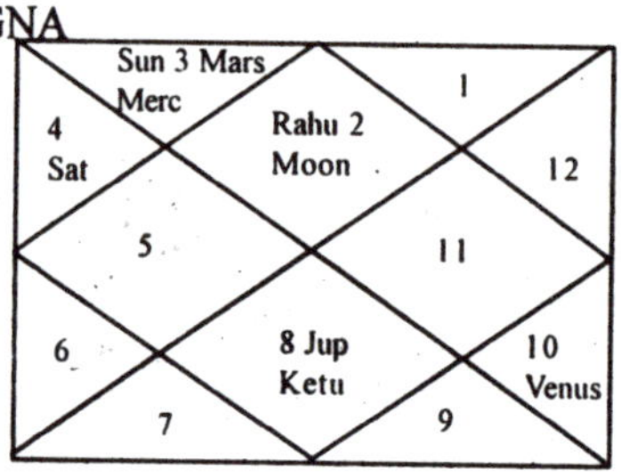

KARKAMSA

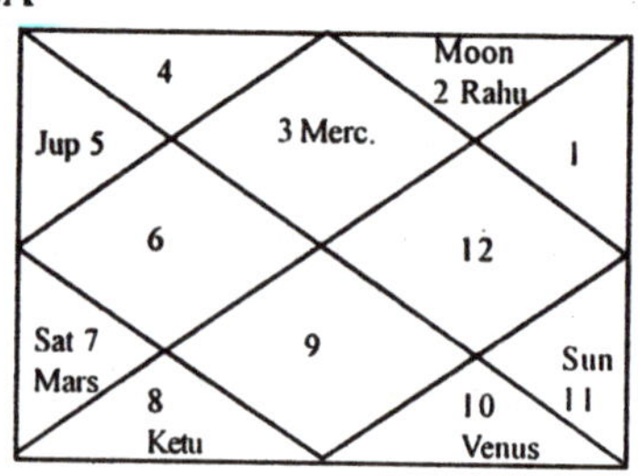

Planetary Position is as following—

Planet	*Sign*	*Degree*	*Kala*	*Nakshatra*	*Charan*
SUN	10	15	32	SHAT BHISHA	3
MOON	1	13	46	ROHINI	2
MARS	10	1	37	DHANISHTHA	3
MERCURY	10	28	42	POORVA BHADRA PADA	3
JUPITER	7	6	28	ANURADHA	1
VENUS	9	1	29	UTTRA SHADA	2
SATURN	3	10	41	PUSHYA	4
RAHU	1	16	28	ROHINI	2
KETU	7	16	28	ANURADHA	4

MOON, RAHU, VENUS, KETU, SUN are in Vargottama Navamsha. Venus is Lord of 8th and 3rd. 3rd house is 8th from 8th house hence Venus in AKARAK and Marak for Pisces Lagna and in KARKAMSA too is in 8th house. Venus is in the Sign of Sun who is great enemy and KARAK for Government. Saturn is in own Nakshatra. Hence Venus antar in Saturn Mahadasa proved fatal to Dig Vijay Singh.

Saturn Mahadasa began from 28-2-1995 and there is Venus antardasa from 21-12-2001 to 21-2-2005.

Dig Vijay Singh was Chief Minister of Madhya Pradesh for 2 terms. 1st term was 1993 to 1998 2nd term was 1998 to 2003 hence in the period of Venus antar in Saturn Mahadasa he had to leave the Chair of C.M. I have hinted about this fact while discussing his 57th year in fortnightly paper JANA-ADHAR issue of February 2003 on Page 65. In Mudda Dasa for 57 Years I had written.

20-10-2003 20-12-2003 and Really UMA BHARTI defeated him and became C.M. of M.P. sworn in on 8-12-2003. This was the period of Venus antar in Saturn Mahadasa and in Solar return Chart for 57 Years to Dig Vijay Singh was the period of Venus Mudda Dasa in which he had to leave the Chair of C.M. JAN-ADHAR is published from Ragho Garh (GUNA) and on 28-02-2003 Mr. Dig Vijay Singh issued this paper in Bhopal.

Hence in these 2 cases I have experienced that Venus antar in Saturn Mahadasa Produces RAJ-BHANG YOGA. Hence Venus antar period in Saturn Mahadasa is dangerous for those who are on high posts as C.M., P.M. etc.

28

Numerology

Persons Born in Number 1

In numerology number one is alloted to Sun. Sun is the main planet in Solar System so is the number one in Numerology. Sun is the main base of this world, life of all animals, human beings and soul or Pran in the body of human beings.

Persons those born on 1-10-19-28 dates of any months are guided by number one. Number one is their birth number and sun is the ground of them. Persons born on 1-10-19-28 are strong intellectuals, have dignity, in dividuality, originality, genius ambitions, brave and hold, having independent personality. Their mind is fertile, their decision are impartial, thoughts incentive, and active. They do not like dependency on others but thousands like to work under their subordination and think themselves grateful.

Number one persons are genius, extra ordinary organiser and to be head of any institution, organisation, Association etc. From very early childhood they try to command small and big societies. They are intutives and have the godgift of knowing others mind activity. They are industrious, farsighted, having magnetic Individuality become the centre of attraction from very early childhood. They are shiming like sun in every field of life, their memory is Sharp. they are Aesthetist, farsight, Psychologist, honest, fond of travelling abroad in the world and making circumstances supporting them. They are born leaders of people. Their insight have scruting power which make them great and number one personality in shining and guiding others in the world.

Number one born persons are very kind hearted, living in always happy moods, through sympathetic to human beings and have high virtuous power. They love honour, discipline and always busy in helping humanity at large level. They surprise the world by their great works and farsight like sun. Coming generation remember their works for a long time and promise to act according to the way of humanity shown by them. They are great proudy independent nationalist of high rank.

For happiness and welfare of mankind is बहुजन हिताय बहुजन सुखाय their motto. They have faith in Veda's words चरैवेति चरैवेति go on go on and words of Shrimad Bhagwat Gita of Lord Shri Krishna 'कर्मण्येवाधिकारस्ते मा फलेषु कदाचन' your right is to work and not in results of therein.

In transit when sun comes in own sign leo, exalted sign aries, friends sign sagittarius, pisces, scorpio etc. native born in number one feels happiness in these above mentioned periods and when sun is in debilitation Sign Libra, inimical signs. Capricorn, Aquarius, taurus etc. then number one person feels unhappiness, gets trouble and dishonour etc. e.g. Late Smt Indira Gandhi Ex Prime Minister of India born in Number one as birth number on 19-11-1917 when sun came in transit in debilitation sign libra she was assassinated on 31-10-1984 because her birth number's lord sun was in weak position.

In Zodiac sun is the lord of 5th sign leo in natural way. Leo represents heart, Abdoman and eyes hence number one person has danger of heart trouble, eye disease, stomach trouble etc. Any kind of intoxication is poisonous to him. As sun and leo are fiery hence there is lot of heat in them hence in life they are never disappointed and never feel fatigued. Their blood circular is Sharp and high so there is fear of high blood pressure too. In the palms of Number one person the sun line is clear and Straight. Mount of sun has square, triangle, straight line on it. The fourth finger Anamika अनामिका is also evilless. Number one produced most ambition and important distinguished personalities in the world.

It is not easy to get victory over number one person born on 1-10-19-28 dates of any month any where in the world. They are fit for executive posts as collector, Sub divisional magistrate civil judge, session judge, Judges of High Court, Commander in chief of Army, Director General of Police or S.P. T.I. etc.

They help others but this world forgets their sympathetic views towards them and have envy, Jealousy of them. Hence their kind heart is broken but they are super human being hence they preserve their Qualities of kind hearted, patient, heping nature etc. as a serpent preserves his 'Mani' jewel.

Born in first date of any months are Alexander, the great who saw the dream of becoming victiorious over the world, German Politician Bismark, Ex-President of U.S.A. Jimmi Karter, Anne Beasent, the famous Hindi poet Rameshwar Shukla "Anchal" Hindi Gazal writer Dushyan Kumar, Liladhar Jagudi, Cricket Player Vadekar, Lady Diana, Central ex-Minister P.A. Sangma.

Born on 10th date of any month are the great freedom fighter, great nationalist, rememberable at morning are Maharana Pratap of Chittorgarh

(Rajasthan) world famous cricket player Sunil Gavaskar, Ex Vice President of India Jatti, Madhav Rao Scindia, Gulamnavi Azad, Arif Mohammed Khan etc.

Born on 19th of any month are the most brilliant, brave and hold lady, the first freedom fighter of India. Queen of Jhansi Maharani Laxmi Bai, the late-prime minister of India Smt. Indira Gandhi, the fast freedom fighter and Hindu pat Maharaj Chhatrapati Shivaji Maharaj of Singh Garh, the world famous Astronomer Copernicus ex-President of India Neelam Sanjeev Reddy, Hindi poet Kumar Narain Dr. Shankar Dayal Sharma etc.

Born on 28th date of any months are the producer of great french Revolution Dante (दांते) the great german poet Goehte, (गोटे) Ex-President of U.S.A. Woodro wilson, the great India freedom fighter Lala Lajpat Ray, the queen of Lyrics Lata Mangeshkar, Noor Zahan (Ex-Queen of India), Ex Prime Minister of India P.V. Narsimha Rao, Dig Vijay Singh Ex Chief Minister of Madhya Pradesh (India).

In this way Number one has given this world. Many famous personalities who made history of their Countries. Freedom fighters, Presidents, Prime ministers, kings, poet, player, musicians, Philosophers, Politicians. Their names will ever shine in the world-history and will inspire others to do great works in this world.

Sunday, Tuesday, Thursday are good days to begin any job. White, Yellow, Light red Colour may give then success. hence they should wear cloths of these colours. They should wear Ruby in Golden ring in fourth finger or Coral in gold or silver in the fourth finger or yellow sapphire in Golden ring in first finger.

Their friendship many be successful with those born on 2-4-9-3 dotes and on Monday, tuesday, thursday etc.

Persons Born in Number Two

In numerology moon represents number two as sun represents number one. Persons born on 2-11-20-29 dates of any months have their birth Number two. These persons gets power, courage, strength, inspiration from moon. Like number one they are also kind hearted, imaginative, peaceful mind, Artist, lover of Nature, fond of travels, independent in love matters. They are also incentive and discoverer like number one but are less impressive.

There is mental strength more in spite of physical strength. They imagine good planning in their minds but in real activity the plannings are not done. To serve humanity is the main quality among them.

They feel difficulties in action due to kind hearted, restless in mind, irregularity in life. They are too much sensitive hence there is lack of strong will power so they feel sadness and are disappointed. Sunday,

Monday, Friday are good for beginning any new job, Industry, or work. They should wear cream colour cloths on their body and pearl in little finger in silver on monday. Blue, Black colours should be omitted.

Their digestive system is weak hence troubles in stomach, gastric trouble, swelling in intestine, Hernia, wounds etc. diseases may weaken their health. Hence they should take simple food. They should take in vegetables Cauliflower, Spinaeh, Cabage, in fruits Cucumber, Grapes, fig, Chestnut, Pineapple, Pomegranate, Plantain, watermelon etc. Number two persons are famous for their imaginative power hence with the strength of imagination they work hard and become famous. They should increase strong will power, self-reliance otherwise being uncontrolled they cannot be successful in life.

Born on 2nd date of october Mahatma Gandhi become great by using his imaginative power in fighting against freedom for India. Born in a very poor family, a father less child Lal Bahadur Shastri become the prime minister of India, American President Harding was also born on 2nd, Chief Justice of India R.C. Lahoti.

Those born on eleventh of any month are the Inventor Edition, Mahatma Phule, Musician K.L. Sahgal, Acharya Rajneesh, Cricket Player Saleem Durrani, Chief Educationist J. Krishna murti are main.

Those born on twentieth of any month are Ex-Prime Minister of India Shri Rajeev Gandhi, Ex-Chief Minister of Madhya Pradesh, Ex-Governor of Uttar Pradesh Motilal Bora, Among Literary Personalities Late Shri Jagannath Prasad Milind of Gwalior, Poet Trilochan, Dictator Herr Hitlar, Hajrat Mohammad, Nepoleon etc.

Those born on 29th date are late Shri Morarji Bhai Desai Ex-Prime Minister of India, John Cannady Ex-President of U.S.A., Musolini, Gladaston of U.K.

For those born in number two on 2-11-20-29 dates February, May, July, August, November are two not good months to begin any new job etc.

Persons Born in Number Three

Persons born on 3-12-21-30 dates of any months have their birth number 3. Jupiter represents number three. Jupiter is the most powerful, influential Divine Planet among all the plants.

Number three persons are very kind-hearted, ambitious, well-wisher of all humanity are independent and like freedom in every action. They are the great adviser of freedom and originality. They are born leaders. They feel trouble in subordination of others. They are highly ambitious and want world-wide fame. They do not like little work, small job, lower thoughts. They are highly devotee of Guru and God, truely obedient, great nationalist, disciplined and defensive of cultural, religious and social heritage. They are Virtuous, dutiful and maintain responsibilities with law and order Being born in a very poor family they rise very high and due to extraordinary works are remembered for ever. They are pure byheart truthful, honest, virtuous and religious.

They rise high in general administration, Education, organising bodies, leadership, head of an institution by their ambition and morality. There is one danger to command and order others and being strong on their principle. Hence they should remove this fault by self-realisation. If they are far from this fault Number three person do great deeds and surprise the world.

Jupiter transists in 12 years a sign and come on the same sign in 12 years. Hence in 12-13 years of age number 3 persons have progressive change. Jupiter rules punarvasu, vishakha, Poorva Bhadra Pada Nakshatras hence on 3-12-21-30 dates if there is Monday, Thursday, Friday and Nakshatra of jupiter then the person born on 3-12-21-30 dates the person has extraordinary genuine and becomes distinguished by serving humanity in society; State and World. When Sun transists on Nakshatras of Jupiter e.g. on Punarvasu between 5th July to 21th July, on Vishakha between 6 Nov. to 21 Nov. on Poorva Bhadrapada from 6th March to 21 March if anybody is born in Number 3, i.e., on 12-21 dates then the person influenced by jupiter gets name and fame in World. Those born in these Nakshatras of Jupiter other than Number 3 also make progress e.g. Sunil Gawaskar (10 July), Arjun Singh (5th Nov.), Jawahar Lal Nehru (14 Nov.), Indira Gandhi (19 Nov.), Gajanan Madhav Mukti Bodh (Hindi poet born on 13 Nov.), C.V. Raman (7 Nov.), Chandra Kant Devtale (13 Nov.) Jaganath Prasad Milind (20 Nov.) Yeshwant Rao Chauhan (12 March) Sheikh Muzib (17 March) Vasant Sathe (5 March), Madhav Rao Scindia (10 March), Hindi Poet Agyeyu (अज्ञेय - 7 March), etc. These Persous born in the period of Nakshatra of Jupiter indirectly got benefit of Number 3 as Number 3 is represensed by Jupiter.

Number three person do not know to how by others. They are independent and have their prestige made by any way. Persons born On 1-2-9 numbers are proved good friends because number one represents Sun, Number two represents Moon, number nine represents Mars and these three planets. Sun, Moon, Mars are friends of Jupiter.

Number 3 persons suffer generally ~~from~~ weakness in nerves, gastric trouble, Heart trouble, Skin disease, High blood pressure, fatness, Constipation, Swelling, Stomach trouble, trouble in throat tube. Cough etc. They should take apple, grapes, almond, Garlic, Saffron, Clove, Nutmeg, fig etc. with Simple food. They should wear sapphire (Pukh Raj) in first finger in golden ring.

Born on 3 date Poet laureate (Rashtra Kavi) Maithlisharan Gupta, Music director Jaideo, Amitabh Bachchan. Dr. Rajender Prasad born on 12 date Swami Vivekanand, Abrahim Lincon, Born on 21 Date Boota Singh, Benazir Bhutto, Alfred Novel, Stalin, Padumlal Punnalal Bakshi.

Born on 30 date Churchill, Roosevelt, Jagadish Chandra Basu, Kanhaiyalal Maniklal Munshi, Vinay Mohan Sharma, Dr. Onkar Lal Sharma "Prmad" (writer of this book).

In this way persons born on 3-12-21-30 dates or in the nakshatras of jupiter's period when sun transists in these nakshatras i.e. from 5-21 July (Punarvasu) 6-21 (Vishakha) 6-21 (March) When Sun comes in transit in the nakshatras of Jupiter, representative of number 3. These persons rise high in the field of knowledge, science, religion. Politics, Art, Literature, film etc. and get the name and fame world-wide.

Persons Born in Number Four

In Numerology Number four is represented by Harshal. Number 4 is the number of Revolution, social, political or Philosophical. Persons born on 4-13-22-31 of any month are guided by Harshal, the newly discovered planet. They think just opposite to the present position and want changes in social and political rules and regulation. Thus opposing the present position in every field of life they make many secret enemies. They appose the old customs, superstitions and world social reformation from the family, city, state and Government.

Number 4 person cooperate in the progress of woman specially. They cannot make friends easily. Born in number 1-2-7-8 person attract much them. They are neutral in the matter of wealth and property hence they are not successful in their physical and family matters.

July, August months are auspicious to 4 persons because these two months are of Moon and Sun when sun transits in Cancer ruled by Moon and in Leo ruled by Sun Moon is mind, Sun is soul. Hence if any body is born in July, August on 4-13-22-31 dates then the person have strong individuality and will power due to this reason they are regarded as angles of great social revolution and their name and fame live long. Upanyas samrat Premchand born on 31 July 1880. Gyanpeeth awarded Amrita Pritam born on 31 August 1919. Sant Tyagraj (4 May) Dada Bhai Naoroji (4 Dec.).

In this way Number 4 has given to world great men in the field of politician, literature, Saint, Head of State, Poet, Social Reformers. Gajanan Madhav Mukti Bodh Hindi Pryogvadi Poet, born on 13 Nov. 1917, the famous Indian English poetess and freedom fighter Sarojini Naidu born on 13 February 1879, Famous National Poet Makhan Lal Chaturvedi born on 4 April, the famous poet Venugopal born on 22 October 1942, Shamsher Bahadur Singh born on 13 January 1911 R. Venkat Raman (4 December).

George washington the President of U.S.A. born on 22 February 1732, Fakhruddin Ali, Ex President of India born on 13 May 1905, Ironperson of Indian politics Sardar Ballabh Bhai Patel born on 31 Oct. 1872, Raja Ram Mohan Ray born on 22 May 1772, Lord Churchill of U.K. born on 13 February 1849, Har Kishan Lal Bhagat born on 4 April 1921, Virendra Kumar Saklecha born on 4 March 1930, Shiv Bhanu Solanki born on 13 February 1927. All these personalities were born in number 4 represented by Harshal.

Though person born in Number four are simple and kind by heart and full of sympathy to all human beings but they are some what leftists. Person born in number four should have control over sensitiveness, Anger, should not change ideas again and again. They may suffer by gas trouble, Headache, eardisease, fear from fire and iron. Saturday, Sunday, Monday are auspicious days to begin a new work. They should wear light blue, khaki, brown, light yellow, shining colours. They should worship Lord Ganesh. Lord of Intellect to the Steady of Intellect. Light Digestive food should be taken. Good and bad events may take place in 4-19-22-31-40-49-58-67 years. 1-10-19-28-37-46-55-64 years may be good to them.

India and Number 4

Number 4 has been proved fatal to India. e.g. year 1948, 1966, 1975, 1984, all these years total comes 4 e.g. 1+9+4+8 = 22 = 4; 1+9+6+6 = 22 = 4, 1+9+7+5 = 22 = 4, 1+9+8+4 = 22 = 4. In 1948 Assassination of Father of Nation Mahatma Gandhi in 1966. Accidental Sudden death of Lal Bahadur Shastri, Emergency in 1975; In 1984 Assassination of Indira Gandhi, Bhopal Gas Kand too in 1984 occurred.

Persons born in Number 5

Persons born on 5-14-23 dates of any month are called in Numerology number 5 persons. The youth Planet Mercury is the lord of Number 5. Mercury is representative of speech, Electricity, Business, Computer, Mathematics, Press, Mental power. Budh (mercury) is called Somya सौम्य ग्रह i.e. simple. It makes itself the same with which planet it is seated. Mercury is expert in finding supporting action. They are highly intellectual, sharp intelligence and have magnetic personality. They are good intutor too. They can make friendship easily any where, at any time, in any circumstances. They are sharp in intelligence. They can adjust and make happy others. Their opposite persons too appreciate them after their attendance. Their happy personality influence others by their magnetic sweet speech.

If Mercury is afflicted or with malefics at the time of birth then number 5 person seems openly human but inside becomes very wicked person, cruel, cunning and takes the benefit of opportunities in completing his work. Though when mercury is with benefics or aspected by benefics at the time of birth 5 Number born person live with smiling face. They are not angry for ever. Due to Sharp mental power there is fear of high blood pressure and nervous weakness.

Persons born on 5-14-23 dates or when transit of Sun in Sign of mercury Gemini and Virgo i.e. from 21-5 to 20-6 and 21-8 to 20-9 every year or when Sun transits on the nakshatras of Mercury Ashlekha, Jyeshtha and Rewati, i.e. 4-8 to 17-8, 4-12 to 16-12, 1-4 to 13-4 every year in these periods born persons are influenced by Mercury and become good writer or businessman whether or not they are born on 5-12-23 dates. They are poet, teachers judge, Advocate, Journalist, Publisher, Businessman, Astrologer, Intutor, Engineer of high rank. Mercury influenced persons are often of materialistic views and due to their farsight, psycho-analysis they rise high and surprise others. Their rise of luck is in 23-24 years of age, special rise in 32-33 years of age and full rise of luck comes in the age of 41-42 years of age.

Their analysis is fully scientific their intellect is inventive and their courage as always youth hence they become great early. They can understand. Characteristics of persons only after listening their speech. Mercury also transits near Sun hence effect of Sun light guides them make wealthy and famous soon. There is fear of breaking views of brain due to more mental thinking, more delivering lecture, more diplomacy, cunningness, whether in the field of society, public politics, or Business Industries, hence they should be very careful about this matter. Deep rest by sleeping, taking a little exercise is compulsory for them. They should take in food things containing vitamins B and D. They should not take more saltic things otherwise gastric trouble may increase. They should wear light blue, brown, green colours clothes which give them magnetic power.

They should wear diamond or Emerald in golden ring in middle or little finger on Wednesday or Friday. These two days are also auspicious for them to begin a new job. Mercury is known as the invalid son of moon born to the wife of Jupiter hence imaginative power of moon and divine power of Jupiter both these things make them extraordinary wise man.

Born of 5th are our great philosopher ex-president Dr. Radha Krishnan, ex-President Gyani Jail Singh, Babu Jagjiwan Ram, Arjun Singh, Karl Marx, Bhutto, etc. are main.

Born on 14th are our first Prime Minister Pandit Jawahar Lal Nehru, Dr. Bhim Rao Ambedkar, Sanjay Gandhi, S.V. Chauhan, Ex-President of U.S.A. Eisen Hower, Margret Alwa, Nastre Dam etc. Born on 23rd are Lok

Manya Bal Ganga Dhar Tilak, Netaji Subhash Chandra Bose, Choudhry Charan Singh, English Poet Shakespeare, Historian Dr. Raghuvir Singh, Yogendra Makwara, Satya Shri Sai Baha, Narendra Chanchal, Cricket Player Madan Lal etc.

In the Sign of Mercury Virgo when Sun transited on it Dr. Radha Krishnan was born, in Revti Nakshatra when sun moves on it Jagjiwan Ram was born.

Persons Born in Number Six

Those born on 6-15-24 dates of any month have their birth number as 6 ruled by Venus, the most shining planet in Sky. These person are wealthy of attractive personality, worshipper of beauty, devotee of love and fully materialistic views. All the Arts music, painting, film, Drawing, Poetry, Drama, Come under the area of venus, the deity of beauty. Their speech is sweet and nature is swift. They decorate their homes with latest articles. They have special love with music, drama, poetry, Drawing, painting fine arts, musical instruments. They have much attachment with deep colours. They are very kind-hearted, happy, living in pleasant atmosphere. But if their anger is roused they fight bravely at the last moment though makes friend easily.

Tuesday, Thursday, Friday are auspicious to them to begin a job every year April, October, November Months are Ominlous to them. They rise very high in the field of Art, literature and specially in polities. In their life the years 6-15-24-33-42-51-60-69 years are remarkable.

They should wear diamond, Emerald, blue sapphire in middle in little fingers respectively. They are generally of Cough cold nature hence Cold cough fever, constipation, spleen, liver, gas trouble, deafness, blindmen, hysteria, Insomnia, Paralysis, Gonorrhoea, eye diseases etc. may attack they should have fast on Tuesday and Pradosh (प्रदोष) so that their health may be maintained.

Sometimes born ordinary, Poor family in a Village, little town are seen progressing on extraordinary level.

Those born in the period when sun moves in transit through taurus, Libra (Signs of Venus), on nakshatras of Venus, e.g. Bharni, Poorvaphalguna, Poorva Shada then two the influene of Number 6 is seen indirectly.

Those born on date 6 are poet Pradeep (6 February) U.S.A. ex-president Ronald Regaon (6 February), Cricket Player Kapil Dev (6 January), Bengsarkar (6 April), Motilal Nehru (6 May), Maxmallar (6 December) Poet Kedarnath Agarwal (6 Octobor) Dr. Mukherjee of Indore (6 September) Henry II, Sir waltair Scott, Varen Hestings etc.

Born on date 15 are Arvinda Ghosh, Nepolean (15 August), Naresh Mehta (15 February), William Harshal Astronomer (15 November), Kamal Khan 'Kamal' (15 March), Independent India.

Born on date 24 Sharif Master of Sironj (M.P.) Ex-Panchayat Minister (24 January), Ram Nivas Mirdha (24 August) Mohammed Rafi (24 September) Mohinder Amarnath (24 September) Emperor Akbar (24 November) Banarsidas Chaturvedi (24 December), Queen Victoria (24 May) Cromwell (24 April) Jagannath Mishra of Bihar (24 June).

India became free on 15th August 1947 when we add Number 15 in 1947 we get 1962 when China attacked on our boarder again adding 15 in 1962 we get 1977 when Indira Gandhi had to leave P.M. Chair and Morarji Desai became P.M. of India. Again adding 15 in 1977 we get 1992 when Babri Masjid at Ayodhya was Demolitated again adding 15 in 1997 we get 2005. We have to see impleasant result. Year 2004 also has number 6. It may also be Ominous to India on experimental basis as above.

Persons Born in Number "Seven"

Those born on 7-16-25 dates of any month have their birth number as 7. Number 7 is most important in Indian Astrology as there are 7 days in a month, 7 rounds are taken by Hindu bride - bridegrom on Pavan Vedi of Agni in marriage, There are 7 Rishi called Sapta-Rishis in north Sky going round to Dhruva Tara. There are 52 weeks in a year whose total is 5+2 = 7. There are 7 ocean. In all religion number 7 has been described as influntial, commanding mystically opening the Divine control of nature. In Governing the world there are seven planets Sun, Moon, Mars, Mercury, Jupiter, Venus, Saturn are basically most important..

Number 7 is basically a mystic number directed by the holy divine power of world. Number 7 is ruled by Nepture in Hindi it is called as Varun 'वरुण'. Varun is called as the God of Water.

Persons born on 7-16-25 of any month have some peculiar qualities other than other number's born persons. They are original, Independence, Solitude thinking, inventive tendency, love feelings, Sea-vayages, restlessness, knowledge of all world, surprising power of Intution, Very Shy, Vast heart and sympathetic personality, Inventor, Poet, Philosopher, Writer and Political Leader. Their geninus is mystic, surprising, magnetic and wonderful. They have keen interest in Archeology, Astrology, tantra, mantra. Due to Sharp intution they make their life important knowing the future events before hand.

Neptune, the lord of number 7 is watery navy, ship, river, well, Dam tubewell are represented by Nepture. This life begins with struggle. In the age of 7 and 16 travels are made at Reservoir places with happenings of pleasant changes. He has to live far from parents and family. Struggle till the age 24, then from the beginning of 25 years of age permanence in job is established.

Number 7 persons are cold in nature due to watery neptune. They are affected specially by the imaginative power of Moon. High flight of imagination, ambition for dreaming future sometimes take the form of truth surprisingly. From 21 July to 20 August when Sun transits in cancer sign of moon counting from Sayana system of west, this time is very auspicious to 7 number born person. Sunday, Monday are most important for getting success in work. Thursday and Friday are auspicious, other days are ominous. They should wear light green, yellow and white colour's clothes. Deep colour is not good. It gives restlessness. To remove tension and restlessness they should wear pearl in silver ring or Cat's eye in silver ring.

They have to see many ups and downs in their life to rise. They should be careful with their co-workers. From childhood dysentry, gas trouble, Dropsy, defect in thighs may suffer them. Any kind of intoxication may produce danger in their life. Due to solitude-thinking mentality sometimes undesirable sinful feelings may come in mind, hence they must remove if by self-realisation. Unnatural sexual work may destroy their life hence they should be cautious and careful. Blood trouble, Brainfever, defect in throat, cold, stone, cancer diseases may attack. Hence take care of health. They should take in their food Radish, Lotus seeds, sago, makhane, Rice, Cabbage, cucumber, apple, grapes, pudina, lemon, orange, papaya etc. They should keep themselves away from any kind of temptation.

Persons born on date 7 are musician Pandit Ravishankar, Maha mahopadhyaya Gopinath Kaviraj, Vipin Chandra Pal, C.V. Raman, Charles Dickens, Browning, Chandra Kant Devtale Hindi Paet Heera Nand Sachchidanand Vatsayan *"Ageya"* and great revolutionary Hindi poet Shri Krishna *"Saral"*.

Born on date 16 are Charlicheplin, Rousso, Girja Kumar Mathur, Dr. Shivmangal Singh *"Suman"*, Oscar Wild Ashok Vajpayee.

Born on date 25 are Canady, Arun Nehru, Vishwanath Pratap Singh, Din Dayal Upadhyay, Imran Khan, Newton, Pandit Madan Mohan Malviya, Atal Bihari Vajpayee.

In Numerology Number 1-4 and 2-7 are mutual complimentary to each other. Because Number one's Lord is sun and Number 4's Lord is Harshal both are fiery by nature and produce heat. Number 2's lord is Moon and number 7's Lord is Neptune. Both are watery Planet.

Persons Born in Number '8'

Persons born On 8-17-26 in any english month have their birth and origin number "8" ruled by saturn, lord of two signs capricorn and Aquarius.

In Horoscope the 8th house is the house of Death, age. Saturn is the son of sun and brother of Yamaraj. Though saturn is known as malefic but it gives good results too.

Nowadays in the world there is Democracy in all the countries mostly and saturn is the representative of Poor, down trodden people. Saturn makes a man great thinker, Sympathetic and kind. We are bounded by good or bad deeds of our previous lives and the malefics Sun, Mars, Saturn, Rahu, Ketu these 5 malefies give punishment in the form of diseases, difficulties, accidents, partiality, court, violence, Suicide etc.

Number 8 persons feel solitude. They are very kind hearted and sensitive. Saturn when represents luck then sudden rise or sudden fall is the result.

Number 8 born people are suspective, obstinate, religious and believing in Luck. Openly they seem hard, selfish, cold but by heart very kind and being kind on poor and helpless. They do not believe in propaganda. They think so that people may be attracted towards them and appreciate them. Either they get high success or are very unsuccessful. By sacrifice, tolerance, Patience, hard struggle they may reach the high place and that too after the age of 36 and not before this.

From the worldly point of view number 8 is not lucky. Because they are suffered at each point by humiliation, Insult, loss, dishonesty, when saturn is weak in their horoscope hence in such condition they should have peace, patience, discipline. In the year when sun moves on saturn's sign capricorn, Aquarius, i.e., from 21 December to 20 January and 21 January to 20 February, this time is most important to them. They should begin new job, new planning in this period in auspicious time. Any work begin on Saturday, Sunday, Monday will be helpful and profitable. They should wear blue sapphire and Firoza in middle finger.

Son of Sun, brother of Yamaraj Sun is very powerful planet. They move slowly on one sign in 2 years 6 months. After 30 years they come on the same sign saturn is strong, aspected by benefics then material wealth and happiness too are given by saturn but if saturn's position is bad, afflicted by malefics or with 6-8-12 lords or in 6-8-12 evil houses then saturn brings ups and downs, suddenly accidental bad luck, misfortune etc. When saturn is strong in Demolition condition then it gives the feeling of *"Vairagya"* (leaving the world) then great thinker, Philosopher, Occultist, religious devotee or scientists are produced by saturn. Saturian struggles for justice life long and after death his story is rememberable. I experienced the revised events in number 8 in the life of Shri Lal Bahadur Shastri the ex-Prime Minister of India.

Date of birth 2-10-1904 = 2+1+0+1+9+0+4 = 17 = 1+7 = 8

First time went to jail in the age of 17 = 1+7 = 8

Railway Minister in 1952 = 1+9+5+2 = 17 = 1+7 = 8
Home Minister in 1961 + 1+9+6+1 = 17 = 1+7 = 8
Prime Minister in 1964 on 9th June = 9+6+1+9+6+4 = 35 = 3+5 = 8
Funeral rite on 12-1-1966 = 1+2+1+1+9+6+6 = 26 = 2+6 = 8
Age at the time of death 62 years = 6+2 = 8

One more wonderful activity of Number, which I experienced in the life of Harihar Prasad Singh ex-Chief Minister of Bihar.

He become C.M. of Bihar after 242 days emergency period = 242 = 2+4+2 = 8

Sworn in as C.M. on 26-2-1969 = 2+6+2+1 +9+6+9 = 35 = 3+5 = 8
On 22-6-1969 resigned as C.M. 2+2+6+1+9+6+9 = 35 = 3+5 = 8
He was C.M. for 116 days 1+1+6 = 8
Death in 1988 = 1+9+8+8 = 26 = 2+6 = 8
Age at the time of death 89 years 8+9 = 17 = 1+7 = 8

Those born in 8th number is profitable if they do business of black things and machinary of iron. Sade Sati, Dhaiya, Mahadasa, Antardasa of saturn makes any one highly lucky to other unfortunate person unlucky. Sade Sati for 7½ years Dhaiya for 2½ years, Mahadasa period of Saturn 19 years.

The following famous person are born on '8' number's dates as following :

Born on Date 8 Guru Nanak (8 November)

Dr. Zakir Husain (8 Feb.) Rajgopalachari (8 December)

Bal Krishna Sharma 'Naveen' Bankim Chandra Chaterjee Both born on 8 April

Salim Durrani (8 December)

Born on Date 17 - Sheikh Muzib (17 March)

Benjmin Franklin of U.S.A. (17 January) Smita Patil (17 October) Sir Syed Ahmed Khan (17 October)

Born on date 26 - George warnard Shaw (20 July) Sir Hari Singh Gour (26 November) Mirza Galib (26 December) Prabhakar Machwe (26 December) Guru Govinda Singh (26 December).

Persons born in Number '9'

Persons born on 9-18-27 of any english month have their birth and origin number 9. Nine is the last and important number. It is fully materialistic Number Mars is the ruler of Number. Mars is the son of Earth its colour is Red and it is known as the commander in Chief of Planet's Army.

Mars is fully fighter, obstinate, brave, bold and courageous. Mars is fiery. Number 9 produced number 9 when multiplied to any number e.g. multiplied into 4275 x 9 = 38475 = 3+8+4+7+5 = 27 = 2+7 = 9. In this way number nine person gets soverignty and full influence every where at any time. Mars has magnetic power and nobody can escape whether the result is good or bad.

Persons who has their birth and origin number 9 are very brave and bold, obstinate, Psychologist, selfish and have keen desire to consume everything produced on this Earth. Sometimes when they show more boldness, courage they self invite their destruction. Hence they should work patiencely and within discipline. They like struggle, excess angerness and never are afraid of any kind of trouble but face boldly any kind of challenge given by the opposition or enemies. Though they are very kind but when in anger they give troubles to others being more and more fiery. They have to think again and again and not to do any thing in hurry without thinking deeply.

When in transit Mars comes on cancer sign in debilitation, it becomes weak. In May, July, October too the position of Mars is weak hence in this period the number 9 person born on tuesday should be cautious about struggle, conflict, enmity with other persons and blood trouble, typhoid fever, Vehicle accident, defeat in Legal Case, Separation of executive power, withdrawals of rights etc. May take place. In the same way from 14th January to 14th March too he should be careful about his health becouse in Mars strong enemy saturn's Sign capricorn and Aquarius, Sun transits for 2 months. hence no intoxication should be taken by the native because any kind of intoxication may destroy the whole life of the Number 9 person.

The persons born in number '9' has good organising ability and strength. They can earn name and fame both by organising power using in service of family, society, city, state, country but this is possible when being unselfish leaving hastyness, materialistic view and do any work with full responsibility.

They should keep themself away from vices like disappointment, anger, to speak ill of others, intolerance, breaking tendency and mental balance should not be lost at any point but should work with surity and discipline. gambling and playing cards, speculation etc. are other vices which should be kept away from them.

To begin new job 9-18-27 dates Tuesday, Thursday are auspicious. every year the period w.e.f. 21 march to 20 April and 21 Oct. to 20 Nov. is very favourable becouse sun transits in Aries and Scorpio the signs of Mars this period. Number 3 too is helpful and 3-6-9-12-15-18-21-24-27-30 series give good result.

Their clear colour is Red, light Red colour, Rosy, Light yellow, light white too may be taken. They should have always with them handker chief of light Red and Rosy colour they should wear coral and pearl in finger number 4 and 5 respectively on Tuesday and Monday in silver rings.

Ruby too may wear in gold on sunday which will give them happiness in doing executive and commanding job. They should have fast on tuesday and *Ekadashi* and should be devotee of Shri Hanumanji, Mother *Durga* which will destroy their all difficulties, hindrances, in the way of success.

Number 9 born people have their childhood trouble. Some, Wounds, cuts, bleeding, fever, blood trouble, snake bite etc. may trouble their health. They have natural ability of organisation. They should defence themselves from Violance and struggle. Their profitable line in Government Service is Police, Military, P.W.D., Agriculture, Land records, land revenue etc. In Profession they may prove good in brokery of land, Houses, animal feeding, organising a party. Mars is the son of Earth so land may be acquired by them accidently and land, house, road, grassland concerning work may be profitable to them.

Number 9 is number of struggle, conflict, fight so when ever at any place when 9 number born person reaches, there is trouble to others by his attendance. 2-4-7-8 number born people feel nervousness from there attendance. 1-3-5-6 born people adjust with them. 9 Number persons cannot be won but may be won by love and sympathy. Mars fears the people because it is natural fiery planet hence cruelty, violance, anger are general in his behaviour.

They suffer from defect in lungs, Heart disease, typhoid, Diarrhoea and blood trouble. They like sweet too much in taste hence it should be controlled in youth attachment with young lady neglecting wife will make life troublesome and full of sorrow. Love affairs and intoxication both are negated to them. For fulfillness of passion they do crimes, hence controll on passion is compulsary. In their life surgery and struggle for land and house, property may take place. Hence should be careful.

Those born on date of 9 are Novel prize winner world poet Ravindra Nath Tagore, Bhartendu Harish Chandra, Gopal Krishna Gokhle, Maharana Pratap, Shri Kant Verma. Raghuvir Sahay A.R. Antuley are main.

Those born on date of 18 are Rafi Ahmed Kidwai Ziaul Rehman Ansari, Abdulgafoor, Narayan Dutta Tiwari, Veer Bahadur Singh, T.N. Chaturvedi, Guru Ghasidas, Bhagwat Jha Azad, Nelson Mandela.

Those born on date of 27 are Janardan Pujari, Cricketer Ravi Shastri, Ex-President of U.S.A. Roosewelt, Vishnu Rajoria, Hariwansh Rai Bachchan etc.

In 1971 Bangla Desh Came in Existance after great trouble, struggle, Sacrifise of Sheikh Muzib. In India Middle term poll was declared, in 1980 too middle term poll was due to resignation of Morarji Desai both years 1971 and 1980 wear number 9 as 1+9+7+1 = 18 = 1+8 = 9; 1+9+8+0 = 18 = 1+8 = 9.

29

Unmarried Ladies

In Astrological texts generally there are combination and discrimination of houses and planets of male Horoscopes only. There is very Little reference about females except in female Horoscopy. So the difficult thing is to acertain about the combinations for marriage or non-marriage of females. I have experienced some non-marriage cases in the Horoscopes of females. The important things for such cases are as following :-

1. Jupiter is KARAKA for husband. If Jupiter is weak and Seventh house Lord of Seventh house, Venus are also weak, then there is no possibility of marriage of females. These things should be considered from both ascendant and Moon Sign along with the second and seventh houses. Second house is the house of family. Increase or decrease in the family by means of marriage, birth of a Son, daughter is known through this house. The eleventh house is the house for union of Married Life. Hence benefics in eleventh house pay positive roll in making the family life happy, if malefics then family life disturb and divorce, death, Suicide etc. negative events take place. Hence eleventh house must also be Strong by aspect or position of benefics in eleventh house.
2. If there is no aspect of Jupiter on Seventh house and Lord of Seventh house.
3. If Jupiter and Moon are in 6,8,12 houses or with their Lords.
4. If SUN, Moon, Mars,Venus, Saturn are in odd Signs, i.e., in 1,3,5,7,9,11, Signs.
5. If Lord of Seventh house, Venus is in debilitated Sign or with malefic or in immical planet then there is no possibility of

marriage of females. I am making it clear by giving some experienced examples.

Example-1. Female Born on 7-9-1925 Monday in Scorpio Lagna at 11.43 a.m. at 28.32 N, 72-13 E. Bharmi Nakshatra IInd part. Here Jupiter is in second house aspected by Saturn from 12th house. Venus in 11th (eleventh house) in Virgo is debilitated (Neech Sign) hemmed in between three malefics Saturn in 12th and Sun Mars in 10th house. Venus is Lord of Seventh house too but on Seventh house or on Venus there is no aspect of Jupiter or any other benefic planet Moon, Mars, Sun, Mercury, Saturn all are in odd Signs. Though Jupiter aspects. Moon but Moon is in an evil house 6th aspect by great malefic Saturn. Hence Jupiter and Moon both are powerless due to bad aspect of Saturn on them. Venus the other great benefic is the Lord of Seventh and 12th houses. Seventh house is the MARAKA House. The Sign Libra of Venus has been occupied by Saturn Jupiter has full aspect on Moon and tenth house So the lady served is education department and retired from the post of Principal of a Government Higher Secondary School in M.P. She remained unmarried through out life. From Moon too in 7th house there is Saturn though exalted, but Lord of Seventh i.e. Venus is in 6th house, (the 12th house from 7th house). Hence all these negative combinations for marriage did not allow to marry the lady.

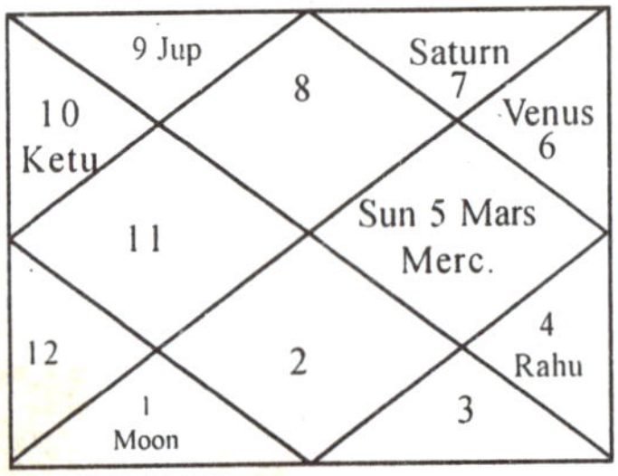

Example-2. Female Born on 3-10-1957 at 11.40 P.M. at 23.32 N 77.50 E in Leo Sign as Lagna Ashwani Nakshatra IInd Pada. Here the Seventh house has been badly afflicted by RAHU-JUPITER combination a Chandal Yoga. The Lord of Seventh Saturn with strong enemy SUN. Venus in an evil house, i.e., sixth house aspected by Mars and Saturn two malefics. From Moon in Seventh there are two malefics Sun and SATURN (enemy of each other). Closing the hope for marriage the most benefic Planets Jupiter and Moon both are badly afflicted by malefics causing no chance for marriage. Though the marriage was settled but the boy refused to marry this girl and engagement was cancelled.

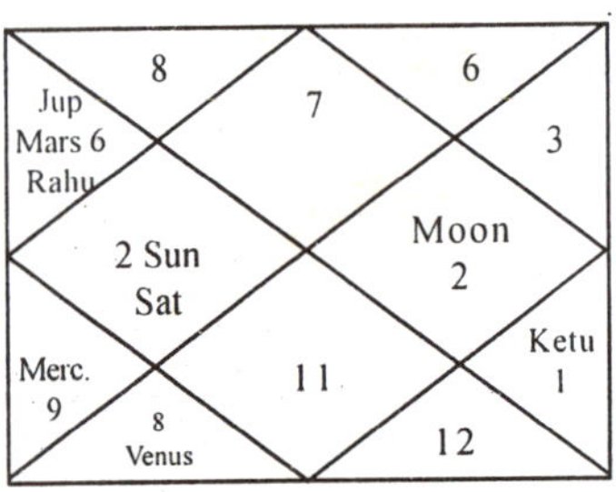

Example-3. Female born in Jyeshtha Shukla Chaturthi Tuesday Vikram Samvot 2013 Ashlesha Nakshatra 2nd Part. Ishtakala 56 ghats' at 26 Palas at 22.40 N 80.20 E in Taurus ascendant. The seventh has been occupied by two malefics RAHU & SATURN Mars the 12th Lord also aspects Lagna, though Mars is the Lord of Seventh house too. Mars, the Seventh Lord is in unimical Sign though aspected by Jupiter a great benefic Jupiter as Lord of 8th house is AKARAKA for Taurus Lagna. Mars and Saturn Lords of Second and Eleventh are under malefic aspect. From Moon Lord of Seventh Saturn too is in unimical Sign with malefic RAHU aspected by SUN and Ketu. All these things include denial of marriage.

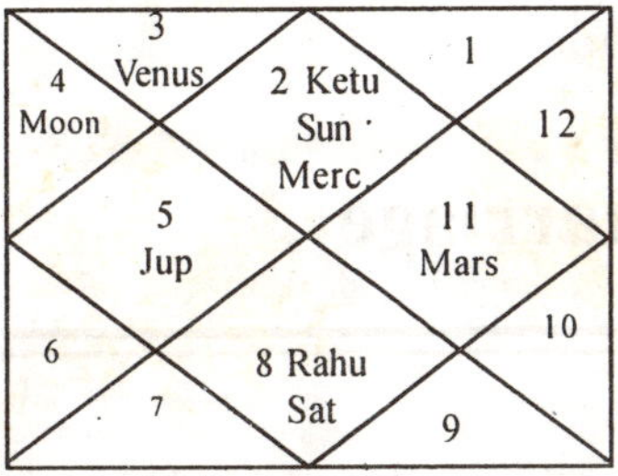

Example-4. Female born on 4-2-1962 of 11.45 P.M. at 23.50 N 78.50 SRAVAN 2nd Charan Libra Lagna 8 Planet combination in Capricorn. RAHU in Cancer in Seventh house. Lord of Lagna, Second, Seventh, eleventh and all evil houses 6,8,12 are in 4th house in Capricorn where JUPITER is in debilitation (NEECHA) MARS is in Exaltation Second and Seventh house's Lord Mars, Lord of eleventh all Karakas and benefics are hemmed between 5 Planets. Her Parents died. She and one elder brother survived. For the sake of her younger brother She did not marry as she played part of Parents for her only younger brother. This is unique example of 8 Planets combinations in One house still unmarried.

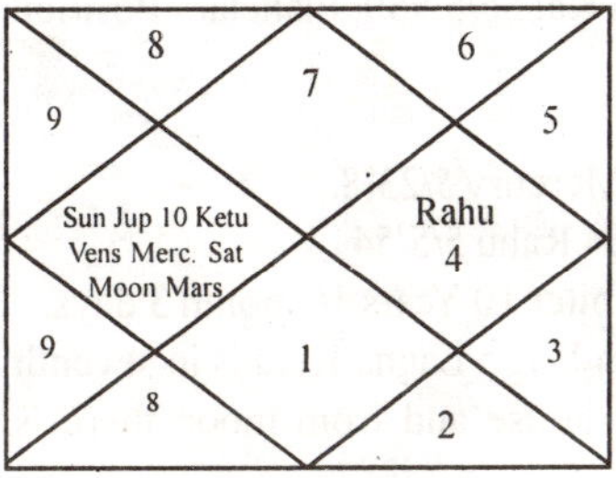

30

Widow's Marriage

From olden times Widow's Marriage is strongly prohibited in upper castes of Hindus. But now a days due to unsecurity of widows upper castes are thinking over the matter seriously and efforts are being made for widow's marriage. Below I am giving an example of widow's marriage whose first husband died of hanging himself due to Suicide. The Lady got remarried with a person who took divorce from his first wife due to her had behaviour and unsocial habits.

Female born on 15-10-1977 at 5.00 a.m. Vikram Samvat 2034 Ashwin Shukla Dwitiya tithi Friday 40/42 Swati Nakshatra 35/29 after which Vishakha Nakshatra Second Quarter Ishta Kal 56/52/30. Planetary Position is as following:-

Sun- 5/27/28; Moon 6/25/06 Mars 3/0/7 Mercury 5/23/8
Jupiter-2/13/40 Venus 5/4/42 Saturn 4/5/54 Rahu 5/5/54
Ketu 11/5/54 Lagna 5/11/8 Balance of Jupiter 10 Years 10 month 3 days.

Here are Sun Rahu two malefics in Virgo Lagna Ketu is in seventh house. Too malefics aspect on Seventh house and from moon there is

Birth Lagna

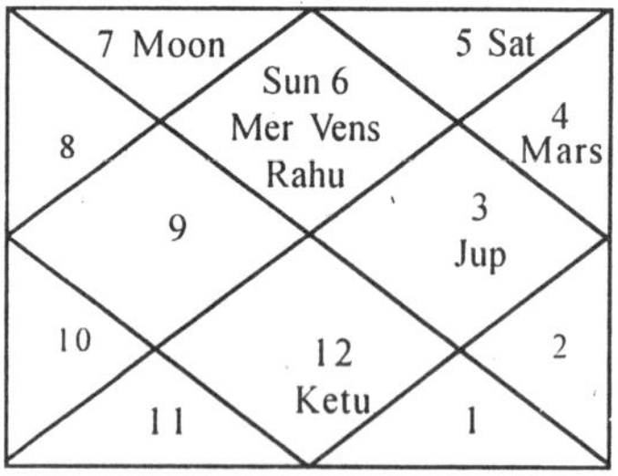

Navamsha

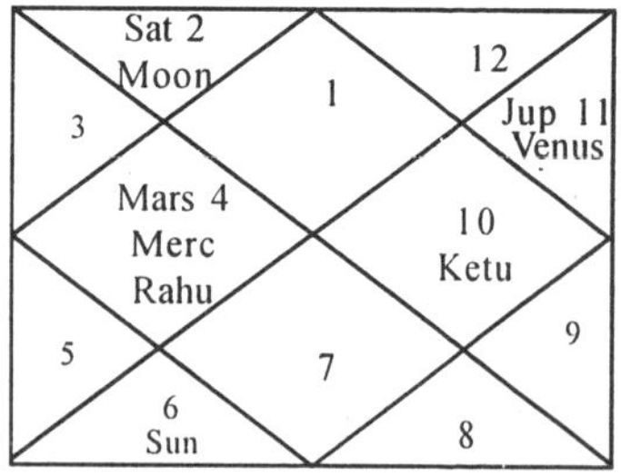

Papa Rasi in 6th house ARIES whose Lord Mars is in NEECHA Sign. There is Saturn with Moon in Navamsa and Mars is with Rahu too in

Navamsa Mars aspects the 7th house and Jupiter with Venus. Thus the husband's house has become weak. Mahadev महादेव pathak in JATAKA TATWA Says सप्रमे भौमे पापध्श्यते विधवा means Mars in Seventh with malefic aspect makes widow in childish. She became widow on 8-7-1994 at the age of Seventeen. Her husband who was mentally disturbed died of Suiciding by hanging himself. She was married in Saturn Mercury period and became widow in Saturn Ketu period. Her first husband did this sinful deed on 8-7-1994 Tuesday at about 2.00 P.M. in Libra Lagna.

The Lord of Lagna and Moon sign are hemmed in between SUN and RAHU and Rahu and Mars. Saturn aspected by Mars aspects the eighth house JUPITER is in NEECHA Rasi retrograded. Hence being in Papa Kartari Yoga Lord of Lagna and Moon with Rahu are badly afflicted by malefics. Lord of seventh Mars is in 12th house in an unimical sign badly aspected by Saturn and retrograded Jupiter. Old Texts Say that when benefics and malefics both aspect the seventh house the lady marries more than one time. In the horoscope of this lady SUN, Rahu, Venus, Mercury aspect the Seventh house and Jupiter the Moon. Saturn too aspects the Moon and Ninth house lord is in Lagna too. Saturn and Jupiter aspect the Lord of Seventh house. Seventh house has been aspected by RAHU too. This Lady was firstly married in 1992. Her second marriage was performed on 28-6-1999. See that the Suicide Lagna Libra Corresponds with the Moon Sign Libra of the Lady.

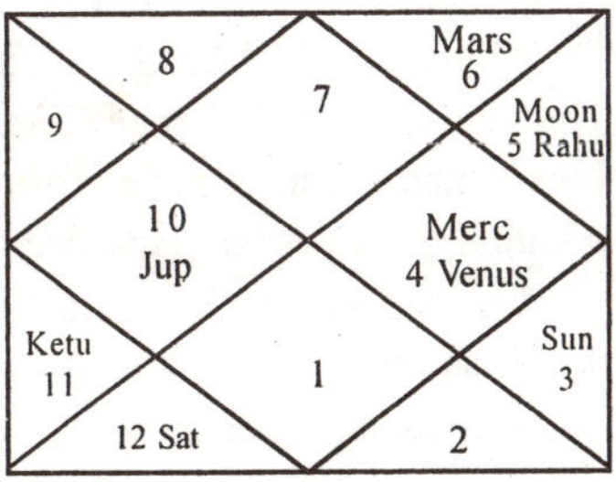

Her Second husband's Horoscope is as following:- Male born on 30-6-1970 at 7.30 P.M. Vikram Samvat 2027 Ashada Krishna Dwadashi Tuesday 33/23 Kritika Nakshatra. 40/4 in Dhanu Lagna Ishtakala 38/52/30 Lagna 8/14/54 Sun 2/14/46 Moon 1/9/16 Mars 2/24/31 Mercury 2/9/58 Jupiter 6/5/51 Venus 3/22/58 Saturn 0/24/49 Rahu 10/12/16 Ketu 4/12/16 with a balance of SUN MAHADASHA 0 Years 4 months 6 days.

During Mars Moon Period he was married first time in June 1987. There was serious accident in 1990 दारे पापे द्विभार्या: which means malefics in seventh gives two marriages. Here are SUN and Mars in 7th house. There are malefics and benefics SUN, Mars, Mercury in Seventh aspected by Jupiter, Rahu and Saturn Surrounded by Moon in 6th house and Venus in 8th house. Moon is hemmed in between Saturn and SUN, Mars. But in

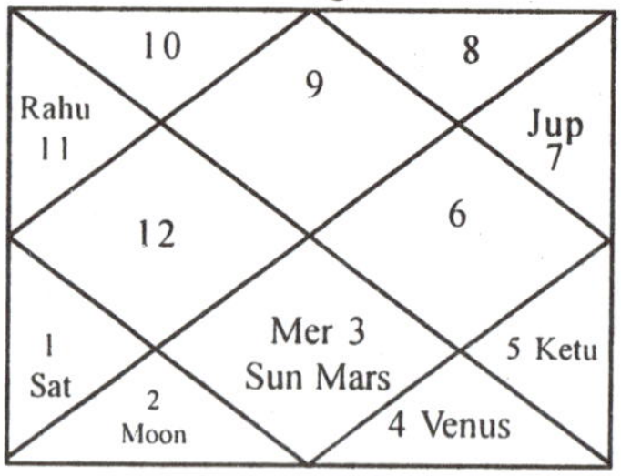

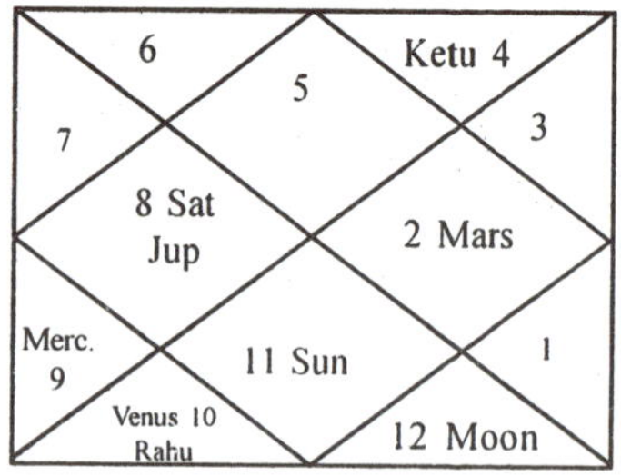

position of 7th house between Moon, Venus aspect of Jupiter, Mercury there in all are those factors which made him husband of 2nd wife.

In NAVAMSA Lagna Atmakaraka is Saturn in KARAMSA. Aspect from Char Rasi by Rahu and Venus on Karkamsa where Jupiter and Saturn are posited made available widow for him to marry. Aspect of Saturn with Jupiter from fixed Sign Scorpio on Seventh Sign Aquarius show that the male will get Lady older than him. The first Lady was older than him. This was done because the father of the first wife showed him another girl and married with another girl than him resembling by face. Secondly the first Lady was mentally disturbed, bad in behaviour, fighting by nature, these things made him to divorce her.

Both husband and second wife are Brahmins. Both were sad and unhappy before this marriage. Second marriage took place in Rahu Mahadashas. Venus antardasha as Rahu and Venus both aspect the lord of seventh Saturn in Navamsa Lagna. In Kakramsa Lagna Venus too is the Lord of Seventh. In Karkamsa Lagna Venus too is the Lord of Seventh and Malefies and benefics Rahu, Saturn, Jupiter, Venus aspect the 7th house where Mars in posited. The Marriage was performed on 28-6-1999 in Gayatri Mandir, They both are happy due to this Second marriage and have a Son by grace of the God.

31

Reunion

In June 2001 a person came to me on 29-6-2001 with the horoscope of his daughter who was living with him for the last 4 years separated from her husband to know that the reunion of my daughter and Son in law is possible or not? The daughter has 2 Sons, one daughter living with her husband. The horoscope of the Lady is as following:-

Female Bornon 18-11-1964 at 10.00 P.M. at 25.14N, 77.36E with the following Planetary position.

Lagna 3-7-20	Pushya-II	JUPITER 0-27-51	Kritika I
SUN 7-2-39	Vishakha-IV	VENUS 5-29-54	Chitra II
MOON 0-20-14	Bharmi-III	SATURN 10-1-48	Dhamishtha III
MARS 4-10-58	Magha-IV	RAHU 2-0-53	Mrigsira III
MERCURY 7-22-47	Jyeshtha-II	KETU 8-0-53	Moola-I

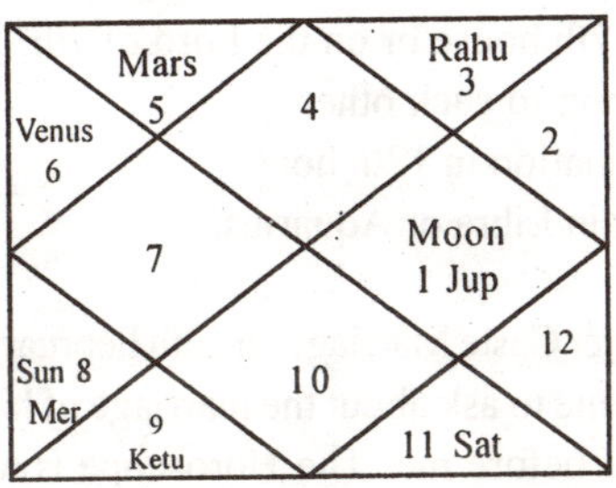

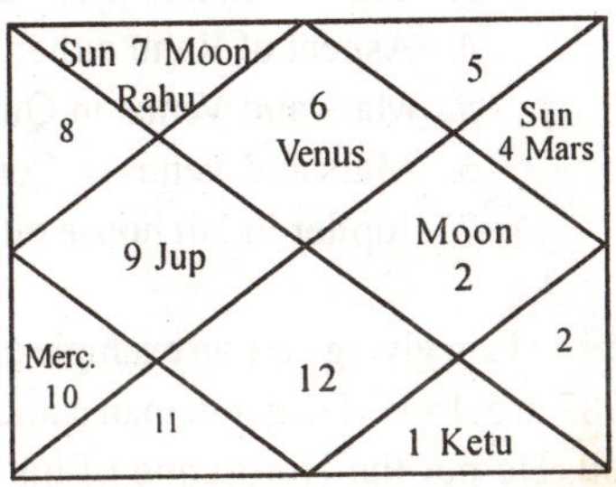

JUPITER-Lord of Bhagya is in retrogression. 9 years 7 months 11 days Balance of Venus Mahadasha From 12-9-1997 Rahu Mahadasha is running. Rahu Mahadasha Jupiter Antar 11.3.2001 to 23.8.2002. From 15-5-2002 to 9-10-2002. Rahu Mahadasha Jupiter Antar, Venus Prityantara Second house increase in family, 7th house pleasure of married Life 11th house denotes reunion and 12th house denotes DIVORCE. Here Mars in IInd house denotes Quarrel in family. Mutual aspect of Mars and Saturn began Quarrel in beginning of Rahu Mahadasha. Moon Jupiter Combination 10th house Produced GAJA KESRI YOGA. After calculating Vimshottari Mahadasha Jupiter antardasha and Venus priyantara reunion is seen. Really the husband of the daughter came in September 2002 and took the daughter with him. Moon Jupiter position is Strong so the Bhagya is strong as Lord of Lagna Moon is with Jupiter in 10th house.

32

INTER CASTE MARRIAGES

Inter Caste Marriages often take place due to mentally and bodily attraction among opposite sexes causing love affairs. Although Communities often oppose these marriages and even the parents and family members feel uneasiness.

I studied some cases of Inter Caste Marriages and found the following Planetary position generally responsible:-

1. Venus Rahu combination either in 6th or 11th houses.
2. Mars in 8th house either from the Lagna or Moon.
3. The Moon and Mars in 6th and 8th houses from each other.
4. Aspect of Rahu either on 7th house or on the Lord of 7th.
5. Mars and Venus in Quadrant to each other.
6. Mars and Venus in Combination in 12th house.
7. Jupiter in 7th house either in Libra or Aquarius.

I am giving here an example of Inter Caste Marriage on 12th February 1987 at 5.15 P.M. a gentleman came to me to ask about the marriage of his Son. He put the Horoscope of his son before me. The Horoscope is as following :-

Male born on 14th August 1960 at 11.00 A.M. at 24.6N; 77.44N. Balance of Venus Mahadasha One month two days. Rahu Mahadasha was running to the Native.

Rahu Mahadasha Rahu antardasha w.e.f.16-9-1983 to 28-5-1986

Rahu Mahadasa Jupiter antardasha w.e.f. 29-5-1986 to 22-10-1988

Here Lord of Lagna Venus is with Rahu in 11th house aspected by Mars from 8th house and by Ketu from 5th house. Mars is in the Sign of Venus. Venus is the Karak for wife is in 11th house. Rahu in Astrology is called VIDHARAMI or person of other Caste or religion. Rahu is aspecting the Moon in 7th house. Mars is aspecting the Lord of 4th house Saturn and Lord of 6th house Jupiter in 3rd house.

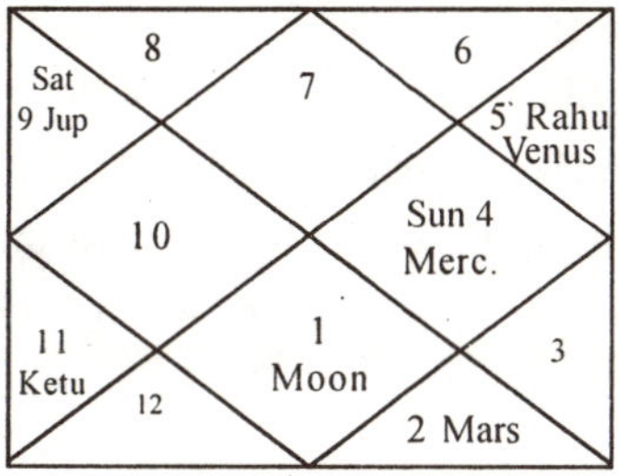

After Judging the Horoscope I told the Querent that his Son has fallen in love with a girl of Super another Caste. So he should try to marry his son immediately in his own caste otherwise within 6 months the Son may marry the girl. Because the antardasha of Jupiter in Rahu Mahadasha has been started Since 28-5-1986 and pratyantar of Saturn is in Jupiter antar will be upto 6-5-1987. So I told him that to be careful in this matter as Jupiter and Saturn both are being aspected by Rahu as well as by Mars. For more clarification I also prepared the time Horoscope as following:-

The Lord of Lagna Moon is in Lagna. Lord of 10th and 5th Mars aspects the Moon, the 4th house and Saturn in fifth house. Moon (Lagna Lord) and 7th Lord Saturn are under the influence of Mars and Rahu as Rahu is also aspecting the Lagna, Lagna Lord, 7th Lord with Jupiter. The Karaka for wife Venus is hemmed in between Sun and Saturn 2 malefics between 6th house. Actually the son of the Querent married a Super Caste Lady on 21-6-1987 according to Arya Samaj System against the will of his parents.

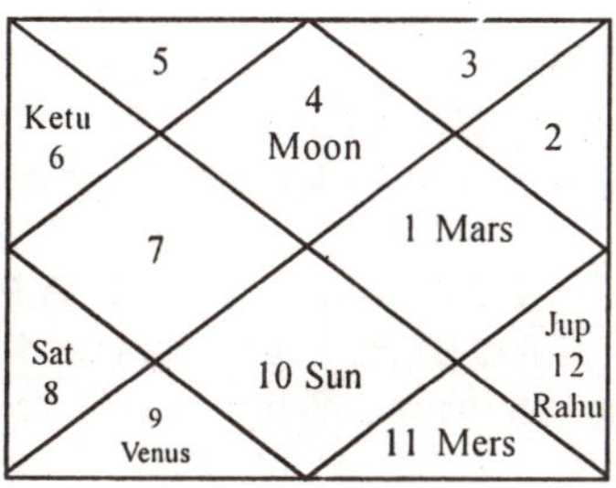

The Querent informed me in July 1987 that the forecast about the inter caste marriage of his Son proved Correct. Tension began in the families and the Querent asked me whether DIVORCE is possible in this Cases. I told him that I had warned you before 4 Months ago to be careful. But you did not care and the Inter Caste Marriage has been performed by your son without your consult. Now Nothing can become. The Son was in Government Service far from his native place where he had fallen in love with a Super Caste lady Professor in College and earning more money than him. I am giving 4 more examples of Inter Caste Marriages.

Example 1. Female born on 28-3-1946 Sravana Nakshatra first Quarter. Born at 23, 30N; 77.50E. At Birth time Mercury, Jupiter, Saturn 3 Planets are in retrogression. Birth Lagna Aries, Lord of Lagna Mars in 3rd house with 2 malefics Saturn and Rahu. The aspect of Rahu on seventh house and Jupiter in seventh house in Libra, Lord of Seventh Venus in 12th house with SUN Mercury. Mars aspects Moon as Moon is in 8th house from Mars all these things are responsible for Inter Caste Marriage.

Birth Lagna 28:3:1946

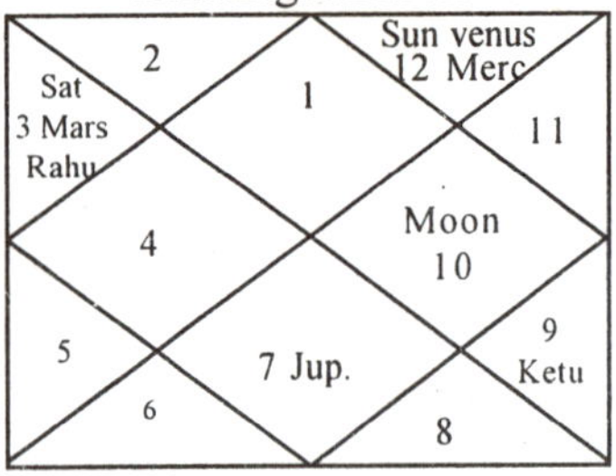

Example 2. Female born on 31-10-1950 Tuesday Mrigsira first Quarter of 41 ghatis 46 Palas at 24.5N 77.44E. Here Lord of Lagna SUN in 3rd house Lord of Seventh Saturn in Second house aspected by Rahu with Ketu. Jupiter in Seventh in Aquarius Jupiter also aspects the Lord of Lagna, Venus, Mercury in 3rd house. Mars is in 7th house from Moon. The seventh house, Jupiter are hemmed in between two malefics Mars and Rahu. All these factors throw light on Inter Caste Marriage.

Birth Lagna 31-10-1950.

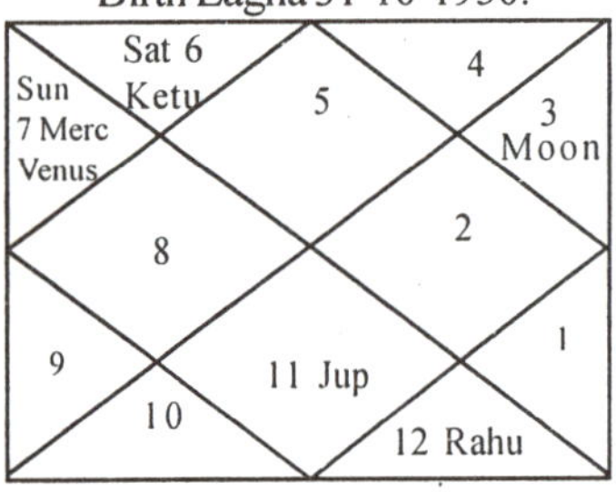

Example 3. Female Born on 15-11-1951 Wednesday at 6.17 A.M. Rohini first Quarter at. 18.56N; 72.51E in Libra Lagna Lagna Libra Lord of Lagna Venus in 12th house with Mars and Saturn two malefics in debilitation aspected by Jupiter from sixth house. Rahu being in fifth house aspects the Lagna where SUN is sitting in debilitation. Though Moon is in exaltation but in 8th house aspected by Mercury. Rahu and Moon are in Quadrants to each other. Seventh house is aspected by its Lord Mars and Sun 2 malefics. These factors show that a lady born at Bombay had fallen in love with a person born in a town near Bhopal in Madhya Pradesh.

Birth Lagna 15-11-1951.

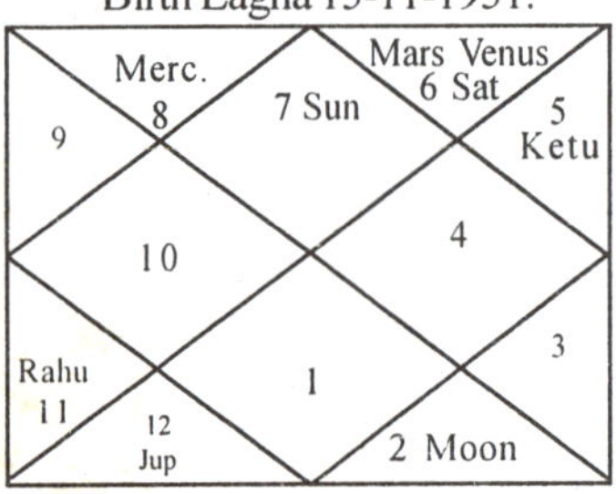

Example 4. Female born on 25-8-1968 Sunday at 8.40 P.M. at 25.57N 81.50E in PISCES Lagna. Uttra Phalguna first Quarter. Mother died when she was only 24 years 6 months

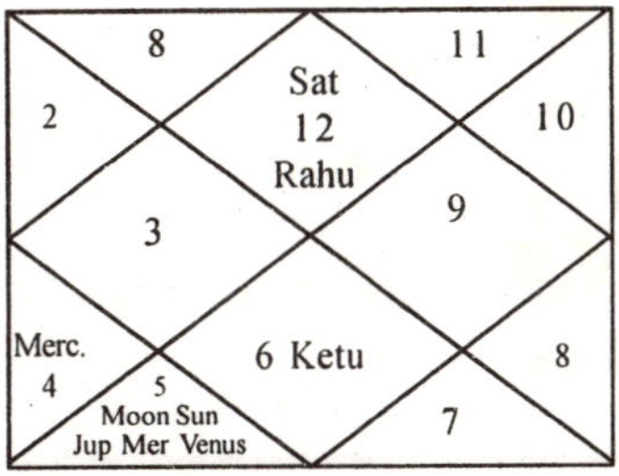

old. See that 2 malefics Saturn and Rahu are sitting in Lagna Lord of Lagna is Jupiter who is in 6th house with Moon, Venus, Jupiter, Mercury. Lord of seventh house Mercury too is in sixth house with Lord of Lagna and Ketu is Present in Seventh house.

33

Divorce

Marriage is recognised as pure family relation between two individuals husband and wife to increase Love, Sympathy, unity in the family but today due to western materialistic influence over Indian families. Differences are increasing and joint family system is badly crushed and Divorce, Rape, Kidnapping, Loot, disrespect of Ladies and Killing them in the name of Dowry System all these unwanted, undesirable things are increasing and breaking the families badly.

Without example only theoretical knowledge of Astrology has no value and its recognition is doubted. I am putting here a case of Divorce to Judge the truth of Astrology for the sake of wise readers.

Male born on 17-4-1968 at 4.35 A.M. Tuesday Jyeshtha Nakshatra third Quarter in Pisces Ascendant with Sun 0-3-38.
MOON-7-25-7 MARS-0-21-43 MERCURY-11-29-05 JUPITER-4-5-37 VENUS-11-17-12 SATURN-11-21-13 RAHU-11-24-53 KETU-5-24-53

At 24.36N; 77.43E : BALANCE OF MERCURY MAHADASHA 8 Years 6 months 0 day.

Birth Lagna

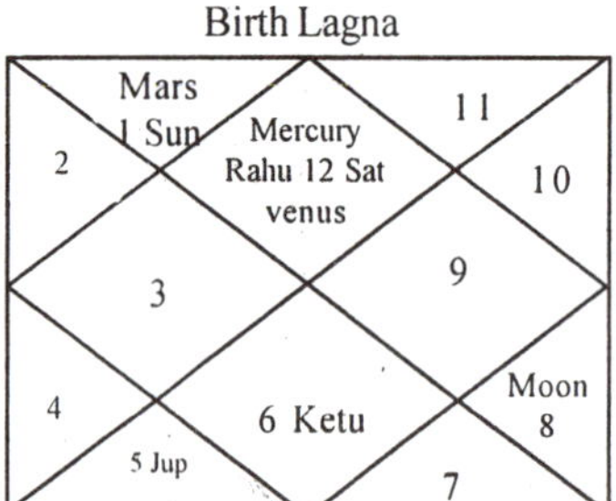

Navamsha

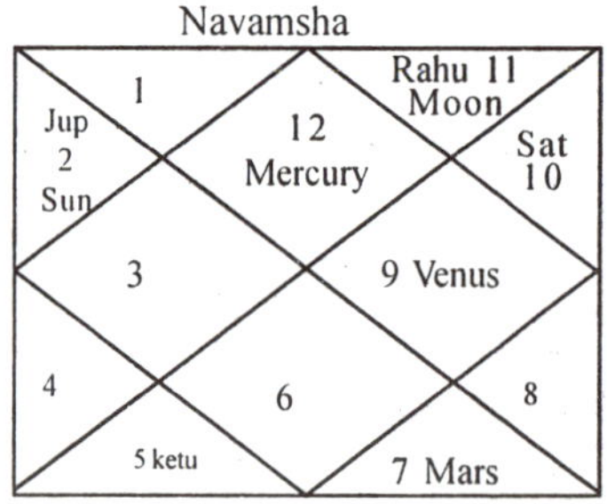

This person was married in February 1999. Divorce Took Place in February 2002. Now See why DIVORCE has taken place? See that PISCES is Birth Lagna and Lord of Lagna Jupiter is retrograded in 6th house an evil house in Leo Sign which is 12th house for 7th house. In birth Lagna Lords of 4,8,12 houses are sitting Mercury Lord and 4th and 7th house is in debilitation Venus as Lord of 8th and 3rd, house, SATURN the Lord of 12th house (DIVORCE) is with the great malefic RAHU. Hence All the 4 Planets Merucury, Venus, Rahu, Saturn have been malefics due to owner ship of evil houses. Second house is the house of family which shows the Position of increase or decrease in the family SUN is Lord of 6th (an evil house) Mars is MARKESH as Lord of 2nd house. Hence in 2nd House (House of family) there are 2 malefics. So just after performance of marriage began struggle in the family. Saturn, Rahu both are dividing Planets (विच्छेदकारक) Twelveth house is house of Divorce. Eleventh house is the hose of UNITY. Hence Saturn did the job of eleventh house (UNITY) and then Divorce (Lord of 12th house) with RAHU in Lagna.

In Venus Mahadasha antardasha of Saturn. Marriage or unity was performed and then in the antardasha of Mercury (Divorce) because Mercury is MARKESH (Lord of Seventh) and is in debilitation (NEECHA) in Lagna and with Mercury two strong malefics or dividing planets sitting. Now See the Horoscope of the Lady-

Female born on 12-10-1974 Saturday Magha Nakshatra third Quarter Ishtakala 4 ghatis 50 Palas in Libra Ascendant at 23.26N 77.42E. with SUN 5-24-20 Moon 4-9-45 MARS-5-23-23 MERCURY (R) 6-11-30 JUPITER (R) 10-16-48 VENUS-5-20-17
SATURN-2-25-30 RAHU-7-19-16 KETU-1-19-16 LAGNA-6-20-10
Balance of KETUMAHADASA 1 Year 10 Months 15 Days.

Birth Lagna

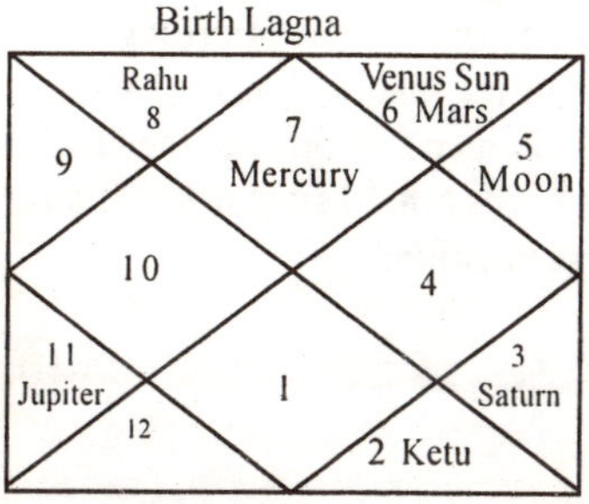

Navamsha

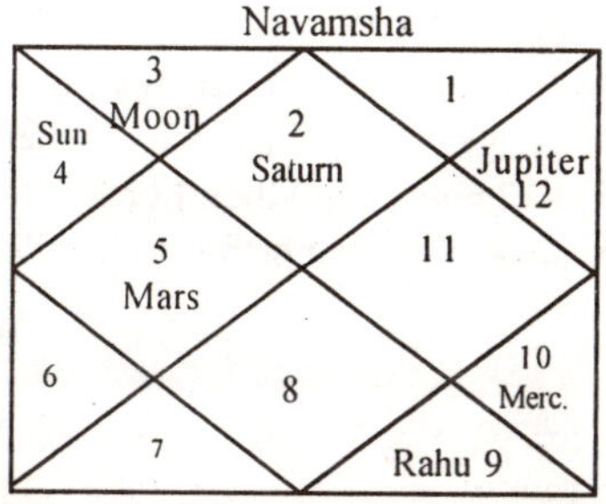

The Lord of 12th house (Dividing Planeter विच्छेदकारक) MERCURY is in Lagna being retrograded. Lord of Lagna Venus is in 12th house PATIKARAK (KARAK for Husband) Jupiter is aspecting the Lagna being the Lord of 3rd and 6th houses. Jupiter is retrograded too. Venus Lord of

Lagna is in 12th house with 2 malefics SUN and MARS being debilitated. Hence exchange of Lagnesh and Lord of 12th is enough for Divorce.

In second house family there is Rahu the great dividing Planet (महा विच्छद कारकग्रह). In this Horoscope there is Pap Kartari Yog because in 2, 12 houses there are RAHU and SUN, MARS. From 27-8-1996 SUNMAHADASA began in Jupiter, 5 antar w.e.f. 15-9-1998 to 3-7-1999. Marriage Ceremony was performed because Jupiter sitting in fifth house aspecting the Lagna and Moon in eleventh house (UNITY HOUSE). Moon in 11th house is aspected by Saturn. Hence in Saturn and Mercury antar the action for Divorce began w.e.f. 27-7-2001 to 27-2-2002. In February 2002 Divorce was in force. Wise Astrologers See that the GUNA MILAN is favourable and 32 gunas are counted. See the position.

Boy		Girl
JYESHTHA		MAGHA-3
SCORPIO	7	LEO
BRAHIMIN	1	KSHATRIYA
KEET	0	VANCHAR
MRIG	2	MOOSHAK
MARS	5	SUN
RAKSHASHA	6	RAKSHASHA
AADI	8	AANTYA
TARA	3	
Total gunas	32	

GRAHA MAITRY is very good. When highest guna Milan was there then why Divorce? The Lods of Nakshatras have no friendship. Then days means Birthdays of both are great enemies Tuesday and Saturday (MARS and SATURN Lords of days). The Astrologers are advised to see not only the total gunas but see that the houses 2 (family) 7 (Marriage) 11 (UNITY) are in beneficial influence or not. See the Position of 6-8-12 houses and their Lords. When Lords 6-8-12 sit in 6-8-12 houses they change the better position in Worst Position.

34

Death by Heart-Attacks

In Shrimad Bhagwat Geeta Lord Krishna says to Arjun that GOD Lives in the heart of all beings.

"ईश्वर: सर्वभूतानां हृद्देशेर्जुन तिष्ठति" So heart is the abode of GOD in the heart of human beings. In the human body heart is the main part of the inner body. Heart is the Centre of Vitality and Longevity. The work of heart is to supply Strength through purifying blood circulation and then to send the pure blood to all the parts of the body. Doctor recognise the work of heart by judging the position of nerves jumping minutely in the root of thumbs near wrist in both hands. So these nerves in both the hands are barometer of life. When heart stops to work then immediately these nerves too stop jumping, pulpitation of hearts stops and the man is declared dead by Doctor.

By Astrological Diagnosis diseases can be known by studying 12 Signs and 27 Nakshatras. When occupied by malefics or 6,8,12 house-lords then in the part of the body represented by particular sign and nakshatra, indicate harms to their part and cause of disease relating to their part of the body. In human body SUN represents Heart and Moon represents Lungs and Mind so when Lagna and its Lord fourth and fifth houses and their Lords, Sun, Moon are afflicted by malefics or by Lords of 6,8,12 houses, in any way either by Conjunction, occupation or aspect heart trouble or heart disease is sure. When heart stops working suddenly heart-attack is the result and the man is declared dead. But if Jupiter aspects the Lagna, fifth, ninth houses and Moon then heart attack is curable and man does not die.

In the Horoscope of great Hindi Poet Shri Krishna *'Saral'* there is Jupiter in fifth house in Leo with Saturn and Ketu is in Ascendant with Venus both are aspected by Jupiter Lord of ninth house, Jupiter also aspects the ninth house so poet Shri Krishna Saral was threatened 3,4 times by heart-attack due to Saturn in Leo in fifth house aspected by Ketu.

But being Jupiter in 5th house he was saved. I am giving below 4 examples of death by Heart-attack. If there are indications of Heart-attack in the horoscope then by remedial measures its attack can be stopped to some extent by means of Japa, recitation of Versese of Shrimad Bhagwat Geeta Chapter II as following :-

> ''क्लैव्यं मा स्म गमा पार्थ नैतत्त्वयुपपद्यते
> क्षुद्रं हृदय दौर्बल्यं त्यकत्वोत्तिष्ठ परंतप''

Japa of Jupiter, Maha Mrityunjaya Mantra, GAYATRI MANTRA, donating food, clothes to poor and beggars, feeding of girls and grass to cows.

Example 1. Male born on 6-9-1928 Thursday Kritika Nakshatra 4th Quarter Balance of Sun Mahadasha 2 years 6 months 15 days. Saturn mahadasha from 21-10-1982 Saturn antardasha upto 24-10-1985. The Native died of Heart-attack on 16-11-1986 in antardasha of Mercury in Saturn Mahadasha.

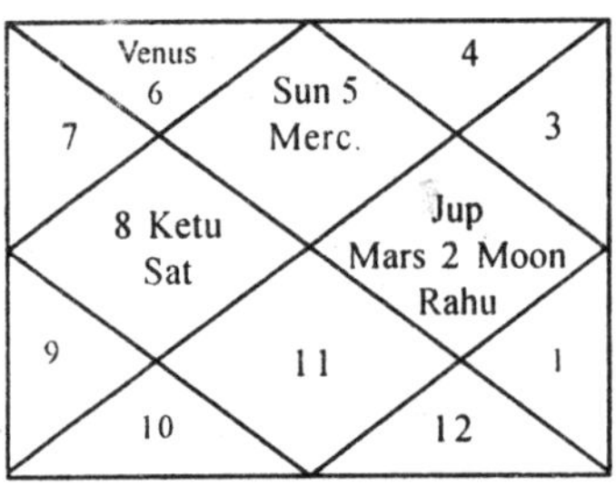

Here Lagna Lord SUN is in Lagna. Two malefics Saturn, Mars aspect SUN and Lagna. Lord of 12th Moon is with Lord of 8th Jupiter with 2 malefics Rahu and Mars aspected by 6,7th Lord Saturn and Ketu. Here SUN, Moon, Leo, Cancer 4th and 5th Houses are badly afflicted by malefics. Mars, Jupiter (Lord of 8th) Moon (Lord of 12th), Rahu aspect 4th house and Mars alone also aspects 5th house. There is strong KALA SARPA YOGA too all the planets between Rahu and Ketu. Heart-attack was in the Mahadasha of Saturn Lord of 6th and Lord of 7th Markesh and antardasha Mercury Lord of 2nd Markesh.

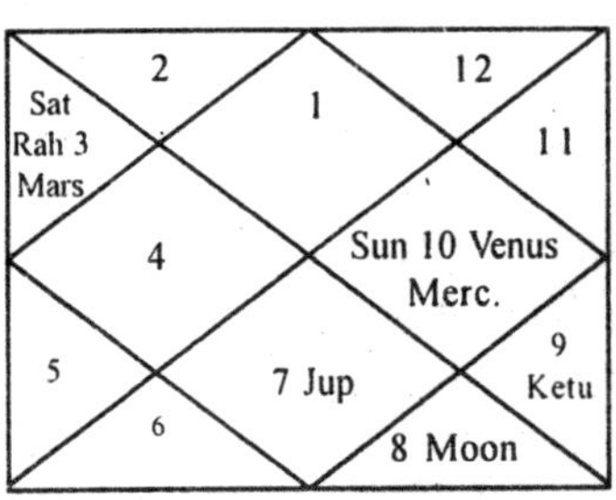

Example-2 Lady born on 29-1-1946 Tuesday Jyeshtha Nakshatra 4th Quarter. Balance of Mercury Mahadasha at birth 0 year 4 months 4 days: Birth Lagna: Lord of Lagna Mars, Moon, Sun, badly afflicted by malefics. Sun with Lord of 2nd Venus (MARKESH) and Lord of Seventh too. Cancer is badly afflicted by aspecting i.e. Sun, Lord of 3rd and 6th Mercury and Lord of 2nd and Seventh (MARKESH) Venus. Moon is in debilitation (NEECHA) Sign. Leo is also aspected by Saturn and its Lord Sun is 10th aspected by Mars. Rahu is with 2 malefics Mars and Saturn in 3rd house (eighth house from 8th) The Lady expired on 5-8-1997 by Heart-attack in Rahu Mahadasha antardasha of Rahu and Prityantardasha of Saturn. Heart attack occurred in Rahu Mahadasha Rahu antar because Rahu is with 2 malefics Saturn and Mars.

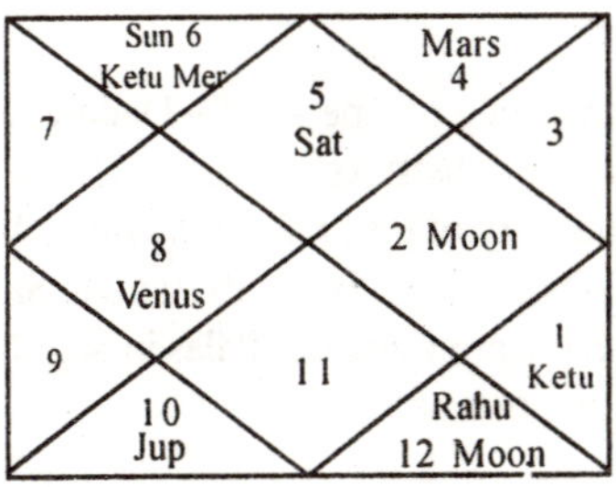

Example-3 Lady born on 10-10-1949 Kritika Nakshatra 3rd Quarter Balance of Sun Mahadasha 1 year 6 months 15 days. Here in Leo Sign (Lagna) Saturn is posited in Lagna aspecting the Moon in tenth house. Sun is with KETU aspected by Rahu. The moon sign Cancer is occupied by Mars. Lord of 6th and 7th Saturn in Lagna Weakens the Lagna and Moon. Mars in 12th, SATURN in Lagna, SUN and Ketu in 2nd created PapaKartari Yoga. The Lady died of Heart-attack on 19-7-1997. Before expiry there was a Sign of Wound on external part of Heart or breast. This seems a case of heart cancer too. Death occurred in Mahadasha of Saturn who is Lord of 6th (disease) and 7th (MARKESH) w.e.f. 25-4-1992 in antardasha of Mercury (Lord of Second MARKESH). Saturn and Mercury both are Markesh.

Birth Lagna

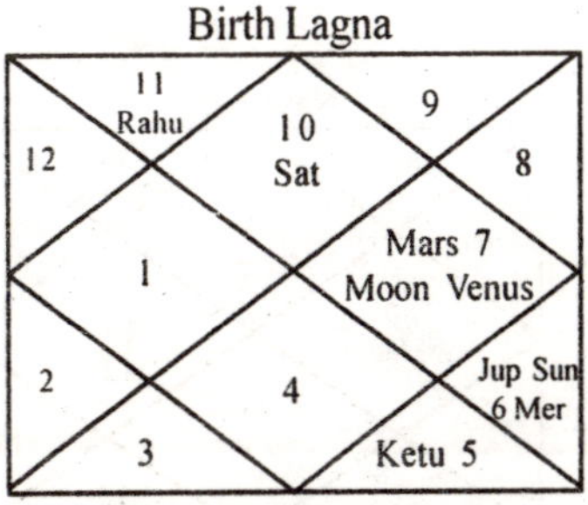

Example-4 Male born on 22-9-1933 Friday in Swati Nakshatra Ist Quarter. Balance of Rahu Mahadasha at birth 14 years 8 months 23 days.

In Lagna, Lagna Lord Saturn is in retrogression aspects the 10th and 4th house. Thus 4th house, its Lord Mars is badly afflicted by Saturn. Mars aspects 4th or 5th house. 5th house Lord Venus is with Mars aspected by Saturn. Aspect of 12th Lord Jupiter on 5th house is also bad. The Native died of heart attack on 13-7-1988 in Mahadasha of Mercury (Lord 6th) antardasha of venus (Lord of 5th) badly afflicted by Mars and Saturn. SUN, KARAKA For heart is hemmed between Ketu and Mars. There is strong kala SARPA YOGA too.

35

Kidnapping

I am giving here a case of kidnapping of a person by Dacoit Amrat Lal On 10-10-1956 in **Dhurra** Village of Distt. Ashoknagar. The person came to me on 29-4-2000 and told the story of his kidnapping himself. He is the son of Late Shri Prabhu Lal Jain born on 26-10-1939 Ashwin Shukla 13 Thursday Uttra Bhadra Pada Nakshatra at 11 ghati 30 Palas in Sagittarius Lagna with the following planetary position:-

Sun	6-8-26	-	SWATI - I
Moon	11-15-32	-	UTTARBHAPRA IV
Mars	9-22-28	-	SHRAVANA IV
Merc.	7-3-54	-	ANURADHA I
Jupiter	11-8-53	-	UTTRABHADRA II
Venus	6-25-21	-	VISHAKHA II
Saturn	11-28-49	-	REWTI IV
Rahu	6-5-19	-	CHITRA IV
Ketu	0-5-19	-	ASHWANI II

Birth Lagna

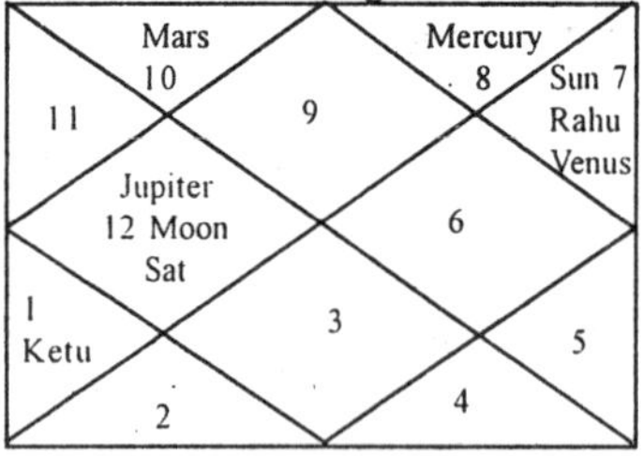

Navamsha

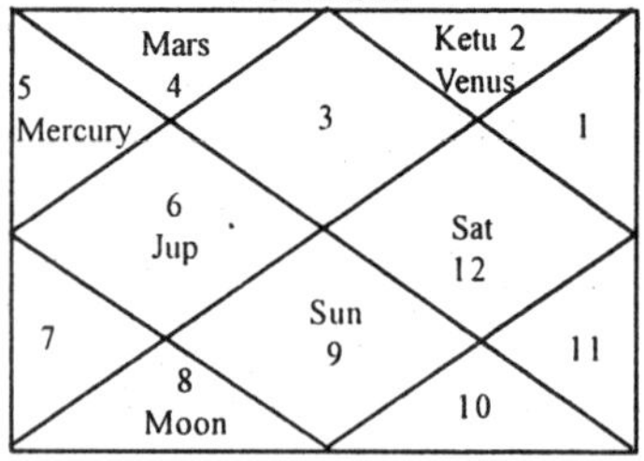

Balance of Saturn Mahadasha (1 year 10 months 24 days)

The event happened in Mercury Mahadasha, Saturn antardasha w.e.f. 11-1-1956 to 20-9-1958. in PRITYANTAR Dasa of Mercury. Dacoit Amrat Lal Entered the house with 40 Persons at 4.00 P.M. and Looted the house for 4 hours with firing Dacoit Amrat Lal took with him this boy then and kept for 6 months i.e., in Prityantar Dasa of Ketu and Venus. DACOIT AMRAT LAL Left him after charging one Lac rupees. It was Wednesday on 10-10-1956. DACOIT AMRAT LAL threatened the Seth PRABHU LAL (Father of this Native) not to inform the Police anyway. Now see that How this event happened? MARS is the representative of DACOITS and LOOT. Mars in exaltation in 2nd house being the Lord of 12th house (expense) and in NAVAMSA too in 2nd house in debilitation being the Lord of 6th and 11th house. Mercury is the Lord of tenth (house of father) posited in 12th house in Mars Sign in NAKSHATRA of Saturn (MARKESH as 2nd Lord) Sitting in NAVAMSA in 10th (House of father) aspected by Jupiter (MARKESH IN NAVAMSA) Jupiter and Saturn Both are retrograded. Ketu and Venus both are under malefics. DACOITS entered the house on 10-10-1956 at 4. P.M. in Aquarius Lagna as following:

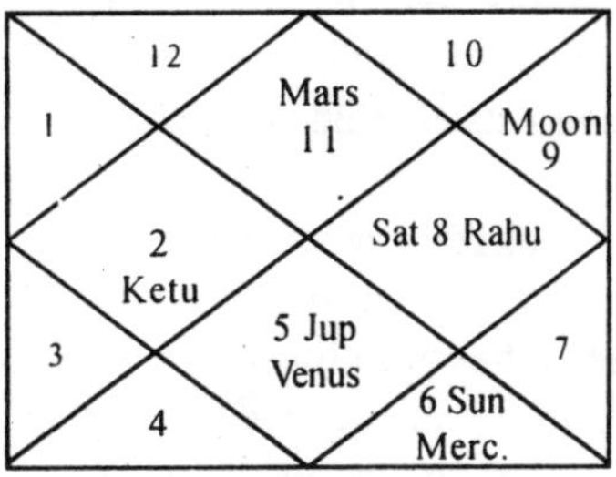

Mars in Lagna, Ketu in 4th, Saturn, Rahu in 10th, JUPITER (MARAK) in 7th with Venus; SUN MERCURY in 8th See that Saturn Mars Rahu Ketu these 4 malefics are in Quadrants 1-4-10. Mars is the main Planet. SUN is with Lord of 8th. Moon as Lord of 6th in 11th house.

36

Jupiter in the 6th House

Jupiter in 6th house from ascendant makes the person victorious over enemies as told in Bhrigu Sutram: शत्रु In Jatakubharana too it is said that Jupiter in 6th house makes one famous and victorious over foes. According to another book of Mana Sagari states जयति शत्रुकुल रिपुग गुरे means the native conquers his foes.

Generally it is told in Astrological books that benefics in 6th house from the ascendant do not produce good results but produce enemies, diseases and hindrances. But practically it has been found that Jupiter, the super benefic planet in the 6th house causes Rajayoga and fame though with struggle, fighting with enemies and at last conquering them.

Our beloved 2nd Prime Minister late *Shri. Lal Bahadur Shastri* born in Scorpio ascendant had Jupiter in 6th house in Aries fully aspected by Venus in Libra in 12th house. His lord of ascendant Mars was in 10th house in Leo with Rahu. With two malefics in 10th house he was debarred of father's love and happiness but due to Jupiter in 6th house, who fully aspects the 10th house and lord of ascendant Mars, Shri Shastri though horn in a very poor family rose to the highest peak of politics and administration in the country. Jupiter is here too lord of the 2nd house and hence from 10th house there is Sagittarius in 2nd house and Jupiter in 9th house. For considering native's rise in politics and career consideration of 10th house, 2nd house, 6th house are important, i.e., trines of 10th house, should also be considered as the play vital role in human growth. Thus this is clear that Jupiter of the 6th house made him the Prime Minister of India and that too very very successful Prime Minister from a very poor and low position.

L.B. Shastri Birth Lagna

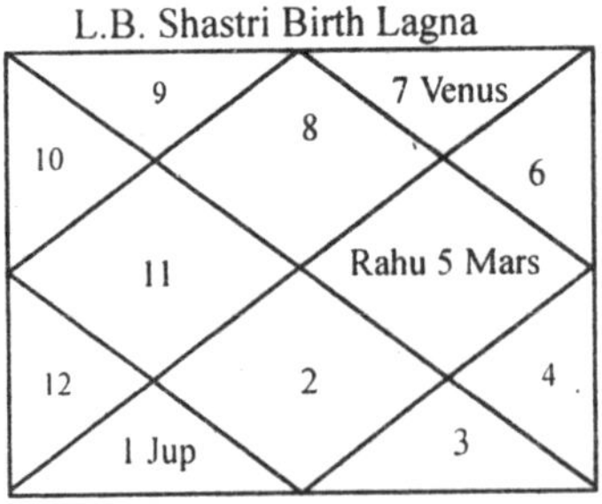

Birth Lagna Sharad Pawar

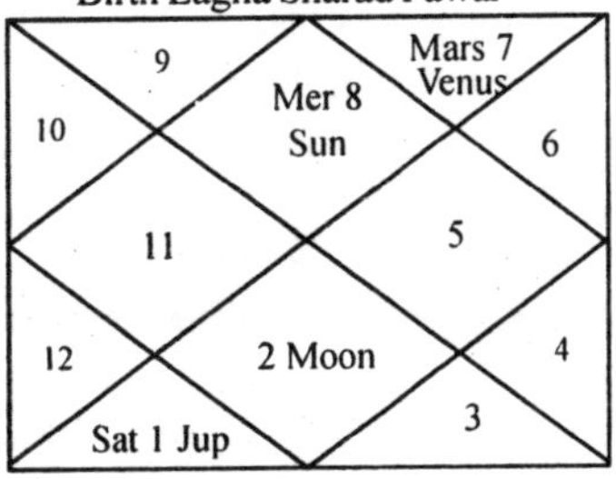

In the present Indian politics, *Shri. Sharad Pawar* born in Scorpio "also has Jupiter in the 6th house in Aries with debilitated Saturn aspected by Mars and Venus from the 12th house. In ascendant Mercury and the Sun produced Budhaditya Yoga: Exalted Moon is in 7th house. The lord of the 10th house Sun is in quadrant from the 10th house.

In the horoscope of *Benazir Bhutto,* the first lady Prime Minister of Pakistan born in Sagittarius ascendant Jupiter is in 6th house in Taurus fully aspecting the 10th house. The 10th lord Mercury in 8th house is being aspected by retrograded Saturn in 10th house in Virgo. This retrograde Saturn fully aspects both the signs of Jupiter, Sagittarius and Pisces. Due to this retrograded Saturn's aspect on Jupiter's both signs Benazir Bhutto was Prime Minister of Pakistan from 2nd December 1988 to 6th August 1990, i.e., for 582 days only when retrograded Jupiter was transiting in Taurus with Navamsa of Pisces and Saturn in Sagittarius in Capricorn navamsa. Thus when both Jupiter and Saturn had full aspect on 10th house she was made Prime Minister and while dismissal Jupiter was in Gemini in Taurus navamsa and retrograded Saturn was in Sagittarius in Sagittarius navamsa. Thus Jupiter was in maraka house in inimical sign of Gemini in 7th house. March 1993 is important to Benazir Bhutto as Jupiter will be retrograde in Virgo and Saturn retrograded in Capricorn. Thus Jupiter will aspect both trinal houses from the 10th house. Again Jupiter in Capricorn and Saturn in Pisces throughout the year 1997 may prove the best period to Benazir Bhutto.

Birth Lagna Benazir Bhutto

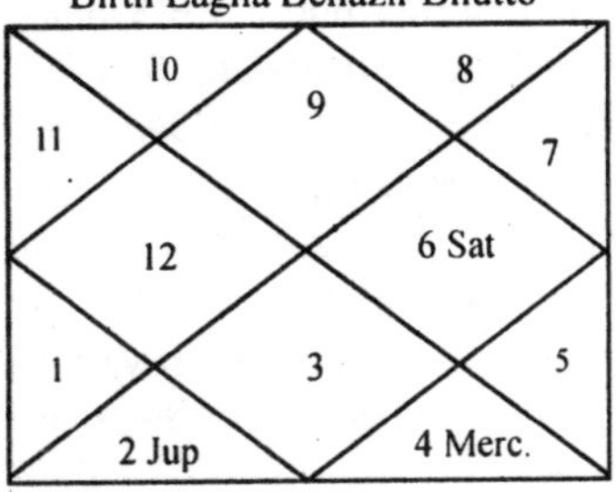

The famous educationist *Mr. J. Krishna Murthy had Jupiter* in 6th house in Gemini sign with Mars and Venus. Retrograded Saturn is in Libra in 10th house being aspected by the Sun.

The super star *Amitabh Bacchan* has exalted Jupiter in 6th house aspecting the 10th house. Saturn is in 4th house in Taurus. Thus Jupiter and Saturn both aspecting the 10th house made Amitabh Bacchan world famous in film field.

Dimple Kapadia, a well known Hindi film actress has Jupiter in 6th house with the Moon. The lord of the 10th Saturn has full aspect on 10th house being present in 8th house. The lord of the ascendant Mars is thereby aspected by Jupiter and Saturn.

The great modern scientist and mathematician *Ramanujam* had Jupiter with Mercury in Scorpio in 6th house. The aspect of the Sun on ascendant, and the aspect of Rahu. Mars and Jupiter on 10th house and the Moon. These factors with Jupiter in 6th house and the Moon in 10th house rose him to glorious height.

Jupiter in Sagittarius in *Raj Kapoor's horoscope* in 6th house with Mercury made him reach the highest peak in the film world.

In the horoscopes of *Chhatrapati Shivaji* and *General Manek Shaw,* Jupiter is in Capricorn in 6th house aspecting the 10th house. Other famous persons in whose horoscope Jupiter is in 6th house are *Sumitra Nandan Pant* (Hindi Poet), *Swami Swaroopanand Saraswati, Tipu Sultan, Guljari Lal Nanda, Prince Charles, Dr. Annie Besant, Hari Deo Joshi, Indu bala Sukhadia, Pandit Shyama Charan Shukla,* etc.

Thus it is proved that Jupiter in 6th house gives good results. Due to shortage of space more examples are not being analyzed. Readers are requested to experience the position of Jupiter in 6th house in various horoscopes with Saturn either in conjunction or with aspect or otherwise relation with Saturn.

These two major planets Jupiter and Saturn play important role in individual's growth and deterioration.

37

Rebirth

AADI SHANKACHARYA Said "पुनरपि जन्म पुनरपि मरणं पुनरपि जननी जठरे शयनं" means again birth and again Death and again to sleep in mother's womb. This means that man dies but takes rebirth again. Rebirth has been proved by many examples. I am giving here 2 cases of Rebirth that I came across.

Example-1 Mr. Suresh Chand Jain, Bharat Radio Service Station Road, Ashok Nagar (M.P.) met me One day and told about his third Son Chandresh Kumar jain born on 23-10-1977 at 2.30 P.M. at Ashok Nagar that while the boy was 3 years old he told the parents that he is Pandit Mishri Lal of PIPRESRA, Tehsil Esagarh Distt. Ashok Nagar. (M.P.) Village Pipresra is about 15k.m. far from District Headquarter Ashok Nagar (M.P.).

The boy pressed the parents to go with him to Pipresra. His parents took him to Village Pipresra. The boy recognised his wife of previous life and children and told many things which were true.

I (the writer of this article) knew very well late Pandit Mishri Lal Personally. He was a Katha Vachaka (Narrator of Mythological Stories). When I was student of High School Inter Classes at GUNA and lived in Jat Mohalla in 1949 to 1953. Pandit Mishrilal used to go there and Read Shri Mad Bhagwat there. I used to listen Shri Mad Bhagwat from his Sweet tongue for 2-3 years Continuously. Slowly I was in contact with him and he also loved me as younger brother. After passing my Intermediate examination from GUNA in 1953 I went to GWALIOR for doing B.A. and M.A. courses. Then I came in Government Service on March 12 year 1956 and lived outside of home till 30th December 1994. In January 1995 I came to my native place Ashok Nagar. During the period I was Quite unknown about where about of Pandit Mishri Lal. The birth particulars of the boy Chandresh Kumar Jain in as follows. Born on 23rd October 1987 Vikram Samvat 2034 Shaka Samvat 1899 Ashwin Shukla Paksha Chaturdashi Sunday Shatdisha Nakshatra. Birth Nakshatra Poorva Bhadra Pada second

Quarter Balance of Jupiter Mahadasha 11 years 6 months 7 days. Planetary Position is as follows:-

SUN-6-5-51
MOON-11-23-44
MARS-3-4-8
MERCURY-6-8-6
JUPITER-2-13-54
VENUS-5-15-2
SATURN-4-6-34 BALANCE OF JUPITER MAHADASHA
RAHU-5-20-38 11 Years 6 Months 7 days.
KETU-11-20-38

Birth Lagna

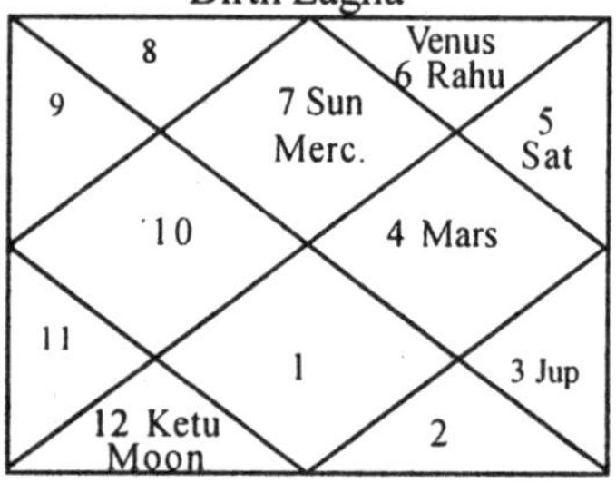

According to "Phala Deepika" the 9th house represents previously born life means Rebirth or Punar Janma, Cause, can be found from 9th house 5th house represents future life. The Lord of ninth house Mercury is in Lagna aspected by Divine planet Jupiter in 9th house. 5th house Lord saturn aspects the 5th house. Moon is in Jupiter's sign PISCES in 6th house with ketu. Jupiter in 9th reminds about previous life. Lagna Lord venus with Rahu aspected by Moon and Ketu. Jupiter is in Navamsha of saturn sign. Aquarius and moon too is with Jupiter in Navamsha 5th house represents future life.

Example-2 Male born on 7-4-1987 in Cancer Lagna Name Madan Mohan Rawat. Father's name Lakhan Singh Rawat Village Raw Kala P.O. Layakna Tehsil Narwar Distt Shivpuri (M.P.). This boy speaks fluently on Ramayana GEETA. His memory is wonderful. He came with his father at my native Place ASHOK NAGAR (M.P.) last year in 1996 his programme was settled for 7 days at Ashok Nagar. The boy says that he remembers 5 previous lives. I met his father and asked about his birth date and time of birth. He told that he was born at 12.00 Noon On Ram Navmi on 7-4-1987 with following Planetary Position:

SUN-11-25-29
MOON-3-20-30
MARS-1-7-44
MERCURY-11-0-14
JUPITER-11-15-42
VENUS-10-19-10
SATURN-7-25-57
RAHU-11-1739
KETU-5-17-39

Birth Lagna

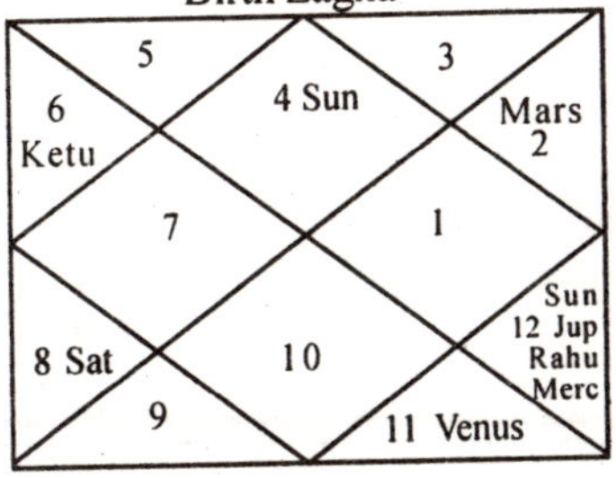

In 9th house in Pisces 4 Planets SUN, Mercury, Jupiter, Rahu are present. Rahu and Jupiter aspect the Lagna, Moon, 3rd house and fifth house. Venus is in 8th house as in Example No. 1 SATURN is in 5th house in Scorpio aspecting Mars. In Navama SUN, Saturn are in KARKAMSA. Jupiter is in Quadrant in 10th house. Previous life from 9th, 12th and their Lords, Speech from second house.

38

Life Span

In Astrology the most difficult task is the determination of age through horoscope when there is loss of life or no age of the native or there is Balarishta yoga (बालारिष्ट योग). Then what is the necessary to prepare Horoscope of such natives who have Balarishta (in fantile mortality yoga or short life yoga (अल्पायु योग).

Hence the first and important work of the astrologer is to find out the Span of life of the native so that astrology and astrologer may not be cause of dishonour. First of all the astrologer should see that whether there is Balarishta yoga upto 4 years, 8 years or 12 years or Alpayu yoga as the case may be he should not prepare the horoscope but ask politely the parents of child that the Horoscope will be prepared after the expiry of Balarishta Yoga period after 4, 5, 6, 8 years of age as the case may be.

According to Classical books available in Astrology it is said that Balarishta Yoga is of 3 kinds.

1. Upto 4 years due to Sins of mother.
2. Upto 8 years of age due to the Sins of father.
3. Upto 12 years of age due to the Sins the native himself. I am giving here 3 Yoga's of Balarishta experienced by me for the knowledge of the readers.

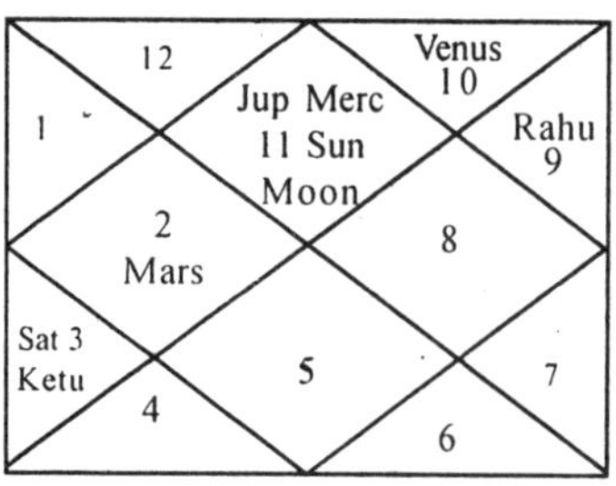

Example-1 A child was born on 23rd February 1974 at 6.30 a.m. in Kumbha Lagna. It was the first tithi of lunar month after amavasya. On this day the Lagna and Nakshatra proceed together it was falguna shukla paksha. According to ancient Sages (Lagna is Aquarius) the first ghatika of first tithi of Phalguna

Shukla Paksha is known as inauspicious. There is trividh gandanta dosha (त्रिविघ गण्डांत दोष) because Lagna, nakshatra, and tithi Proceed together. It was Saturday and 2 1/2 ghatis of the beginning of the day, i.e., one hour and thirty minutes of Saturday is knonwn as Kala ghatis (कालघड़ी) the male child was born on 23-2-1974 at 6.30 aim in trividha gandanta. It is said about gandanta "पौष्णादि गण्ड भवो हिमर्त्य:" Means one born gandanta is inauspicious to Parents and elder brothers. It means that the Parents and elder brothers of the native may die due to Some reason. In Man Sagri it is Said "लग्नात् चतुर्थग्न पापी यदि स्यात् बलवत्तर: तदा मातृवघं कुर्यात्केन्द्र वा न परो यदि" means when there is Strong detrimental malefic Planet in the 4th house the mother of the native dies soon after giving birth to the child because there is Mars in the fourth house.

In Sarvartha Chinta Mani it is said that Moon in Aries 23°, Taurus 21°, Gemini 22°, Cancer 22°, Leo 27°, Virgo 1°, Libra 4°, Scorpio 10°, Sagittarius 18°, Capricorn 22°, Aquarius 20°, and Pisces 10°, Produce Balarishta Yoga.

Kalyan Verma too emphasised on the Moon's degrees in different rasis as following- Aries 8°, Taurus 9°, Gemini 22°, Cancer 12°, Leo 5°, Virgo 1°, Libra 4°, Scorpio 23°, Sagattarius 18°, Capricorn 20°, Aquarius 21°, Pisces 10°. Sarvartha Chinta Mani and SARAVALI show the Same degrees of the Moon at the time of birth they are Gemini 22°, Virgo 1°, Libra 4°, Sagattarius 18°, and Pisces 1°.

In the above mentioned Chart Moon is in 21° (twenty one degrees) in Aquarius hence Balarishta Yoga is present. In Gemini Sutras जैमिनी सूत्र Chapter II verse 36 says क्रूरग्रहेषु यद्योरिष्टम् means if there are malefics in 3,6,8,12 houses from 6th house or from Lord of 6th house, it is very inauspicious and arishta is sure. Cancer is in 6th house from Lagna, from 6th house Rahu is in 6th Sun is in 8th, Saturn and Ketu are in 12th house. Hence all these indication a Balarishta Yoga are present. Malefic in 4th house too produced Balarishta Yoga and it is Said चतुर्थे हन्यते माता means malefic in fourth house kills the mother. Mother of the child died soon after giving birth. In SARAVALI it is Said "पापस्त्रिकोण केन्द्रे सौम्या: षटव्ययगाश्च सूर्योदये प्रसूता सद्य प्राण त्यजति जन्तु" means malefics in 5,9,1,4,7,10 house and benefics in 6th or 12th with birth at Sun rise produce Balarishta and the Child dies early. Here SUN, MARS, RAHU all malefics are in 5,9,1,4,7,10 houses, Mercury Lord of 8th is in Lagna. Venus in 12th Lord of birth and Moon Lagna i.e. Saturn is in 5th house with Ketu aspected by Rahu all of which are inauspicious. Due to all these arishta Yogas Mother died Soon after giving birth and the native too died in infancy period, i.e., on 9 March 1974.

According to Mansagri यदि लग्नेराहु क्रूरा षष्टे वाप्यष्टमे शशि तदा सद्योभवेन्मृत्यु: जातस्य न संशय:'' means malefics in Lagna (RAHU) moon in 6 or 8 the native dies soon. Moon being Lord of 6th house is in Lagna.

Example-2 Male born on 12-1-1971 at 10.35 P.M. Magha Krishna Paksha Pratipada (प्रतिपदा) Pushya Nakshatra Virgo Lagna. In SARAVALI ARISHTA YOGA Adhyay Verse 5 it is Stated ''वक्रीशनि भौमग्रहं प्रपन्नश्चन्द्रेष्ट षष्ठेथ चतुष्टये वा कुजेन सम्प्राप्त बलेन दृष्टो वर्षद्वयं जविति प्राजातं'' means if Retrograde Saturn is in the Sign of Mars and Moon is in 6th 8th or in Quadrant aspected by Mars the native lives for 2 years. Here Saturn in the Sign of Mars Aries in 8th house retrograded aspected by the eighth Lord Mars. Moon is in Cancer in 12° is also the Cause of early death The Lord of the 8th house Mars is in inimical Sign Libra aspected by retrograded Saturn, the Lord of 6th. According to MANSAGRI, JATKABHARAN too malefic in 6th or 8th house aspected by a malefic causes early death. This child died on 12-11-1972 before completing the age of 2 years.

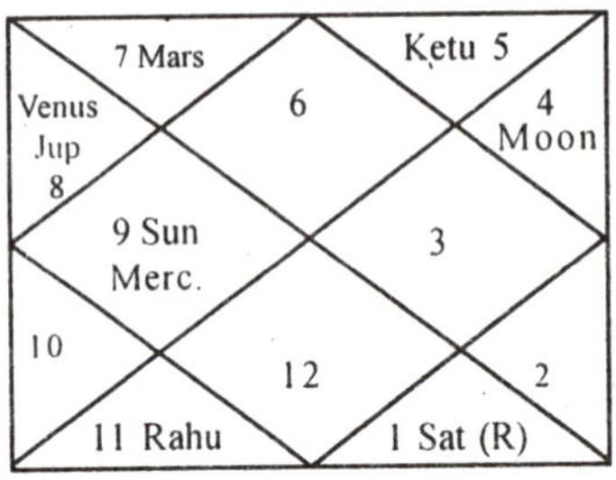

EXAMPLE-3 Male born on 10-12-1969 at 8.00 P.M. MARGSHEERSHA Shukla Paksha Pratipada tithi Wednesday Mool Nakshatra. Here Jwalamuhki Yoga as per Hindi aphorism पडवा मूल पांचै भरणी आठै कृतिका नवै रोहिणी दस अश्लेषा ये नक्षत्र ज्वाला मुखी कहिये। जन्मे तो जीवै नहीं, वसै तो ऊसर होय। means moola on Padwa, Bharni on Panchmi, Kritika on Ashthmi, Rohini on NAVMI, Aslesha on DASMI TITHI are Jwalamukhi If born, no life. If lives then no fruitful life. This male Child too died before completing the age of 2 years. MARS and RAHU two malefics are in 8th house aspected by the Lord of 6th house Jupiter who is in inimical Sign. The Lord of 8th house is in debilitation (NEECHA) in Aries. The Lagna Lord Moon is in 6th house with Mercury the Lord of 12th house. These 3 examples are of BALARISHTA of children born on Pratipada have very short Life as proved by 3 examples. Secondly in two cases Saturn the KARAKA for life is in debilitation (NEECHA) aspected by malefics.

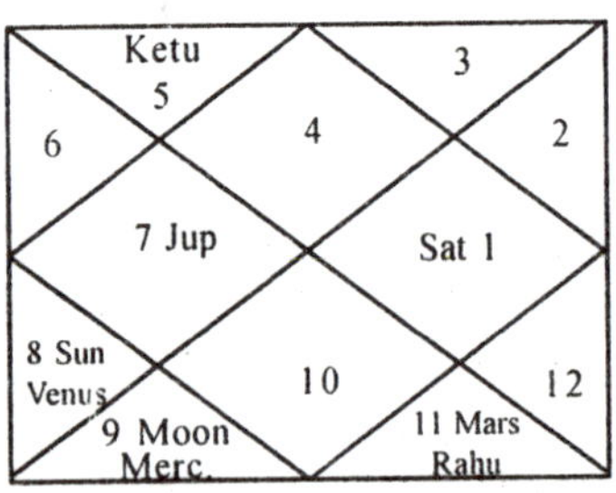

Alpayu Yoga Example-4 Alpayu Yoga is upto 12 years of age. I am giving an example Female born on April 3 year 1949 Chaitra Shukla Paksha Panchmi Rohini NAKSHATRA. MANSAGRI Says—मित्रक्षेत्र गतेलाभे दशमे वा यदि गुरू शत्रुक्षेत्रे अथवा शुक्रो द्वितीय द्वादशे भवेत एक विंशति वर्षायुजायते बालकं ध्रुवम् Jupiter is in friend's Sign in 10th or 11th Venus in inimical Sign in 2 or 12 houses The Native lives for 21, years only. This girl died at the age of 21. ALPAYU YOGA is Present as RAHU the first grade malefic in Lagna, Lord of Lagna Mars in 12th. KARAKA For Life Saturn is in Leo retrograded an inimical Sign. 8th Lord Mars in 12th. Hence loss of life in Alpayu of 21 year only.

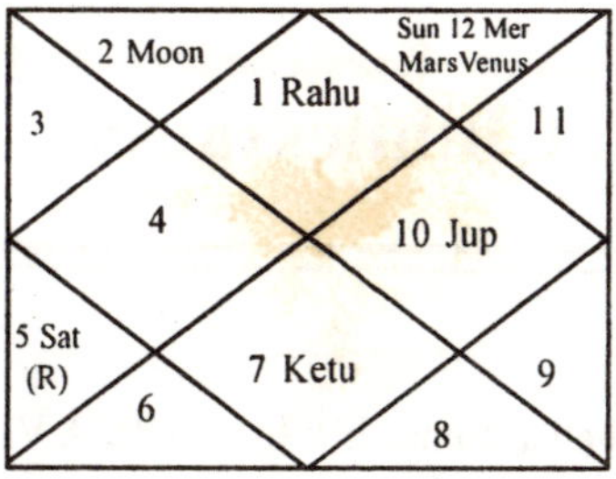

Madhyayu Yoga Example-5 Mrigsira Nakshatra 4th Quarter Born on 8-8-1986 Tuesday died on 4-4-1954 at the age of 58 years. According to जासकालंकार if Moon is in 6,8,12 houses Lord of Lagna in Navamsa of Saturn, the Native Lives upto 58 years. This person was murdered in running train in Mahadasa of Saturn antardasha of Jupiter. Mars in 4th in Chara Sign aspected by Saturn and their mutual aspect too indicates accidental death. Mars also aspects the Lord of 8th house SUN. Venus the KARAKA for Vehicle is in 8th house aspected by RAHU. Saturn also aspects the 8th Lord Sun in 7th house.

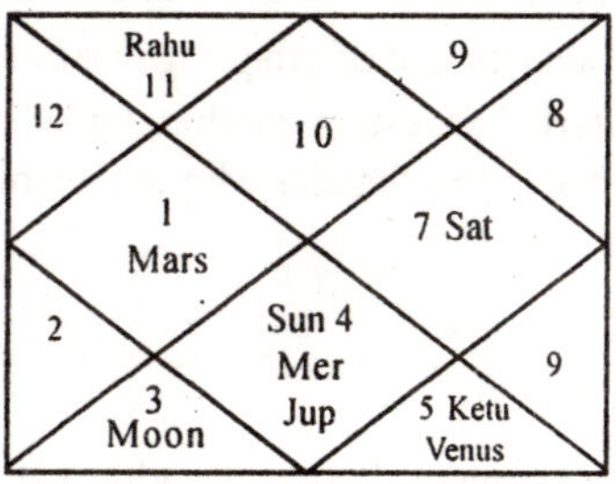

39

Astrology and Childlessness

A home without progeny is a hell in human life. In "KARMA VIPAK SAMHITA" कर्मविपाक संहितां It is said.

मर्त्या: सर्वे जगज्जाता कर्म कुर्वन्ति सर्वदा।
स्वकर्माणि ततो देवि भुज्यन्ते देवमानुषै:।।

Lord Shiva Says to Deity Parvati that those who are born in this world always do Karma and get results according to their Actions or work whether they are Devtas or men.

Those who are devoid of Son and daughter Killed their teachers and members of their family in Previous life. According to Santan Deepika 'संतान दीपिका' Male and female are also devoid of offspring due to curse of serpent, GODS. Maternal and Paternal ancestors, mother, father etc. I am giving here some cases of such males and females who are devoid of offspring.

CHARTS 1 AND 2

Husband born on 16-11-1953 Sunday Poorva Bhadrapada first Quarter.

Wife born on 18-6-1961 Sunday Magha 3rd Quarter.

In Husband Horoscope Jupiter the Karaka for Son and Lord of 5th is in eleventh house in inimical Sign. Lord of Lagna SUN is in 3rd house in debilitation, Lord of Ninth house Mars is in 2nd house in inimical Sign. Moon is hemmed in between RAHU and Mars (Mars aspects the 8th house). Mahadev Pathak in "JATAKTATWA" Says:- सुरेशे त्रिके लग्नेशे नीचे पाप युते चन्द्र मातृ शापाद् विपुत्र:'' means if Lord of fifth is in Trik houses, Lord of Ascendant in debilitation, Moon with malefics or afflicted the native will be devoid of offspring due to Curse of mother. Here Lord of 5th is in

Birth Chart - Husband

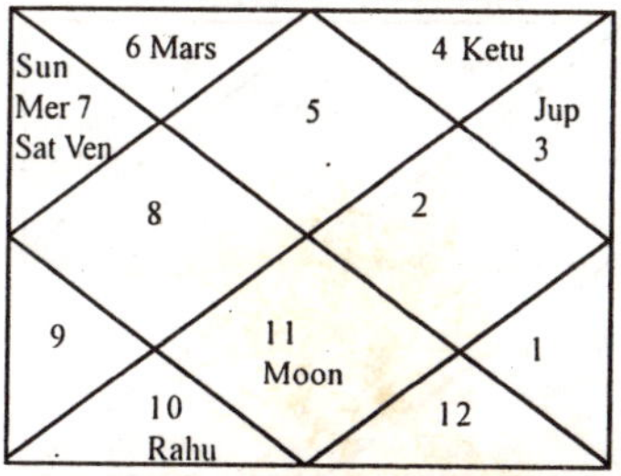

Birth Chart - Wife

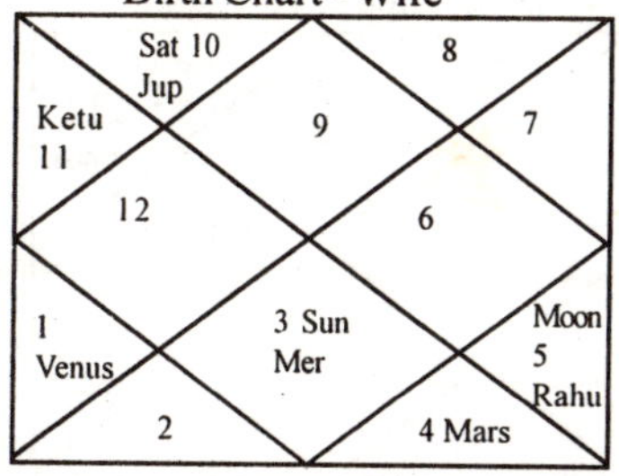

eleventh, Lord of Lagna in debilitation and Moon in Aquarius hemmed in between malefics. "जीवात्सुते पापे सन्तान सुखाभावो नान्यथा" means if there are malefics in 5th house from Jupiter then there is no happiness of Children. Here from Jupiter in 5th house there are 3 malecfics SATURN (Lord of 6th & 7th) Mercury (Lord of 2nd Markesh, Venus (Lord of 3rd house). SUN is in debilitation the Lord of Lagna. "पंचमे जीवर्क्षे सुतसुखं नं" Means if there is sign of Jupiter in fifth house then there is no happiness of Son. In Husband's Horoscope there is Sagittarius a sign of Jupiter is in fifth house. Hence the native still at the age of 51 is without offspring, though the Lord of 5th House Jupiter and Lord of ninth house Mars both aspect the 5th house, but both are in inimical Signs hence they are helpless.

In wife's horoscope Chart No. 2 Lord of Lagna Jupiter and Lord of 5th house Mars both are in evil houses in Neecha (debilitation) Sign's aspecting each other with SATURN Markesh aspecting the 5th Lord Mars too. Besides Lord of 5th house Mars is hemmed in between 2 malefics Sun and Rahu. Moon is with great enemy Rahu. Rahu aspects the 5th house too. "सपापे अंगेशे त्रिके सुखेशे विपुत्र:" means Lord of Lagna with malefic and Lord of fifth in Trik (6,8,12) make the native childless. In the wife's horoscope Lord of 5th is in 8th house in debilitation. Lord of Lagna Jupiter too in debilitation with Saturn a malefic aspected by the other malefic Mars. Mars in 8th house in Neecha Rasi aspected by Saturn has became Malefic.

In this way in both horoscopes there is Strong yoga for Childlessness.

CHARTS 3 and 4

Husband born on 21-11-1943 Sunday Uttra Phalguan 1st Quarter wife born on 16-9-1946 Poorva Shada first Quarter. Saturn-Mars Combination:- नीचे गुरौ भृगौ वा समे ज्ञे विषमेर्के सुत सौख्यं न means if Jupiter and Venus are in dehilitation, Mercury in even sign, Saturn is in odd sign

Birth Chart - Husband

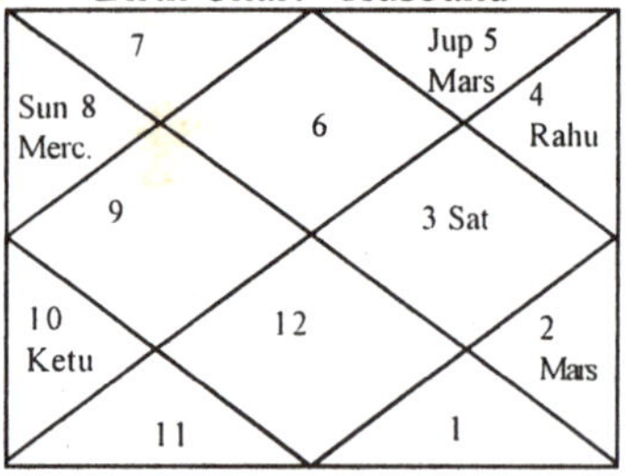

Birth Chart - Wife

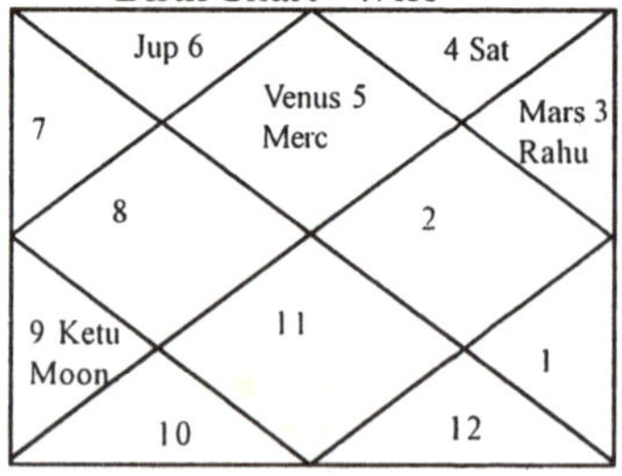

there is no happiness of Son. 'अन्त्यांगर्थे सुते सहजपे सुत सुखं न' means if Lord of third is in 12,1,2 or 5 houses then there is no happiness of Son. सुते शुक्र भौमसुते दृष्टे द्वित्रिविवाहे वप्य सन्तानः means if Venus or devoid of 5th house then after marrying 2 or 3 times the native will be devoid of offspring.

In husband's horoscope Lagna Lord Mercury is in 3rd house aspected by Mars and RAHU 2 malefics. With Mercury there is SUN too who is also aspected by 2 malefic RAHU and MARS. SUN is Lord of Twelfth house. Lord of 5th is Saturn is in Tenth house surrounded by 2 malefic RAHU and Mars. Ketu is in 5th house. RAHU aspects the 5th house Lord of Ninth Venus is in debilitation. Hence 5th and 9th houses, their Lords are badly afflicted.

In wife's horoscope the Lord of 5th Jupiter is in 2nd house aspected by 2 malefics Saturn and Mars. Moon in 5th is with KETU aspected by 2 malefics MARS and RAHU. Thus in both the horoscopes Jupiter is aspected by Saturn and Mars. RAHU aspects the 5th house in both the horoscopes. Though in both the Horoscopes there is GAJA-KESHRI YOGA but the KARAKA for Son JUPITER is badly afflicted by Mars and Saturn. Hence due to these Yogas the natives are devoid of offspring.

CHART-5

Male born on 3-1-1942 Friday Punarvasu Ist Quarter 'पुत्रस्थे मदनाद्दिपे वितनयो जायाविहीनो ऽथवा means if Lord of fifth is in Seventh house then the native is devoid of offspring and wife. Here the Lord of 5th house. Saturn is in seventh house in inimical Sign in debilitation aspecting the Lagna, ninth and fourth houses. With the Lord of Lagna Venus, Lord if ninth Mercury, Moon. Rahu too aspects the fifth house and its Lord Saturn.

Birth Chart 3-1-1942

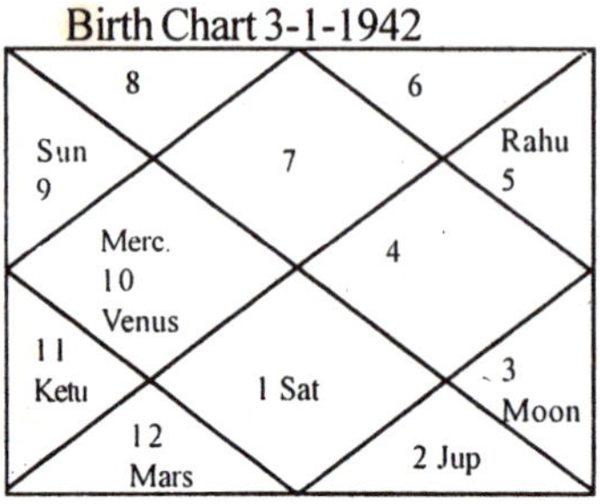

Jupiter the Karaka for Son and Mars the Lord of Seventh are in eighth and sixth houses (evil Houses). Though the native is married still at the age of 62 is devoid of the happiness of offspring.

CHART-6

Born on 31-3-1938 at 11.35 P.M. Aridra 3rd Quarter सुते पापयुते दुष्टे गर्भ च्युतिः means if there are malefics in fifth house then there is ABORTION.

Birth Chart 31-3-1938

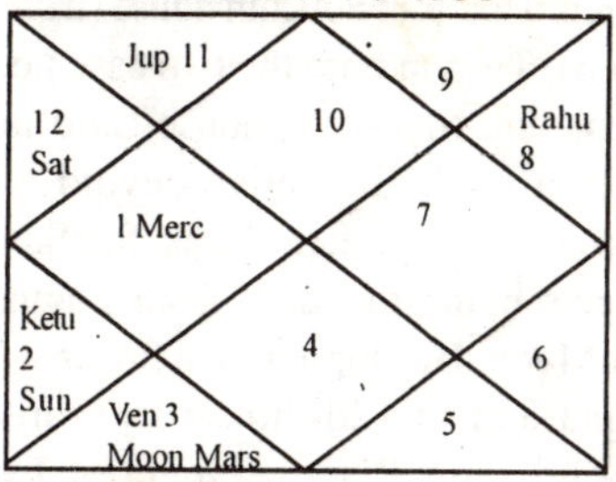

Lord of Lagna Saturn in 3rd house aspected by RAHU and Lagna aspected by Mars are not good. On 5th house Saturn and Rahu 2 malefics are aspecting. 6th Lord Mercury in fourth house and fourth Lord Mars in sixth is with Moon and Venus. The Lord of eighth SUN in 5th with Ketu aspected by Rahu, Lord of twelfth Jupiter. These combination kept the native devoid of offspring. The native is handicapped too. The wife was once Pregnant Abortion in March 1972 took place. Something left in the Ovary operations also held in June 1972. Since then his wife could not conceive.

CHART-7

Female born on 12-4-1948 at 2.00 a.m. Bharni Nakshatra fourth Quarter. The lady gave birth to a daughter who died at the age of 18-19 years. Her Horoscopes is as following:

Birth Chart 12-4-1948

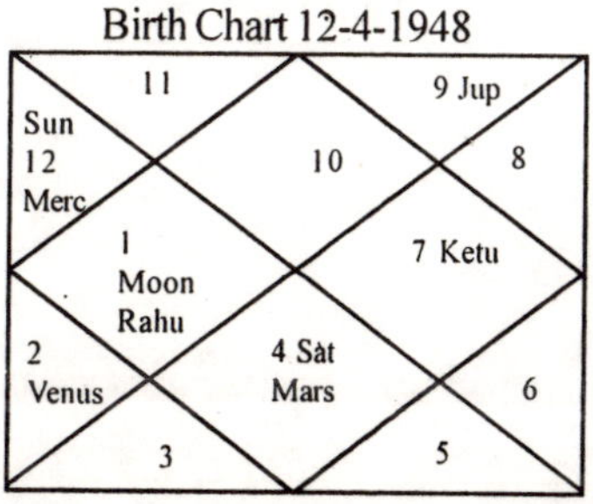

The Lord of Lagna Saturn and Lord of fourth house Mars are bitter enemies. These two malefics combined in 7th house is not good. The Moon in 4th with Rahu aspected by Saturn and Ketu and Lord of 12th house Jupiter from 12th house. Venus being in even sign in fifth house in own sign could make the native give birth to a daughter but she too could not survive because Venus is aspected in retrogression position by Saturn. The Lady is devoid of offspring तुर्यो मन्दारौ दत्त पुत्रः Saturn and Mars in fourth house from Moon give the native adopted Son. Here both Planets are in fourth to fourth house. She had adopted a Son. The husband is alive.

CHART-8

Female born on 16-8-1942 at 4.P.M. Shat Bhisha Nakshatra Ist Quarter. Her Horoscope is as following:-

In "JATAK PARIJAT" it is said पुत्र मदनाधिपे वितनयो जाया विहीनो means if lord of fifth is in Seventh house the native is devoid of offspring and wife. Here Lord of fifth is in seventh house in an inimical sign. The Lady had adopted a on. From Moon in fifth house is Mars, whose Lord Mercury too is in Seventh house (from moon). Thus in both the two case i.e. Lagna and Moon 5th house Lord in seventh made the native devoid of Son. Though Jupiter Karak for Son aspects both 5th Lords from Lagna and Moon. But Jupiter is in 3rd from Lagna and in 12th house from his second sign Pisces aspected by enemy Mercury. Mercury is hemmed in between RAHU and Venus (Neecha) Venus as Lord of sixth in 10th house too is not good. The Lord of 8th house Moon with Jupiter too lost the chances of son birth. Moon sign is badly afflicted by malefics RAHU and Saturn.

Birth Chart 16-8-1942

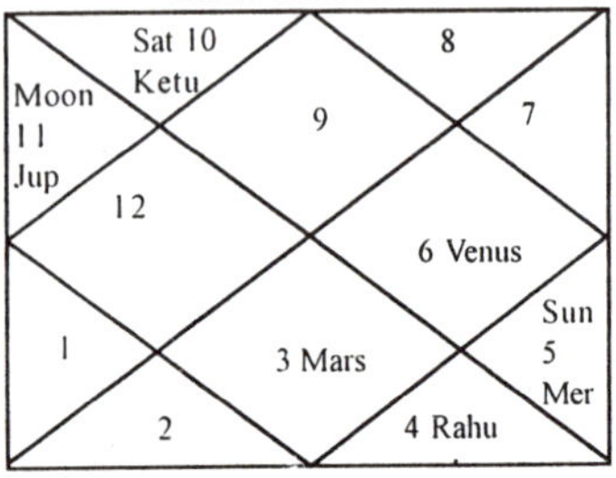

40

The Patwa Ministry in Madhya Pradesh

Mr. S.L. Patwa of B.J.P. was sworn in as the chief minister of Madhya Pradesh on 5-3-1990 at 4.30 p.m. in Bhopal.

The Sun, the lord of the Ascendant, though in an inimical sign with Mercury, the lord of 2nd and 11th houses, is in exaltation in Navamsa with the aspect of Jupiter. Saturn is in the 5th aspecting the lord of the Ascendant Sun. The influence of Saturn and Jupiter on the Moon, and on the lord of the Ascendant is not desirable as Saturn is the lord of the 6th and 7th houses and Jupiter is the lord of the 8th house.

In Navamsa too, Saturn, as lord of the 10th house, is in the 8th in Scorpio aspecting the 10th house. Venus, the 10th lord, in Rasi is in Capricorn (the house of enemy) with two malefics Mars and Rahu and in Navamsa in Aquarius without any benefic aspect. Thus there is no benefic in *kendra* either in Rasi or in Navamsa charts. There is Gajakesari Yoga in both Rasi and Navamsa charts.

Though the Ascendant of the swearing-in time is *sthira or* an immovable sign, the Navamsa Ascendant is *chara* or movable.

Therefore, it looks like Mars and Rahu will defeat enemies but will also create problems which may produce a critical situation in July 1990 when Jupiter will transit in Cancer in the 12th house with the Sun and Ketu and earlier in April 1990 when Mars will transit Aquarius aspecting the 10th house. Saturn's retrogression will create difficulties in the way of Mr. Patwa. Hence there is fear of the ministry changing in July 1990. Mr. Patwa may not complete his term.

Rasi : Leo – Ascendant; Sun and Mercury in Aquarius; the Moon in Aridra and Jupiter in Gemini; Marse, Venus and Rahu in Capricorn; Saturn in Sagittarius; and Ketu in Cancer. *Navamsa;* Aries; Ascendant with Sun; Jupiter and the Moon in Sagittarius; Saturn in Scorpio; Mars, Ketu and Mercury in Capricorn; Venus in Aquarius; and Rahu in Cancer.

41

Indra Kumar Gujral's Swearing Ceremony

Mr. Indra Kumar Gujral's swearing in ceremony as Prime Minister of India was held on 21-4-1997 between 10.00 a.m. and 10.02 a.m. at Delhi in Gemini Ascendant, a dual and uncertain sign. The Moon is also in a dual sign Virgo with Rahu and is caught between malefics Rahu, Ketu and Saturn. The 10th lord Jupiter is in debilitation in the 8th in Capricorn. The 10th' house has 8th lord Saturn and Ketu aspected by Mars, Rahu and the Moon, the three malefics. The Moon though strong in Pakshabala, but with Rahu and aspected by 8th lord Saturn, has been turned into a malefic. The Ascendant lord Mercury is in Aries with the 3rd lord Sun and 12th lord Venus. The lord of Ascendant Mercury and 5th lord Venus in the llth is a good combination especially with the Sun in exaltation. It will somehow carry the Ministry but not with certainty, because the Ascendant and Moon have no benefic aspect. Though Jupiter aspects the Moon, he is a Maraka lord and also has Kendradhipati Dosha and is turned into a malefic for Gemini Ascendant.

In Navamsa, the Ascendant lord Mercury is with Mars in 8th and Saturn, lord of Navamsa Ascendant, is in Scorpio in the 10th house. Chaturdasi Tithi is ominous for swearing-in ceremony.

Hence the Gujral Government has no certainty and there will be struggle and tension after 10-6-1997 when Mars will transit Virgo and 10th lord Jupiter becomes retro grade from 23-7-1997. It looks like that this Government too will not complete its term and may be short-lived. It will be a hard and tough period for the Government between December 1997 and February 1998.

42

Planets and the V.P. Singh Government

Mr. V.P. Singh took oath as Prime Minister of India on 2nd December 1989 at 12.15 p.m. at Delhi in Aquarius Ascendant. The lord of the Ascendant Saturn is in the llth house in Sagittarius fully aspecting the Ascendant. The Moon is in Capricorn in the 12th house with Rahu. The Sun and Mercury are in the 10th house in Scorpio. Mars is in the 9th house in Libra. Jupiter is in the 5th house in Gemini aspecting the Ascendant and its lord Saturn. Ketu is in Cancer in the 6th house.

Mars and Saturn transit Capricorn in March 1990. Mars—Saturn combination in the 12th house may produce some typical problems in the way of Mr. Singh. Jupiter, the 2nd lord, will be transiting Cancer in exaltation in July 1990.

Jupiter will be with Ketu though aspecting the lord of Ascendant. Nevertheless March 1990 and July 1990 may prove the most troublesome periods to Mr. V. P. Singh.

43

Benazir Bhutto

Ms. Benazir Bhutto, was sworn in on 2-12-1988 as the first lady Prime Minister even of Pakistan and of a Mulsim country. After 11 years of military dictatorship under General Zia democracy has been introduced in Pakistan. She was born on 21-6-1953 at 7.43 p.m. at Karachi. Her horoscope is Ascendant - Sagittarius, Rahu in Capricorn, Venus in Aries, Jupiter in Taurus, the Sun and Mars in Gemini, Mercury and Ketu in Cancer, retrograde Saturn in Virgo and the Moon in Libra.

The lord of the Ascendant Jupiter in Rohini in Taurus in the 6th house aspects, the 10th, 12th and the 2nd houses. The 2nd house from the 10th house is Libra where the Moon is aspected by Venus from the 5th house. The Ascendant is fully, aspected by the lord of the 5th Mars and lord of the 9th Sun. Retrograde Saturn has also a full aspect on the Ascendant. Saturn as 2nd lord plays an important part being in the 10th house. Hence in this horoscope the combination of lords of 5th and 9th houses, Mars and the Sun, are important.

Saturn Dasa to begin from 3-10-1990 may shake the position of Benazir Bhutto as Saturn is a *maraka* here. The sub-period of Saturn may be positively harmful. The period of Rahu's transit of Capricorn may show wide fluctations in Ms. Bhutto's political life.

44

Horoscope of Smt. Maneka Gandhi

Mrs. Maneka Gandhi was born on *26-8-1956.

The lord of the Ascendant Moon is in the 9th house in Pisces *Vargottama.* The lord of the 5th *(trikona)* and the 10th *(kendra)* Mars (Yogakaraka for Cancer Ascendant) is in Aquarius retrograde in the 8th house aspecting the 2nd house, its lord Sun and the 9th lord Jupiter. The mutual aspect of Mars and Jupiter with Sun (Rajyakaraka) produces Raja Yoga. There is an exchange of signs between Mars and Saturn which is not favourable.

Mars in the 8th house in a female horoscope is not good for the longevity of husband. It is said *Krureshtameca vidhava papakshetre visheshatah,* meaning that if there is a malefic in the 8th, especially a cruel planet, widowhood results. Mars here, a cruel planet, is in inimical sign Aquarius whose lord is Saturn. Besides Saturn is also in Scorpio and Rahu is with Saturn. Saturn represents air, Rahu unexpected event and Mars crash. Sanjay Gandhi died in an air-crash unnaturally.

According to Vimshottari Dasa the death of Sanjay Gandhi occurred in Venus major, Mercury sub and Venus inter. Here Venus represents vehicle. In Navamsa, Venus is in the 8th house in Aries, Mars is in Gemini in the 10th house aspecting the lord of the 7th and Patikaraka Jupiter.

The Moon Dasa started in August 1989. As the Moon is the lord of the Ascendant, his Dasa brings fortune, fame, glory and influence to the person. Rahu as *karaka* for Cancer Ascendant aspects the Ascendant and its lord Moon.

The Dasa of Mars may produce difficulties as being the 5th and 10th lord and Yogakaraka for Cancer, he is in the 8th house in an inimical sign. From August 2006 Rahu Mahadasa will start.

**Rasi:* Cancer - Ascendant; Leo - Sun and Jupiter; Virgo - Mercury; Scorpio - Saturn and Rahu; Aquarius -Mars; Pisces - Moon; Taurus - Ketu; and Gemini - Venus. *Navamsa:* Virgo - Ascendant and Jupiter, Libra - Rahu and Sun; Aquarius - Mercury; Pisces - Moon; Aries - Venus and Ketu; Gemini - Mars; and Cancer - Saturn.

45

Rajiv Gandhi's Death

I was astonished when I read in the Astrological Magazine February 1993 issue on page. 193 where Mr. K.N. Rao writes "In fact I was the only astrologer, other than an almanac maker of Assam etc..."

Perhaps Mr. K.N. Rao has not read my article "Rajiv Gandhi-Evam Jyotish Visleshan" published in Bhavishya Alok (Hindi) In March 1989 wherein I had hinted about the tragedy on page 123 before 27 months ahead of the incident in Bhavishya Alok (monthly Hindi) published from Agra (U.P.).

Besides in another article published in Bhavishya Alok, Agra, "वर्तमान गोचर में शनि मंगल की भयावह स्थिति"

In April 1991 under the title *"Varthman Gochar Men Sani-Mangal Ki Bhayavah Sthithi"*, I had clearly hinted that on 21st May 1991 an unavoidable, terrible, fateful incident was going to happen due to retrogression of Saturn.

The learned editor of Bhavishya Alok, Sri N.V. Rajagopalan has clarified about this fact in Bhavishya Alok, June 1991 on page 172 under the title "Rajiv Gandhi – Kuch Jyotish Prasna" and declared that my forecast about the tragedy with late Mr. Rajiv Gandhi came correct as hinted by me published in March 1989 issue of Bhavishya Alok.

46

Horoscope of Bhagwan Shri Ganesh Ji

In the beginning of any auspicious work lord of intellect, sea of knowledge, killer of hindrances, by remembering giving fruitful success are worshipped. The Horoscope of Bhagwan Ganapati, Gana Nayak, Shri Ganesh is as following :

Birth Chart : Ganesh Ji

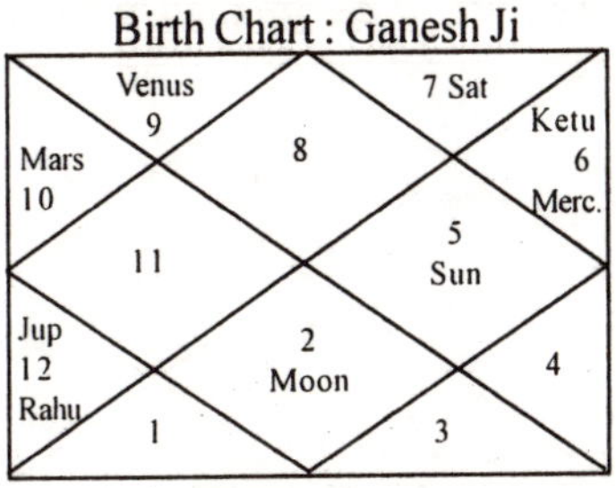

Moon Sign : Ganesh Ji

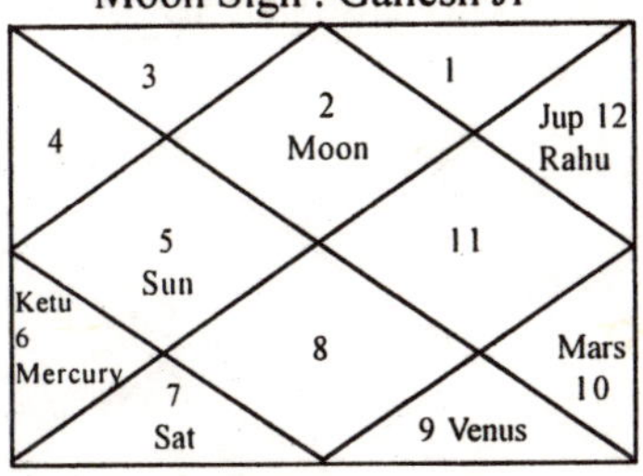

Navamsha : Ganesh Ji

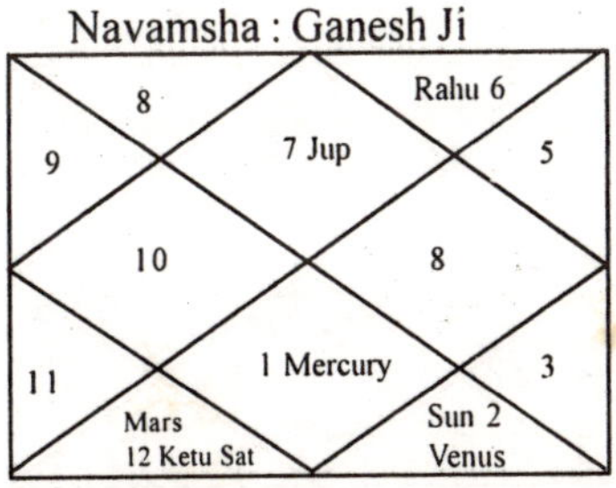

From the time immemorial Shri Ganesh the first worshipped God, Son of Shrimati Parvatiji and Lord Shiva were born in Scorpio Lagna. Lord of Lagna, the great warrior, Brave and Bold, killer of enemies, Mars is in 3rd house in exaltation, being very strong in strong position aspecting the 9th and 10th houses. Mars also aspects the 6th house, house of disease, Enemy and Debt crushing handly these 3 hindrances for men. Lord of 2nd

8 speech), 5th (Mind) knowledged Jupiter is posited in strongly in own sign in 5th house with Rahu. Rahu is a diplomatic planet so with Jupiter mind has been super, knowledge strongly increased. On 5th lord Jupiter aspect of mercury, the Kạrak of speech, knowledge etc. Jupiter aspects the 9th house, 11th house and Lagna. Hence 1-5-9 Trikona houses have been most strong. Lord of ninth moon in exaltation in seventh house aspecting the Lagna. In this way Jupiter. Rahu and Moon have full aspect on Lagna. Saturn in 12th exalted aspects the 2-6-9 houses. Lord of tenth sun in own house is increasing fame in the whole world.

In the horoscope of Shri Ganesh Moon, Mars, Mercury, Saturn these 4 planets are in exaltation, Sun, Mercury, Jupiter in their own signs strong. Saturn Mars aspecting the 6th house are crushing enemies strongly. In Navamsa too Mars, Saturn, Ketu are destroying enemy, debt, diseases. In Navamsa Moon, Mercury, Jupiter are in Quadrants with Gaja-Keshri Yoga.

''लम्बोदरं' नमस्तुभ्यं सततं मोदकं प्रियं-निर्विघ्नं कुरू मे देव सर्वकार्येषु सर्वदा''

47

Horoscope of Acharya Chatursen Shastri

Birth Lagna: 26-8-1891

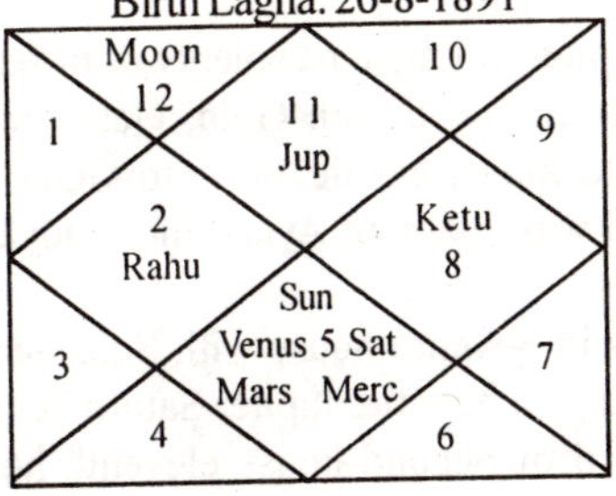

I am specially interested in lives and Horoscopes reading of Literary Personalities, Saints, Poets, Philosophers, Social Workers and great men. While reading the Autobiography of ACHARYA CHATURSEN SHASTRI 'MERI ATMA KAHANI'. I found his birth date 26th August 1891 and the relevant horoscopic Chart in it. He was a great Hindi writer, Poet, Novelist, Story writer, dramatist and Ayurvedic Doctor. A vaidya by occupation he was noble by heart, highly brilliant wrote 186 books in Hindi. He lived for 70 years and gave the best books to Hindi world, e.g., Vayam Rakshama (वयं रक्षाम:) SOMNATH (सोमनाथ) Vaishali Ki Nagarwadhu (वैशाली की नगर वधु) etc. Born on 26th August 1891 Sunday in GODHULI VELA at 32 ghatis 13 Palas in CHANDOKH VILLAGE of Buland Shahar District of U.P. in a Kshatriya family of Kewal Ram in Revti Nakshatra 3rd Quarter with a balance of Mercury Mahadasa 8 years 0 month 0 days. Planetary Degrees could not be found as Panchanga of that year was not available. His birth Lagna is as following:- According to Satya Charya Kumbha Lagna is not auspicious but According of CHANAKYA it has not dosha. Kumbha Lagna Native is sensitive, thinker and a Philosopher. Many great men are born In KUMHA LAGNA e.g. RAMKRISHNA PARAM HANSA, KARL MARX, AMITABH BACHCHAN, G.D. BIRLA, BRAHMAN AND REDDY, YESWANT RAO CHAUHAN, SHIVAJI GANESHAN, BRIJNARIAN 'BRIJESH'etc. About Kumbha Lagna is said—

दातो ऽ लस़: कृतज्ञश्च गज वाजि धनेश्वर:
शुभ दृष्टि सदा सौम्यो धन विद्या कृतोद्यम:
पुव्याठ्या ख्यात कीर्तिश्च धन योगी स्व शक्ति न:
शालूरकुक्षि निर्मीत: कुंभे जातो भवेन्तर:

Means a Person born in Kumbha Lagna is donar, idle, faithful, owner of Elephants, Horses, Wealth, good eye sight, Noble, busy in getting knowledge and money, virtuous, famous, Consumer of Self-earned money, brave and has waist like Lion. Jupiter is in Lagna. It is said about Jupiter in Lagna.

विविध वस्त्र विपूर्ण कलेवर: कनक रतन धन प्रियदर्शन:
नृपति वंश जनस्य च क्ल्लभो भवति देवगुरु तनुगे नर:।।

Means a Person born with Jupiter in Lagna has plenty of different clothes and a beautiful body. He is endowed with Gold, Gems and a Charming appearance. He is dear to kings, has devotion to GOD and teachers. Acharya Chatursen Shastri was a famous Ayurvedic Vaidya So he was related to many royal families.

The Lord of Lagna Saturn is in Seventh house with Sun, Venus, Mercury, Mars all these are aspected by a benefic. Jupiter Saturn being a Karak for diseases aspected by Lord of Second house eleventh house Jupiter indicates income through curing diseases.

In the second house there is Moon in Pisces who is the Lord of sixth house (House of diseases) indicates income through curing of diseases. In seventh house (House of Spouse) there is combination of 5 Planets SUN, SATURN, MARS, MERCURY, VENUS. This combination with Lord of Lagna made him to marry four times and wandering here and there in search of income. Mercury and Venus in seventh gave him happiness of 4 wives, fame and money. SUN and Saturn 2 malefics with Lord of eighth in seventh house made him to loose 3 wives. Venus as karak for Spouse is hemmed in between SUN, MARS, SATURN, MERCURY four malefics and has Kendradinpati Dosha too being Lord of 4th house, a Kendra.

RAHU in fourth house does not allow the native to live at a place peacefully but made the native to wander here and there in search of livelihood and domestic peace. Rahu in fourth alone also allows the native to have a daughter only. The native had 4 brothers and two sisters. His Childhood was spent in village. He began his education in a town but there are 3 benefics in Kendras, i.e., Jupiter, Venus and Mercury. So in 1908 in Venus Mahadasha he ran away to Kashi and studied there Sanskrit, Vyakaran, Logic. In 1910-11 in Venus Mahadasha Sun antar he came to Jaipur Sanskrit College where he studied Ayurveda, Sanskrit.

His first marriage occurred in Venus Mahadasa Moon Antardasa with TARA DEVI on 28th April 1912 at the age of 21. In 1913 in Venus Mahadasha Mars antardasha he started AUSHDHALAYA in Kinari Bazar, DELHI. In 1914 he served in Seth Samal Das Vidyalaya and Passed ACHARYA and SHASTRI Examination in Venus-Rahu Period. In Venus-Jupiter he served as Ayurveda Professor in D.A.V. College, Lahore. Then Leaving Professorship started AUSHD HALAYA at Ajmer. His sister Kala Devi died of fever and he too suffered from fever. This was due to the fact Lord of 3rd house Mars is hemmed in between three malefics SUN, SATURN, MERCURY (as Lord of 8th houses and aspected by a markesh Jupiter Lord of 2nd and who is the Lord of 12th house from 3rd house (House of younger ones)

During Venus-Saturn and Venus-Mercury periods his brother Bhadra Sen suffered and first wife TARADEVI died on 14-6-1923. During Venus-Mercury he and his younger brother married. At the time of second marriage. He was 32 years old and his second wife Priyambda was 23. He lived in Bombay for 4 years from 1920 to 1924 and then returned to Delhi and started Aushdhalaya again. His mother expired on Ram Navmi in 1927 as Lord of fourth Venus is in inimical Sign with Lord of that Sign Sun and Venus hemmed in between 3 malefics. Mother expired in Venus-Moon Period Sun is the Lord of 4th house from 4th house and Sun-Moon are in 6-8 position to each other. From Sun's Position Moon Sign Cancer in 12th During Sun-Mercury brother Bhadra Sen expired. In 1931 he came to Lucknow from Delhi and started Aushdhalaya there Published a book "AROGYA SHASTRA", From 10th to 10th house there is Sun the Karaka for occupation, there is Lord of 10th Mars is too with him and in 10th house there is Ketu. Hence, in Connection with occupation and earning money the native wondered here and there throughout his life. In beginning of Moon Mahadasa be returned to Delhi again and Started Aushdhalaya there at Fawwara Chowk. During Moon-Mars his second wife Priyamvada expired on 18th October 1933. In Moon-Rahu Period he married third time with Gayatri Devi on 3rd May 1934 at the age of 44. His 3rd wife's age 21. On 8th June his father expired.

During Moon-Saturn in 1939 he suffered from pain in Chest and breathing Passage From 1942 to 1949 in Mars Mahadasha the year 1944 was very bad on 21st January 1944 his foot got injured in horse-cart accident. His 3rd wife Gayatri Devi too expired on 8th Dec. 1944.

On 7th June 1945 during Mars-Saturn his fourth marriage was celebrated with 22 Year old Kamla, the younger sister of his third wife Gayatri. He was 32 years older than his fourth wife i.e. He was 54 years old.

In 1946 he was slightly injured in a Car accident but recovered Soon. On 8th April 1952 he met with Dr. Rajendra Prasad the first President of India and talked about 45 minutes to him. In RAHU-JUPITER Period the only daughter Jyoti took birth on 29-9-1955. In Nov. 1957 his finger crooked and fracture in arm was there. He was respected by means of Public Honour अभिनिन्दन on his 65th Anniversary by Bhartiya Chhatra Samagam. In 1959 he went to Madras to attend the Conference of writer's Association. After returning from Madras he fell ill and was admitted to IRVIN HOSPITAL, Delhi and breathed his last on 12th January 1960. This is the Horoscopic story of a brave man who struggle after struggle did not loose temper in any way but was always busy in writing books, curing Patients, though he wandered throughout his life. He wrote 186 books and died at the age of 70. Such Courageous Personalities are rare and just far and few to come across, who lightened their lamp of life in bitter circumstances of life.

48

Horoscope of Netaji Subhash Chandra Bose and Poet Shri Krishna Saral

The Great revolutionary nationalist Patriotic Netaji Subhash Chandra Bose's horoscope and great revolutionary poet Rasatra Kavi Shri Krishna 'Saral's horoscope have many peculiar similarities. Both are born in Aries Ascendant.

Horoscope of Netaji Subhash Chandra Bose,
Date of Birth 23-1-1987.

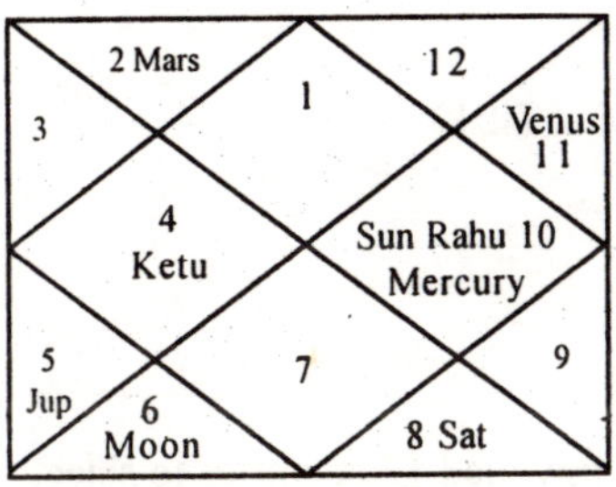

Horoscope of Poet S.K. Saral

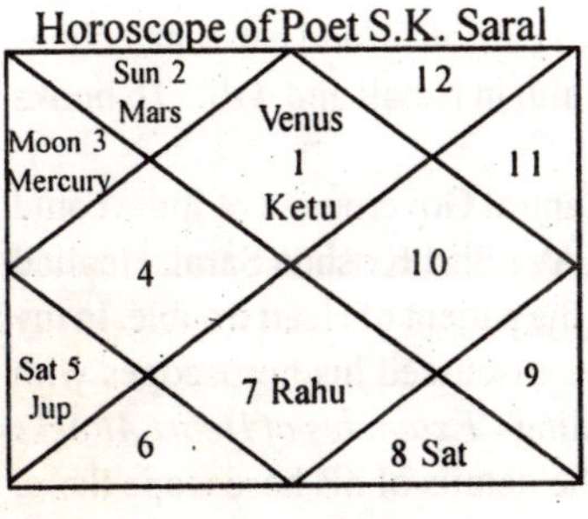

In both Horoscopes the peculiar similarities are as following:-

1. Both are born in Aries Lagna

2. The most benefic and divine planet Jupiter is in 5th house of both Horoscopes aspecting the Lagna.

3. Jupiter aspects the other benefic planet Venus in both horoscopes.

4. In both horoscopes RAHU aspects the Lagna Lord Mars and Lagna.

5. In both horoscopes Jupiter is in fifth house. In Netaji Horoscope where Saturn (Lord of tenth house) has full aspect on fifth house where Lord of ninth house Jupiter is in fifth house. In Saral's horoscope Lord of ninth Jupiter and Lord of tenth Saturn are in fifth house.

6. In both Horoscopes Moon is in Mercury's Sign. In Netaji Subhash's horoscope Moon is in Virgo in 6th house and in Saral's horoscope Moon is in Gemini. The Lord of Virgo and Gemini is Mercury.

Netaji's Sudden death in air crash is due to the fact that Lord of Ascendant Mars and Lord of tenth house Saturn in eighth house having mutual aspect. In Saral's horoscope too Mars and Saturn have mutual aspects. Saturn is Karaka for air, Mars is Karaka for fire and iron. Hence it is justified that death of Netaji was due to this fact in crashing of airplane. In Netaji's Horoscope Mars the Lagna Lord has full aspect On ninth and tenth Lords Jupiter and Saturn. This aspect gave him World wide fame and great deeds.

The great revolutionary poet of Hindi Shri Krishna 'Saral' born on 7-6-1921 at ASHOKNAGAR (M.P.) wrote 12 Epics. He made world record of writing 12 Epics in any Language of the world. He wrote two epics on Netaji and 14 other books too wrote on Netaji. Besides this He wrote 112 books. His 12 Epics are as following:

1. Shaheed Bhagat Singh
2. Chandra Shekhar Azad
3. Subhash Chandra Bose
4. Jai Subhash
5. Shaheed Asfaac Ali Khan
6. Vivek Shri (On Vivekananda)
7. Swaraj Tilak (On Bal Ganga Dhar Tilak
8. Kranti Jwal Kama
9. Bagi Shaheed Kartar Singh
10. KRANTI GANGA
11. TULSI MANAS
12. SARAL RAMAYANA.

The great poet Shri Krishna Saral travelled 12 countries to select facts on the Life of Netaji on his own expenses. Besides all the 112 Books published on his own expanses and sold them in India travelling here and there. Thus poet Shri Krishna Saral evolved patriotism and national feelings among the youths of India. He had great faith in Netaji and wrote 16 books on Netaji.

The state Government as well as Central Government of India could not honour this great poet RASHTRA KAVI Shri Krishna Saral. He died on 2nd September 2000 in Ujjain. He was the patient of Heart trouble. In my Book *"MEDICAL ASTROLOGY"* I have discussed his horoscopes with details on Pages 56,57,58 under the Heading *"Examples of Heart Attacks and Heart trouble."* Readers may read the details of his horoscope there.

49

Horoscope of Jagadguru Shankaracharya Swami Jayendra Saraswati

The Jagadguru Shankaracharya of Kanchi Kam Kotti Peetham Swami Jayendra Saraswati's name is in media and Newspapers who has been arrested on 11-11-2004 in Mehboob Nagar (A.P.) in case of assassination of SHANKAR RAMAN, a worker of Kanchi Kam Kotti on 3rd September 2004. His horoscope was published in Naidunia Hindi newspaper published from Indore on Page 9 of 6-12-2004.

Jayaendra Saraswati Ji was born on 18-7-1935 at 7.30 P.M. in a village in Tanjaur District of Tamil Nadu in Capricorn Lagna Dhanishtha Nakshatra Ist Quarter having Balance of Mars Mahadasha in Vimshottari system 5 Years 7 Months 18 Days according to my calculation.

Vikram Samvat 1999 Shaka 1857 Shravana Krishna Paksha 2 Thursday 0/57 Dhanishta 47/57 Preeti Yoga 52/33 gar karana 0/57. Birth Lagna and Planetary position is as following:

Birth Lagna

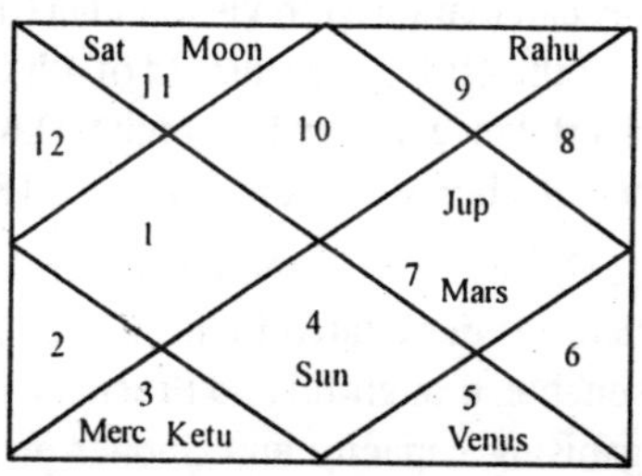

Moon Lagna

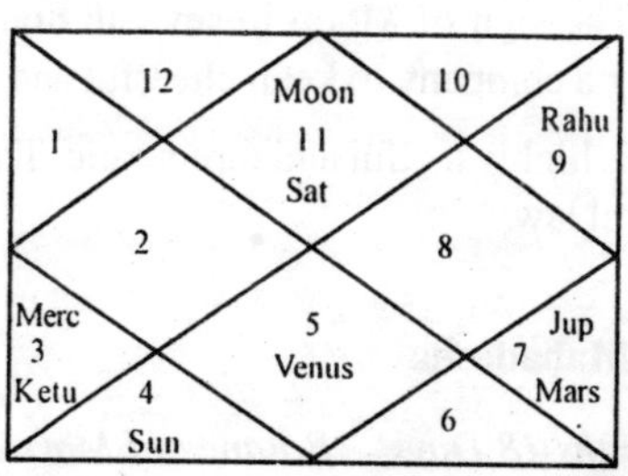

ATMAKARAK-Moon : Karkamsa - Leo :

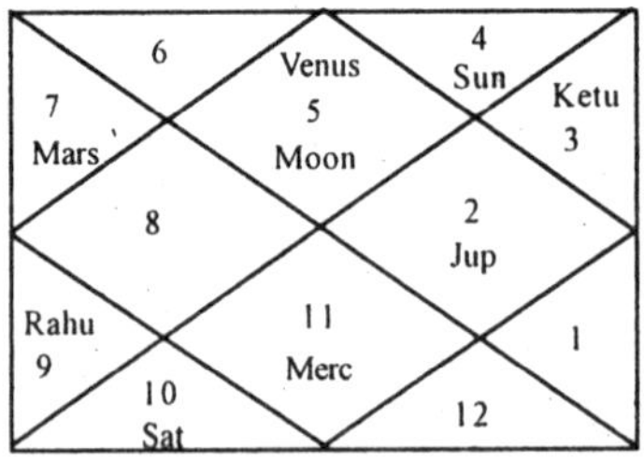

SUN, RAHU, KETU, VENUS in Vargottama Navamsha Though RAHU is in debilitation. Sign of Jupiter.

Planetary Position is as following:

Planet	*Sign Degree*	*Kala*	*Nakshatra*	*Charan*
Sun	3-1°	19	Punarvasu	1
Moon	9-25°	57	Dhamishtha	1
Mars	6-1°	14	Chitra	3
Mercury	2-15°	6	Aridra	3
Jupiter	6-23°	56	Vishakha	2
Venus	4-15°	20	Poorva Phalguna	1
Saturn	10-12°	54	Shat Bhisha	2
Rahu	8-28°	49	Uttra Shada	1
Ketu	2-28°	49	Punarvasu	3

According to my calculation Moon is found in Capricorn instead of Aquarius and in Dhanishtha-Ist Quarter instead of 4th Quarter. There was given Mars Mahadasha Balance 0 Year 11 month 9 Days but according to my calculation Balance of Mars is 5 Years 7 Months 18 Days.

Capricorn is the sign of sacrifice. Moon in Capricorn is said to be in enemy's house. Capricorn is debilitated in this Sign. Persons born in this Sign are Prudent reasonable, thoughtful and Practical minded. They work patiently. He has organising capacity and Sooner or later becomes the head of Institution. The. sign of Moon in seventh house shows that one will be always having a company to keep cheerful and active.

Capricornian is highly tactful and diplomatic. They work for others and abide by the moral law.

Vim Shottari Mahadasha

5 Years 7 Months 18 Days Balance of Mars Mahadasha
18—0—0 Rahu Mahadasha till 6-3-1959

16—0—0 Jupiter Mahadasha till 6-3-1975
19—0—0 Saturn Mahadasha till 6-3-1994

58—7—18 From 6-3-1994 Mercury Mahadasa

1935—7—18 is running. Antardasha in Mercury

1994—3—6 Mahadasha is as following—

6-3-1994
27—4-2
3-8-1996 Mercury antar in Mercury Mahadasha
27-11-0
30-7-1997 Ketu antar in Mercury Mahadasha
0-10-2
30-5-2000 Venus Antar in Mercury Mahadasha
6-10-0
6-4-2001 Sun Antar in Mercury Mahadasha
0-5-1
6-9-2002 Moon Antar in Mercury Mahadasha.
6-9-2002
27-11-0
3-9-2003 Mars Antar Mercury Mahadasha
18-6-2 Rahu antar Mercury Mahadasha
21-3-2006

Mercury the Lord of Mahadasha is in 6th house of enemy in own sign in Nakshatra of Rahu aspected by RAHU in debilitartion from 12th house. It is clear that Rahu is expert in occurring suddenly falling in evil cases. As Rahu is a Chhaya grah and is in the Nakshatra of Sun. Sun represents Government. Hence Rahu indicates harassment by Government in scandal of assassination case. Now see the Pratyantar dasa of Rahu antar in Mercury Mahadasha from 3-9-2003 to 21-3-2006

3-9-2003
18-4-0
21-1-2004 Mercury Mahadasha Rahu antar Rahu Pratyantar
2-4-0
23-5-2004 Mercury Mahadasha Rahu antar Jupiter Pratyantar
25-4-0
18-10-2004 Mercury Mahadasha Rahu antar Saturn Pratyantar
10-4-0
28-2-2005 Mercury Mahadasha Rahu antar Mercury Pratyantar
24-1-0
22-4-2005 Mercury Mahadasha Rahu antar Ketu Pratyantar

3-5-0

25-9-2005 Mercury Mahadasha Rahu antar Venus Pratyantar

16-1-0

11-11-2005 Mercury Mahadasha Rahu antar Sun Pratyantar

16-2-0

27-1-2006 Mercury Mahadasha Rahu antar Moon Pratyantar

24-1-0

21-3-2006 Mercury Mahadasha Rahu antar Mars Pratyantar

In Saturn pratyantar the assassination case occurred and in Mercury Pratyantar he was arrested on 11-11-2004 and is still under judicial arrest. His case has been put up for bail in Supreme Court by Tamil Nadu High Court Chennai. He was released on bail on 11-1-2005 by the order of Supreme Court of India from Venus Pratyantar time in favourable.

50

Horoscope of Chief Justice Supreme Court of India

Honourable Shri Ramesh Chand Lahoti

The honourable Chief Justice of Spreme Court of India. Shri Ramesh Chand Lahoti was born on 1-2 November 1940 at 3.25 A.M. at GUNA (Madhya Pradesh). His father Late Shri Ratan Lal Lahoti was the famous Advocate and freedom fighter. Samvat 1997 Shaka 1862 Kartik month Shukla Paksha Second Tithi 41/40 Friday Vishakha Nakshatra 14/21 after Anuradha Nakshatra 4th Quarter Saubhagya Yoga 32/420 after Shoban Yoga Valab Karna 14/13 Ishta Kal 52 ghatis 26 Palas Virgo Lagna 6 degrees. His birth Lagna and Planetary Position is as following:

Birth Lagna R.C. Lahoti

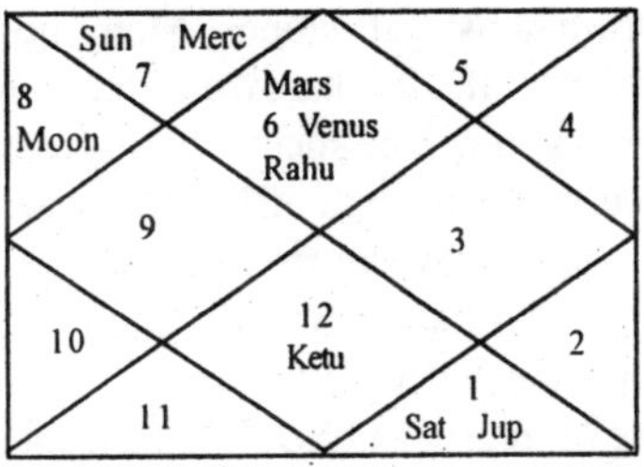

Moon Lagna R.C. Lahoti

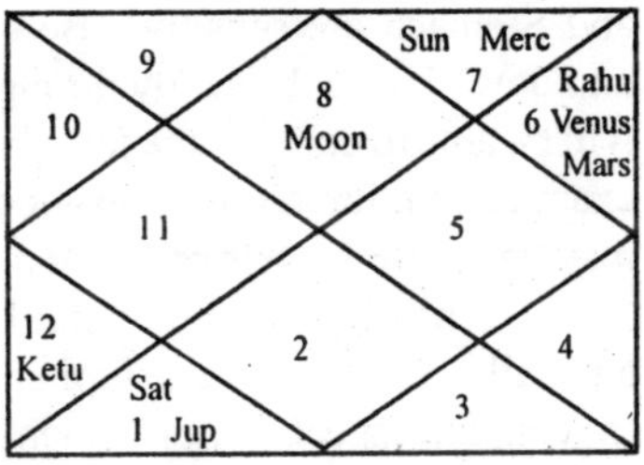

KARAKAMSA-Lagna ATMAKARAK-MARS

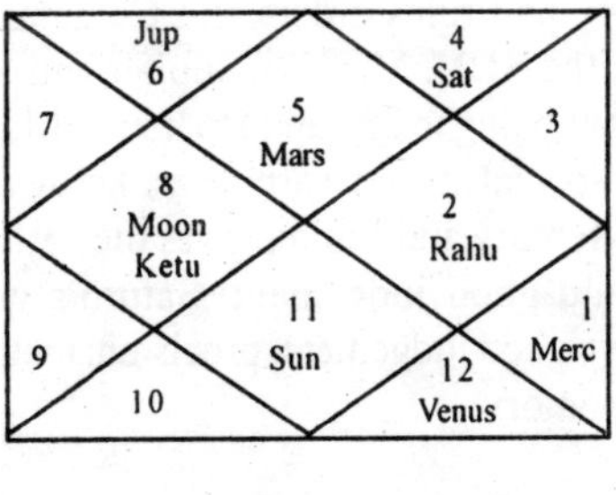

Planetary Position

Planet	*Sign*	*Degree*	*Kala*	*Vikla*	*Nakshatra*	*Charan*
SUN	6	16	04	58	Swati	3
MOON	7	14	00	57	Anuradha	4
MARS	5	24	20	17	Chitra	1
MERCURY	6	·22	13	06	Vishaka	1 +
JUPITER	0	18	59	01	Bharni	2 +
VENUS	5	7	2	47	Uttra Phalguna	4
SATURN	0	13	11	1	Ashwni	4 +
RAHU	5	15	39	56	Hasta	2 +
KETU	11	15	39	56	Uttra Bhadrapada	4

SUN, MOON, VENUS, SATURN four Planets are in debilitation. Rahu in Moon's Nakshatra own Sign Virgo, Ketu in Saturn's Nakshatra own sign Pisces. Mars in own Nakshatra enemy Sign Jupiter and Mercury in Bharni and Vishaka Nakshatra in friends Sign.

Virgo Lagn: Person born in Virgo is shy and self-conscious. He is very conscientious and very capable of handling even unfortunable conditions. He is practical and discriminative. He is Self Pity and Quick at finding fault with others. He is tall and genius. He analyses, dissects and goes deep into the matter. It is said that Virgo is the goddess of agriculture and of legislation and social order. He is governed by intellect as Mercury is exalted in Virgo. He is very analytical and in conversation will give lengthy discription. He is himself a good judge. Malefics in Virgo suffer from dysentery, typhoid, and space during their periods. Nervous system and Stomach are sensitive. Be on guard against gall stones. Many ups and down in life. It is only through your own talent as hardwork that you will be able to come to the top. As a lawyer you will be successful in cross examination. Jupiter forming good aspects with the Lords of 2-6-10 houses may have law as their profession. They work in law courts very wisely.

Tenth house: Good and bad aspects to Saturn Show a good rise and fall. The benevolent Jupiter well. Connected with the Tenth house (having full aspect on Lord of tenth house Mercury with SUN) is a definite indication of high honour, favour of those in high position. Jupiter being the Planet of Justice and high Morals. One's moral Standard will be high. It includes all positions of distinction, trust and responsibility. The tenth house is called *"AGYA"* and rules orders and Commands issued. From tenth house, its owner, the SUN, Mercury, Jupiter and Saturn there four Planets aspects each other being in 2nd and 8th house. Means of livilihood, fame, knowledge of the special art and learning are known from 10th house. Good aspect between Mercury and Jupiter gives the native clear thinking, correct fore-thought and good judgement. Saturn's good aspect with Mercury offers the native good judgement, precision, methodical approach to any subjects good memory.

Jupiter rules over law so one will be law a biding true, honest and dutiful one will be logical and broadminded. Sun forming good aspect with Jupiter gives the native a Broad out look. Honorary posts are offered either by SUN or by Moon forming good aspects with Jupiters Mercury and Jupier in favourable aspect are an asset in the native's life, even in his times of adversity he will keep his spirits, the mind will be ever-broad. He will be versatile, will form a good judgement by intelligent deliberation. He will reason out correctly. He may be slow to form an opinion due to Mercury. But his decision due to Mercury will be found incontroversihed.

If Mercury were to give the native a promotion then the higher official will be transferred and that vacancy will be filled up by him. If Saturn has to promote him his senior mostly will pass away and he will be promoted. If Jupiter offers him a promotion in its period there may be expansion and he may be lifted by creating a post and in the chain of promotion he will have his promotion also. Mars gives enough of energy, authority responsibility, tact, push and activity.

The Lords of Quadrants 1-4-7-10 Mercury and Jupiter both are aspected by each other. Lord of ninth Venus and Lord of tenth Mercury have produced great Rajyoga by exchanging their signs Venus in Virgo and Mercury in Libra.

In Karkamsa Mars is ATMAKARAK strong in SUN's. Sign Leo aspected by SUN. The Lord of ten Venus is in exaltation in 8th house aspected by Lord of ninth Mars and Lord of fifth Jupiter. Moon is in Vargottama Navamsha aspected by Lord of Ninth (house of Luck) Mars. Mercury the Lord of Second house (Speech) is in ninth house and in second house is Lord of fifth house Jupiter.

Vimshottari Mahadasha—

3 Years 9 Months 11 days	Balance of Saturn Mahadasha.
17—0—0	Mercury Mahadasha till 13-8-1961
7—0—0	Ketu Mahadasha till 13-8-1968
20—0—0	Venus Mahadasha till 13-8-1988
6—0—0	Sun Mahadasha till 13-8-1994
10—0—0	Moon Mahadasha till 13-8-2004

He started his carrer as an advocate, then A.D. Judge, then again High Court advocate, then High Court Judge, Justice in Supreme Court and then at last in June 2004 sworn in as Chief Justice of India in Moon Mahadasha, Sun antar. Jupiter aspects Sun in Second house and 4th house. In Second house there is Sign of Lord of luck (9th house) Venus, where is Sun with Mercury. The Journey of an advocate from advocacy to the highest post of law Chief justice of Supreme Court of India is most Surprising. Sun in Swati and Moon in Anuradha Nakshatras both are of Rahu and Saturn's Nakshatra. Rahu gives sudden rise and in gochar too Rahu was transiting in Aries and Saturn in Gemini in tenth house.

51

Horoscope of Honourable High Court Judge Shri Abhaya Gohil

The honarable High Court Juge Shri Abhaya Gohil was born on 12-1-1945 at 4.42 P.M. at Sironj Dist. Vidisha (M.P.) Samvat 2001 Shaka 1866 Magh Krishna Paksha 13 Friday 12/20 Mool Nakshatra 52/32 Dhruva Yoga 40/50 Vava Karam 12/20 in Gemini Lagna. His birth Lagna and Planetary position is as following: his father Shri Keshri Mal Jain was also a Freedom fighter and leader.

Birth Lagna

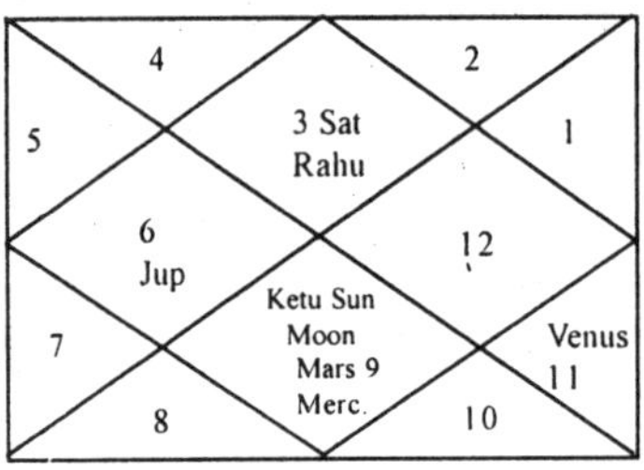

Moon Lagna

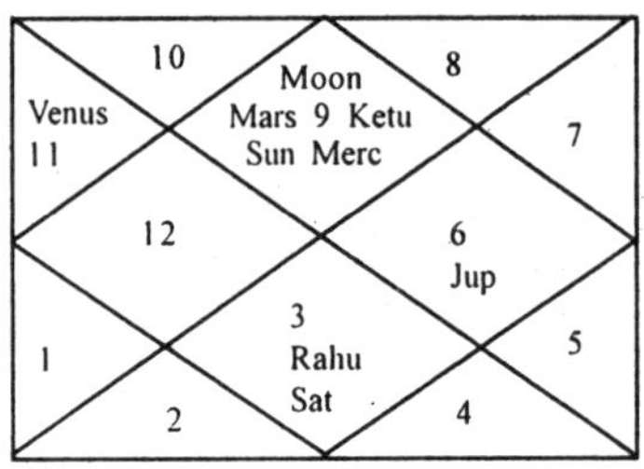

Karkamsa-SAGITTARIUS, Aatma Karak-SUN

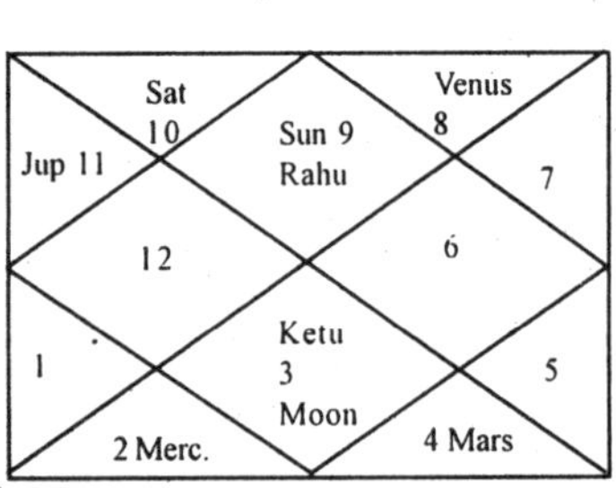

Planetary Position is as following:

Planet	*Sign*	*Degree*	*Kala*	*Vikla*	*Nakshatra*	*Charan*
SUN	8	29	28	.	Uttra Shada	1
MOON	8	7	22	.	Mool	3
MARS	8	10	28	.	Mool	4
MERCURY	8	4	19	.	Mool	2
JUPITER	5	5	56	.	Uttra Phalguna	3
VENUS	10	15	24	.	Shat Bhisha	3
SATURN	2	14	38	.	Aridra	2
RAHU	2	28	51	.	Punarvasu	2
KETU	8	28	51	.	Poorva Shada	2

Lord of Lagna Mercury in Mool Nakshatra in Jupiter Sign with Sun, Moon, Mars, Ketu are aspected by Saturn, Rahu is Strong in Quadrant. The Lord of Lagna Mercury aspects the Lagna, the Lord of tenth house Jupiter aspects fully the tenth house and is in Nakshatra of Sun. Jupiter also aspects the eighth and twelfth houses. Marls also aspects the tenth house.

As there is Sign of Jupiter, Pisces in tenth house Jupiter is the Planet of law and Justice. Jupiter has been related with Lord of Lagna being in Quadrant from Lagna and being in the Sign of Lagna Lord Mercury. The Second Sign of Mercury is Virgo. Thus the position of Lord of Lagna Mercury, Lord of Seventh and tenth house being aspected by Mars, Saturn, and the position of Venus in 9th house (house of luck) in the Sign of Saturn. Thus Sun, Saturn, Mercury, Jupiter, Mars, Venus all these favourable Planets are present in Square and triangle Signs. Saturn Lord of eleventh, Venus Lord of fifth house, Mercury and Jupiter as Lords of Lagna and tenth house are strongly posited. The Lagna, second, ninth, tenth houses are respresented strongly by their Planetary position.

Moon—Jupiter in Square position produced Gaja Keshri Yoga. Aspect of Jupiter and Saturn with Mars on tenth house made him high Court Judge. He started his Career as an High Court advocate at Bhopal and was connected with Bar Council of Madhya Pradesh for many years.

Vimshottari Mahadasha

3 Years 1 Month 18 Days	**Balance of Ketu Mahadasha**
20—0—0	Venus Mahadasha
6—0—0	Sun Mahadasha
10—0—0	Moon Mahadasha
7—0—0	Mars Mahadasha
46—1—18	Rahu Mahadasha Started with effect
45—1—12	from 2-3-1991 to 2-3-2009
1991—3—2	

In Rahu Mahadasha the antardasha chart is as following:

2-3-1991	
12-8-2	
14-11-1993	Rahu antar in Rahu Mahadasha
24-4-2	
8-4-1996	Jupiter antar in Rahu Mahadasha
6-10-2	
14-2-1999	Saturn antar in Rahu Mahadasha
18-6-2	
2-9-2001	Mercury antar in Rahu Mahadasha
18-0-1	
20-9-2002	Ketu antar in Rahu Mahadasha
0-0-3	
20-9-2005	Venus antar in Rahu Mahadasha
24-10-0	
14-8-2006	Sun antar in Rahu Mahadasha
0-6-1	
14-2-2008	Moon antar in Rahu Mahadasha
18-0-1	
2-3-2009	Mars antar in Rahu Mahadasha

He was Sworn in as High Court Judge on 23-4-1999 at High Court Bench Indore of M.P. High Court in Mercury antar in Rahu Mahadasha. Mercury is Lord of Lagna in Mool Nakshatra in Jupiter Sign and Rahu is in Nakshatra of Jupiter in Lagna. Hence Rahu has been paying the roll of Karak for Lagna and tenth house as tenth house Lord is Jupiter and Rahu is in the Nakshatra of Jupiter. Now Mr. Abhaya Gohil is working at Gwalior Bench of M.P. High Court.

See the position of Karkamsa Lagna where too Rahu is posited with Sun in Jupiter Sign.

52

Horoscope of Mahesh Bohre (A Famous Advocate)

Born on 16-4-1946 at 5.00 A.M. Vikram Samvat 2003 Shaka 1868 Chaitra Shukla Paksha 14 Monday 21/16 Hasta 38/31 Vyaghat 29/7 VaVa 21/16 Birth Nakshatra Chitra—2nd Quarter.

Birth Lagna PISCES

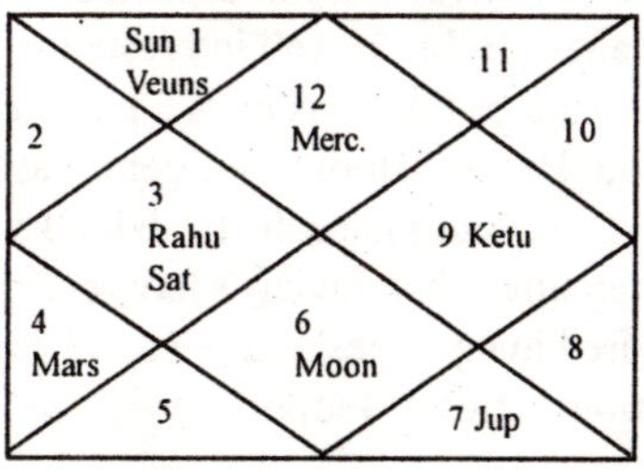

Moon Lagna

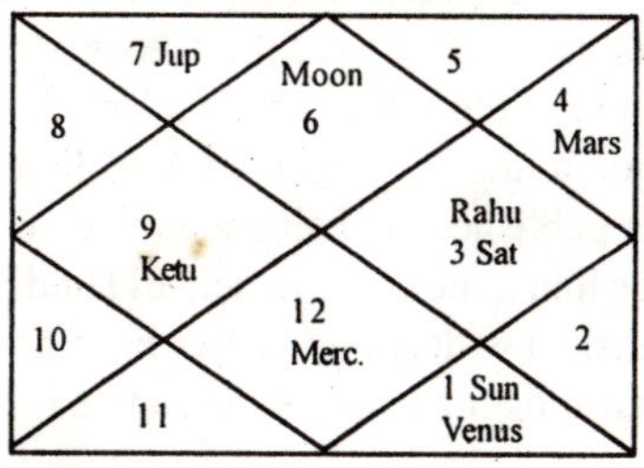

Karkamsa-VIRGO, Atmakarak-MOON

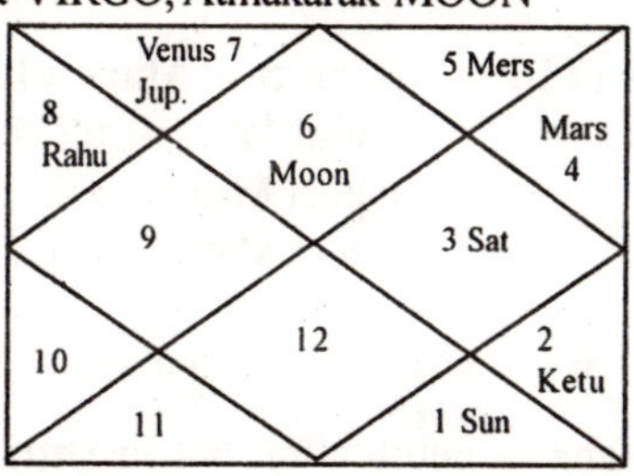

Planetary Position

Planet	*Sign*	*Degree*	*Kala*	*Nakshatra*	*Charan*
SUN	0	2	11	Ashwini	1
MOON	5	27	43	Chitra	2
MARS	3	2	41	Punarvasu	1
MERCURY	11	5	9	Uttra Bharda Pada	1
JUPITER+	6	0	42	Chitra	3
VENUS	0	20	19	Bharni	3

SATURN	2	26	42	Punarvasu	3
RAHU	2	4	34	Mrigsira	4
KETU	8	4	34	Mool	2

See that 5 Planets are in Vargottama Navamsa and they are Sun, Moon, Mars, Jupiter and Saturn.

Lagna Pisces—The lord of Pisces is the divine Planet Jupiter hence the person born in Pisces is philosophical, restless, dreamy imagining, honest, outspoken, helpful and humane he forgives the enemies as Pisces is a watery Sign. He is helpful to everybody He cannot think of harm to any. He is sweet-tempered and socially inclined. He is polite and modest. Venus in 2nd house (house of Speech) makes him poet. He plans in many ways to help the suffering people. He is desirous of study the occult Science, divine life. He is frank and fearless. As he earns, so he spends equally. He may travel abroad and may go even to foreign lands. Seventh house is ruled by Mecury for Astrologer and there is Moon aspected by Mercury Lord of Seventh. Hence Mr. Mahesh Bohre is well interested in Astrology too.Advocacy is his profession and besides this he is a poet, a singer, a literary person an Astrologer too. His two Books on Poetry has been published (1) Sahitya Sanjeevni (2) Doha KusumanJali. Both books made him famous in the field of Hindi Literature. Their review's have been published widely and he has been honoured many times as a poet and as an astrologer by various societies in various cities of India.

VimShottari Mahadasa

4 Years 8 Months 12 Days	**Balance of Mars till 28-12-1950**
18—0—0	Rahu Mahadasa till 28-12-1968
16—0—0	Jupiter Mahadasa till 28-12-1984
19—0—0	Saturn Mahadasa till 28-12-2003

From 28-12-2003 Mercury Mahadasa is running.

Mercury is in Lagna in debilitation but in Uttra Bhadra Pada Nakshatra, of Saturn. Hence Mercury will give the fruits of Saturn (Nakshatra Lord) and of Jupiter (Sign Lord). Saturn aspects the tenth house and Mercury and Jupiter too aspects Saturn. Hence the Mahadasa of Mercury will give him fame and name, travels, divine thinking as Saturn too is in the Nakshatra of Jupiter. Ketu in tenth house in Nakshatra of Jupiter being aspected by Rahu and Saturn will also help him in sudden rising in life.

53

Horoscope of Member (Judicial) Railway Claim Tribunal Bhopal Bench Honourable Shri Prakash Chand Jain

This is the horoscope of honourable member (Judicial) Shri Prakash Chand Jain Railway Claim Tribunal Bhopal Bench Born on 2-3-1946 Vikram Samvat 2002 Shaka 1867 Phalgun Krishna Paksha 13 Friday 46/7 Shravana 44/58 Parigh 55/32 Gar 15/57, Istakal 58 ghatis 55 Palas.

Aquarius Lagna

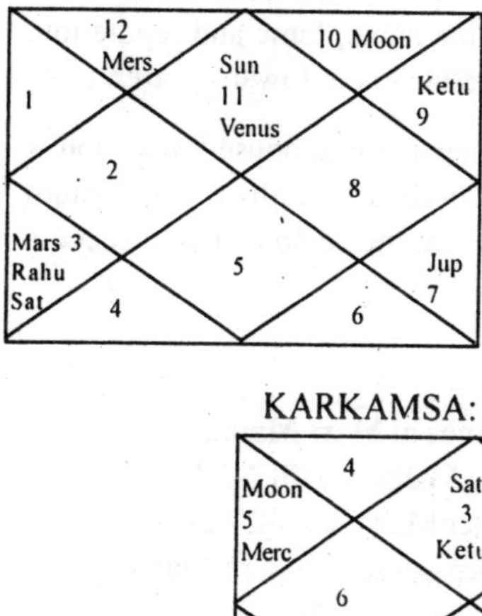

Moon Lagna

KARKAMSA: ATMAKARAK SATURN

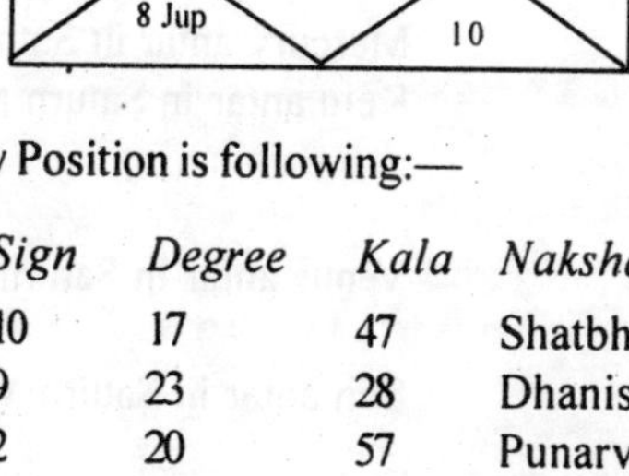

Planetary Position is following:—

Planets	*Sign*	*Degree*	*Kala*	*Nakshatra*	*Charan*
SUN	10	17	47	Shatbhisha	4
MOON	9	23	28	Dhanishtha	1
MARS	2	20	57	Punarvasu	1

MERCURY	11	3	36	Uttra Bhadrapada	1
JUPITER+	6	5	28	Chitra	4
VENUS	10	26	40	Poorva Bhadrapada	2
SATURN	2	26	42	Punarvasu	3
RAHU	2	6	54	Aridra	1
KETU	8	6	54	Mool	3

The Lagna Aquarius Sign is an airy Sign. It is the Sign of recovery from Sinking life, regaining life again delighted. Aquarius is an intelligent person. Nobody can make them fool. They are successful readers of characters of others. First they watch see the results they act after that. They are a bit slow in grasping fresh ideas but they cannot forget easily as they have good retentive power. They have broad out look, out spoken, unselfish, humane. They are silent workers in any society. They are shrewed, clear headed, Quick witted. They are always new in their thoughts and desires. They have own way of thinking. They have intution. They succeed in long run. Jupiter as Lord of 2 and 11 blesses the native with good family and money Mars Lord of 3 and 10 inclines towards study, research work, bold and courageous attains name, fame and reputation. Venus Lord of 4 gives higher education, attachment towards parents.

If Sun-Saturn are aspected by Jupiter in ninth house the person is Judge. Jupiter—Moon in 4-10 Position produced Gaja Keshwri Yoga. Saturn is in Vargottama Navamsha which shows that the person will get success after the age of 36.

VimShottari Mahadasa

6 Years 11 Months 5 Days	**Balance of Mars Mahadasa**
18—0—0	Rahu Mahadasa till 7-2-1971
16—0—0	Jupiter Mahadasa till 7-2-1987
From 7-2-1987	Saturn antar in Saturn Mahadasa
3-0-3	
10-2-1990	Saturn antar in Saturn Mahadasa
9-8-2	
19-10-1992	Mercury antar in Saturn Mahadasa
9-1-1	Ketu antar in Saturn Mahadasa
28-11-1993	
0-2-3	
28-1-1997	Venus antar in Saturn Mahadasa
12-11-0	
10-1-1998	Sun antar in Saturn Mahadasa
0-7-1	

10-8-1999	Moon antar in Saturn Mahadasa
9-1-1	
19-9-2000	Mars antar in Saturn Mahadasa
6-10-2	
25-7-2003	Rahu antar in Saturn Mahadasa
12-6-2	
7-2-2006	Jupiter antar in Saturn Mahadasa

The native was an advocate in SIRONJ Distt Vidisha till December 1987. He came to me in December 1987 at my home then I was Principal at SIRONJ) and Said that my date of birth is 2-3-1946 born in night after 12. Hence time is uncertain Please tell me about my future. I saw the Panchang of Vikram Samvat 2002 and after some Important Queries fixed the Aquarius result Saturn Mahadasa was begun from 7-2-1987. He told me that on 1-1-1988 there is my Interview for the Post of Deputy Legislative counsel in Law Department Government of India. I told him that there is full hope of your selection as Mahadasa of Saturn is running now and Saturn is the Lord of Lagna posited in 5th house in Gemini Sign in Nakshatra of Jupiter. Hence Saturn is to give the result of Jupiter.

He was fortunate and really selected for the post which he joined on 9-5-1988 and on 6-9-1996 Promoted as legislative counsel superseded in 1998. Thus his life changed fully and he become happy, healthy and wealthy.

For the present post of member (Judicial) Railway claims tribunal he gave interview on 22-6-2002 in the Supreme Court of India. He was retired from the previous post on 6-3-2003 and on 7-3-2003 joined at Railway Claims tribunal Bhopal Bench as member (Judicial). Till then he is working on this post. He is now getting total Rs. 40,000/- P.M. He is also a writer in law Books. He has written *Chawla's Elections law and Practice* Published by Bahri Publication printed 1st edition in 1967 Now 6th edition of this volume has been published in 2004. Which has 2776 Pages with H.B. cover Price Rs. 1495/-. See that the Saturn in this horoscope is in Vargottama Navamsha. Hence just from beginning of Mahadasa of Saturn the native is going on progressing his life more and more.

54

Horoscope of a Genius Bhuvan Sharma

I am analyzing here a special Horoscope of a genius student BHUVAN SHARMA Son of DR. R.B. Sharma Superintendent Medical College Meerut (U.P.).

Born on 12-9-1978 Tuesday at 10.35 A.M. at Jalaun (U.P.) Vikram Samvat 2035 Shaka 1900 Bhadra Pada DASHMI Tithi Tuesday 14/47 Poorva Shada Nakshatra 21/30 Saubhagya yoga 27/23. GAR KARN 14/47 With following Planetary Position in LIBRA LAGNA.

Planetary Position is as following:-

Planet	*Sign*	*Degree*	*Kala*	*Nakshatra*	*Charan*
SUN	04	25	01	Poorva Phalgunna	4
MOON	08	24	21	Poorva Shada	4
MARS	06	00	14	Chitra	3
MERCURY	04	11	51	Magha	4
JUPITER	03	09	39	Pushya	2
VENUS	06	10	05	Swati	2
SATURN	04	14	34	Poorva Phalguna	1
RAHU	05	03	29	Uttra Phalguna	3
KETU	11	03	29	Uttra Bhadra Pada	1

Birth Lagna

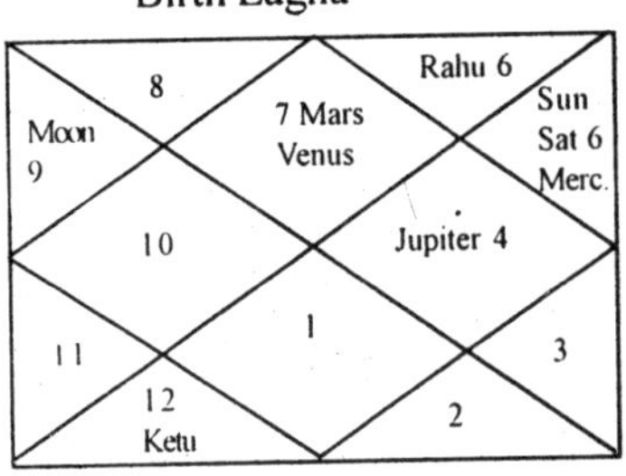

Moon Lagna

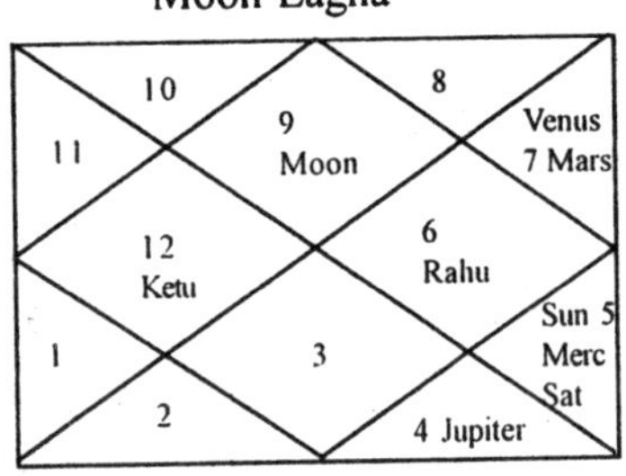

Karkamsha:-Scorpio Atmakarak Sun

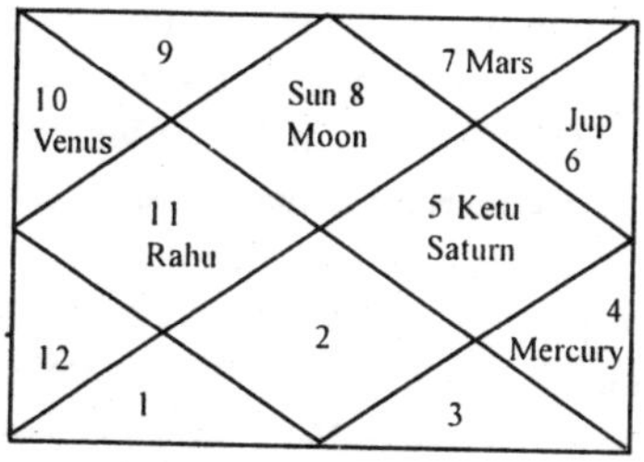

Jupiter is in Exaltation in 10h house. Here there is Lord of Lagna Venus is in Lagna being in Star of Rahu. Rahu is strong in Virgo in 12th house Rahu gives sudden rise because is in the Star of Venus Poorva Phalguna, Karak for foreign travel. Hence Venus and Rahu both are Mutually in Stars of each other.

JUPITER in Cancer in Star of Saturn. Saturn is the Lord of 5th house of education aspecting 5th house with SUN and Mercury. Long Journeys are known through the 9th and 10th houses. 9th Lord is Mercury who is in Ketu's Star and Ketu in 6th house indicates foreign lands Ketu aspects Rahu. Hence this genius student Passed his B.E. Examination from Indian Institute of Technology and went to England for M.E. Degree. He passed M.E. and now is doing research work for Ph.D. Degree in England. He is in service too in England with doing Ph.D.

Balance of VimShottari Mahadasa :

3 Years 5 Mouth 21 Days Venus Mahadasa

6-0-0	Sun Mahadasa
10-0-0	Moon Mahadasa
19-5-21	
1978-9-12	
1198-3-3	
From 3-3-1998	Mars Mahadasa begins Antardasa is as following
27-4-0	
30-7-1998	Mars Mahadasa Mars Antardasa
18-0-1	
18-8-1999	Mars Mahadasa Rahu Antardasa
6-11-0	
24-7-2000	Mars Mahadasa Jupiter Antardasa
9-1-1	
3-9-2001	Mars Mahadasa Saturn Antardasa
27-16-0	
30-8-2002	Mars Mahadasa Mercury Antardasa

In Saturn and Mercury antar he went to England for further studies after taking degree of B.E. from IIT. Here Saturn is Lord of 5th house of education and Mercury is Karak for education, Lord 9th house (house of luck) and Lord of 12th too. Saturn is in Star of Venus (Lord of Lagna) and Mercury is in Star of Ketu. Ketu aspects Rahu in Virgo Sign (Sign of Mercury, the Karak for education. Hence due to Rahu, Venus, Saturn, Mercury, Suddenly programme of foreign Journey made by these stars. Mahadasa Nath is Mars. It is said that if Malefics are the Lords of 1-4-7-10 houses they give good results. Here Mars is the Lord of 7th house. Seventh house denotes short Journeys, ninth and tenth denote long travels. Hence due to this combination of Planets Mr. Bhuvan Sharma is in now in England serving as Engineer and doing Ph.D.

From	
30-8-2002	
27-4-0	
Till	
27-1-2003	Mars Mahadasa Ketu Antardasa
0-2-1	
Till	
27-3-2004	Mars Mahadasa Venus Antardasa
6-4-0	
Till	
3-8-2004	Mars Mahadasa Sun Antardasa
0-7-0	
Till	
3-3-2005	Mars Mahadasa Moon Antardasa

From 3-3-2005 Rahu Mahadasa will begin Exalted Jupiter in Cancer in 10th house gives fame due to good deeds, honour and dignity and the native is wealthy, devotee to parents. World wide fame and earning through high level post.

55

Horoscope of Miss Universe Susmita Sen

It is said ("न विद्या न च पौरूष भाग्य फलति सर्वदा") means that neither education nor Endeavour but luck is fruitful every time in the course of human life since childhood to old age according to the deeds of previous lives. This does not mean that man should not work at all and sit silently. It means broadly that though every person acts, tries and works hard even then does not get success. Then we have to say that Luck is the fruit or result of action done by a man in his previous lives. Sushmita Sen of India was selected Miss Universe of the age of eighteen and proved the above axiom. She is lucky so she got name, fame and wealth so early.

Sushmita Sen was born on 19th Nov. 1975. At 7:15 a.m. having the following planetary position.

नारी भवेद् वृश्चिक लग्न जाता सुरूप गाता नयनाभिरामा ।

Which means female born in Scorpio ascendant is very beautiful with handsome, attractive eyes.

According to BHAVARTHA RATNAKAR 9-14-2

तृतीय भाग्यगो मन्दो योग प्रद इति स्मृताः

Means Saturn being Lord of third house is beneficial YOGAPRADA gives much wealth. Here Saturn is in 9th house in Cancer and is exalted in Navamsa Lagna in Libra.

Lord of ninth moon and Lord of tenth SUN when posited mutually in quadrant in 1-7 position aspecting each other make the native Lucky and famous. Here SUN is in birth Lagna in 1st house and Moon in 7th house in exaltation.

According to BHAVARTHA RATNAKAR. B.R. Rajyoga-20

भाग्य राज्याधिप यत्र सप्तमथौ च लग्नगो

Which means if Lords of 9th and 10th house are in Lagna or 7th give Rajayoga. Karaka and Lord of 10th house SUN, Lord of third, fourth in 9th, i.e., Saturn in 9th house aspected by 2nd and 5th house Lord Jupiter, This yoga make the JATAKA World famous and is hard to find.

According to UTTAR KALAMRITA of Kalidasa 4-22

रन्ध्रेशो व्ययषष्ठगो रिपुपतौ रन्ध्रे व्यये वा स्थिते जातोऽसौ नृपति प्रशस्ति विभवो राजाधिराजेश्वर

Which means if Lord of 8th house is in 12th/6th house, or Lord of 6th in 8th/12th house and Lord of 12th house is in 8th house, then the native born in this planetary position is famous, most wealthy and emperor. This is called VIPAREETA RAJYOGA which if found even in the horoscope of a poor make the native Happy, wealthy and equal to king's king.

In the Horoscope of Sushmita Sen Lord of 6th house Mars is in 8th house and Lord of 8th house Mercury is in 12th house. But Lord of 12th house Venus is not in 6th or 8th house. Hence this yoga is applicable 2/3 of Vipareeta Rajayoga which also make the native equal to king as regards in wealth, property and fame. This yoga is here due to Mars and Mercury's positions, which denote adultage (Mars) and young age (Mercury).

Sushmita Sen in the early age of eighteen got name, fame and wealth due to this yoga present in her horoscope for her excellent beauty. According to JATAKA TATWA of Mahadev Pathak Vide 9-84

धर्मे शुभे दृष्टाधिक्ये सर्वदेशे भाग्योदयः

"During Venus-Moon period (year 1994), India will try to beautify her face on International level and that is welcome thing" - Rajeshwari Shankier (In "Roses for the year 1994-95" appeared in Express Star Teller, January 1994 Issue)

Which means aspect of a beneficial in 9th house rises the Luck of the native in all countries. Here the most divine and beneficial planet Jupiter aspects the 9th house.

According to Version 10-9 of JATAKA TATWA of Mahadev Pathak

खे खपे शुभ संबधे मानी

Means if 10th house or its lord receive benefic aspect from natural benefics, then person acquires honourable position. Here Lord of 10th houe Sun is in Lagna in friend's sign and aspected by Deva guru Jupiter. Hence Sushmita Sen got honor and then became honorable due to grace of Jupiter J.T. 10/47. A planet in own signs makes the native Chief in family. Here Jupiter is in own signs Pisces in trine in 5th house. J.T. 10/50

लाभ बलाढ्ये शुभ ग्रहै दृष्टे श्रीमान

Means if 11th house is strong and is aspected by a benefic then the native is highly respectable and wealthy. Here Venus is in 11th house, though in debilitation but aspected by strong Jupiter (Lord of trine).

CHART 1

N-R	RASI	DEGREE	LRD	NAK	SUB	S-S	CUSP	RASI	DEGREE	LRD	NAK	SUB	S-S
SUN	SCO	2:40:25	MAR	JUP	RAH	VEN	1	SCO	7:53:47	MAR	SAT	KET	SAT
MON	TAU	4:14:1	VEN	SUN	SAT	MON	2	CAG	8:13:55	JUP	KET	JUP	MER
MAR-R	GEM	5:5:41	MER	RAH	RAH	VEN	3	CAP	11:32:31	SAT	MON	MAR	MER
MER	LIB	27:0:37	VEN	JUP	VEN	SUN	4	AQU	15:56:12	SAT	RAH	VEN	MAR
JUP-R	PIS	22:5:26	JUP	MER	SUN	KET	5	PIS	17:36:23	JUP	MER	MER	MON
VEN	VIR	16:33:2	MER	MON	SAT	VEN	6	ARI	14:35:18	MAR	VEN	VEN	JUP
SAT-R	CAN	9:36:36	MON	SAT	VEN	SAT	7	TAU	7:53:47	VEN	SUN	VEN	VEN
RAH-R	LIB	28:28:58	VEN	JUP	VEN	MER	8	GEM	8:13:55	MER	RAH	RAH	VEN
KET-R	ARI	28:28:58	MAR	SUN	MAR	MAR	9	CAN	11:32:31	MON	SAT	MON	SAT
URA	LIB	10:52:25	VEN	RAH	SAT	MER	10	LEO	15:56:12	SUN	VEN	SUN	SAT
NEP	SCO	17:31:32	MAR	MAR	MER	MON	11	VIR	17:36:23	MER	MON	SAT	JUP
PLU	VIR	17:32:10	MER	MON	SAT	JUP	12	LIB	14:35:18	VEN	RAH	KET	VEN

Fortuna TAU 9:27:23. Ayanamsa : 23:25:33. Balance of Dasa : SUN 2 Years 7 Months 3 Days

LAGNA

JUP	KET	MON	MAR
			SAT
	ASC SUN NEP	MER RAH URA	VEN PLU

CUSPAL CHART

JUP	MON KET	MAR	SAT
			VEN PLU
	ASC NEP	SUN MER RAH	URA

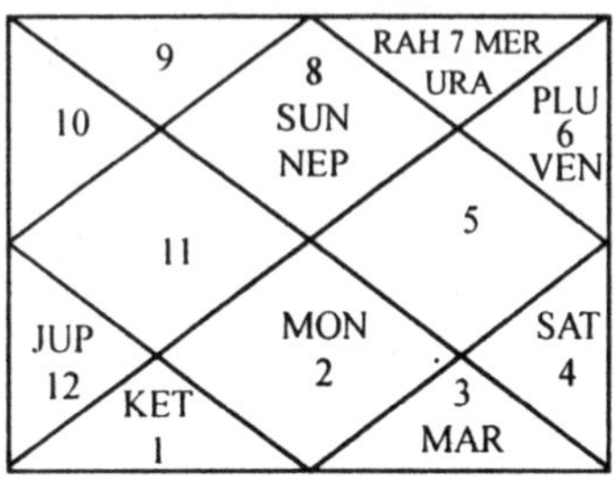

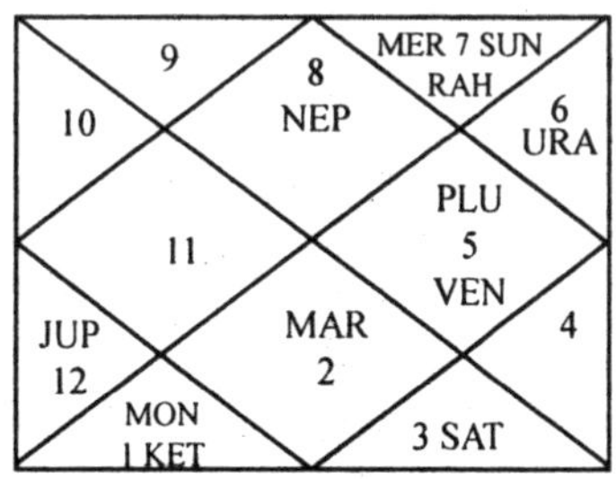

Though Lord of Lagna Mars is in Exaltation in Navamsa and Venus is aspected by Lord of fourth (Saturn) and fifth (Jupiter) hence got strength inspite of its neecha Position. Lord of eleventh has relation with Lord of 12th than it became YOGADA.

लाभ व्ययाधिपत्याश्च योगदा भवेत्

Here Lord of 11th Mercury and Lord of 12th Venus both are related being in Mutual exchange of signs.

Again BHVARTHA RATNAKAR says-

वाक्स्थानपो वाकपतिश्च केन्द्र कोणेषु संस्थितौ
रभा पूज्यश्च सपूर्ण विद्यावान भवति ध्रुवम्

Means if Lord of 2nd house and Jupiter are in Quadrant and trine than the native is respectable in assembly, is educated. Venus as Lord of 7th and 12th is Karaka for poetry, beauty, film, dance or beauty, art etc. She is in Lord of 12th sign, aspected by Jupiter, is beneficial both in birth Lagna and Navamsa in the signs of Mercury. w.e.f. 7-9-88 to 7-9-95. Mars Mahadasa (Dasa of Lagna Lord) was in course, hence she was successful Model at the age of fifteen. In seventeen selected *"MISS INDIA"* and in eighteen *"MISS UNIVERSE"*. Her father was in air force because Karaka for air Saturn is posited in 9th house, Saturn is the Lord of 4th house (House of vehicle). In the direction of Mahesh Bhatt in Dastak film she worked as an actress. Now w.e.f. 7-9-95. Rahu Mahadasa is in course. Rahu is Karaka for foreign language, foreign countries and is in 12th house. Hence her fame widely spread in foreign countries.

द्वितीयेश दशा काले व्ययेशो मारको भवेत्

Means in Mahadasa of Lord of second, such period of Lord of 12th house may prove maraca. Jupiter is Lord of 2nd house and Mercury is Lord of 12th house. Hence in Mahadasa of Jupiter, such period of Mercury may prove her fatal. Moon, Saturn, Venus are exalted in Sapta Vargas. Venus is exalted in two Vargas. Hence being Karaka for beauty Sushmita Sen has to work in films.

The fame in lower age is only available to those who are really lucky. Her birth Number too is number one (19=1+9=10=1+0=1) like Smt. Indira Gandhi in the same month November. So at the very age of 19 she became world famous. The great Hindi Poet *TULSIDAS* has correctly said.

"सकल पदारथ हैं जगमाही कर्म हीन नर पावत नाही"

Means there are all things in the world but those do not get who looser of action or unlucky in other words. Only lucky person gets all things in the world.

56

Horoscope of Smt. Sonia Gandhi

Lady of International Fame

The Present President of India National Congress and United Progressive Alliance (UPA) Smt. Sonia Gandhi was born on 9-12-1946 Monday at Lusiyana Village in Italy. Her Birth Lagna, Moon Lagna, Karkamasa is as following:

Birth Lagna

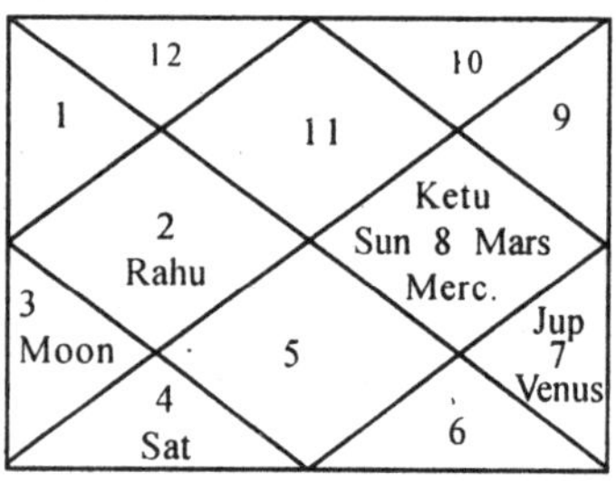

Moon Sign

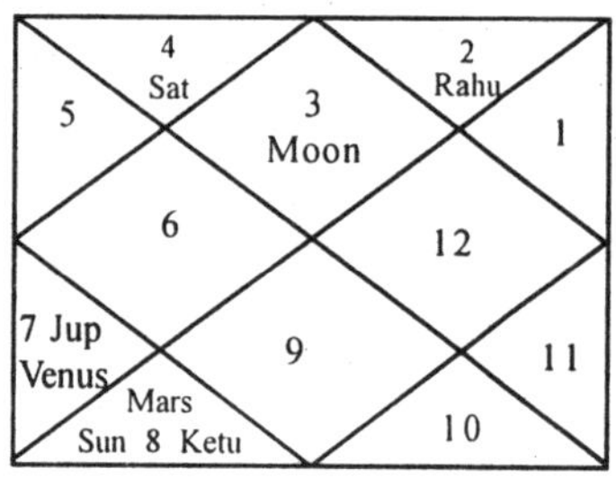

Karkamsa - Pisces; Aatmakarak - Mars

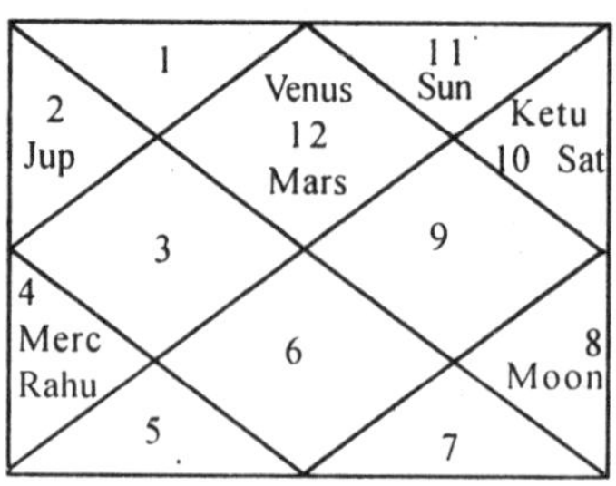

Planetary position is following:

Planet	Sign	Degree	Kala	Nakshatra	Charan	
Sun	7	24	32	Jyeshtha	3	in Enemy sign in Navamsa
Moon	2	5	53	Mrigsir	4	in Neecha Navamsa
Mars	7	29	0	Jyeshtha	4	in own sign in friends sign Navamsa
Mercury	7	2	49	Vishakha	4	in enemy sign in enemy Nakshatra
Jupiter	6	24	17	Vishakha	2	in venus sign in Navamsa too venus sign
Venus	6	18	35	Swati	4	in own sign in uchcha in Navamsa
Saturn	3	12	0	Pushya	3	in own Nakshatra in own sign Navamsa
Rahu	1	21	57	Rohini	4	in enemy Nakshatra
Ketu	7	21	51	Jyeshtha	2	in enemy Nakshatra

Aquarius Lagna born have fixed intellect, excellent heart, soft body and happy. Moon in 3rd house happy, wealthy, wise. Sun in 10th house have many good qualities. Sun in karak for 10th house have a prestige, profession, state. Mars in 10th house is (निजकुल जयबारी) means gives triumph to own family, kuldeepak (light of family). Mercury in 10th well wisher of self with teachers, wealthy with own earning speaks with serious thinking, but little. Jupiter in 9th aspects the lagna and moon. Native is the best among men, wealthy like king. Venus in 9th house beautiful, happy, devotee to God and Virtuous people happy by self-earned money and is lucky.

Saturn in 6th defeats enemies. Rahu in 4th house in friends sign leaves his home and goes to other places. Lives being head of the institution, village, city or company.

Ketu in Scorpio in 10th defeats enemies. Sun, Mars, Mercury in 10th house make the native bold, famous, hard heart, happy with wealth and son.

She came first time in New Delhi on 13-1-1968. Married with Rajiv Gandhi on 25-26 February 1968.

Vimshottari Mahadasa:

0 year 7 month 7 days Mars Mahadasha in Balance
18 year 0 month 0 days Rahu Mahadasha till 16-7-1965
16 year 0 month 0 days Jupiter Mahadasha till 16-7-1981

From 16-7-1981 to 16-7-2000 Saturn Mahadasha. In Venus antar w.e.f. 7-4-1988 to 7-6-1991. Her husband Rajiv Gandhi was assassinated on 21-5-1991 in ketu pratyantar. Saturn is in own nakshatra, Venus in Rahu's

Nakshatra; Ketu in Mercury (Lord of 8th) Nakshatra: Rahu aspects her lord of seventh house Sun with Mars, Ketu, Mercury. Hence sudden unnatural death of her husband occurred.

From 16-7-2000 Mercury Mahadasha begins. Mercury is lord of 5th (Trikona) with Sun in tenth house made her popular and a strong leader of congress. Her Sun, Mars, Ketu are very strong in 10th house. Now she is all in all for congress party. In Ketu antar w.e.f. 13-12-2002 to 10-12-2003 she became most powerful and in Venus antar till 10-10-2006 will have excellent period. Sun and Moon antar may produce some obstacles and hindrances as Sun is in 12th in Karkamsa in enemy house, Moon is in Neecha Navamsa in 9th house in Karkamsa.

57

Horoscope of Sachin Tendulkar

Sachin Tendulkar made Ten thousand runs in Test Cricket in Kolkata on 16th March 2005. He is the second Indian cricket player who made Ten thousand runs.

In the age of 16 in 1989-90 when he started his test career while on tour to Pakistan this was the 122nd match. Before him Sunil Gawaskar made 10122 runs. See the horoscope of Sachin Tendulkar. Born on 24-4-1973 at 2:35 p.m. at Mumbai Tuesday. His birth lagna is Leo and Lord of Lagna Sun is in 9th house in the house of luck aspected by Mars in exaltation.

Birth Lagna

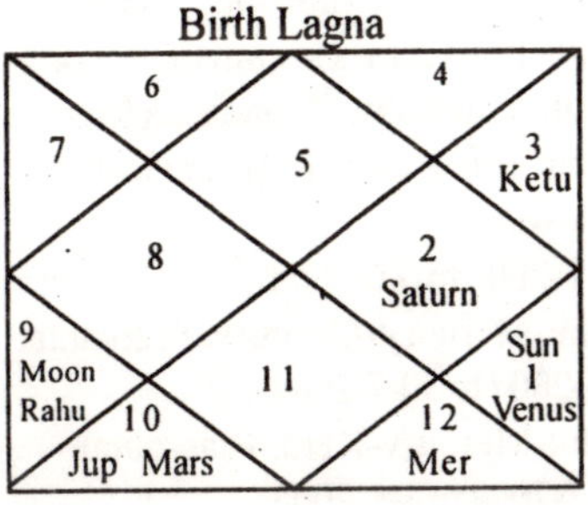

Moon Lagna

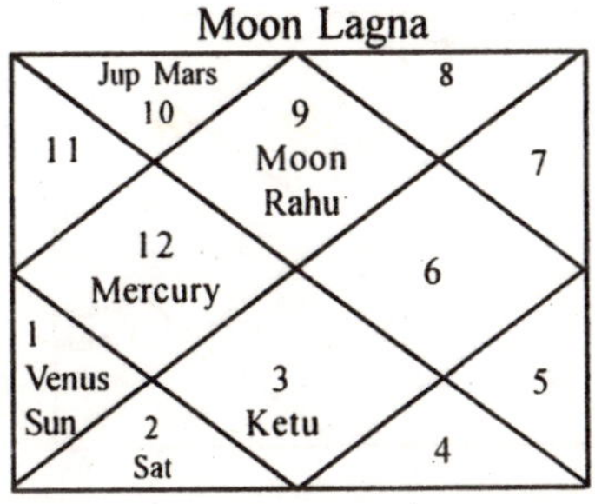

Vimshattari Mahadasa

5 years 9 months 20 days

Sun Mahadasa	Till -14-2-1979
Moon Mahadasa	Till 14-2-1989
Mars Mahadasa	Till 14-2-1996

Planetary Position:

Planet	Sign	Degree	Kala	Nakshatra	Charan
Sun	0	10	35	Ashwini	4
Moon	8	27	06	Uttrashada	1
Mars	9	26	27	Dhanishtha	2
Mercury	11	20	21	Rewti	2
Jupiter	9	17	47	Shravana	3
Venus	0	16	7	Bharni	1
Saturn	1	24	39	Mrigsir	1
Rahu	8	17	43	Poorvashada	2
Ketu	2	17	43	Rohini	3

Lagnesh Sun in exaltation in 9th house (house of luck).
Moon is in Vargottama Navamsha.
Mars is in 6th house in exaltation aspecting the Lord of Lagna Sun.
Mercury in debilitation in eighth house.
Jupiter in debilitation in sixth house but debilitation has been cancelled by exalted Mars.
Venus in own nakshatra but in Navamsha in enemy house.
Saturn in Mrigsir in Navamsa of enemy.
Rahu in Venus Nakshatra in Navamsha in own sign Virgo.
Ketu in Moon Nakshatra in Navamsha in own sign Pisces.

Karkamsha : Sagittarius; Aatma Karak : Moon

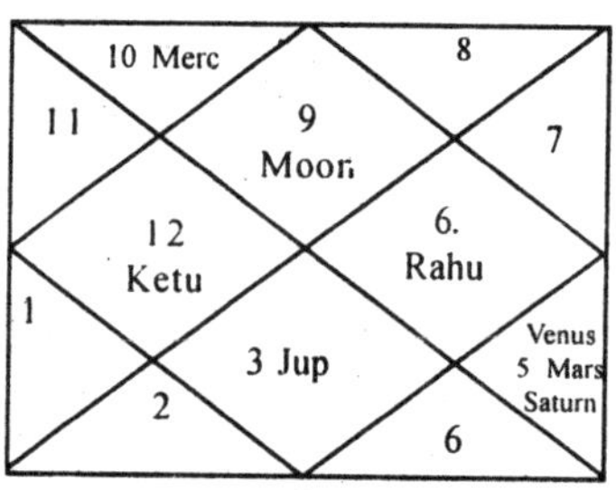

From 14-2-1996 to 14-2-2014 Rahu Mahadasha is running. Rahu is in tenth house in karkamsha strongly posited. In Rahu Mahadasha Mercury antar the Pratyantar period is as following:

26-1-2004 to 6-6-2004
Rahu-Mercury-Mercury, Pratyantar
6-6-2004 to 30-7-2004
Rahu-Mercury-Ketu, Pratyantar
30-7-2004 to 3-1-2005
Rahu-Mercury-Venus, Pratyantar

3-1-2005 to 19-2-2005 Rahu-Mercury-Sun, Pratyantar
19-2-2005 to 5-5-2005 Rahu-Mercury-Moon, Pratyantar
5-5-2005 to 29-6-2005 Rahu-Mercury-Mars, Pratyantar

On 16th March 2005 was Wednesday, Rohini Nakshatra, Moon in Taurus sign and Sachin Tendulkar made ten thousand complete runs in Rahu-Mercury-Moon period i.e. w.e.f. 19-2-2005 to 5-5-2005. Hence on 16th March Wednesday and moon sign is fit day. The success made in Rahu major mercury minor is due to the fact that Rahu in Navamsha is in Virgo whose Lord is Mercury.

Sachin Tendulkar became famous in world in little age. In 1999 he was awarded with "Padam Shri". After this "Rajiv Gandhi Khel Ratan". At the age of 17 won the match by 119 runs in England was awarded "Man of the Match". At the age 21 he was a great batsman awarded world cup at the age of 23 in 1996 making 200 runs. Sixth house in the house of sport where exalted mars in posited and aspecting Lord of Lagna Sun who is exalted in 9th house. Coming next years are important for him. I wish him best wishes and more bright future.

58

Horoscope of Nicolas Dejenne

French Ph.D. student in Indology from Paris University Mr. Nicolas Dejenne is doing Research work on 'Parashuram' He received the copy at my Hindi Mahakavy (जंय पशुराम) Jai Parashu Ram from Mr. Siddhinath Awasthi, President Kanya Kubja Mahasabha, Janak Puri, New Delhi. He is extremely interested in the rewriting of the whole Parashuram Story in my Hindi Maha Kavya and has decided a part of Ph.D. to it.

He came on 14th April 2005 to my home at Ashok Nagar (M.P.) with Dr. Anu Radha Bhattacharya to discuss the various narrative and ideological points of my book on the life of Parashuram Ji. I asked him about his birth particulars which are as following:

Born on 7-10-1974 at 8.25 p.m. in Nantes 047:12 North 001:33 West

Birth Lagna

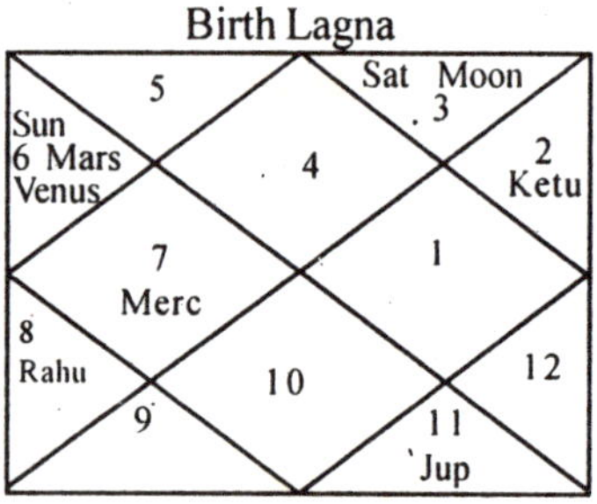

Moon Sign

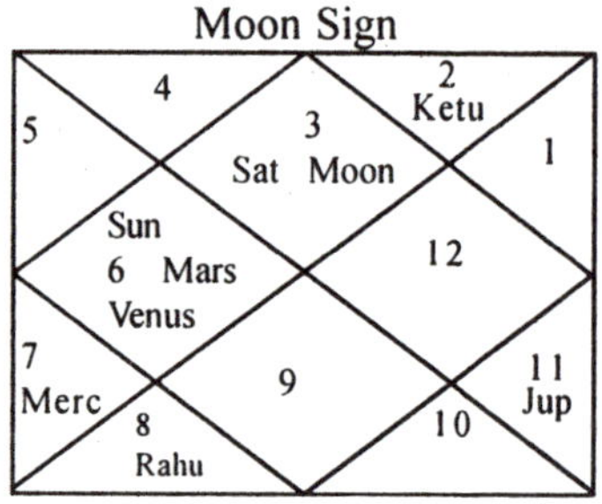

in North France 400 k.m. from Paris in Cancer Lagna.

Karkamsha: Taurus

Aatmakarak: Saturn

Birth Lagna

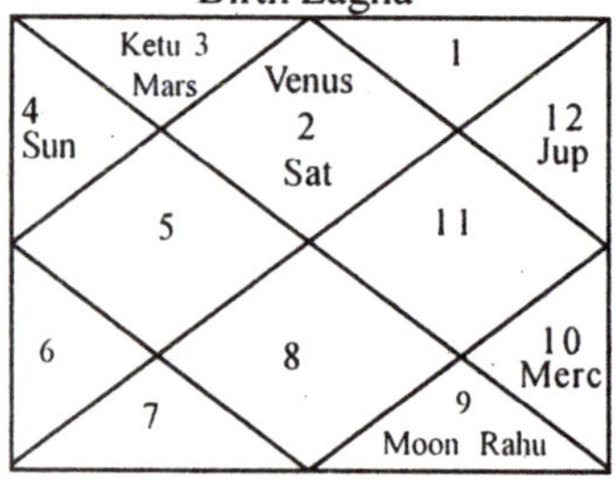

Plahetary position is as following

Planet	*Sign*	*Degree*	*Kala*	*Nakshatra*	*Charan*
Sun	5	20	10	Hasta	4
Moon	2	8	42	Aridra	1
Mars	5	19	28	Hasta	3
Mercury	6	12	17	Swati	2
Jupiter	10	17	17	Shat Bisha	2
Venus	5	13	34	Hasta	1
Saturn	2	25	17	Punarvasu	2
Rahu	7	19	33	Jyeshtha	2
Ketu	1	19	33	Rohini	3

According to 'Sarawali'

र्कक लग्न परदेशगः सुधीरः साहसकर्मा जलाधिगतवित्त ।

स्त्रीं भूषणाम्बर सुखैभेगिश्च समन्वितौ भवाति ।

Means person born in Cancer goes to foreign land, patient, bold, getting money from water, happy from wife, wealth and ornaments. Born in IInd Hora of Cancer wanders here and there is truthful. Born in III rd Drekkana of Cancer dear to wife, wealthy, living in foreign lands, has beautiful eyes, happy in forest and near water.

Saturn in Gemini aspected by Jupiter: Sincere to king, full of all good qualities, dear to virtuous people.

Aspect of Jupiter on Moon in Gemini:

विद्याशास्त्राचार्य, विख्यातं, सत्यवाच मति रूपम् ।

मान्यं वाग्मिन्दु करोति गुरू वीक्षितो मिथुने ।।

Means wise with full knowledge of old texts, famous, truthful, beautiful, recognised, expert in speech, respected.

Sun in Virgo: Writer, sweet speech, wise devotee to teacher, God.

Mars in Virgo: Worshipped, wealthy, wise sweet speech, fond of old culture.

Venus in Virgo: Expert in Arts, sweet speech.

Mercury in Virgo: Expert in debate and technique, going to foreign lands, devotee to God, saints, teachers, writer, patriot. Mr. Nicolas has all these qualities and is virtuous.

Vimshottari Mahadasa – Balance of Rahu Mahadasa

15 years 0 month 27 days till 4-11-1989

From 4-11-1989 Jupiter Mahadasa is running till 4-11-2005. Now Rahu antar is running in Jupiter Mahadasa. From Jupiter Rahu is in 10th house and 10th house is the house of travelling as said "रमध्यातप्रवासो". So Mr. Nicolas Dejenne is on tour in foreign countries. He is true devotee of God Parashuram and fond of old Indian and east religion and culture. I wish him good luck and bright future in all the matters of life. His address is 13 fonkevard du Val-si-cherine, 44800 Saint Herblain – France.

59 List of Important Horoscopes

S.	*Name*	*Lagna*	*Sun*	*Moon*	*Mars*	*Mercury*	*Jupiter*	*Venus*	*Saturn*	*Rahu*	*Ketu*
1	Bhagwan Shri Ram	4	1	4	10	2	4	12	7	6	12
2	Bhagwan Mahavir Swami	10	1	6	10	1	4	2	7	4	10
3	Gautam Buddha	4	1	7	1	2	1	1	1	3	9
4	Guru Nanak	5	8	2	8	8	6	7	2	9	3
5	Christ	7	5	2	12	9	7	10	3	9	3
6	Sant Tulsidas	7	5	7	4	5	11	5	6	8	2
7	Swami Ram Tirtha	12	7	7	9	7	6	6	10	1	7
8	Baba Ram Dev	8	8	12	6	8	8	8	6	7	1
9	Ram Krishna Param Hansa	11	11	11	11	11	3	12	7	8	2
10	Swami Vivekanand	10	10	6	1	10	7	10	6	8	2
11	Arvinda Ghosh	4	5	9	4	5	4	5	9	2	8
12	Prathvi Raj Chauhan	1	12	6	7	10	10	10	5	3	9
13	Maharana Pratap	10	2	3	6	3	4	3	6	11	5
14	Chhatrapati Shivaji	5	11	6	3	11	10	12	7	3	9
15	Rana Ranjit Singh	4	8	2	6	8	7	6	8	1	7
16	Tipu Sultan	9	8	1	11	8	2	7	8	8	2
17	Haidar Ali	7	8	8	8	8	8	10	8	3	9
18	Changej Khan	4	6	7	6	6	6	6	6	1	7
19	Alexander	1	5	3	7	4	7	5	2	11	5
20	Bal Gangadhar Tilak	4	4	12	8	3	12	4	3	12	6
21	Mahatma Gandhi	7	6	5	7	7	1	7	8	4	10
22	Subhash Chandra Bose	1	10	6	2	10	5	11	8	10	4

23	Rani Laxmi Bai	7	8	7	4	7	2	9	7	2	8
24	Pt. Motilal Nehru	4	1	12	2	1	4	1	5	9	3
25	Pt. Jawahar Lal Nehru	4	8	4	6	7	9	7	5	3	9
26	Sardar Ballabh Bhai Patel	1	7	2	10	7	7	7	10	12	6
27	Rajgopala Chari	8	8	2	7	9	10	8	12	10	4
28	Dr. Rajendra Prasad	9	8	2	9	9	5	7	3	6	12
29	Dr. Radha Krishnan	6	5	5	8	6	8	6	4	4	10
30	Lal Bahadur Shastri	8	6	6	5	6	1	7	10	5	11
31	Smt. Indira Gandhi	4	8	10	5	8	2	9	4	9	3
32	Morarji Desai	3	11	5	11	10	10	10	7	7	1
33	Chaudhry Charan Singh	9	9	6	6	9	10	9	10	6	12
34	Guljarilal Nanda	1	3	9	1	3	6	4	8	9	3
35	V.V. Giri	7	4	8	1	4	3	3	6	12	6
36	Sanjiva Reddy	9	2	7	12	1	9	1	2	12	6
37	Atal Bihari Bajpai	7	9	8	12	9	9	8	7	4	10
38	C.D. Deshmuk	6	10	10	9	10	4	8	7	11	5
39	V.K. Menon	9	1	10	11	2	4	1	7	11	5
40	Din Dayal Upadhyay	9	6	5	7	6	1	4	4	10	4
41	Shyama Prasad Mukher Ji	2	3	11	6	4	9	4	9	7	1
42	Dr. Sampoorna Nand	1	9	1	7	10	9	9	5	3	9
43	Lata Mangeshkar	2	6	4	6	6	2	5	8	1	7
44	Shivaji Ganeshan	11	6	10	3	7	1	7	8	2	8
45	Ashok Kumar	10	6	3	2	6	7	5	1	1	7
46	Raj Kapoor	4	8	4	12	9	9	7	7	4	10
47	Jamshedji Tata	4	11	6	6	11	6	12	8	12	6
48	Jugal Kishore Birla	3	2	9	1	2	3	1	2	7	1
49	R.K. Dalmia	3	12	9	2	12	1	12	6	1	7

50	Dacoit Man Singh	8	7	4	3	6	8	6	11	1	7
51	Kaka Hath Rasi	3	6	6	5	5	3	7	11	4	10
52	Shri Krishna 'Saral'	1	2	3	2	3	5	1	5	7	1
53	Gen. Maner Shaw	5	12	3	3	11	10	1	2	11	5
54	Sheikh Muzib	12	12	10	7	12	4	11	5	7	1
55	Maharani Victoria	2	2	2	12	1	4	1	12	12	6
56	George Vth	12	2	6	4	1	9	12	7	7	1
57	Warnard Shaw	2	4	2	7	3	12	4	3	12	6
58	Shakespear	9	1	1	3	12	4	2	4	2	8
59	George Washington	3	11	9	8	10	6	12	12	9	3
60	Roosevelt	5	10	3	3	11	1	10	1	8	2
61	John Canady	6	2	5	1	1	2	2	4	9	3
62	Nixon	5	9	10	9	9	9	11	2	12	6
63	Hitlar	7	1	9	1	1	9	1	4	3	9
64	Karl Marx	11	1	1	4	2	9	12	11	1	7
65	Stalin	7	9	12	1	8	11	7	12	9	3
66	Sushmita Sen	8	8	2	3	7	12	6	4	7	1
67	Cheiro	8	7	5	4	8	10	8	7	6	12
68	Brijnarain "Brijesh"	11	5	7	7	6	1	4	4	10	4
69	Chandra Shekhar	3	1	7	3	12	11	2	8	3	9
70	Madhavrao Scindia	8	11	9	10	12	6	3	1	3	9
71	B.V. Raman	11	4	2	5	5	8	5	2	12	6
72	Goswami Girdharilal	3	5	5	3	6	2	6	4	3	9
73	Lal Krishna Adwani	11	7	1	7	7	12	6	8	2	8
74	Chhatra Shal	8	2	12	8	1	6	2	8	2	8
75	Shyama Charan Lahidi	7	6	3	9	7	7	4	4	6	12
76	Ravindranath Tagore	12	1	12	3	1	4	1	5	3	9

77	Ishwarchandra Vidyasagar	9	6	2	7	6	11	4	12	10	4
78	Sumitra Nandan Pant	4	2	10	1	1	8	3	9	8	2
79	Bhartendu Harish Chandra	5	5	7	6	6	6	7	12	4	10
80	Harivansharai Bachchan	7	8	4	11	7	4	8	11	3	9
81	Benazir Bhutto	9	3	7	3	4	2	1	6	10	4
82	Menka Gandhi	4	5	12	11	6	5		8	8	2
83	Jai Prakash Narain	4	6	10	4	7	10	6	9	1	7
84	Chandra Shekhar Azad	9	4	4	4	5	3	5	11	4	10
85	Madanmohan Malviya	4	6	6	10	9	6	10	6	3	9
86	Aadi Shankracharya	3	1	3	12	1	1	1	9	8	2
87	Gopal Krishna Gokhle	7	1	11	12	1	10	2	7	6	12
88	Sant Gyaneshwar	2	5	2	10	6	4	6	7	9	3
89	Sant Tyagraj	4	1	4	3	1	5	11	11	10	4
90	Vikrmaditya Samrat	4	1	2	11	2	4	2	7	9	3
91	Sant Kavir Das	2	12	2	11	12	4	12	7	6	12
92	Hajrat Mohammed	11	1	5	4	1	7	2	8	2	8
93	Rajiv Gandhi	6	5	5	6	5	5	5	3	4	10
94	Jai Shankar Prasad	11	10	2	10	10	10	10	5	3	9
95	Shri Hanuman Ji	12	1	10	2	12	4	12	12	2	8
96	Hari Singh Gaur	9	8	4	4	8	10	7	7	6	12
97	Sant Tukaram	12	10	12	11	10	4	8	8	3	9
98	Sharad Pawar	8	8	2	7	8	1	7	1		
99	Vir Sawarkar	9	2	11	1	3	3	1	2	7	1
100	Samrat Akbar	7	8	3	10	9	7	7	7	11	5
101	Vinoba Bhave	7	5	10	1	6	3	5	7	12	6
102	Rajesh Khanna	3	9	5	8	9	3	9	2	5	11

103	Amitabh Bachchan	11	6	7	6	6	4	6	2	5	11
104	Ramanujan	3	9	2	6	8	8	7	4	4	10
105	C.B. Raman	7	7	7	1	8	11	6	12	9	3
106	Jagdish Chandra Basu	2	8	6	10	9	2.	9	4	11	5
107	Radhey Shyam Kathawachak	4	8	1	10	8	10	8	5	2	8
108	Meena Kumari	5	4	3	3	5	5	3	10	11	5
109	Nargis	1	2	11	4	2	2	1	9	1	7
110	Bal Gandharva	9	3	10	6	3	8	3	4	4	10
111	Dilip Kumar	1	8	10	7	8	9	9	12	7	1
112	R. Santhanam	8	2	1	4	1	4	1	3	4	10
113	Ravi Shankar Shukla	5	4	1	11	4	9	5	11	3	9
114	Kailashnath Katju	4	3	1	2	3	7	4	3	4	10
115	Dr. Shankar Dyal	5	5	9	7	5	3	4	4	8	2
116	Jainmuni Vidyanand	7	1	1	2	1	9	1	7	4	10
117	Swatantra Bharat	2	4	4	3	4	7	4	4	2	8
118	Bhaironsingh Shekhawat	2	7	12	6	6	8	7	7	5	1
119	Jainmuni Vidyasagar	4	6	12	7	7	7	7	4	2	8
120	Dr. Shiv Mangal Singh "Suman"	9	4	6	3	4	12	4	3	10	7
121	Hema Malini	4		12	8	7	9	5	5	1	7
122	Joy Lalita	3	11	5	5	11	9	12	4	1	7
123	Sachin Tendulkar	5	1	9	10	12	10	1	2	9	3
124	Jayendra Saraswati	10	4	11	7	3	7	5	11	9	3
125	Acharya Chatur Sen Shastri	11	5	12	5	5	11	5	5	2	8
126	Chief Justice R.C. Lahoti	6	7	8	6	7	1	6	1	6	12
127	Smt. Sonia Gandhi	11	8	3	8	8	7	7	4	2	8
128	M. Nicolas Dejenne	4	6	3	6	7	11	6	3	8	2

Index